Green Management

EMERALD STUDIES IN FINANCE, INSURANCE, AND RISK MANAGEMENT

Series Editor: Simon Grima

Books in this series collect quantitative and qualitative studies in areas relating to finance, insurance, and risk management. Subjects of interest may include banking, accounting, auditing, compliance, sustainability, behavior, management, and business economics.

In the disruption of political upheaval, new technologies, climate change, and new regulations, it is more important than ever to understand risk in the financial industry. Providing high quality academic research, this book series provides a platform for authors to explore, analyze, and discuss current and new financial models and theories, and engage with innovative research on an international scale.

Previously published:

Uncertainty and Challenges in Contemporary Economic Behaviour
Ercan Özen and Simon Grima

New Challenges for Future Sustainability and Wellbeing
Ercan Özen, Simon Grima, and Rebecca Dalli Gonzi

Insurance and Risk Management for Disruptions in Social, Economic, and Environmental Systems: Decision and Control Allocations Within New Domains of Risk
Simon Grima, Ercan Özen, and Rebecca Dalli Gonzi

Public Sector Leadership in Assessing and Addressing Risk
Peter C. Young, Simon Grima, and Rebecca Dalli Gonzi

Big Data Analytics in the Insurance Market
Kiran Sood, B. Balamurugan, Simon Grima, and Pierpaolo Marano

Big Data: A Game Changer for Insurance Industry
Kiran Sood, Rajesh Kumar Dhanaraj, B. Balamurugan, Simon Grima, and R. Uma Maheshwari

The Adoption and Effect of Artificial Intelligence on Human Resources Management, Part A
Pallavi Tyagi, Naveen Chilamkurti, Simon Grima, Kiran Sood, and B. Balamurugan

The Adoption and Effect of Artificial Intelligence on Human Resources Management, Part B
Pallavi Tyagi, Naveen Chilamkurti, Simon Grima, Kiran Sood, and B. Balamurugan

Contemporary Studies of Risks in Emerging Technology, Part A
Simon Grima, Kiran Sood, and Ercan Özen

Contemporary Studies of Risks in Emerging Technology, Part B
Simon Grima, Kiran Sood, and Ercan Özen

The Framework for Resilient Industry: A Holistic Approach for Developing Economies
Narinder Kumar, Kiran Sood, Ercan Özen, and Simon Grima

VUCA and Other Analytics in Business Resilience, Part A
Deepmala Singh, Kiran Sood, Sandeep Kautish, and Simon Grima

VUCA and Other Analytics in Business Resilience, Part B
Deepmala Singh, Kiran Sood, Sandeep Kautish, and Simon Grima

Finance Analytics in Business: Perspectives on Enhancing Efficiency and Accuracy
Sanjay Taneja, Pawan Kumar, Kiran Sood, Ercan Özen, and Simon Grima

Enterprise Risk Management in Today's World: Enterprise-wide Risk Management and Strategy, Part A
Author: Jean-Paul Louisot; Editor: Simon Grima

Enterprise Risk Management in Today's World: A Current and Futuristic View of the Complexity, Resilience, Responsibility, and Tools in ERM, Part B
Author: Jean-Paul Louisot; Editor: Simon Grima

Green Management: A New Paradigm in the World of Business

EDITED BY

SWATI GUPTA
Chitkara Business School, Chitkara University, Punjab, India

SANJAY TANEJA
Graphic Era Deemed to be University, India

ERCAN ÖZEN
University of Uşak, Turkey

KIRAN SOOD
Chitkara Business School, Chitkara University, Punjab, India; Women Researchers Council, Azerbaijan State University of Economics (UNEC), Baku, Azerbaijan

AND

SIMON GRIMA
University of Malta, Malta

emerald PUBLISHING

United Kingdom – North America – Japan – India – Malaysia – China

Emerald Publishing Limited
Emerald Publishing, Floor 5, Northspring, 21-23 Wellington Street, Leeds LS1 4DL.

First edition 2025

British Library Cataloguing in Publication Data
A catalogue record for this book is available from the British Library

ISBN: 978-1-83797-443-6 (Print)
ISBN: 978-1-83797-442-9 (Online)
ISBN: 978-1-83797-444-3 (Epub)

Printed and bound by CPI Group (UK) Ltd, Croydon, CR0 4YY

Contents

About the Editors

Swati Gupta is a dynamic individual with a doctoral degree, working as an Assistant Professor at Chitkara Business School, Chitkara University, Punjab, India. She has vast experience in imparting knowledge across various educational institutions and universities in diverse locations. She specializes in teaching subjects such as consumer behavior, market research, marketing management, organizational behavior, sales and distribution management, services marketing, and retail management. Known for her energy and dedication, she possesses excellent analytical, problem-solving, and decision-making skills. Having served as the editor for various books under renowned publishing houses including NOVA, Emerald, IGI Global, and AAP, she has contributed significantly to the academic field. Additionally, she has undertaken the role of a Reviewer for IGI Global and has books and chapters indexed in Scopus covering topics in marketing, digital marketing, green business management, robo-advisors in management, consumer behavior, among others. Furthermore, she holds patent and copyrights under her name.

Sanjay Taneja is a Post Doctorate from University of Usak, Usak, Turkey and Ph.D. from Chaudhary Devi Lal University, Sirsa, India. He has joined the Department of Management Studies, Graphic Era (Deemed to be University) as an Associate Professor in 2023. He has a vast experience in the area of teaching and research. He has worked as a faculty member for more than 11 years and has taught finance, banking, insurance, and research courses to B.Com./M.Com./B.B.A./M.B.A./Ph.D. students. He has published several research papers in various international journals. His research interests include sustainable finance, fin tech, insurance, risk and banking, also published numerous research papers in the Scopus, Web of Science, ABDC, and refereed journal. He received research excellence award from Chandigarh University in the year 2023. He organizes several conferences. He is an active reviewer of various refereed journals. Additionally, in view of his recent substantial creative contribution in the area of sustainable finance, he has been invited as a guest speaker in various renowned organizations in India as well as Europe. He is Guest Editorial Board member of IJEI, IJSDP, JFRM, FINTECH, IJTM&SD, and Reviewer Board of *Journal of Family Business Management* (Emerald).

Ercan Özen received his B.Sc. in Public Finance (1994), M.Sc. in Business-Accounting (1997), and Ph.D. in Business Finance (2008) from University of AfyonKocatepe. Now he is Professor of finance in the Department of Finance and Banking, Faculty of Applied Sciences, University of Uşak, Türkiye (Turkey). His current research interests include different aspects of finance. He served as co-editor for books by eminent international publishing houses. He has publications of more than 100 and participated in many international conferences. He is board member of five international conferences and workshops besides, Chair of International Applied Social Sciences Congress, co-editor of two international journals (*Journal of Corporate Governance, Insurance, and Risk Management (JCGIRM) and Opportunities* and *Challenges in Sustainability (OCS)*). He is also the certificated accountant, a member of Agean Finance Association, and a member of TEMA (Turkey Combating Soil Erosion, for Reforestation and the Protection of Natural Resources Foundation).

Kiran Sood is a Professor at Chitkara Business School, Chitkara University, Punjab, India. She received her undergraduate and postgraduate degrees in commerce from Panjab University, respectively, in 2002 and 2004. She earned her Master of Philosophy degree in 2008 and Doctor of Philosophy in Commerce with a concentration on product portfolio performance of general insurance companies in 2017 from Panjabi University, Patiala, India. Before joining Chitkara University in July 2019, she had served four organizations with a total experience of 18 years. She has published various articles in various journals and presented papers at various international conferences. She serves as an Editor of the refereed journal, particularly the *IJBST International Journal of BioSciences and Technology, International Journal of Research Culture Society*, and *The Journal of Corporate Governance, Insurance, and Risk Management (JCGIRM)*. Her research mainly focuses on regulations, marketing, and finance in insurance, insurance management, and economics and management of innovation in insurance.

Simon Grima is the Deputy Dean of the Faculty of Economics, Management, and Accountancy, an Associate Professor, and the Head of the Department of Insurance and Risk Management. He is also a Professor at the University of Latvia, Faculty of Business, Management and Economics, and a Visiting Professor at UNICATT Milan.

About the Contributors

Rohitha Abeysinghe, Rear Admiral, currently serves as the Director of General Training in the Sri Lanka Navy. He was the Commanding Officer of SLNS Gajabahu (SLNS Gajabahu – A ship belonging to the Sri Lanka Navy that provides maritime security and search and rescue operations). He holds a postgraduate degree (M.Sc.) from General Sir John Kotelawala Defence University, a Fellowship of Counter Terrorism Studies from DKI Asia Pacific Centre for Security Studies, Honolulu, Hawaii, a BSc in Mechanical Engineering from General Sir John Kotelawala Defence University and a successful 33+ year track record of service in the country as a Navy officer. He is currently doing his M.Phil. at the General Sir John Kotelawala Defence University, Sri Lanka.

Shahidul Alam is a Master of Business Administration student in the Department of Business Administration at Premier University Chattogram, Bangladesh. He is an energetic and enthusiastic young researcher who has worked on several projects with the faculty and achieved excellent academic results at his graduation level. He has a vast interest in the research field of fintech and completed his project paper submission on blockchain applications into several business models to achieve his Bachelor of Business Administration degree.

Bimal Anjum is M.Com, M.Phil, Ph.D from Kurukshetra University, Kurukshetra and presently working as Faculty of Commerce & Management at DAV College, Chandigarh. He has been teaching since July 1997, supervised 14 Ph.D research Scholars & 14 M. Phil scholars. He is Former Member of PG Board of Studies of Commerce & Management, Panjab University, during 2017-19, former member of Board of Studies of IKGPTU, Jalandhar during2012-14. He Submitted DSR to MSME-DI (Government of India) for the development of a steel cluster at Mandi Gobindgarh, Punjab. He has been a Resource Person more than 200 times during FDP/Conferences and training programmes. He is a Member of Editorial Boards in more than 15 National/International Journals. He is a Visiting faculty in various Educational and Training Institutes in the field of Accounting and Finance.

Rupali Arora is working as a Professor in Chandigarh University since 2012, presently handling the role of Doctoral Research Coordinator. She has obtained M.B.A. from Punjab Technical University, UGC Net Qualified, and Ph.D. from Kurukshetra University. She is the Founder Editor of Bi-annual refereed management journal *Management Edge* and on the advisory and review board of various national and international journals. She has more than 40 publications to her credit in various national and international journals. She has also organized and attended and presented papers in more than 40 seminars, national and international conferences.

Vlora Berisha is an accomplished Assistant Professor of Accounting and Finance at Business College – UHZ, with a Ph.D. degree in Bank, Accounting, and Finance from the University of Pristina "Hasan Prishtina," and a Fulbright Visiting Scholar postgraduate degree from Northern Arizona University. She also has a postdoctoral candidacy at Malta University. She has contributed to several TEMPUS and ERASMUS + Projects, including CONSUS and T2P and CTPE Projects. Beyond academia, she has worked as a financial manager at Woman Wellness Center and served as a liaison officer for the Kosovo NGO network for gender equality and against domestic violence under IOM project. Her work has been published in numerous journals and presented at many conferences, and she is a member of the prestigious European Cooperation in Science and Technology.

Iva Rani Das is a highly experienced professional in education and research, currently serving as an Assistant Director at the Daffodil Institute of IT and as a Guest Faculty at the Asian Institute of Business and Technology in Dhaka. She is also pursuing an M.Phil. in Marketing at the University of Dhaka, focusing on marketing, management, tourism, and HR management. Her research interests cover many topics, demonstrating her keen intellect and understanding of business interconnections.

Adriana AnaMaria Davidescu is Full Time Professor in the Department of Statistics and Econometrics of the Bucharest University of Economic Studies. She has over 15 years of experience in the analysis of informal economy issues, coordinating or being a member of the research team of over 50 national and international projects. The main areas of interest include, among others: labor market analysis, sustainable development, regional development, analysis and evaluation of public policies and programs, human resources management, etc.

Shuchi Dawra has teaching, consultancy, and research experience of over 18 years in industry and academia. She is an Assistant Dean and Professor of Organizational Behaviour and Human Resource Management, Chitkara Business School, Chitkara University, Punjab, India. Her area of expertise includes global HRM practices, AI in HR, digital transformation, sustainable practices, and high potential workplaces and employees. She is a Doctorate in the domain of HRM and OB from Faculty of Business, Management and Commerce from Panjab University, Chandigarh, India. She has obtained M.Com., M.B.A. (HR), UGC (NET-Commerce) and is HR Analytics certified from the IIM, Rohtak. She has her publications in reputed international and national journals, four registered copyrights and three granted patents, and has successfully supervised three doctoral research. She is also a reviewer and has chaired sessions in the conferences.

Narayanage Jayantha Dewasiri is a Professor attached to the Department of Accountancy and Finance, Sabaragamuwa University of Sri Lanka. Furthermore, he currently serves as the Brand Ambassador at Emerald Publishing, UK, and the Vice President of the Sri Lanka Institute of Marketing. He is a pioneer in applying triangulation research approaches in the management discipline. He is currently serving as the Co-Editors-in-Chief of the *South Asian Journal of Marketing* published by Emerald Publishing, Managing Editor of the *Asian Journal of Finance*, and *South Asian Journal of Tourism and Hospitality* published by the Faculty of Management Studies, Sabaragamuwa University of Sri Lanka.

Hiranya Dissanaike, a Senior Lecturer at the Department of Accountancy, Wayamba University of Sri Lanka, is a Ph.D. candidate in Management (Finance) at the University of Sri Jayewardenepura. Holding an M.Sc. degree in Applied Finance and a B.Com. (Special) Second Class honors degree from the University of Colombo, Hiranya is a Passed Finalist of CIMA and a notable recipient of the CIMA Research Excellence Award in 2022 and Second Runner Up and People's Choice Award at the National Pitching Research Competition in 2021. Having served as the Head of the Department of Accountancy (2018–2019), Hiranya's teaching interests encompass corporate governance, strategic management accounting, sustainability reporting, financial statement analysis, and research methodology. With a research focus on Corporate Governance and Sustainability, Hiranya has made substantial contributions to both international and local journals, addressing critical topics in finance and management.

Le Nguyen Ngoc Dung has a Bachelor degree in the Faculty of Public Finance, Academy of Finance, Ha Noi, Vietnam. He is currently researching a thesis about the procurement of a national budget in the field of public finance in Vietnam. In addition, he also has some projects which contributed to his faculty; therefore, he has had more chances to deeply understand the crucial impact of green public procurement. The development of public procurement is one of his favorite research expertise.

Cristina Maria Geambasu is a Ph.D. student at the Doctoral School of Cybernetics and Statistics and has over seven years of experience in market research, holding various positions in data teams. In the last years, the author focused on data engineering and regional studies around shadow economy. The subject the author studied in the Ph.D. is the Estimation of the shadow economy at regional level for the EU countries.

Liubov Gutsalenko, Doctor of Economic Sciences, a Professor of the Accounting and Taxation Department, National University of Life and Environmental Sciences of Ukraine, teaches the following disciplines: management accounting, accounting and financial reporting by international standards, organization and methods of auditing, and methodology and organization of scientific research. Her scientific interests are related to the formation of a system of accounting and control of business entities. She is the author about 198 scientific works, including 12 monographs and 13 tutorials ORCID: 0000-0001-5181-8652.

Phung Thu Ha, Ph.D., has nearly 10 years of experience in the fields of finance and banking in Vietnam. She works as a Lecturer in the Faculty of Public Finance, Academy of Finance, Ha Noi, Vietnam. She also works as a Senior Researcher at Viet Analytics Co., Ltd., then she has had more chances to deeply understand the public financial management in Vietnam. The green public procurement is one of her favorite research expertise. She published several papers on this subject.

Nargiz Hajiyeva (https://orcid.org/0000-0002-9448-5613), Political Scientist, the Director of the Organization of Scientific Activities Unit, and the Chair of the Women Researchers Council at the Research Center of Azerbaijan State University of Economics (UNEC). She is the first female political scientist from Azerbaijan and also serves as the Co-Director of the "Empirical Methods" Working Group at the Swiss Political Science Association in Switzerland. She worked as an Independent Researcher at Corvinus University of Budapest, Cold War History Research Center. Additionally, she is an honored alumna of the European Academy of Diplomacy in Warsaw, Poland. She is a recipient of various academic scholarships and grants in Europe.

Anuradha Iddagoda is a Senior Lecturer at the University of Sri Jayewardenepura, Sri Lanka. She holds a Ph.D. from the University of Sri Jayewardenepura Sri Lanka, an M.B.A. in Human Resource Management from the Postgraduate Institute of Management, University of Sri Jayewardenepura, a Master of Information Technology postgraduate degree, a Bachelor of Information Technology both from Charles Sturt University, Australia. She has been a Guest Researcher at the Department of Sociology and Work Science at the University of Gothenburg, Sweden.

Mohammad M. Jaber is an experienced researcher, educator, and advocate with over a decade of experience. He holds a Ph.D. in Economics and a Master's degree in Environmental Sciences and Management. His expertise spans climate change and energy economics. He has published numerous papers and has extensive experience as a lecturer and technical advisor. He is deeply committed to promoting environmental awareness and sustainability. He enjoys exploring new areas and contributing to the development of solutions. With his multifaceted skills and passion for creating positive environmental impact, he is a prominent figure in his field ORCID: 0000-0001-8808-4170.

Arvinder Kaur is working as an Assistant Professor at the University School of Business, Chandigarh University, in the field of Finance since 2016. She has done Masters in Finance and Control with distinction Masters and graduation in commerce. She is a qualified member of Institute of Company Secretaries of India. Also, she has a license as a distributor of Mutual Funds under NISM. She is currently pursuing Ph.D. from Punjabi University, Patiala. She has seven years of academic experience and expertise in teaching specialized subjects like taxation, financial accounting, corporate accounting, and GST. She has 20 research papers presented (national and international conferences) and published in various renowned journals and seven book chapters. She attended 16 faculty development programs and workshops in her tenure. Her area of interest is Fintech.

Reet Kaur, an accomplished professional, holds a Bachelor's and Master's degree in Commerce, complemented by an M.B.A., and is UGC-NET Commerce qualified. She also holds Ph.D. degree in Commerce. With over 12 years of teaching expertise in finance and marketing, she is dedicated to academic excellence. She has contributed significantly to her field, presenting and publishing research papers in national seminars, international conferences, and journals. Her commitment to education and the dissemination of knowledge is evident in her impactful contributions, driven by a commitment to excellence, she continues to inspire and impart valuable insights in the realms of commerce, making a lasting impact in the academic arena.

Simranjeet Kaur is pursuing a Ph.D. in Human Resource Management from Chandigarh University, having experience in teaching for more than three years. She has done M.Com. (Hons) from Punjab University and UGC Net Qualified. She has been a high achiever throughout her educational career. She has authored research articles in journals in Scopus/Web of Science. She has also attended and presented papers at national and international conferences.

Game Kankanange Krishani Kaushalya is a graduate of the Department of Accountancy and Finance, Sabaragamuwa University of Sri Lanka.

Pawan Kumar with 18 years of experience as an academician, researcher, innovator, and quality assessor, he has a wealth of knowledge and skills to offer. His professional journey has been marked by numerous accomplishments, including supervising six Ph.D. students in commerce and management. He has published more than 40 research papers.

Sanjeev Kumar is a Professor, School of Hotel Management and Tourism, Lovely Professional University, Punjab, India. He holds a Bachelor's degree in Hotel Management from Osmania University. He earned his Master's degree in Tourism Management from Madurai Kamaraj University and his Doctorate from Amity University Rajasthan. He has worked as a teacher for the past 18 years. He has 20 research articles and has presented more than 12 papers at national and international conferences. He also traveled throughout the country to attend international and national conferences.

Eduard Mihai Manta is a Ph.D. student at the Doctoral School of Cybernetics and Statistics and has over seven years of experience in IT, holding various positions in data teams. In the last years, the author focused on machine learning and data science. The subject the author studied in the Ph.D. is the COVID-19 – an accelerator of the implementation of sustainable development concepts, resilience, green, and inclusive of the global economy.

Uliana Marchuk, Candidate of Economic Sciences, Associate Professor of the Accounting and Taxation Department, State Higher Educational Institution "Kyiv National Economic University named after Vadym Hetman," teaches the following disciplines: methodology and organization of research in accounting, audit and taxation, financial accounting, enterprise accounting policy, and financial analysis (in English). Her scientific interests are related to the management, accounting, control, and audit in Ukraine. She is the author of 98 scientific works (four of them are the publications in periodicals, included to Scopus and Web of Science databases) and the co-author of five monographs and three tutorials ORCID: 0000-0003-0971-1303.

Adalat Muradov (https://orcid.org/0000-0002-7461-3761) is the Rector of Azerbaijan State University of Economics (UNEC). He is also the Chairman of the Dissertation Council operating at UNEC. On March 5, 2014, and he was appointed as the Rector of the UNEC. By the Decree of the President of the Republic of Azerbaijan dated September 24, 2020, on the occasion of the 90th anniversary of the UNEC and in recognition of his services in the development of education in Azerbaijan, he was awarded the Order of Glory. His research fields include world economy, green economy, economic theory, macroeconomics, and related fields ORCID: 0000-0002-7461-3761.

Nguyen Hoang Oanh, a Bachelor in the Faculty of Public Finance, Academy of Finance, Ha Noi, Vietnam, is currently researching a thesis about the procurement of a national budget in the field of public finance in Vietnam. In addition, she also has some projects which contributed to her faculty. Therefore, she will have more chances to deeply understand the crucial impact of green public procurement. The development of public procurement is one of her favorite researching expertise.

Vidhi Pathak is a keen researcher and a fourth year student of Integrated Programme in Management, B.B.A.+M.B.A. at Chitkara Business School, Chitkara University, India.

Mananage Shanika Hansini Rathnasiri is a Lecturer, attached to the Department of Marketing Management, Faculty of Management Studies, Sabaragamuwa University of Sri Lanka.

Jathun Dahanayaka Kaushalyani Ruwandika is a Lecturer attached to the Faculty of Management Studies at the Sabaragamuwa University of Sri Lanka.

Albulena Shala works as an Assistant Professor at the University of Pristina "Hasan Prishtina." She is a Professor of courses in Banking and Finance. She has published several papers in credible journals. She attended Teaching Principles and Practices 1, CERGE-EI Foundation Teaching Development, 2018. Also, she attended the Digital Transformation and FinTech House of Training in Luxembourg in 2022. She is an external expert in Cost Action 19130. She attended several conferences in FinTech. She was a member of the jury in the "Best WI-FI 2023 Young Researcher Paper: FinTech Contest."

Jyotsna Sharma is working as Associate Professor in RIMT University. She is a postgraduate in Business Management and holds Doctorate in the area of Banking. She also holds a postgraduate diploma in International Business and qualified UGC-NET. She has work experience of over 15 years and actively involved in teaching for more than 12 years in diverse areas of business management, finance, and marketing. She has authored a book Titled "Career Planning and Management." She has published various research papers in various journals, seminars/conferences of national and international repute. Also, she has contributed research papers which have been included as in chapter in different books with ISBN number. She has participated in several Faculty Development Programmes. ORCID: 0000-0002-1846-3201

Preeti Sharma is working as an Assistant Professor in University School of Business, Chandigarh University. She is a double postgraduate in Business Management and Business Economics and is perusing Ph.D. Her major areas of interests are human resource analytics and finance. She is a dedicated and focused academician, having over more than 10 years of experience in teaching commerce and management graduate and postgraduate students. She has served as a Trainer and Resource Person at Institute of Chartered Accountants of India, Chandigarh chapter, North region. Also, she has a solid Research background and has presented papers and articles at many national and international conferences. She has won the Best Research Paper Award in international conference.

Sandhir Sharma, Ph.D. in Strategic Management, has 24 years in higher education and 5 years in telecom. With over 150 research publications in national and international journals and conferences, he focuses in strategy design. He is Pro Vice Chancellor of Chitkara Business School and a Visiting Professor at Binus University, Indonesia and University of Applied Sciences, Osnabruck, Germany. He advises SMEs on strategy. He advises 10 academic and industrial Ph.Ds. Eight of his pupils have Ph.Ds in Neuromarketing, Consumers, Foods, Organic Foods, Work Engagement, Brands, Brand Personality, Brand Love, Television, Broadcasting, Digital Television, Green Marketing, and Consumer Behavior. His 27 patents and 14 copyrights include health, life, social, technical, and industrial products.

Mariya Shygun, Doctor of Science in Economics, a Professor, and an Auditor of Ukraine. She is an author of more than 240 publications. She is a leader and participant in more than 12 research on accounting, auditing, and taxation. She has been awarded for CIMA Employability Excellence Award 2021 – Regional Champion (Europe) and for Distinguished Contribution 2020 "Conceptual Changes in Accounting" for the CIMA Research Excellence Award, presented by the CGMA Global University and Academic Center of Excellence. She was awarded as a recognized expert in the field of audit by the "Honor of the Audit Chamber of Ukraine" (2016). Her research interests include theory and methodology of accounting and auditing, modeling of accounting system, and strategic management accounting and control ORCID: 0000-0003-1660-9534.

Afroza Sultana is an Assistant Professor in Finance at the Department of Business Administration, Premier University Chattogram, Bangladesh. She is also an Offshore Diploma Teacher at the University of Technology, Sydney. She is an M.Phil. Research Fellow at the University of Chittagong. She has an enormous interest in the research field of financial inclusion, financial literacy, and the adaptation of technologies into business processes. She has several articles published in renowned local and international journals and 10 years of teaching experience in financial accounting, corporate finance, and financial engineering at the undergraduate and postgraduate levels.

Tekla Szép, Ph.D., is an Associate Professor and Deputy Director of the Institute of World and Regional Economics, Faculty of Economics, University of Miskolc, and a Research Fellow at UNEC Women Researchers Council. She is an economist, and her research interests are focused on energy economics with special emphasis given to the sustainable energy transition. In addition to her work, she has also directed a variety of national and international EU funded projects. She has vast experience in proposal writing, project management and evaluation, and policy monitoring. She has been cooperating with consortium partners and colleagues from different European universities, companies, and national and international organizations. She holds a Ph.D. in Management and Business Administration ORCID: 0000-0001-9985-1881.

Mohammad Badruddoza Talukder is an Associate Professor at the College of Tourism and Hospitality Management, International University of Business Agriculture and Technology, Dhaka, Bangladesh. He completed his Ph.D. in Hotel Management at the School of Hotel Management and Tourism, Lovely Professional University, India. He has been teaching in Tourism and Hospitality domains at various universities in Bangladesh since 2009. His research areas include tourism management, hotel management, hospitality management, food and beverage management, and accommodation management, where he has published research papers in well-known journals in Bangladesh and abroad.

Anita Tanwar is working as an Assistant Professor in Chitkara University. She has done her M.B.A. from, Maharishi Dayanand University and M.Phil. and Ph.D. in the area of banking. She has a corporate experience of two years in The Ambala Central Cooperative Bank and an experience of nine years in teaching. She is presently working in Chitkara University. Moreover, she has published many research papers in UGC Care listed journals and Scopus indexed journals and has attended many national and international conferences and seminars. She has been awarded NCC "C" certificate and moreover best cadet award. Furthermore, she reviewed six papers for Academy of Management, and she is a reviewer in *Global Business and Finance Review-Scopus indexed Journal*.

Nitin Thapar is a management professional having more than 17 years of experience in banking, financial services, and academics. His areas of expertise are finance, quantitative techniques, accounting, and derivatives.

Ngo Duc Tien, Ph.D., has more than 10 years of experience in the fields of finance and banking in Vietnam. He works as a Lecturer in the Faculty of Banking and Insurance, Academy of Finance, Ha Noi, Vietnam. He also works as a data analytics lecturer at Magic code institute Vietnam, and he has had more chances to deeply understand the crucial impact of green credit on banking operations. The implication of green credit is one of his favorite research expertise.

Rajesh Tiwari is currently working as a Professor, Academic Coordinator, and Chair Head-Finance in Department of Management Studies, Graphic Era (Deemed to be University). He has over 20 years of rich experience in academics and industry. He has obtained M.B.A. (Finance), Chartered Financial Analyst, UGC-NET, Ph.D. in Management. He has previously worked as Director in Indus University, Ahmedabad, United Group-Greater Noida (Affiliated to Guru Gobind Singh Indraprastha University, New Delhi), Sai Balaji Group-Pune. He has been Academic Coordinator for Management Programs of Staffordshire University, UK and other reputed B Schools. He has 51 research publications in national and international journals.

Ekrem Tufan is interested in behavioral finance and behavioral economics. He is the head of Health Management Department and Health Economics Master Program. He has been delivering project cycle management and strategic planning private courses. He has improved a unique estimation method and successfully applied for political elections. The author has been working as an academic for 30 years where he spent most of the time at Çanakkale Onsekiz Mart University (Türkiye).

Cu Hoang Lam Vu graduates from the Faculty of Public Finance, Academy of Finance, Ha Noi, Vietnam. He was the Formerly President of the Science Club of Students at the Academy of Finance. And he is currently researching on the procurement of a national budget in the field of Public finance in Vietnam. In addition, he also has a number of research projects contributing to his academy, so he has the opportunity to gain a deeper understanding of the important impact of green public procurement. The development of public procurement is one of his favorite research specialties.

Simbiya Hevage Madu Lakmini Walakumbura is a Lecturer attached to the Department of Accountancy and Finance at the Sabaragamuwa University of Sri Lanka.

W. P. Richard Wickramaratne has been working as a Professor in the Department of Human Resource Management, Faculty of Management at the University of Peradeniya, Sri Lanka.

Foreword

In recent years, the necessity for sustainable business practices has experienced exponential growth, prompting industries worldwide to reassess their operations from an environmentally conscious perspective. The emergence of green management as a new paradigm in the world of business underscores this shift toward ecological responsibility. This book, *Green Management: A New Paradigm in the World of Business*, delves into various facets of green management and its implications for businesses globally.

The compilation of chapters within this book offers a comprehensive exploration of diverse topics pertinent to green management. From examining the trends and regulations surrounding green finance to investigating the impact of sustainable human resource management practices on employee retention, each chapter contributes valuable insights into the multifaceted nature of green management. One chapter delves into the discussion of sustainability within healthcare systems amidst the backdrop of the COVID-19 pandemic, comparing the approaches of Germany, France, Italy, and Turkey. Another chapter explores the intersection of internal and external corporate social responsibility with organizational competitive performance, particularly within the banking sector in Sri Lanka.

The book also examines the integration of green energy sources and initiatives for sustainable development, employing bibliometric analysis to assess their adoption. Furthermore, it explores the intersection of artificial intelligence (AI) and green human resource management practices, offering a systemic review of AI's influence on evolving green HRM strategies. Additionally, the book evaluates the application of green economy policies, such as those observed in Switzerland, to regions like the Karabakh area of Azerbaijan. It also scrutinizes the role of energy in human well-being through a case study from Jordan and explores green public procurement practices in Asian countries. Moreover, the book delves into various other topics, including green credit policies in Vietnam, sustainable development in healthcare management and accounting within Ukraine, and the role of green energy in the economic aspects of sustainable development. Finally, it addresses the significance of shareholder engagement, the evaluation of the 2030 Agenda's progress, and the adaptation of blockchain technology in financial arrangements from an Asian perspective.

Green Management: A New Paradigm in the World of Business serves as an invaluable resource for academics, policymakers, and practitioners seeking to navigate the complexities of sustainable business practices. Its diverse array of chapters offers a comprehensive understanding of the challenges and opportunities inherent in adopting green management principles across various industries.

I commend the authors for their insightful contributions, and I trust that readers will find this book to be a guiding light in their journey toward a greener, more sustainable future.

Prof. Ass. Dr Fisnik Morina, Post-Doc
Vice-Dean for Teaching, Student Affairs and Scientific Research at Faculty of Business and Professor at University "Haxhi Zeka" – Kosovo

Preface

Green Management: A New Paradigm in the World of Business is an attempt to analyze sustainability's influence on corporate operations. It considers the strategic, process, and attitudinal changes businesses need to sustain ecology-conscious trading.

This book is about the theory and a real instrument designed for adopting sustainable thinking in every existing organization, be it a small company or a big producer. Such a line of thought gives a fuller outline of the green management principles. It has a very diverse range of skills, which it imparts using practical examples, real-life examples, and proven strategies from leading companies across the globe.

The book will be a voyage of discovery for the readers, proving that having an environmentally aware mindset is one of the ways to solve the problems that are our planet's consequences. One of the advantages is the ability to invest and grow, build and support the brand's reputation, be prepared, and respond rapidly to any global issue. Moreover, "Green Management" attaches great importance to the ethics work of enterprise to take the position of environmental guardians, which means their duty toward environmental conservation is morally recognized to guarantee a sound ecological future for the next generations.

Today, we are struggling to deal with this ecological disaster and upcoming economic boon, which is important for future green management prospects. This book performs the function of a persuasive appeal and advises businesses on innovation, creativity, and responsibility as they strive toward that future, namely, the one with environmentally friendlier and more economic-sound policies.

Green Management: A New Paradigm in the World of Business explores the concept of business as more than just an idea to be executed. It serves as an inspiration and incentive for individuals and organizations to embrace the environmentally friendly transition that is currently underway. The ultimate outcome of the relationship between the economy and the ecosystem necessitates a comprehensive cooperation to promote the interests of both industry and the environment as a whole.

Swati Gupta
Chitkara Business School, Chitkara University, Punjab, India

Sanjay Taneja
Graphic Era Deemed to be University, India

Ercan Özen
University of Uşak, Turkey

Kiran Sood
Chitkara Business School, Chitkara University, Punjab, India;
Women Researchers Council, Azerbaijan State University of Economics (UNEC), Baku, Azerbaijan

and
Simon Grima
University of Malta, Malta

Chapter 1

Green Finance: Trends and Regulation

Albulena Shala[a] *and Vlora Berisha*[b]

[a]*University of Pristina, "Hasan Prishtina", Kosovo*
[b]*University of Peja, "Haxhi Zeka", Kosovo*

Abstract

Purpose: This chapter highlights the key findings about the development of green finance in Central and Eastern European (CEE) countries. The main purpose is to analyze the policy to promote green financing, the role of financial institutions and regulators in the green finance agenda, and the challenges of green financing.

Need for the study: Through this study, we will identify the level of development of green finance in CEE countries. It is also necessary to know the role and contribution of central banks in the development of green finance.

Methodology: Using the comparative methodology, we analyzed the following indexes: green economic opportunities, the Green Growth Index, the Global Climate Risk Index, and the Green Central Banking Scorecard in the G20. We included 17 countries from Central and Eastern Europe (CEE): Albania, Bulgaria, Bosnia and Herzegovina, Croatia, Czech Republic, Poland, Estonia, Romania, Hungary, Latvia, Lithuania, Kosovo, Montenegro, North Macedonia, Slovenia, Slovakia, and Serbia.

Findings: The results show that the countries of the Western Balkans do not have a satisfactory performance compared to other countries, although they stand well in terms of legislation.

Practical implications: Studying green finance in a group of countries would bring new insights to their economies and to all other countries wishing to develop green finance markets. Their exposition, especially for the countries of the Western Balkans, will bring new knowledge and practices to the Central Bank and relevant institutions.

Keywords: Green finance; green central banking; climate risks; low carbon; regulation; green investment; green growth

JEL Classifications: E5; E5; G2; G4; Q5

Green Management: A New Paradigm in the World of Business, 1–21

Published under exclusive licence by Emerald Publishing Limited
doi:10.1108/978-1-83797-442-920241001

1. Introduction

Green finance is a relatively new topic that offers a more creative form of funding for people, companies, and governments wanting to take part in low-carbon or green ventures. Today, we are aware that the possibility of the financial system collapsing is increased by the risks related to climate change. A rising number of global financial stakeholders are incorporating an evaluation of climate change into their risk management processes. This process might be more straightforward with the increased participation of macroprudential authorities, such as central banks, primarily by coordinating the shift to a low-carbon economy. Central banks are beginning to assess the risks associated with climate change and are incorporating them more and more into their broader policy agenda. The monetary policy strategy reviews and reserve management by central banks are becoming increasingly influenced by climate change issues. The strategy of central banks' monetary policy reviews and reserve management is becoming increasingly influenced by climate change issues. Involving the financial sector and the regulatory bodies in charge of it will be essential to achieving a green transformation toward low-carbon, sustainable growth and development.

Green finance is becoming more critical in the banking industry due to the need to protect banks and society from unforeseen future economic issues brought on by unexpected global financial events, climate catastrophes, social unrest, and corporate scandals (Ziolo et al., 2019). Furthermore, the paradigm of traditional banking is changing to emphasize the supply of environmentally friendly goods (Dikau & Volz, 2021).

Including climate change risk concerns in current monetary and macroprudential frameworks is necessary because central banks are accountable for financial and macroprudential stability. To promote green financing, central banks can use various practical policy tools. Numerous financial regulatory tools can be adjusted to either mandate or incentivize financial organizations to consider climate and environmental risks when making decisions about loan origination or financial stability. Investments must shift from carbon- and resource-intensive to sustainable to meet the goals of the 2030 Agenda for Sustainable Development and Paris Climate Accord. The central bank has implicit or explicit responsibility for maintaining financial and macroeconomic stability; as such, it should take a systemic approach to mitigate climate-related and other environmental risks. Moreover, central banks have a solid position to encourage the creation of sustainable finance strategies and ensure that financial firms price environmental and carbon risk appropriately because of their regulatory control over money, credit, and the financial system (Volz, 2017).

Against this background, this paper offers a theoretical analysis of green finance, different indicators, and the pros and cons of central banks' obligations to environmental objectives. The paper also explores how central banks, through monetary policies, can influence decisions in the distribution of credit in activities that affect green financing. The countries included in this study are from Central and Eastern Europe (CEE) (Bosnia and Herzegovina, Bulgaria, Croatia, Albania, the Czech Republic, Estonia, Hungary, Kosovo, Latvia, Lithuania, Poland, Romania, Northern Macedonia, Montenegro, Serbia, the Slovak Republic, and Slovenia).

The primary purpose of this study is to research the level of legislation and the relevant indicators in the Western Balkans countries to determine the current level, the challenges, and the recommendations that these countries should follow.

The paper is structured as follows: Section 2 briefly reviews the literature. Then, Section 3 covers data and methodology. Section 4 then discusses the range of different indices that indicate the performance of the countries involved and the legislation of these countries. Section 5 ends with some recommendations and conclusions for the proper work of central banks and other public institutions to achieve the standards set by the relevant institutions.

2. Literature Review

Humanity is facing a severe threat from climate change in this century, and its impacts are becoming increasingly visible. Funding green initiatives can decrease carbon emission levels (Li et al., 2021). Institutional investors engaged in impact investment will profit from green finance (Barber et al., 2021; Tang & Zhang, 2020). Investors in the corporate and Treasury markets can benefit from diversification through green financing (Reboredo, 2018). Funding for fossil fuel operations that endanger the environment and climate change can be decreased by increasing green financing (Ozili, 2022; Sachs et al., 2019). As defined by Höhne et al. (2012), green finance is a catch-all word for financial investments made in environmental products, policies that support the growth of a more sustainable economy, and programs and activities related to sustainable development.

Additionally, the literature mentions a broader variety of other environmental objectives, such as water cleanliness, biodiversity protection, or industrial pollution control. Pricewaterhouse Coopers Consultants (2013) states that green finance refers to financial products and services considering environmental factors in lending decisions, monitoring, and risk management. These promote environmentally responsible investments and low-carbon technologies, projects, industries, and businesses, as mentioned by other authors (Li et al., 2012; Lindenberg, 2014) if a "traditional" financial product, service, or instrument is used to collect money for environmentally friendly investments, initiatives, or activities. It can be considered "green." According to the literature, green finance requires that financial resources be allocated to the protection of the environment, clean energy, green building, climate change, social inclusion, and corporate governance in all sectors of the economy (Urban & Wójcik, 2019; Yuan & Gallagher, 2019). In order to get a competitive edge in the market, banks should strategically select and market green finance products (Raberto et al., 2019). According to Ozili (2021), green finance is funding initiatives that improve the environment and generate money. Green finance is defined by Wang and Zhi (2016) as financing that combines financial gains with environmental preservation.

A green loan or credit is a unique form of short- to medium-term financial support provided by banks to start-ups, small enterprises, and multinational organizations to support their research and development of innovative products (Díaz-García et al., 2015).

Growing the proportion of green investments (GIs) goes beyond just meeting medium-term climate goals. The need to improve energy security, lessen the negative health consequences of air pollution, and discover new business opportunities are some reasons given by proponents of investing in low-carbon energy sources (Alva & Bhat, 2018). Furthermore, bank products such as green long-term investment accounts and sustainable investment accounts enable clients to save enough money to support environmentally conscious long-term investment ventures in agriculture and other sectors of the economy (He et al., 2019). According to recent data, banks enable businesses and people to engage in renewable energy projects, contributing to the rise in investment in this area (He et al., 2019). Trading and investing in "carbon emission rights" and their derivatives is known as "carbon finance." Li and Liu (2011) say it differs from conventional financial activity. To lessen the damaging effects of carbon emissions on the environment, many banks in countries that export coal are issuing more carbon finance and fewer conventional loans on fossil fuels, such as coal (Ganda, 2018; Glomsrød & Wei, 2018).

Central banks are critical financial sector players to make appropriate climate change decisions. According to Chenet et al. (2021) central banks have started to enforce banks to obtain green certifications, green credit scores, environmental innovation, and social inclusion. Competitively, the central bank offers tax breaks and other incentives to banks that comply with these rules.

The term "green central banking" refers to how central banks can respond to the threats presented by climate change. In its climate agenda, the European Central Bank (ECB) lists three goals to which central banks might contribute, even though it recognizes that governments and lawmakers bear primary responsibility for addressing climate change: First, central banks can assist with financial risk. Second, central banks can contribute by providing financial resources for the change. Third, to promote more extensive behavioural changes, central banks might exchange their expertise (Spinaci et al., 2022).

Climate change could impact the economy in general and the financial system in particular, according to climate finance and economics research. The two main ways that climate risks manifest are: (1) physical risk, events as a result of climate change that will damage infrastructure and the properties of businesses and households; and (2) transition risk, effects on the financial system and the economy as a whole as a result of the shift to a low-carbon economy (Cipollone, 2022). Climate change could impact the economy in general and the financial system in particular, according to climate finance and economics research. Suddenly unpredictable climate episodes (such as extreme weather-related events or climate-related disasters) give rise to "physical risk," which first appears as negative supply- and demand-side shocks to output and prices that hurt the balance sheets of households and businesses (Molico, 2019). According to Bolton et al. (2020), Rijal et al. (2024), and Kaur et al. (2024), physical risks are the financial losses and costs associated with catastrophic weather events and the results of long-term environmental changes. Capital depreciation can occur due to asset damage, which can cause a sudden repricing of entire asset classes. For example, the deterioration of financial companies' balance sheets following weather disasters (a physical risk) lowers their profitability and debt servicing capacity, which raises credit risk. Physical risk has the potential to directly or indirectly affect financial stability from a systemic standpoint because extreme weather events can result in increased liabilities, insurance claims, and bankruptcies that cause significant losses to the financial system. Financial stability can be affected in various ways by physical and transitional risks. The duration of the steps taken to address climate change and how quickly they are taken will determine the impact of these risks. In this context, the October 2018 progress report (NGFS, 2019) from the Network of Central Banks and Supervisors for Greening the Financial System emphasizes that climate change risks are a source of financial risk. It demands that supervisors and central banks ensure the financial system resists these threats.

Inflation targets are usually kept low by central banks, which implement monetary policy and manage the country's money supply. In light of the significant investments that must be made quickly to move toward a sustainable financial system, there has been a public debate about whether or not central banks should play a key role in addressing this issue. In order to achieve the primary objectives of price stability and financial stability, sustainability factors may be considered even in cases where environmental objectives are not explicitly mentioned in a central bank's mandate.

Central banks are uniquely positioned to shift resources away from carbon-intensive sectors and toward green investment because of their regulatory authority over money, credit, and the financial system. Central banks, particularly those in developing nations, usually have a solid institutional position that allows them to influence policy outcomes in ways other public institutions, like environmental ministries, are unlikely to be able to. Climate policies (mitigation measures to achieve a low-carbon economy and adaptation measures to address physical risks) impact monetary policy in addition to climate shocks (Boneva et al., 2021). The central bank can use various tools to enhance green investments, such as unconventional and traditional monetary policy tools. Additionally, using their power, central banks may push financial institutions to build the resources necessary to address environmental and climatic risks. According to Schoenmaker et al. (2015), macroprudential supervision should detect ecological imbalances that could result in material financial risks and account for externalities that could lead to financial instability. Limiting credit extensions to specific carbon-intensive or polluting activities would be a simple solution to reduce environmental, systemic risk.

A bank's credit allocation may be influenced, and green investments may be encouraged by differential reserve requirements that are correlated with the portfolio compositions of the bank, permitting lower (or higher) required reserve rates for portfolios skewed toward greener. Financial authorities impose capital requirements on financial institutions, which typically form a capital-to-risk (weighted) asset ratio, requiring them to keep a specific amount of capital for risk-weighted assets. Capital requirements may apply higher risk weights to carbon-intensive assets. "Carbon certificates" is another strategy that will provide an incentive to increase green investment. They can be distributed to low-carbon projects (Rozenberg et al., 2013). Banks can control how much credit they offer to different industries and what assets they invest in. This means they can decide which industries they want to support financially. This will limit the flow of resources to businesses or sectors that exceed predetermined carbon-emission targets. One technique used in macroprudential regulation to limit financial institutions' exposure to assets with high risks – in the case of green financing, a high carbon intensity – is exposure limitations by counterparty, industry, or geographic area (Ndekwa et al., 2023; Schoenmaker & Tilburg, 2016; Sood & Ozen, 2024; Yerpude et al., 2022). The central banks in the eurozone are making a concerted effort to incorporate climate change concerns into their missions. The shared agreement encourages disclosure and knowledge of the risks associated with climate change. The European Central Bank (ECB) has reviewed banks' self-assessment of their procedures, clarified its expectations for climate risk management and disclosure in the previous few years, and, most recently, introduced a supervisory climate-risk stress test. The European Commission is working to put environmental, social, and governance (ESG) issues at the center of the financial system to convert the European economy into a circular economy (European Commission, 2018). Currently, the ECB's responsibility might be to mandate the adoption of ESG risk management standards by banks and other financial institutions (Dikau & Volz, 2018). Furthermore, according to Cecot (2019), commercial banks may use ESG risks as a criterion in their credit approval procedures. To consider the potentially harmful environmental effects of financial products and services, banks and other financial institutions should incorporate ESG risk management principles into their governance frameworks (Cecot, 2019).

3. Data and Methodology

The methodology is based on a comparison of the relevant indices. Three possible case counts can be compared: few-, single-, or many-countries. In the same way, Landman (2008) offered a three-part classification of comparative studies: single-country studies, studies that compare a single country, and studies that compare numerous countries. The research conducted by Shala et al. (2018), Shala and Qehaja (2021), and Shala and Perri (2022) employed a consistent methodology. The study scrutinized several key indexes, including the Green Economic Opportunities, the Green Growth Index, the Global Climate Risk Index, and the Green Central Banking Scorecard in G20. The analysis was focused on 17 countries situated in Central and Eastern Europe (CEE), such as Albania, Bulgaria, Bosnia and Herzegovina, Croatia, Czech Republic, Poland, Estonia, Romania, Hungary, Latvia, Lithuania, Kosovo, Montenegro, North Macedonia, Slovenia, Slovakia, and Serbia.

Since comparative analysis applies to almost any topic and may be found in almost all disciplines, it plays a significant part in studying almost every topic (Azarian, 2011). Three phases were involved in the comparative methodology used in our study:

1. analyzing each index separately, including all countries;
2. analyzing the rankings of all countries in these indices; and
3. concluding which countries made more progress in green finance.

Specifically, we analyzed the legislative frameworks on energy and climate in Western Balkan countries, which are part of the NGFS. Meanwhile, we also mentioned G20 members' results for the Green Central Banking Scorecard.

4. Analysis of Results and Discussions

The Green Growth Index is a tool used to evaluate how Central and Eastern European countries are performing regarding social inclusion, green economic opportunities, natural capital protection, and efficient and sustainable resource use. The index is scored on a scale of 1–100, with 1–20 indicating abysmal performance, 20–40 indicating low performance, 40–60 indicating moderate performance, 60–80 indicating excellent performance, and 80–100 indicating perfect performance. When a country achieves a green density score of 100, it meets the sustainability objectives.[1] Table 1.1 displays the Green Growth Index scores for Central and Eastern Europe (CEE) countries.

As can be seen from the latest data on the Green Growth Index (2022), the five countries with the best performance are the Czech Republic, Slovakia, Hungary,

Table 1.1. The Green Growth Index in CEE Countries.

Country	Sub-region	2010		2022	
		Index	Rank	Index	Rank
Czech Republic	EE	72.82	4	75.13	5
Slovakia	EE	70.25	6	74.04	7
Hungary	EE	68.41	10	69.75	12
Latvia	NE	66.39	16	68.85	14
Lithuania	NE	64.60	20	68.57	15
Estonia	NE	65.71	17	68.27	17
Croatia	SE	61.12	27	68.07	19
Romania	EE	65.60	19	68.01	20
Slovenia	SE	62.94	24	67.68	22
Poland	SE	63.45	23	66.66	24
Macedonia	SE	61.60	26	64.93	26
Bulgaria	EE	60.14	30	63.93	29
Serbia	SE	60.57	28	63.49	30
Bosnia and Herzegovina	SE	55.06	36	60.53	31
Albania	SE	60.40	29	60.48	32
Montenegro	SE	45.82	39	58.14	35

Source: Acosta et al. (2022). Green Growth Index 2022 – Measuring performance in achieving SDG targets, GGGI Technical Report No. 27 (link https://greengrowthindex.gggi.org/).

Note: NE – Northern Europe; EE – Eastern Europe; SE – Southern Europe.

[1] *Source*: Green Growth Index – Measuring performance in achieving SDG targets (gggi.org).

Latvia, and Lithuania, while Bulgaria and the five countries of the Western Balkans have recorded the weakest performance. Unfortunately, there is no data for Kosovo.

The dimensions of green economic opportunities are green investment, trade, employment, and innovation. Green investment is defined as both public and private investment that advances sustainable development and green growth by supporting, directly or indirectly, the conservation of natural capital through environmental protection and climate action, as well as the sustainable use of resources, including land, water, energy, and materials (Obradović, 2019). Meanwhile, green trade is defined as the ability of a nation to manufacture and export environmentally friendly products that support green growth, climate action, environmental protection, and sustainable development (European Parliament, 2019). "Green jobs" are jobs that come from more activities that support an environmentally sustainable economy. Green jobs also help preserve the environment, reduce people's environmental impact, and offer respectable working conditions (ILO, 2015). Green innovation is considered product, process, and service innovations that positively impact the environment (Gao et al., 2018). These innovations include energy conservation, pollution prevention, waste recycling, and green product designs.

Regarding green economic opportunities, as seen from Table 1.2, the countries with the best performance during 2020–2021 are the Czech Republic, Slovakia, Hungary, Latvia, and Lithuania. These countries have offered good opportunities for green investment and green employment (see Table 1.2). In the countries of the Western Balkans, there is a lack of general data; however, from the data that has been presented, it can be seen that the best performance is in green investment (see Table 1.2).

The Global Climate Risk Index evaluates and ranks how extreme weather events (storms, floods, heatwaves, etc.) linked to climate change have impacted different nations and areas. The Global Climate Risk Index indicates a level of exposure and vulnerability to extreme weather events, which countries should understand as warnings to be prepared for more frequent and severe future events. The countries with the highest rankings experience extreme weather events the most, and they should use the CRI as a warning indicator that they could have either regular occurrences or uncommon but catastrophic disasters (Eckstein et al., 2019). The CEE countries with the highest scores in 2019 are Albania, North Macedonia, Kosovo, Lithuania, and Romania (see Table 1.3).

Positive Money and Green Central Banking produced the Green Central Banking Scorecard, which rates and ranks all the green policies and programs the G20 central banks have adopted. Research and Advocacy, Monetary Policy, Financial Policy, and Leading by Example are the four main categories used to assess the green policies of G20 central banks and regulators. Presenting environmental papers, joining the NGFS, and embracing key ideas can advance research and advocacy. Monetary policy includes interest rates and reserve requirements, funding and refinancing plans, collateral frameworks, direct credit allocation, green policies related to assets and monetary reserves, and coordination with fiscal authorities. Financial regulation includes capital and liquidity tools, disclosure and stress-testing green policies, and impact regulation of financial firms. Setting an

Table 1.2. Green Economic Opportunities by Region and Rank in CEE Countries.

Country	Regional Rank	Green Economic Opportunities	Green investment	Green Trade	Green employment	Green innovation
		Indicator categories (Percent)				
2020						
Czech Republic	**3**	65.49	67.61	53.02	88.86	57.74
Slovakia	**7**	58.58	60.73	36.77	77.74	67.85
Lithuania	**9**	52.2	68.81	34.65	42.77	72.80
Hungary	**10**	62.24	72.68	53.37	69.53	55.64
Slovenia	**11**	51.34	69.55	35.93	62.56	44.44
Estonia	**13**	50.48	75.17	34.85	25.25	98.15
Latvia	**14**	41.95	61.19	20.43	39.78	62.27
Poland	**16**	55.05	68	34.05	60.35	65.74
Romania	**18**	54.01	56.06	56.33	49.58	54.35
Croatia	**21**	45.91	72.58	21.35	52.09	55.04
Bulgaria	**27**	41.46	73.39	22.02	45.75	39.98
Serbia	**28**	40.91	59.32	26.83	68.31	25.75
Montenegro	**36**	12.75	–	6.36	24.96	13.04
Bosnia and H	**37**	9.54	–	28.02	30.94	1
Albania	**35**	9.44	53.91	1.15	13.54	–
Macedonia	–	–	72.82	100	–	–

(Continued)

Table 1.2. (*Continued*)

Country	Regional Rank	Indicator categories (Percent)				
		Green Economic Opportunities	Green investment	Green Trade	Green employment	Green innovation
2021						
Czech Republic	**3**	55.38	65.91	58.32	87.47	27.97
Slovakia	**6**	51.49	64.53	40.42	80.26	33.58
Hungary	**11**	48.63	72.54	58.71	63.95	20.53
Estonia	**12**	51.66	71.75	38.3	43.58	59.46
Latvia	**13**	35.56	57.73	22.41	42.57	29.04
Lithuania	**14**	43.46	66.42	38.08	43.16	32.67
Croatia	**17**	39.4	70.75	23.42	54.42	26.73
Romania	**18**	46.62	61.19	61.97	49.09	25.37
Slovenia	**19**	41.34	64.54	39.49	59.69	19.21
Poland	**22**	46.97	67.54	37.42	58.79	32.77
Bulgaria	**27**	39.43	67.51	24.16	48.33	30.68
Serbia	**29**	30.30	50.97	29.46	66.95	8.38
Montenegro	**36**	9.22	–	8.87	24.47	3.61
Albania	**31**	8.86	53.71	1.7	7.59	–
Bosnia H.	–	–	–	30.77	31.69	–
Macedonia	–	–	77.44	100	–	–

2022						
Czech Republic	**5**	40.09	55.24	61.45	87.47	8.7
Slovakia	**7**	38.30	50.55	47.09	80.26	11.26
Hungary	**12**	32.67	58.94	51.18	63.95	5.91
Latvia	**14**	24.07	46.01	22.41	42.57	7.64
Lithuania	**15**	30.91	58.28	38.08	43.16	9.53
Estonia	**17**	32.90	67.66	42.25	43.58	9.4
Croatia	**19**	25.48	58.68	23.42	54.42	5.63
Romania	**20**	32.72	48.22	71.06	49.09	6.81
Slovenia	**22**	31.21	58.92	39.49	59.69	6.83
Poland	**24**	32.66	57.96	37.42	58.79	8.93
Macedonia	**26**	39.59	65.63	100	–	9.45
Bulgaria	**29**	32.07	57.53	27.12	48.33	14.02
Serbia	**30**	31.02	47.35	29.47	66.95	9.91
Bosnia and H	**31**	27.76	–	35.74	31.69	18.88
Albania	**32**	9.63	35.46	1.7	7.59	18.74
Montenegro	**35**	21.29	–	8.87	24.47	44.42

Source: The Global Green Growth Institute. The data were collected by the author (https://greengrowthindex.gggi.org/?page_id=2547).

Table 1.3. The Global Climate Risk Index in CEE Countries.

Country	CRI Rank 2017	CRI score 2017	Losses in US$ million (PPP) Rank	Losses per unit GDP in % Rank	CRI Rank 2018	CRI score 2018	Losses in US$ million (PPP)	Losses per unit GDP in %	CRI Rank 2019	CRI score 2019	Losses in US$ million (PPP)	Losses per unit GDP in %
Lithuania	124	116	124	124	19	29.33	23	10	**130**	118	130	130
Romania	63	64.33	50	61	89	81.67	80	109	**123**	104.5	77	116
Bulgaria	53	58.17	75	78	116	101	85	88	**119**	101	98	109
Croatia	53	58.17	38	17	126	108.33	101	102	**107**	92.83	63	88
Slovenia	90	81.67	70	48	51	57.83	58	46	**103**	91.83	85	74
Latvia	22	34.5	64	33	44	50	32	8	**98**	86.83	79	62
Poland	29	37.83	21	34	41	49	22	55	**93**	80	40	85
Slovakia	64	64.67	77	81	102	88.33	132	131	**87**	77.17	87	97
Estonia	124	116	124	124	108	90.5	76	61	**83**	75.67	92	72
Hungary	114	99	84	93	123	107.17	134	133	**81**	75.17	51	41
Czech Republic	41	51.5	51	58	35	46.83	28	28	**81**	75.17	51	41
N. Macedonia	105	86.67	118	118	135	125	135	135	**130**	118	130	130
Kosovo	124	116	124	124	135	125	135	135	**130**	118	130	130
Albania	24	35.83	43	13	125	108	124	124	**130**	118	130	130
Serbia	32	42.67	22	8	61	65.5	44	35	**105**	92	78	78
Montenegro	124	116	124	124	114	98.17	104	70	**89**	78	126	123
Bosnia & H.	58	61	28	7	129	109.67	113	100	**48**	57.83	45	20

Source: Global climate risk index 2017–2019. The data were collected by the authors (https://www.germanwatch.org/en/cri).

example entails revealing the environmental risks related to central banks, greening non-policy portfolios, endorsing and putting into practice taxonomies and standards, providing education on environmental risk and green finance, and incorporating environmental values into routine operations (Eames & Barmes, 2021). In each of the four categories, the impact of green policy is divided into three levels: high, medium, and low (which means their impact is away from economic activities that cause climate crises). The ranking of the G20 countries is presented in Table 1.4.

Table 1.4. The Green Central Banking Scorecard in G20.

Rank	**Country**	**Aggregate Score**	**Grade**	**Research and Advocacy**	**Monetary Policy**	**Financial Policy**	**Leading by ex.**
		(out of 130)	**(A+ to F)**	**(out of 10)**	**(out of 50)**	**(out of 50)**	**(out of 20)**
1	**France**	70	B−	10	12	31	17
2	**Italy**	61	C+	10	12	31	8
3	**Germany**	60	C+	10	12	30	8
4	**European Union**	58	C	10	12	28	8
5	**United Kingdom**	56	C	10	10	27	9
6	**Brazil**	53	C	10	18	18	7
7	**China**	53	C	10	12	31	0
8	**Japan**	35	D+	10	6	14	5
9	**Indonesia**	30	D+	10	1	14	5
10	**Canada**	28	D	10	2	14	2
11	**Mexico**	23	D	10	4	4	5
12	**India**	21	D	10	0	10	1
13	**S. Korea**	19	D−	10	1	6	2
14	**Russia**	18	D−	8	0	8	2
15	**Australia**	17	D−	10	0	4	3
16	**United States**	16	D−	10	0	6	0
17	**Turkey**	14	D−	10	0	2	2
18	**S. Africa**	13	D−	10	0	2	1
19	**Argentina**	6	F	6	0	0	0
20	**S. Arabia**	0	F	0	0	0	0

Source: Eames and Barmes (2021). The green central banking scorecard 2022 edition, p. 8 (https://positivemoney.org/publications/green-central-banking-scorecard-2022/).

The total score is the sum of the scores in each category. There is a 130-point maximum score that is possible. The nation's overall score is then used to determine grades ranging from A+ to F. France, Italy, and Germany are in the top 20 countries on the list of G20 central banks.

In 2017, the Network for Greening the Financial System was created to manage environmental and climate risks in the financial sector. The NGFS has modified them since 2020 to assist supervisors and central banks in investigating potential effects on the financial system and the economy. There are 127 central banks and supervisors who are members of the NGFS. The following table lists all CEE countries that are part of NGFS. As we see from Table 1.5, Bosnia and Herzegovina, the Czech Republic, Kosovo, and Poland still need to be part of it.

Apart from the central banks and their policies, other institutions also need to contribute to the legislation and protection from risks that come from climate change. In Table 1.6, strategic and legislative frameworks in Western Balkans are presented. As we see from Table 1.6, all countries have laws on climate change.

Table 1.5. Member of NGFS from Central and Eastern Europe Countries.

Central bank of	Membership of NGFS
Albania	Yes
Bulgaria	Yes
Croatia	Yes
Estonia	Yes
Hungary	Yes
Latvia	Yes
Lithuania	Yes
Romania	Yes
Northern Macedonia	Yes
Montenegro	Yes
Serbia	Yes
Slovak Republic	Yes
Slovenia	Yes
Bosnia and Herzegovina	**No**
Czech Republic	**No**
Kosovo	**No**
Poland	**No**

Source: https://www.ngfs.net/en/about-us/membership

Note: According the website of Central Bank of Kosovo (CBK), they applied to be part of NGFS (https://bqk-kos.org/governor-ismaili-unveils-the-annual-presentation-for-2023-to-the-media/?lang=en).

Table 1.6. Strategic and Legislative Frameworks on Energy and Climate.

Country	The development of national energy and climate plans (NECPs)	Energy Strategy *(Energy Efficiency Strategy)*	Renewables Development Strategy	Climate-change Law *(Low-carbon Development Strategy)*
Albania	In place/Limited progress	National Energy Strategy 2018–2030	National Action Plan for Renewable Energy Resources in Albania 2019–2021	**Law on Climate Change (adopted in December 2020)**
		National Energy Efficiency Action Plan expired in 2020		*National Climate Change Strategy (endorsed in 2019)*
Bosnia and Herzegovina	Limited progress/Limited progress	Framework Energy Strategy 2035 *Action Plan for Energy Efficiency of Bosnia and Herzegovina 2019–2021 (NEEAP BiH) (final draft)*	National Renewable Energy Action Plan 2020	**Climate Change Adaptation and Low Emissions Growth Strategy 2025**
Kosovo	Limited progress/Limited progress	Energy Strategy of the Republic of Kosovo 2022–2031	National Renewable Energy Action Plan (NREAP 2019–2021)	**Law no. 08/l-250 on climate change (05.01.2024).**
		National Energy Efficiency Action Plan (NEEAP) 2019–2021 (draft)		Climate Change Strategy 2014–2024
Montenegro	In place/Limited progress	The Law on Efficient Use of Energyno. 3/2015 from 21.01.2015.	National Renewable Energy Action Plan to 2020	**In December 2019, the "Law on Protection from the Negative Impacts of**

(Continued)

Table 1.6. (*Continued*)

Country	The development of national energy and climate plans (NECPs)	Energy Strategy (*Energy Efficiency Strategy*)	Renewables Development Strategy	Climate-change Law (*Low-carbon Development Strategy*)
		Energy Efficiency Action Plan of Montenegro for 2019–2021	Montenegro	**Climate Change" (Climate Law) entered into force** in Montenegro. Montenegor is making its own low-carbon development strategy.
		The fourth Energy Efficiency Action Plan of Montenegro		
North Macedonia	In progress/limited progress	Energy Development Strategy 2030 Fourth National Energy Efficiency Action Plan (NEEAP) (adopted)	Renewable Energy Action Plan Until 2025	**Law on Climate Action (draft)** Long-term Strategy on Climate Action and National Action Plan on Climate Change (drafts)
Serbia	In place/Limited progress	Energy Sector Development Strategy for the Period until 2025; Energy Development Strategy 2040 (draft ongoing)	National Renewable Energy Action Plan 2020 (adopted in 2013)	**Law on Climate Change (adopted in 2021)**
		Fourth National Energy Efficiency Action Plan(NEEAP) (until 2021) (adopted)		Draft low-carbon development strategy

Source: Adapted from OECD (2011), Multi-dimensional Review of the Western Balkans. From Analysis to Action, April 2021, section 14.2. (https://www.oecd-ilibrary.org/sites/6727544d-en/index.html?itemId=/content/component/6727544d-en); https://energetska-efikasnost.me/zakon-o-efikasnom-koriscenju-energije/; https://www.energy-community.org/implementation/reporting/MO.html; https://icapcarbonaction.com/en/members-observers;me.rks-gov.net; https://gzk.rks gov.net/ActDetail.aspx?ActID=85112; https://climate-laws.org/

Governments must ensure that energy reform unifies and clarifies the current set of policies, plans, and objectives. Every economy in the Western Balkans has either created or implemented a low-carbon development plan. However, these frequently conflict with alternative frameworks, such as energy policies that permit the construction of new coal rather than the phase-out of existing coal (as in the case of several economies in the region, such as Kosovo).

5. Conclusion

The central bank is just one of several governmental entities that can affect the outcomes of green investments, and in many countries, it is not always the best institution to do so. Other important stakeholders include public institutions with development or environmental objectives, the finance ministry, which can reroute investment using tax laws and subsidies, and the environment ministries, which have the power to prevent investments that threaten the environment. Moreover, entities endorsing the financial sector must likely counsel industry participants and offer directives concerning disclosure, sustainable lending, and additional matters.

Shortly, the objectives of the central banks in Central and Eastern Europe (CEE) countries, the factors that influence the achievement of these objectives, and the policies they have undertaken for climate risk can be researched in detail. The countries with the highest scores on the Global Climate Risk Index from CEE countries 2019 are Albania, North Macedonia, Kosovo, Lithuania, and Romania. Meanwhile, Bosnia, Herzegovina, the Czech Republic, Kosovo, and Poland must still be part of NGFS. Countries must adopt measures that mitigate their climate risk index, participate in the NGFS, endorse initiatives about green finance, and integrate them into their objectives. The repercussions of climate change on financial stability and its effects on price stability provide a compelling case for central banks to deliberate on environmental risks and proactively address sustainability issues as required.

Minimizing climate change's impact requires incorporating environmental risks into the financial system. Central banks should be at the forefront of this effort, given their responsibility to maintain financial stability. They must also proactively identify and address sustainability issues and associated risks by developing frameworks incorporating environmental risks into their decision-making processes, including stress testing, scenario analysis, and disclosure requirements.

By embracing sustainable practices, countries can reduce their vulnerability to climate change and promote economic growth and financial stability. As such, policymakers and financial institutions must work together to address the challenges of climate change and facilitate the transition to a greener economy.

References

Acosta, L. A., Nzimenyera, I., Sabado, R., Jr., Munezero, R. M., Nantulya, A., Shula, K., Quiñones, S. G. L., Luchtenbelt, H. G. H., Czvetkó, T., Lee, S., Adams, G. P., Astralaga, M., Bhatt, A., Cantore, N., Cavatassi, R., Chonabayashi, S., Eaton, D., Eboli, F., Esambe, G., Farnia, L., ... Zarnic, Z. (2022). *Green growth index 2022 – Measuring performance in achieving SDG targets*. GGGI Technical Report No. 27. Retrieved February 20, 2024, from https://greengrowthindex.gggi.org/

Alva, H., & Bhat, S. (2018). Accenture–Understanding sustainable business strategies. *International Journal of Case Studies in Business, IT and Education (IJCSBE)*, *2*(1), 54–63.

Azarian, R. (2011). Potentials and limitations of comparative method in social science. *International Journal of Humanities and Social Science*, *1*(4), 113–125.

Barber, B. M., Morse, A., & Yasuda, A. (2021). Impact investing. *Journal of Financial Economics*, *139*(1), 162–185. https://doi.org/10.1016/j.jfineco.2020.07.008

Boneva, L., Ferrucci, G., & Mongelli, F. P. (2021). To be or not to be "green": how can monetary policy react to climate change?. *ECB Occasional Paper* (2021/285). http://dx.doi.org/10.2139/ssrn.3971287

Cecot, M. (2019). *Climate emergency and central banks*. Retrieved February 18, 2024, from http://dx.doi.org/10.2139/ssrn.3509012

Chenet, H., Ryan-Collins, J., & Van Lerven, F. (2021). Finance, climate-change and radical uncertainty: Towards a precautionary approach to financial policy. *Ecological Economics*, *183*, 106957. https://doi.org/10.1016/j.ecolecon.2021.106957

Cipollone, P. (2022). *The role of central banks for green finance.* Retrieved February 12, 2024, from https://www.bis.org/review/r220321b.pdf

Díaz-García, C., González-Moreno, Á., & Sáez-Martínez, F. J. (2015). Eco-innovation: insights from a literature review. *Innovation*, *17*(1), 6–23. https://doi.org/10.1080/14479338.2015.1011060

Dikau, S., & Volz, U. (2018). *Central banking, climate change and green finance*. Tokyo: Asian Development Bank Institute. ADBI Working Paper No. 867. Retrieved from https://eprints.soas.ac.uk/26445/

Dikau, S., & Volz, U. (2021). Central bank mandates, sustainability objectives and the promotion of green finance. *Ecological Economics*, *184*, 107022. https://doi.org/10.1016/j.ecolecon.2021.107022

Eames, N., & Barmes, D. (2021). *The green central banking scorecard: How green are G20 central banks and financial supervisors? positive money*. Retrieved February 1, 2024, from The Green Central Banking Scorecard: 2022 Edition – Positive Money

Eckstein, D., Künzel, V., Schäfer, L., & Winges, M. (2019). *Global climate risk index 2020*, Bonn: Germanwatch (pp. 1–50). Retrieved February 1, 2024, from Microsoft Word – 20-2-01e Global Climate Risk Index 2020 (germanwatch.org)

European Commission. (2018). *Proposal for a Regulation of the European Parliament and of the Council on the establishment of a framework to facilitate sustainable investment*. EUR-Lex. Retrieved February 11, 2024, from EUR-Lex – 52023PC0443 – EN – EUR-Lex (europa.eu)

European Parliament. (2019). *Plurilateral environmental goods agreement (EGA)*. europa.eu. Retrieved February 10, 2024, from Carriages preview | Legislative Train Schedule (europa.eu)

Ganda, F. (2018). The influence of carbon emissions disclosure on company financial value in an emerging economy. *Environment, Development and Sustainability*, *20*, 1723–1738. https://doi.org/10.1007/s10668-017-9962-4

Gao, Y., Tsai, S. B., Xue, X., Ren, T., Du, X., Chen, Q., & Wang, J. (2018). An empirical study on green innovation efficiency in the green institutional environment. *Sustainability*, *10*(3), 724. https://doi.org/10.3390/su10030724

Glomsrød, S., & Wei, T. (2018). Business as unusual: The implications of fossil divestment and green bonds for financial flows, economic growth and energy market. *Energy for Sustainable Development*, *44*, 1–10. https://doi.org/10.1016/j.esd.2018.02.005

He, L., Liu, R., Zhong, Z., Wang, D., & Xia, Y. (2019). Can green financial development promote renewable energy investment efficiency? A consideration of bank credit. *Renewable Energy*, *143*, 974–984. https://doi.org/10.1016/j.renene.2019.05.059

Höhne, N., Khosla, S., Fekete, H., & Gilbert, A. (2012). *Mapping of green finance delivered by IDFC members in 2011*. Cologne. Retrieved from https://idfc.org/wp-content/uploads/2019/03/idfc_green_finance_mapping_report_2012_06-14-12.pdf

ILO. (2015). *Two defining challenges for the twenty-first century. In decent work, green jobs and the sustainable economy* (pp. 1–8). International Labour Organization. Retrieved from Rapport V_Sustainabledev…and greenjobs-ENG.indd (ilo.org)

Kaur, S., Kumar, R., Singh, K., & Huang, Y. L. (2024). Leveraging artificial intelligence for enhanced sustainable energy management. *Journal of Sustainable Energy*, *3*(1), 1–20. https://doi.org/10.56578/jse030101

Landman, T. (2008). *Issues and methods in comparative politics: An introduction* (3rd ed.). Routledge. Retrieved August 14, 2023, from http://debracollege.dspaces.org/bitstream/123456789/466/1/comparative%20politics.pdf

Li, Z. Z., Li, R. Y. M., Malik, M. Y., Murshed, M., Khan, Z., & Umar, M. (2021). Determinants of carbon emission in China: how good is green investment?. *Sustainable Production and Consumption*, *27*, 392–401. https://doi.org/10.1016/j.spc.2020.11.008

Lindenberg, N. (2014). *Definition of green finance*. Retrieved February 10, 2024, from MultiLink (archive.org)

Molico, M. (2019). *Researching the economic impacts of climate change*. Retrieved February 9, 2024, from https://www.bankofcanada.ca/2019/11/researching-economic-impacts-climate-change/?_ga=2.146

Ndekwa, A. G., Kalugendo, E., Sood, K., & Grima, S. (2023). An analysis of agribusiness digitalisation transformation of the sub-Saharan African countries small-scale farmers' production distribution. *Research on World Agricultural Economy*, 4(3), 63–78.

NGFS. (2019). *A call for action Climate change as a source of financial risk*. NGFS. Retrieved February 10, 2024 from First comprehensive report « A call for action » | NGFS

Obradović, S. L. (2019). Environmental investments. In *Climate action* (pp. 1–12). Springer. https://doi.org/10.1007/978-3-319-71063-1_67-1

OECD. (2011). *Towards green growth*. OECD Publishing. Retrieved February 10, 2024, from http://www.keepeek.com/Digital-Asset-Management/oecd/environment/towards-green-growth_9789264111318-en

Ozili, P. K. (2021). Digital finance, green finance and social finance: is there a link?. *Financial Internet Quarterly*, *17*(1), 1–7. https://doi.org/10.2478/fiqf-2021-0001

Ozili, P. K. (2022). *Theories of sustainable finance; Managing global transitions*. SSRN. Retrieved March 1, 2022, from SSRN: https://ssrn.com/abstract=4055371

Pricewaterhouse Coopers Consultants (PWC). (2013). *Exploring green finance incentives in China, PWC*. Retrieved February 10, 2024 from https://silo.tips/download/exploring-green-finance-incentives-in-china#

Raberto, M., Ozel, B., Ponta, L., Teglio, A., & Cincotti, S. (2019). From financial instability to green finance: the role of banking and credit market regulation in the Eurace model. *Journal of Evolutionary Economics*, *29*, 429–465. https://doi.org/10.1007/s00191-018-0568-2

Reboredo, J. C. (2018). Green bond and financial markets: Co-movement, diversification and price spillover effects. *Energy Economics*, *74*, 38–50. https://doi.org/10.1016/j.eneco.2018.05.030

Rijal, S., Nursaputra, M. A. C., & Dari, H. U. (2024). Flood susceptibility analysis using frequency ratio method in Walanae watershed. *International Journal of Sustainable Development and Planning*, *19*(3), 823–832. https://doi.org/10.18280/ijsdp.190302

Rozenberg, J., Hallegatte, S., Perrissin-Fabert, B., & Hourcade, J. C. (2013). Funding low-carbon investments in the absence of a carbon tax. *Climate Policy*, *13*(1), 134–141. https://doi.org/10.1080/14693062.2012.691222

Sachs, J. D., Woo, W. T., Yoshino, N., & Taghizadeh-Hesary, F. (2019). Importance of green finance for achieving sustainable development goals and energy security. *Handbook of Green Finance: Energy Security and Sustainable Development*, *10*, 1–10.

Schoenmaker, D., & Tilburg, R. V. (2016). What role for financial supervisors in addressing environmental risks? *Comparative Economic Studies*, *58*(3), 317–334. https://doi.org/10.1057/ces.2016.11

Schoenmaker, D., van Tilburg, R., & Wijffels, H. (2015). *What role for financial supervisors in addressing systemic environmental risks?* Sustainable Finance Lab Working Paper, Sustainable Finance Lab, Utrecht. Retrieved February 17, 2024 from What Role for Financial Supervisors in Addressing Systemic Environmental Risks.pdf (greenpolicyplatform.org)

Shala, A., Ismajli, H., & Perri, R. (2018). A comparative study of prudential regulation on loan classification and provisioning of the south east European countries. *Acta Universitatis Agriculturae et Silviculturae Mendelianae Brunensis*, *66*(5), 1337–1346. https://doi.org/10.11118/actaun201866051337

Shala, A., & Perri, R. (2022). Regulatory barriers for fintech companies in Central and Eastern Europe. *Eastern Journal of European Studies*, *13*(2), 292–316. https://10.47743/ejes-2022-0214

Shala, A., & Qehaja, A. B. (2021). The practices and corporate governance frameworks: comparative evidence from south-eastern European countries. *Eastern Journal of European Studies*, *12*(1), 31–52. https://doi.org/10.47743/ejes-2021-0103

Sood, K., & Øzen, E. (2024). A systematic review of ESG in the insurance industry: Navigating the path to sustainability. *International Journal of Sustainable Development and Planning*, *19*(3), 807–821. https://doi.org/10.18280/ijsdp.190301

Spinaci, S., Höflmayr, M., & Hofmann, L. (2022). *Green central banking* (pp. 1–12). European Parliamentary Research Service. Retrieved on February 20, 2024.

Tang, D. Y., & Zhang, Y. (2020). Do shareholders benefit from green bonds? *Journal of Corporate Finance*, *61*, 101427. https://doi.org/10.1016/j.jcorpfin.2018.12.001

Urban, M. A., & Wójcik, D. (2019). Dirty banking: Probing the gap in sustainable finance. *Sustainability*, *11*(6), 1745. https://doi.org/10.3390/su11061745

Volz, U. (2017). *On the role of central banks in enhancing green finance*. Inquiry Working Paper 17/01. Retrieved from https://wedocs.unep.org/handle/20.500.11822/16803;jsessionid=903D3F0E1ED346E0CDEE4610EC4C0604

Wang, Y., & Zhi, Q. (2016). The role of green finance in environmental protection: Two aspects of market mechanism and policies. *Energy Procedia*, *104*, 311–316. https://doi.org/10.1016/j.egypro.2016.12.053

Yerpude, S., Sood, K., & Grima, S. (2022). Blockchain-augmented digital supply chain management: A way to sustainable business. *Journal of Risk and Financial Management*, *16*(1), 7.

Yuan, F., & Gallagher, K. P. (2019). Greening development lending in the Americas: trends and determinants. In *Development Banks and Sustainability in the Andean Amazon* (pp. 75–101). Routledge.

Ziolo, M., Filipiak, B. Z., Bąk, I., & Cheba, K. (2019). How to design more sustainable financial systems: The roles of environmental, social, and governance factors in the decision-making process. *Sustainability*, *11*(20), 5604. https://doi.org/10.3390/su11205604

Websites

Retrieved January 2, 2024, from https://www.oecd-ilibrary.org/sites/6727544d-en/index.html?itemId=/content/component/6727544d-en

Retrieved January 22, 2024, from https://energetska-efikasnost.me/zakon-o-efikasnom-koriscenju-energije/

Retrieved February 12, 2024, from https://www.energy-community.org/implementation/reporting/MO.html

Retrieved January 8, 2024, from https://icapcarbonaction.com/en/members-observers

Retrieved January 10, 2024, from me.rks-gov.net; https://gzk.rks gov.net/ActDetail.aspx?ActID=85112; https://climate-laws.org/

Retrieved February 10, 2024, from https://www.ngfs.net/en/about-us/membership

Retrieved February 26, 2024, from https://bqk-kos.org/governor-ismaili-unveils-the-annual-presentation-for-2023-to-the-media/?lang=en)

Retrieved February 3, 2024, from https://positivemoney.org/publications/green-central-banking-scorecard-2022

Retrieved January 18, 2024, from https://www.germanwatch.org/en/cri)

Retrieved January 21, 2024, from https://greengrowthindex.gggi.org/?page_id=2547

Retrieved January 17, 2024, from https://greengrowthindex.gggi.org/

Retrieved February 10, 2024, from Green Growth Index – Measuring performance in achieving SDG targets (gggi.org)

Chapter 2

An Empirical Study on the Impact of Sustainable Human Resource Management Practices on Employee Retention

Simranjeet Kaur and Rupali Arora

University School of Business (USB), Chandigarh University, India

Abstract

Purpose: The chapter explores the impact of sustainable human resource management (SHRM) practices such as green job design, recruiting and selection, training, green HR operations and onboarding processes, and compensation and rewards for initiatives related to sustainability on employee retention in the education sector.

Need for the study: SHRM practices actively align human resources with sustainability goals. Green human resource management (GHRM)-implemented organisations can attract and retain top individuals, giving them a competitive edge. The impact of GHRM policies on employee retention is crucial for organisations seeking sustainable growth, ethics, and a pleasant workplace culture.

Methodology: Examination of the data is done using partial least squares structural equation modelling utilising SMART-PLS 4.0

Findings: Sustainable HRM directly affects employees' intentions to leave (employee retention). The consequences of the results, future prospects, and the research limits are highlighted.

Practical implications: The study suggests that organisations are better able to retain their employees when they actively incorporate eco-friendly work designs, recruitment and hiring practices, training programmes, and incentives for eco-friendly work.

Green Management: A New Paradigm in the World of Business, 23–33

Published under exclusive licence by Emerald Publishing Limited
doi:10.1108/978-1-83797-442-920241002

Keywords: Sustainability; employee retention; SMART-PLS; green recruitment and selection; sustainable human resource management practices (SHRM); green human resource management (GHRM); education sector

JEL Classifications: O15; Q01; I23; Q56

Introduction

Social exchange theory is applied to illustrate the association between green human resource management (GHRM) and employee retention. This idea specifies the conditions under which individuals, i.e., employees, are obligated to reciprocate when they individually profit from organisations or other individuals. Kenkel et al. (1959) developed SET (social exchange theory), which has been utilised as the theoretical foundation for employee turnover and stay analysis to understand better the way workers and their employers interact (Coyle-Shapiro & Conway, 2005). Employees have a proclivity to return to human resource management practices through their dedication, loyalty, positive mindset, and actions. In addition, this indicates that employees' productivity increases if their superiors are supportive. The essential premise of SET is that an individual, i.e., an employee, forms a social connection characterised by a shared understanding.

Consequently, intentions of an employee leaving the organisations would fluctuate based on how many opportunities the workers have been provided at the workplace, so this is also referred to as a mutual exchange of benefits between staff and employers. In this way, value support and fulfilling employee expectations will foster increased employee commitment and loyalty, diminishing their intention to depart. Hence, this study hypothesises that GHRM methods might be having an impact on preferences for employee turnover. Also, the same is recognised as advantageous to employees and should be mandated by organisations, and intent to leave may be reduced.

In recent years, organisations worldwide have increasingly recognised the importance of aligning their HR practises with their environmental and social responsibilities, leading to the prominence of sustainable human resource management (SHRM), which also influences an organisation's ability to retain its employees (Ndekwa et al., 2023; Sood & Özen, 2024; Yerpude et al., 2022).

Green Job Design and Employee Retention: Green job design entails making job positions comply with environmental sustainability objectives. Green job workers frequently express more significant levels of job satisfaction, enhanced motivation, and a strong feeling of purpose, all of which can contribute to improved employee retention. The latest research (e.g., Fazal-e-Hasan et al., 2023) indicates that the workforce in positions specifically tailored to support sustainability is more inclined to maintain their dedication to their organisations, resulting in reduced employee turnover rates.

Green Recruitment and Selection: Efficient methods are crucial in attracting and maintaining environmentally aware staff that align with the organisation's commitment to sustainability in green recruitment. A recent study conducted by Qadri et al. (2022) showed that organisations that adopt environmentally conscious recruitment techniques observe a decrease in turnover rates and an enhancement in staff retention. Furthermore, individuals chosen based on their dedication to sustainability are better inclined to maintain their involvement and contentment with their positions.

Green Training and Employee Retention: Allocating resources towards green training programmes enables employees to acquire the necessary information and skills to participate actively in sustainability projects. Judeh and Khader (2023) demonstrated that staff training in sustainable practices exhibits higher engagement, loyalty, and commitment towards their organisations. These employees possess superior capabilities to adopt sustainability objectives, leading to increased employee retention rates.

Compensation and Rewards for Green Initiatives: As per latest study by Islam et al. (2022), providing remuneration and incentives for eco-friendly activities motivates employees to actively engage in sustainability endeavours, they highlighted organisations that acknowledge and incentivise employees for their efforts in promoting environmental sustainability likely to see more excellent employee retention rates. So, the staff who consider their contributions appreciated are more inclined to remain with the organisation.

The literature review emphasises the increasing significance of SHRM, like green job design, recruitment and selection, green training, and remuneration and rewards for green activities, in positively impacting employee retention. The amalgamation of current research highlights the capacity of these practices to augment employee loyalty and dedication, ultimately benefiting organisations in terms of long-term viability and competitiveness. Nevertheless, despite the growing fascination in this domain, there are areas for improvement in our comprehension. Further investigation is needed to thoroughly examine the precise mechanisms by which these practices impact employee retention and explore potential factors that may moderate these effects (Kaur et al., 2024; Rijal et al., 2024)

Research Methodology

The study focuses on employee retention as the dependent variable, with green human resource management as the independent variable. This study sample comprises all educational institutions in Punjab and Haryana. As mentioned in the latest study's research design, this is an experimental, quantitative, questionnaire-based study. The gathered data are also quantitatively examined. Utilisation of Smart PLS version (4.0) analysed the data in this research. Following the quantitative research design, primary data are obtained by a standardised survey form. To generate responses from participants, various questions about the variables in the investigation are provided. The questionnaire comprises closed-ended questions, and the interval scale is employed to assess the responses since this scale is appropriate for measuring the responses in quantitative research studies. Measures of green job design, recruitment and selection, training, HR operations and onboarding process, and compensation and rewards for green initiatives and staff retention are included in the survey. A seven-point Likert scale is used for evaluating comments, with results ranging from (1) "strongly agree" to (7) "strongly disagree." The investigators were able to collect 752 filled relevant survey questionnaires from private university employees.

Data Analysis

Assessment: Measurement Model

The chapter explores the external specifications of the model using internal dependability and converged validity assessments. Reflective modelling was utilised in the partial least square equational modelling for green HRM practices. In the first stage of two thoughtful evaluations, Mode A was used to evaluate the latent variable scores of all five sustainable human resource capital criteria. Thus, a second-order composite was developed to assess the effect of the same on employee retention. The measurement model of the study is shown in Figure 2.1.

The metrics of Cronbach's Alpha, Dijkstra and Henseler's rhoA (Dijkstra & Henseler, 2015), and composite reliability (CR) were used to assess internal dependability. All of these measures surpassed the threshold of 0.70, (Ali et al., 2018). As in Hair et al. (2017, 2020) instead for no construct well below the mentioned term; however, the result of rho A was over the 0.70 threshold prove the constructs' reliability. Table 2.1 displays the outcomes of the internal reliability and converged validity assessments, which demonstrated that the AVE scores for all reflective constructs in the model were significantly higher than the threshold

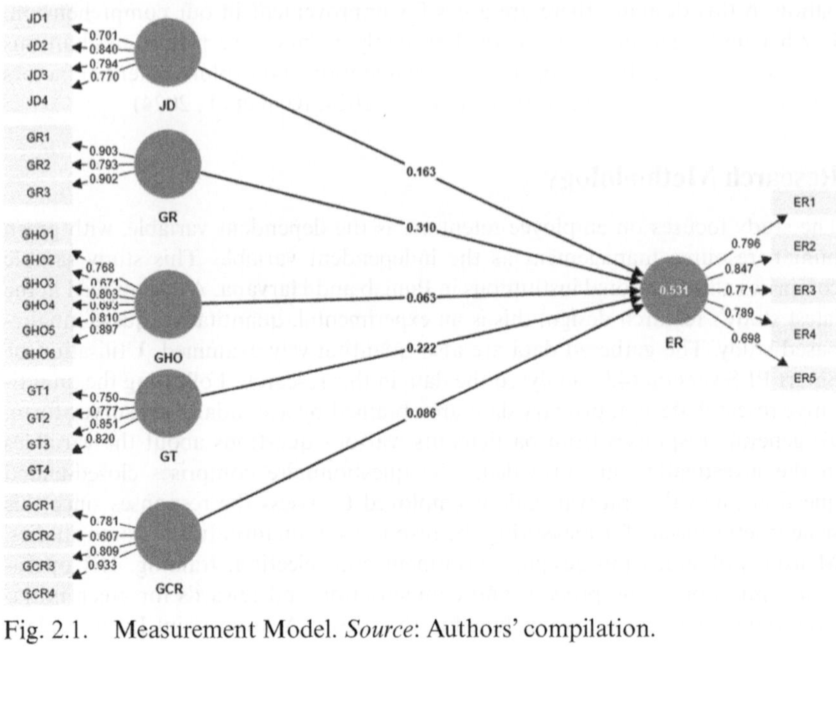

Fig. 2.1. Measurement Model. *Source*: Authors' compilation.

Table 2.1. Reliability and Validity Analysis.

Construct	Items	Loadings	Alpha	rho_A	CR	AVE
Job Design	JD1	0.701	0.784	0.805	0.859	0.605
	JD2	0.840				
	JD3	0.794				
	JD4	0.770				
Green Recruitment	GR1	0.903	0.839	0.849	0.901	0.753
	GR2	0.793				
	GR3	0.902				
Green Training	GT1	0.750	0.814	0.830	0.877	0.641
	GT2	0.777				
	GT3	0.851				
	GT4	0.820				
Green Human Resource Operations	GHO1	0.768	0.868	0.888	0.901	0.604
	GHO2	0.671				
	GHO3	0.803				
	GHO4	0.693				
	GHO5	0.810				
	GHO6	0.897				
Green Compensation and Reward	GCR1	0.781	0.791	0.814	0.867	0.626
	GCR2	0.607				
	GCR3	0.809				
	GCR4	0.933				
Employee Retention	ER1	0.796	0.843	0.852	0.887	0.611
	ER2	0.847				
	ER3	0.771				
	ER4	0.789				
	ER5	0.698				

Source: Author's calculations.

Note: CR refers to Composite Reliability, and AVE stands for Average Variance. Obtained.

value of 0.50, as recommended by Fornell and Larcker (1981) and Hair et al. (2019).

Applying Fornell and Larcker's Criterion (1981), discriminant validity was inspected further by determining that the under-root of AVEs for diagonal constructs was more significant than the inter-item correlation values. Table 2.2

Table 2.2. Fornell–Larcker Criterion and HTMT.

	ER	GCR	GHO	GR	GT	JD
ER	**0.782**	0.633	0.591	0.713	0.731	0.710
GCR	0.538	**0.791**	0.717	0.697	0.713	0.795
GHO	0.552	0.603	**0.777**	0.748	0.748	0.646
GR	0.668	0.581	0.656	**0.868**	0.824	0.830
GT	0.637	0.580	0.642	0.691	**0.800**	0.821
JD	0.619	0.642	0.560	0.695	0.677	**0.778**

Source: Authors' compilation.

Note: The square root values of the AVE are shown in diagonal and bold. The connections among the construct values are below the diagonal elements, whereas the HTMT values are above the diagonal.

demonstrates a clear difference between each construct, allowing the study to proceed with the last assessment. The further conventional approach for analysing the discriminant validity of variables, a novel parameter, the heterotrait–monotrait (HTMT) ratio, is applied. According to a stricter note, the mentioned ratio of correlations must not exceed 0.85 (Henseler et al., 2015). In this analysis, the HTMT values for all constructs were between 0.591 and 0.830, indicating distinctiveness in each construct as per empirical norms.

Structural Model assessment

Validating Reflective–Reflective Higher Order Construct – Green Human Resource Management Practices

The relationship between constructs and their ability to predict outcomes was examined in assessments of structural models (Hair et al., 2017). The green HRM practice framework is initially analyzed as a reflecting scale within the structured inner model. SHRM practices were evaluated as a second-order based on the latent variable scores of 5 reflective constructs. Cronbach's alpha, component reliability, and average variance extracted (AVE) were below the required level (see Table 2.3). All second-order aggregate outer weights were found to be significant and distinct from 0 at the 1% level.

As per Table 2.4, the discriminant validity of the higher-order construct is established using both methods of discriminant validity (Fornell and Larcker and HTMT). Fig. 2.2 depicts the evaluations of the structural model.

As per Table 2.5, tolerance and variance inflation factor (VIF) values are less than 2.847, which is below the threshold limits (less than five) to indicate that the study did not contain any collinearity concerns (Hair et al., 2017).

The R-square for the dependent construct (employee retention) was moderate to high at 49.8%, showing green HRM methods strongly influencing employee retention. The proposed model's effect size (f2) and relevance (Q2) were used to evaluate predictive significance. The proposed limitations for assessing the change in R2 resulting from the influence of independent construct on dependent

Table 2.3. Factor Loadings, Reliability and AVE for Higher Order Construct (GHRMP).

	Outer loadings	Cronbach's alpha	Composite reliability	Average variance extracted (AVE)
JD <- GHRM	0.848	0.894	0.898	0.703
GR <- GHRM	0.865			
GHO <- GHRM	0.811			
GT <- GHRM	0.861			
GCR<- GHRM	0.803			

Source: Authors' calculations.

Table 2.4. Discriminant Validity.

HTMT		
	ER	GHRMP
GHRMP	0.775	
Fornell and Larcker Criterion		
	ER	GHRMP
GHRMP	0.706	0.838

Source: Authors' calculations.

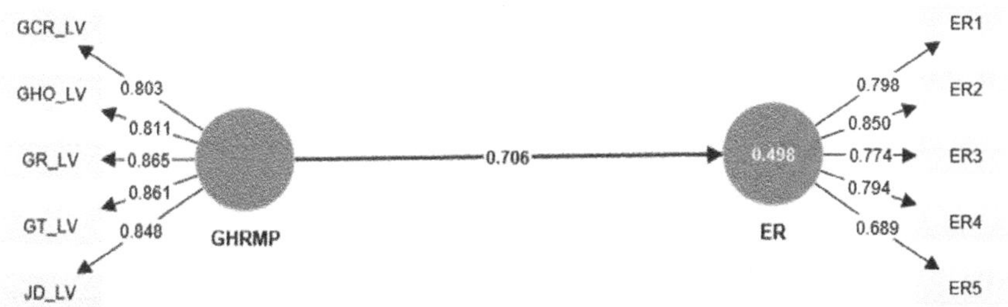

Fig. 2.2. Structural Model. *Source*: Author's compilation.

variables are 0.02 (for minor effects), 0.15 (for moderate effects), and 0.35 (for substantial impacts) (Cohen, 1988). The analysis reveals an F-square value of 0.992 (significant as per Cohen, 1988)

Stone-Q2 Geisser's value (Geisser, 1975; Stone, 1974) was used to assess the predictive significance of the structural model, which was determined to be 0.496, which indicates a substantial degree of predictive relevance (Hair et al., 2013).

Table 2.6 explains the predictive relevance assessment well. A value more excellent than 0.02 generalizes outcomes while forecasting capacity (Richter et al., 2016), which

Table 2.5. Collinearity Statistics (VIF) Outer Model.

	VIF
ER1	1.942
ER2	2.847
ER3	2.159
ER4	1.967
ER5	1.243
GCR	2.050
GHO	2.129
GR	2.539
GT	2.467
JD	2.459

Source: Authors' calculations.

Table 2.6. Explanatory Power of Structural Model.

	R-square		
	R-square	R-square adjusted	
ER	0.498	0.497	
	F-square		
	ER	GHRMP	
ER			
GHRMP	0.992		
	Q-square		
	Q^2 predict	RMSE	MAE
ER	0.496	0.712	0.539

Source: Authors calculations.

states that different views contribute to the basic model of the study, in addition to the fact that the outcomes can be categorized into many scenarios in the future.

The testing of hypotheses is shown in Table 2.7. To determine the requisite p-values for the hypotheses posed in the study, the bootstrapping method with the suggested 5000 bootstraps was utilised (Hair et al., 2020).

The results of Table 2.7 indicate that green HRM practises positively influence employee retention ($\beta = 0.706$, $p < 0.001$), supporting the study's hypothesis.

Table 2.7. Hypothesis Testing.

	Beta coefficients	**Sample mean**	**Standard deviation**	**T statistics**	**P values**
GHRMP -> ER	0.706	0.706	0.018	40.074	0.000

Source: Authors' calculations.

Findings

This study examined the effects of GHRM practices on employee retention in the education sector. The statistical results indicate that the mentioned method directly impacts the faculty members' choice to quit their positions. SmartPLS investigations constantly indicate a strong and statistically significant correlation between adopting sustainable human resource methods and employee retention. This implies that organisations that actively integrate environmentally friendly work design, environment-friendly recruitment and selection, training, and remuneration and awards for related efforts are more able to retain their staff.

Furthermore, the study advocates for more research on the enduring consequences of these practices on staff retention and organisational sustainability, given the limited exploration in this domain. As organisations increasingly prioritise sustainability, the impact of SHRM practices on employee retention will continue to be an essential topic of study. This area of research presents significant opportunities for academics and professionals to make valuable contributions. Developing methods related to the latest study is a strategic approach that improves employee retention, hence contributing to the long-term sustainability and competitiveness of the organisation. This can result in financial benefits related to less employee turnover, enhanced efficiency, and a more dedicated workforce.

Conclusion and Future Research

Although this chapter has offered valuable insights, there are still opportunities for further research. Researchers can further investigate the particular aspects of sustainable human resource management methods that exert the most substantial influence on employee retention. Moreover, future research should prioritise investigating the enduring consequences of these policies on employee retention and evaluating their impact on the organisation's overall sustainability.

Smart PLS has demonstrated its efficacy as a robust instrument for evaluating the impact of GHRM on the employees' stay. The capacity to simulate intricate connections, intervening processes, and moderating factors has enhanced our comprehension of this crucial association. The utilisation of SmartPLS in SHRM research will continue to be essential as organisations increasingly adopt sustainability and acknowledge the significance of retaining their workforce. This approach enables evidence-based decision-making and practises that benefit organisations and employees.

References

Ali, F., Rasoolimanesh, S. M., Sarstedt, M., Ringle, C. M., & Ryu, K. (2018). An assessment of the use of partial least squares structural equation modeling (PLS-SEM) in hospitality research. *International Journal of Contemporary Hospitality Management*, *30*(1), 514–538. https://doi.org/10.1108/ijchm-10-2016-0568

Cohen, J. (1988). Set correlation and contingency tables. *Applied Psychological Measurement*, *12*(4), 425–434. https://doi.org/10.1177/014662168801200410

Coyle-Shapiro, J. A., & Conway, N. (2005). Exchange relationships: Examining psychological contracts and perceived organizational support. *Journal of Applied Psychology*, *90*(4), 774–781. https://doi.org/10.1037/0021-9010.90.4.774

Dijkstra, T. K., & Henseler, J. (2015). Consistent partial least squares path modeling. *MIS Quarterly*, *39*(2), 297–316. https://doi.org/10.25300/misq/2015/39.2.02

Fazal-e-Hasan, S. M., Ahmadi, H., Sekhon, H., Mortimer, G., Sadiq, M., Kharouf, H., & Abid, M. (2023). The role of green innovation and hope in employee retention. *Business Strategy and the Environment*, *32*(1), 220–239. https://doi.org/10.1002/bse.3126

Fornell, C., & Larcker, D. F. (1981). Structural equation models with unobservable variables and measurement error: Algebra and statistics. *Journal of Marketing Research*, *18*(3), 382. https://doi.org/10.2307/3150980

Geisser, S. (1975). The predictive sample reuse method with applications. *Journal of the American Statistical Association*, *70*(350), 320–328. https://doi.org/10.1080/01621459.1975.10479865

Hair, J. F., Howard, M. C., & Nitzl, C. (2020). Assessing measurement model quality in PLS-SEM using confirmatory composite analysis. *Journal of Business Research*, *109*, 101–110. https://doi.org/10.1016/j.jbusres.2019.11.069

Hair, J. F., Ringle, C. M., & Sarstedt, M. (2013). Partial least squares structural equation modeling: Rigorous applications, better results and higher acceptance. *Long Range Planning*, *46*(1-2), 1–12. https://doi.org/10.1016/j.lrp.2013.01.001

Hair, J. F., Risher, J. J., Sarstedt, M., & Ringle, C. M. (2019). When to use and how to report the results of PLS-SEM. *European Business Review*, *31*(1), 2–24. https://doi.org/10.1108/ebr-11-2018-0203

Hair, Jr., J. F., Matthews, L. M., Matthews, R. L., & Sarstedt, M. (2017). PLS-SEM or CB-SEM: Updated guidelines on which method to use. *International Journal of Multivariate Data Analysis*, *1*(2), 107. https://doi.org/10.1504/ijmda.2017.10008574

Henseler, J., Ringle, C. M., & Sarstedt, M. (2015). A new criterion for assessing discriminant validity in variance-based structural equation modeling. *Journal of the Academy of Marketing Science*, *43*(1), 115-135. https://doi.org/10.1007/s11747-014-0403-8

Islam, M. A., Mendy, J., Haque, A. K., & Rahman, M. (2022). Green human resource management practices and millennial employees' retention in small and medium enterprises: The moderating impact of creativity climate from a developing country perspective. *Business Strategy & Development*, *5*(4), 335–349. https://doi.org/10.1002/bsd2.202

Judeh, M., & Khader, J. (2023). Green training and development and job delight as determinants of green employee behavior and employee retention: An empirical study on hotels and tourism corporations. *International Journal of Sustainable Development and Planning*, *18*(1), 221–228. https://doi.org/10.18280/ijsdp.180123

Kaur, S., Kumar, R., Singh, K., & Huang, Y. L. (2024). Leveraging artificial intelligence for enhanced sustainable energy management. *Journal of Sustainable Energy*, *3*(1), 1–20. https://doi.org/10.56578/jse030101

Kenkel, W. F., Thibaut, J. W., & Kelley, H. H. (1959). The social psychology of groups. *The American Catholic Sociological Review*, *20*(4), 345. https://doi.org/10.2307/3709294

Ndekwa, A. G., Kalugendo, E., Sood, K., & Grima, S. (2023). An analysis of agribusiness digitalisation transformation of the Sub-Saharan African countries small-scale farmers' production distribution. *Research on World Agricultural Economy*, *4*(3), 63–78.

Qadri, S. U., Bilal, M. A., Li, M., Ma, Z., Qadri, S., Ye, C., & Rauf, F. (2022). Work environment as a moderator linking green human resources management strategies with turnover intention of millennials: A study of Malaysian hotel industry. *Sustainability*, *14*(12), 7401. https://doi.org/10.3390/su14127401

Richter, N. F., Cepeda, G., Roldán, J. L., & Ringle, C. M. (2016). European management research using partial least squares structural equation modeling (PLS-SEM). *European Management Journal*, *34*(6), 589–597. https://doi.org/10.1016/j.emj.2016.08.001

Rijal, S., Nursaputra, M. A. C., & Dari, H. U. (2024). Flood susceptibility analysis using Frequency Ratio method in Walanae watershed. *International Journal of Sustainable Development and Planning*, *19*(3), 823–832. https://doi.org/10.18280/ijsdp.190302

Sood, K., & Özen, E. (2024). A systematic review of ESG in the insurance industry: Navigating the path to sustainability. *International Journal of Sustainable Development and Planning*, *19*(3), 807–821. https://doi.org/10.18280/ijsdp.190301

Stone, M. (1974). Cross-validatory choice and assessment of statistical predictions.*Journal of the Royal Statistical Society: Series B (Methodological)*,*36*(2), 111–133. https://doi.org/10.1111/j.2517-6161.1974.tb00994.x

Yerpude, S., Sood, K., & Grima, S. (2022). Blockchain-augmented digital supply chain management: A way to sustainable business. *Journal of Risk and Financial Management*, *16*(1), 7.

Chapter 3

Discussing the Sustainability of Health Systems in the Context of the COVID-19 Pandemic: A Comparison Between Germany, France, Italy, and Türkiye

Ekrem Tufan

Health Management Department, Çanakkale Faculty of Applied Sciences, Çanakkale Onsekiz Mart University, Türkiye

Abstract

Purpose: The purpose chapter emphasizes the need to explore the relationship among health, well-being, and the impact of COVID-19 on different countries. It highlights the inadequacy of GDP as a sole indicator and introduces the Human Development Index (HDI) and Gross National Happiness Index (GNH) for a comprehensive understanding.

Need for the study: This chapter underscores the challenges faced during the COVID-19 pandemic and its impact on global well-being. It delves into the disparities in death rates, hospital capacity, and health services, posing essential questions about the perception and approach towards health.

Methodology: The study focuses on comparing the health financing systems of Germany, Italy, France, and Türkiye, comparing facts like GDP, GINI Index, happiness scores, and COVID-19 death data. A brief history of each country's healthcare system is presented, highlighting key developments and structural elements.

Findings: Findings reveal differences in health financing systems, GDP, happiness scores, and COVID-19 death tolls among the selected countries. Notably, Türkiye, with lower GDP and happiness scores, shows a lower COVID-19 death toll compared to Germany. This prompts further exploration into the correlation between health system structures and pandemic outcomes.

Green Management: A New Paradigm in the World of Business, 35–50

doi:10.1108/978-1-83797-442-920241003

Practical implications: National governments in ensuring universal health coverage (UHC) and addresses the challenges of profit-centered healthcare systems. It advocates for a trustworthy, transparent, and state-supported health system to enhance overall well-being.

Keywords: Health and well-being; COVID-19 impact; Human Development Index; Gross National Happiness Index; health financing systems; comparative analysis; universal health coverage

JEL Classifications: I140; I150; I180

Introduction

The world population is categorized into developed, developing, and undeveloped countries. It is important to note that this categorization is based on the economy rather than the quality of life. While the quality of life is indeed significant, we face challenges in measuring and describing it in comparison to the quality of life of others. Economists, such as Ul Haq, build upon Amartya Sen's work on human capabilities, which focuses on whether individuals can "be" and "do" desirable things in life. This approach encompasses three main dimensions, as outlined by the Human Development Report (https://hdr.undp.org/about/human-development, 2023):

> Beings: Being well-fed, sheltered, and healthy.
> Doings: Engaging in work, education, voting, and community life.
> Freedom of choice is central to this approach.

Gross domestic product (GDP) is commonly used as a proxy to categorize countries economically. However, GDP alone is insufficient to describe overall well-being. The first Human Development Report introduced the Human Development Index (HDI) as a measure of achievement in the fundamental dimensions of human development across countries (https://hdr.undp.org/about/human-development). However, even this index only partially captures the meaning of life. Researchers have studied the topic and introduced the happiness index to achieve a more accurate calculation. The United Nations Department of Economic and Social Affairs describes the Gross National Happiness Index. This description is:

> […] concept implies that sustainable development should take a holistic approach towards notions of progress and give equal importance to non-economic aspects of wellbeing. The Gross National Happiness Index (GNH) (https://sdgs.un.org/partnerships/gross-national-happiness-index, SGDS UN, 2023) is a single-number index developed from 33 indicators categorized under nine

> domains. The GNH Index is constructed based on a robust multidimensional methodology known as the Alkire-Foster method. The nine domains are psychological well-being, health, education, time use, cultural diversity and resilience, good governance, community vitality, ecological diversity and resilience, and living standards. The domains represent each of the components of the well-being of the Bhutanese people, and the term wellbeing here refers to fulfilling conditions of a "good life" as per the values and principles laid down by the concept of Gross National Happiness. (SGDS UN, 2023, https://sdgs.un.org/partnerships/gross-national-happiness-index)

To survive is the primary aim of humans, stemming from evolutionary tracks. However, more than merely survival is needed for modern humans who seek happiness and fulfillment. This is where well-being and health come into play.

The COVID-19 pandemic serves as a litmus test for our wellbeing and health. Since the outbreak began in China, 6,817,478 deaths have been reported to the World Health Organization as of February 3, 2023 (WHO, 2023b). Although vaccines have been developed against COVID-19 and its variants, deaths due to the virus continue.

Regarding Table 3.1, the highest death count is observed in the Americas, which comprises 35 countries, including the US, Canada, Mexico, and Brazil. The second-highest death toll is observed in Europe. It can be asserted that the COVID-19 pandemic has impacted the world's wealthiest regions, except Japan. Two main dimensions are contributing to this observation.

The first dimension involves deaths directly resulting from COVID-19 and those indirectly caused by the saturation of hospital capacity and lack of usual care. For instance, data from available statistical regions (NUTS 3) indicate that

Table 3.1. Global COVID-19 Pandemic Overview.

WHO Region	Cases-Cumulative Total	Deaths-Cumulative Total	Persons Boosted per 100 Population
GLOBAL	754,018,841	6,817,478	30,61
Europe	271,830,048	2,183,152	34,45
Western Pacific	199,856,908	391,240	53,74
Americas	188,848,009	2,914,796	41,71
South-East Asia	60,757,143	803,683	20,28
Eastern Mediterranean	23,244,448	349,341	17,58
Africa	9,481,521	175,253	3,89

Source: Adapted from WHO (https://covid19.who.int).

at least one week of double the usual mortality was experienced in half of the regions (EU, 2023, https://cohesiondata.ec.europea.eu). The second dimension relates to the elderly population. Why have wealthy countries faced a shortage of intensive care units and health workers? For example, in Germany, the physician-to-bed ratio is comparatively low, and the nurse-to-bed ratio is one of the lowest in the European Union (European Commission, 2021, p. 10). In this case, the main argument revolves around how we perceive and approach health services. If we consider Health a commodity that can be traded, the question arises: who pays the bill? Conversely, if we view health services as a human right, the challenge lies in determining how to distribute the costs equally.

How do We Define Health, and Who is Responsible for Our Well-being?

According to the World Health Organization (WHO), achieving a state of complete physical, mental, and social well-being involves individuals or groups being able to identify and pursue aspirations, meet their needs, and adapt to or cope with their environment (WHO, 2023c, https://portal.who.int/triplebillions/PowerBIDashboards/Countries).

Health is a fundamental aspect of the Human Development Index and Gross National Happiness Index. For humans to survive and experience happiness, good health is crucial. However, healthcare services are costly, and their demand is expected to rise. So, the question arises: Who will bear the healthcare expenses? Around the world, we observe different systems, including state-funded, individual-based, and mixed payment systems.

This paper compares the health financing systems and their success in managing the COVID-19 pandemic. For this purpose, three of the most populated EU member countries, namely, Germany, Italy, and France have been chosen. Additionally, Türkiye has also been considered due to its population within Europe.

Here are some facts about these countries:

These three EU countries have also recorded the highest number of COVID-19 deaths (Worldmeters, 2023, https://www.worldometers.info/coronavirus/#countries).

At a glance, we can observe that Türkiye is the poorest country presented in Table 3.2, and its population does not report high levels of happiness. Regarding GDP, Türkiye has a five times lower score than Germany, and its happiness score is eight times lower in the rankings. The COVID-19 death data show that Germany has lost 167,387 people (0.0019% of the population), while Türkiye has reported 101,419 deaths (0.0011%). Although Germany and Türkiye have similar population sizes (Germany: 84.3 million and Türkiye: 85.2 million), there are significant differences in terms of happiness, wealth, Gini coefficients, and total COVID-19 death numbers (assuming the numbers are accurate). Interestingly, Türkiye (101,419) seems to have a lower COVID-19 death toll than Germany (167,387). Could this difference be attributed to differences in the health systems of both countries?

Table 3.2. Country Rankings by Some Facts.

Country 2022	Ranking by GDP	Real GDP growth 2022 (%)	GINI Index 2018	GDP per capita, Current prices 2022	Happiness score	Happiness ranking
Germany	4	1,8%	31.7	65,870	7,034	14
France	7	0,7%	32.4	58,420	6,687	20
Italy	12	0,9%	35.2	52,830	6,467	31
Türkiy	19	3% (2023)	41.9 (2019)	40,880	4,744	112

Source: Author compilation from World Bank, IMF, and World Happiness Report webpages.

Brief History of the German Healthcare System

The history of the modern German healthcare system traces back to the medical reform movement of the 1840s. During the nineteenth Century, most hospitals were public institutions administered by cities or local communities (Bleker, 2002, p. 20).

> In 1854, employers had to pay part of the (industrial) auxiliary insurance premiums. As a result of this history, three elements of health insurance institutions developed: compulsory health insurance or compulsory membership in local or in-trade health insurance organizations, financial participation of employers in their employees' insurance payments, and the extraordinary political significance for the labor of the independent management of their health insurance funds. (Labisch, 2002, p. 40)

Otto von Bismarck established the first health insurance system in Europe, which covered laborers (German History in Documents and Images, 1922). This system is essential in Europe, and some countries have copied it.

> During the 19th Century, the German system was still based mainly on public foundation. Poor citizens who cannot afford to pay for health services could apply for poor relief funds. Local authorities and communities have sponsored these funds. The system as it exists today traces its historical development, which can be divided into a period of rapid expansion after World War II, followed by one increasingly centering on cost containment starting in the mid-1970s and continuing up to the present. After World War II, German statutory health plans played a passive role. Plans focused on premium collection and administration, and access to health insurance plans increased markedly. In 1925, only 51% of all citizens were enrolled in statutory plans. By 1960, 83% were covered, rising to almost 90% enrolment in 2000. While the number of subscribers increased, the number of statutory health plans declined through consolidation. (Porter et al., 2012, pp. 56–57)

In addition, health insurance was first introduced in Germany in 1883 (https://www.ncbi.nlm.nih.gov/books/NBK298834). Historically, the German healthcare system has transitioned from a primarily public-based system to a more private one. However, this shift does not imply a complete overhaul of the system. Germany is home to the oldest social health insurance (SHI) system in the world, with approximately 11% of the population covered by private health insurance (PHI) and 89% by SHI (European Commission, 2021).

The German healthcare system is divided into three main sectors: outpatient care, inpatient care (hospitals), and rehabilitation facilities (National Library of Medicine, 2018, https://www.ncbi.nlm.nih.gov/books/NBK507320/figure/Ch3-f0001). This is mapped out in Fig. 3.1.

Today, Germany is the most populous and affluent country in the European Union, with a population of 80,523,700, and its GDP per capita stood at nearly 51,237.64 U.S. dollars in 2021 (Statista, 2023, https://www.statista.com/statistics/295465/germany-gross-domestic-product-per-capita-in-current-prices/).

Are there many differences between the countries' health financing systems and organization structures?

Brief History of the French Healthcare System

The French healthcare system has been predominantly based on private financing, even after the French Revolution in 1789. Doctors formed unions to protect their economic rights and opposed the establishment of tariff schedules, arguing that the fees charged to clients should be a matter of the doctors' conscience and the client's financial means (Hildreth, 2018). According to Hildreth, even a century later, the debate over the payment system for health services between local governments and physicians' unions continued. The French healthcare system follows a similar pattern to the German system (Ndekwa et al., 2023; Sood & Özen, 2024; Yerpude et al., 2022).

> […] today, the French health care system is structurally based on a Bismarckian approach, with goals of universality and solidarity that have led to an increasingly Beveridge system style. Social Healthcare Insurance currently covers almost 100% of the resident population. We can divide the French healthcare system. (Chevreul et al., 2015; Magri et al., 2019)
>
> - The state: the parliament and the government, specifically the Ministry in charge of Health;
> - SHI; and
> - local communities to a lesser extent, particularly at the regional level ….

This is mapped out in Fig. 3.2.

Today, France has a 65.81 million population and 42,646.03 US dollars (Statista, 2023, https://www.statista.com/statistics/295465/germany-gross-domestic-product-per-capita-in-current-prices).

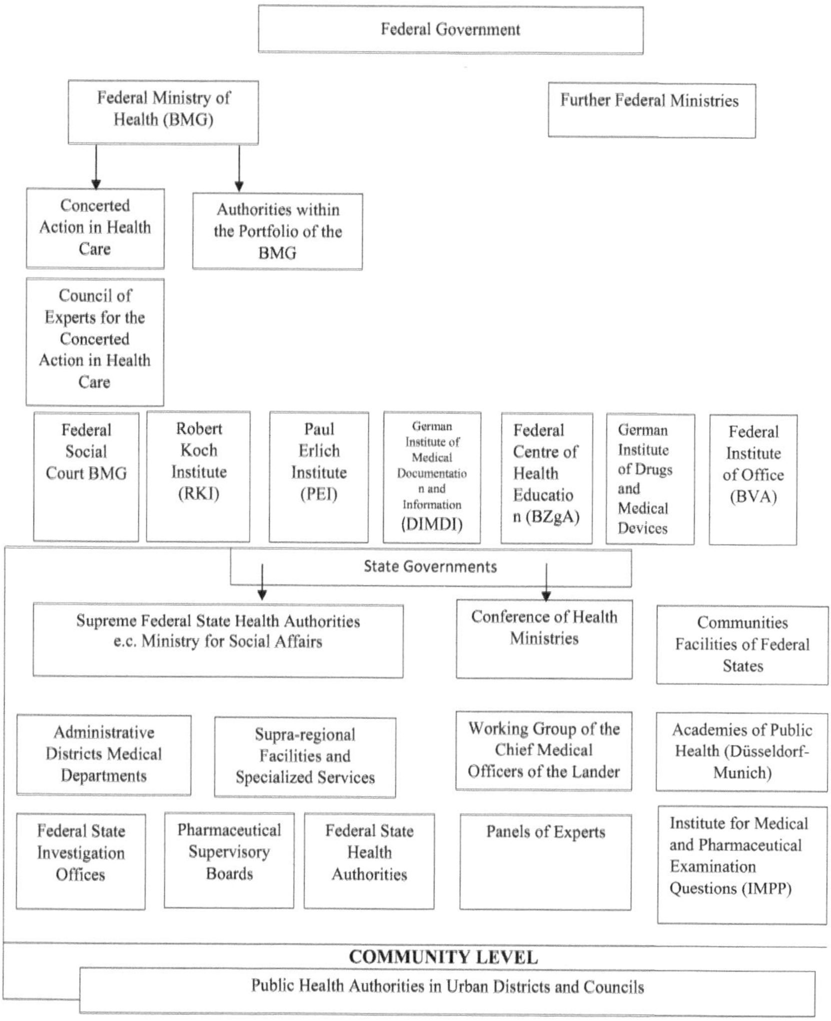

Fig. 3.1. Organization of the Public Health Service in Germany. *Source*: Rechel et al. (2018).

The organizational structure of the French health system differs from that of Germany due to Germany's federal government system.

Brief History of the Italian Healthcare System

With its significant historical importance, Italy is among the countries that have taken the necessary initial steps in healthcare. The country has a longstanding tradition of public health and health promotion. In 1888, the Law on Hygiene, Health Protection, and Public Health was conceptualized and co-signed by Luigi Pagliani, the first Italian Professor of Hygiene and founder of the Italian Society

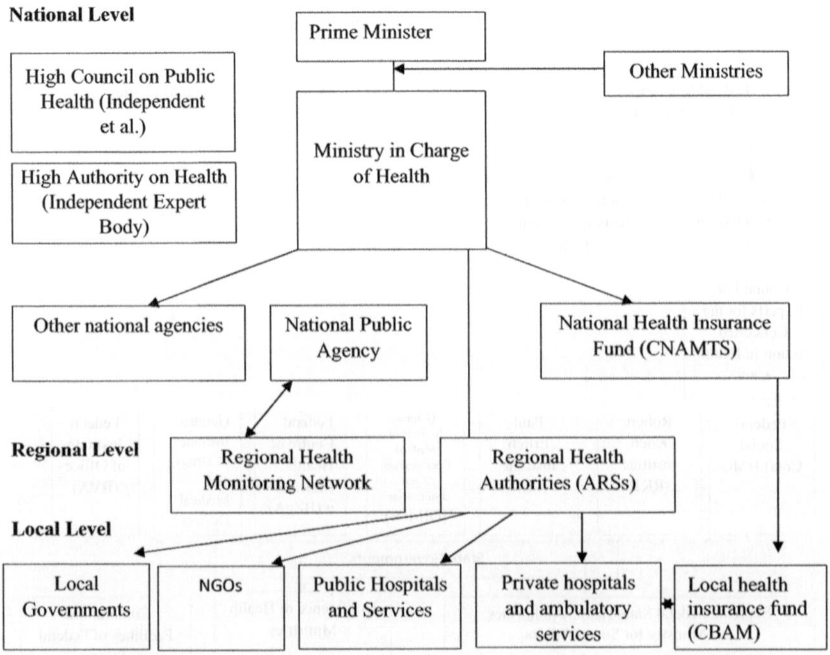

Fig. 3.2. Organization of Public Health Services in France. *Source*: Rechel et al. (2018).

of Hygiene, Preventive Medicine, and Public Health (SItI) established in 1878. This law laid the foundation for Italy's first modern health system, focusing on sanitation, hygiene, and disease prevention (Cilliers & Retief, 2002; Paniga, 2022).

Today, Italy has a regionalized National Health Service (SSN) that offers universal coverage, with most services provided free at delivery. However, some services and goods may require a co-payment. Italy has a long history of high life expectancy, consistently ranking among the highest in the European Union (Ferre et al., 2022). This may be attributed to the Mediterranean-type nutrition prevalent in the country. The central government and local authorities share the responsibility for health services. However, unlike other European countries, Italy does not have an overarching Public Health Act or a central public health agency (Rechel et al., 2018). This is mapped out in Fig. 3.3.

The Italian health system has similarities with France's system. In addition, all three countries have divided their health system at regional and national levels (Kaur et al., 2024; Rijal et al., 2024).

Brief History of the Turkish Healthcare System

Before the establishment of the modern Republic of Türkiye, an institutional healthcare service cannot be considered to have existed. The healthcare system during that time was quite rudimentary, especially compared to the systems in European countries, and it mainly provided services to the emperor and wealthy

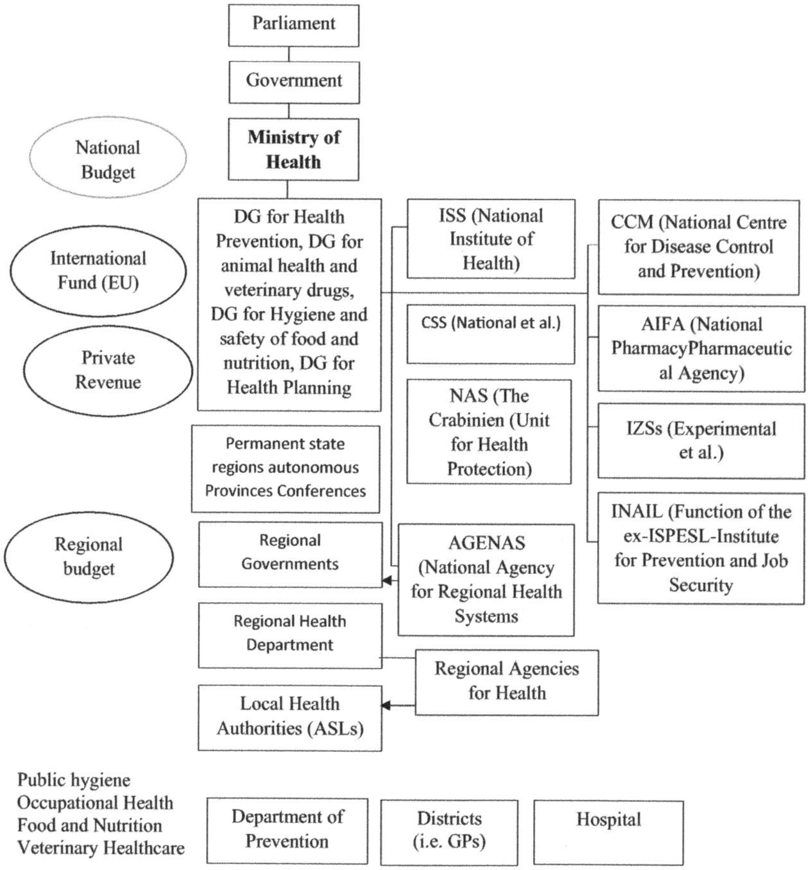

Fig. 3.3. Administrative Structure of Italian Public Health Services. *Source*: Poscia et al. (2023).

citizens (Çavmak & Çavmak, 2017). The concept of a modern health institution dates back to 1920, when the Ministry of Health was inaugurated (OECD and IBRD/World Bank, 2008).

- The foundations of the current public health system for Türkiye were established during 1923–1946.
- During 1946–1960, health centers, which were supposed to provide integrated health services to the Turkish population, were established, and all hospitals were transferred from local administrations to the Ministry of Health.
- In 1961, the Law on Socialisation of Health Services (Law 224) was adopted.
- In 1963, for the first time, Health was included in the five-year development plans.
- In 1978, a Law on Full-time Practice for Public Sector Doctors was adopted, and doctors were prevented from working in the private sector.

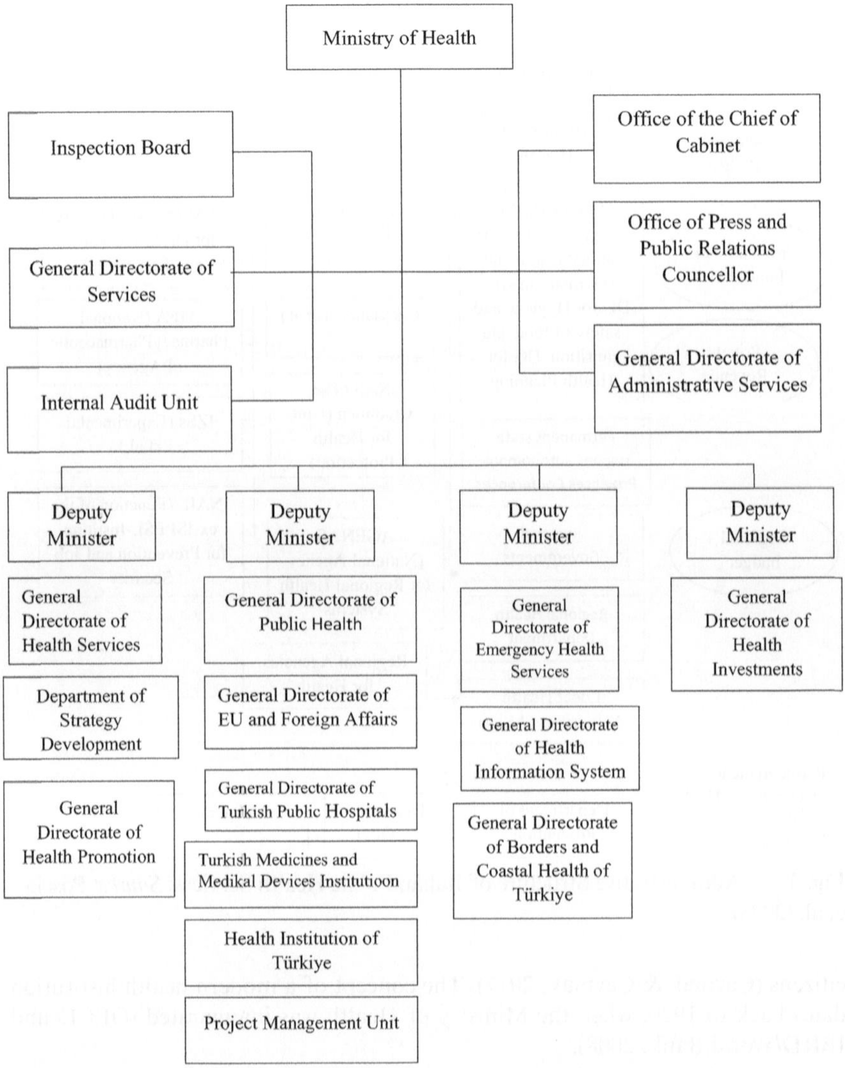

Fig. 3.4. Administrative Structure of Turkish Public Health Services. *Source*: Ministry of Health of Türkiye (2023).

- During 1980–2002, Turkish citizens were granted critical constitutional rights about access to social security and health services.
- Between 1986 and 1989, the government adopted the Basic Law of Health Services (1987) and the Law on Launching Health Insurance through Ba-Kur (the Social Insurance Agency for Merchants, Artisans, and Self-employed).
- During 1988–1993, the MoH and the State Planning Organisation (SPO) conducted a significant health reform study to understand needs and identify reform directions.

- Healthcare reforms continued to be included in the various development plans during this period. For example, the seventh development plan 1996–2000 aimed.
- The Health Transformation Programme (HTP) of the Ministry of Health includes the implementation of Universal Health Insurance (UHI), covering 2003–2013.

If we compare the Turkish health system with the other three countries, we can assert that the Turkish health system is separate from regional and national levels.

COVID-19 Pandemic, Health System Performance and Happiness Index

First, we should look at the COVID-19 pandemic performance of the four countries by considering cases, death toll, and persons boosted per 100 population.

As seen in Table 3.3, regarding the 0.32% rate of deaths per population, the worst country is Italy, while the most successful is Türkiye. The proportion of the elderly population in these countries is:

Germany 65 > 22% (2022)[1]
France 65 > 21.7% (2022)[2]
Italy 65 > 24% (2021)[3]
Türkiye 65 > 9.9% (2022)[4]

Table 3.3. COVID-19 Performance of Germany, France, Italy, and Türkiye.

	Cases Cumulative Total	**Deaths Cumulative Total**	**Deaths per Population (%)**	**Persons Boosted per 100 Population**
Germany	38,359,611	171,059	**0.20**	62,38
France	38,735,658	162,055	**0.23**	60,91
Italy	25,695,311	189,089	**0.32**	75,3
Türkiye	17,004,677	101,416	**0.11**	33,55

Source: https://covid19.who.int/table (WHO, 2023a, accessed on 06 April 2023).

At a glance, we can assert that the percentage of the elderly population has played a significant role in the number of deaths per population rather than the number of vaccinated individuals per 100. It is worth noting that COVID-19 vaccines were provided free of charge in all these countries: Germany (YES), France

[1]https://knoema.com/atlas/Germany/Population-aged-65-years-and-above.
[2]https://knoema.com/atlas/France/Population-aged-65-years-and-above
[3]Italy/Population ages 65 and above. https://data.worldbank.org/indicator/SP.POP.65UP.TO.ZS?locations=IT
[4]https://data.tuik.gov.tr/

(YES), Italy (YES), and Türkiye (YES). Therefore, we cannot argue that the cost of the vaccine has had an effect.

With the lowest death count, Türkiye seems fortunate, and its citizens may be happier than their counterparts. However, it is essential to note that happiness is not solely based on avoiding death but is also related to overall well-being. The health system financing in all four countries is similar, with costs primarily covered by the state, but out-of-pocket payments still exist. According to the World Health Organization (WHO), in Türkiye, the population with household expenditures on Health exceeding 10% of total household expenditure or income decreased from 6% in 2006 to 3.2% in 2016, while those exceeding 25% decreased from 1.1% to 0.4% in the same period (https://portal.who.int).

As shown in Table 3.4, although there is no data available for France, we can argue that lower out-of-pocket payments, which indicate higher public spending on health expenditures, result in a lower death rate from COVID-19. Among the developed countries, except for Türkiye, Italian citizens spend the most out-of-pocket money on their Health. This suggests that the health system financing in Italy is based on less public financing than in Germany and France, yet it has the highest death toll.

On the other hand, Italy is less happy compared to Germany and France. As shown in Fig. 3.5, Türkiye's happiness index has decreased over the past six years. The reason for this decline appears to be related to constitutional changes. 2017, a referendum was held, and since July 2018, the system has undergone a complete transformation. Following this date, the happiness index has been on the decline. Additionally, Türkiye's income diversity rate is quite significant, making it challenging for ordinary citizens to afford the health system.

The Happiness Index shows the effect of the COVID-19 pandemic. Türkiye's happiness indices indicate that the pandemic has significantly impacted happiness. Even though it has the lowest death toll among the four countries, its citizens are not happy, and the indices have been decreasing during and after the

Table 3.4. Health Expenditures Financing in Türkiye, Germany, France, and Italy.

	Türkiye	**Germany**	**France**	**Italy**
Population with household expenditures on Health >10% of total household expenditure or income %	3.2% (2016)	1.5% (2010)	–	9.3% (2010)
Proportion of population with >25% household expenditures on Health	0.4% (2016)	0.1% (2010)	–	1.1% (2010)
Domestic general government health expenditure (% of general government expenditure)	9.5% (2019)	20.1% (2019)	15.1% (2019)	13.2% (2019)

Source: Author compilation from WHO.

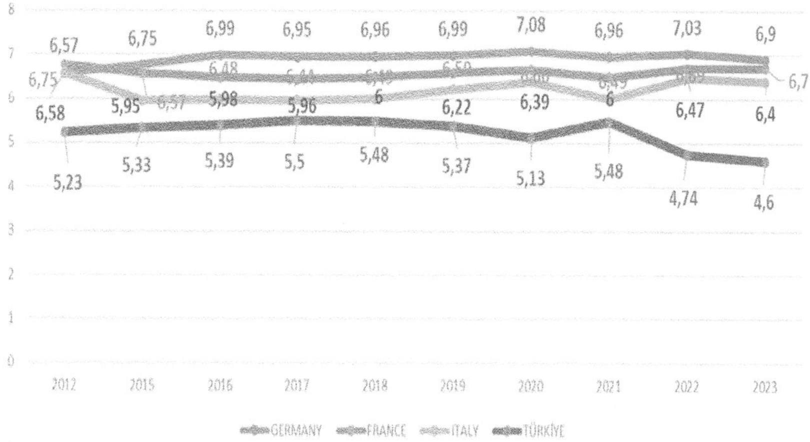

Fig. 3.5. Happiness Index Ranking. *Source*: https://worldhappiness.report/data/ (accessed on 07 April 2023).

pandemic, which is unique in the group. So, we can claim that happiness is also related to economic conditions.

The average Happiness Index for the four countries is 6.23. Italy falls slightly below the average with a score of 6.19, while Türkiye is significantly lower at 5.22. Türkiye is the least happy country among the group, even though its Human Development Index has improved and ranked from 1990 to 2021, as shown in Fig. 3.6.

As we compare the two figures, we can claim that increasing the human development index does not lead to an increase in happiness in the country.

Conclusion

All societies have faced challenges in health system financing. Capitalism considers Health a tradable good, where individuals must pay for it when needed. To achieve a balance between people's income and their health expenditures, insurance systems have been introduced. In countries like the United States, where almost the entire health system is financed out of pocket, there are certain pitfalls, such as the difficulty for citizens to determine the best health insurance option. Additionally, pension funds collected by insurance companies are often invested in stock exchanges, which can lead to the loss of funds during economic crises.

Health is a fundamental human right that cannot be compromised. This idea is a concept that has been widely recognized.

> [...] The Sustainable Development Goal on Health (SDG 3) comprises 13 specific targets relating to maternal and child health, communicable diseases such as HIV/AIDS, tuberculosis, and hepatitis, as well as non-communicable diseases such as cancers and diabetes, to services relating to mental Health as well as sexual and reproductive health and rights, to the health impacts of pollution, traffic and tobacco consumption as well as the research

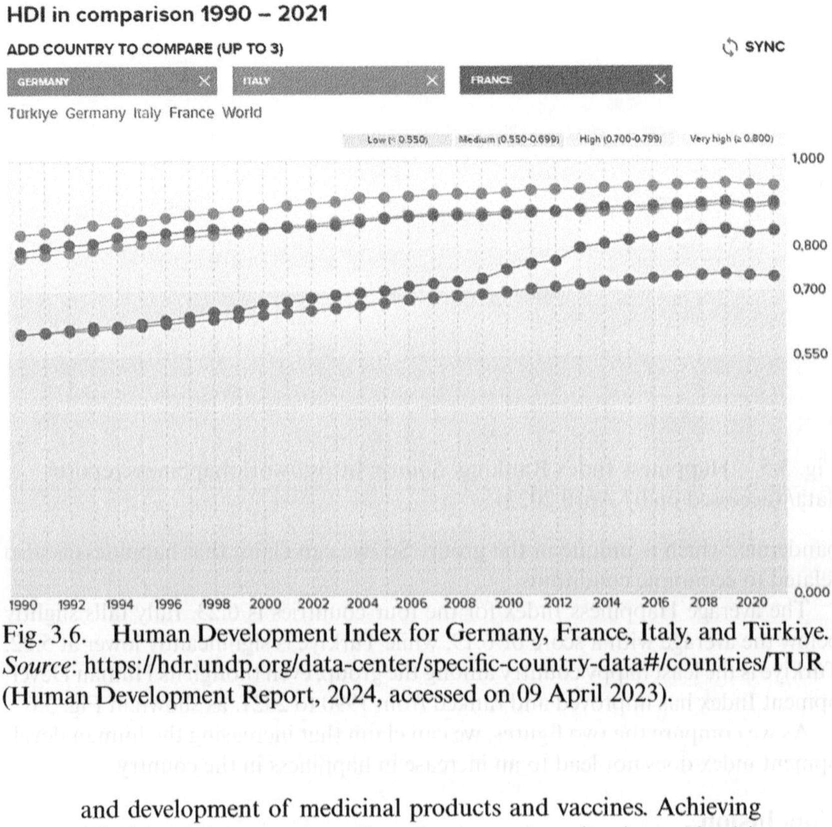

Fig. 3.6. Human Development Index for Germany, France, Italy, and Türkiye. *Source*: https://hdr.undp.org/data-center/specific-country-data#/countries/TUR (Human Development Report, 2024, accessed on 09 April 2023).

> and development of medicinal products and vaccines. Achieving SDG 3 relies on targets such as the expansion of universal health coverage, access to affordable, high-quality essential vaccines and medicinal products, sustainable financing, the provision of a sufficient and qualified health workforce, and capacity-building to prevent and overcome health emergencies .... (https://www.bundesgesundheitsministerium.de)

Is achieving goals such as expanding universal health coverage by implementing a profit-centered capitalist health system possible? If not, how can we achieve these goals? Health is considered a fundamental aspect, and proponents of profit-centered ideas argue that establishing a private insurance system can solve all problems, much like other views, such as the socialist idea of Health. However, there is a fundamental difference between these two political systems. A profit-based system considers citizens as customers who must pay for healthcare and generate profit. In order to make a profit, citizens must be ill; otherwise, the system becomes unsustainable. On the other hand, a non-profit-based system does not prioritize profit or view patients as customers; its objective is to prevent citizens from falling ill and promote their overall Health.

National governments must play a crucial role in public health by providing financial funds. The system must be trustworthy, accountable, transparent, and satisfactory and cover the entire population. Universal health coverage (UHC) can be a starting point for improving the quality of health systems, which could save over 8 million lives each year (Kruk et al., 2018).

Other than public health financing by the state, what can explain Türkiye's COVID-19 achievements compared to Germany, France, and Italy?

References

Bleker, J. (2002). In G. C. B. Manfred and J. Cocks (Eds.) *Medicine and modernity* (2nd ed.). Cambridge University Press, Cambridge, ISBN: 978-0521564113.

Çavmak, Ş., & Çavmak, D. (2017). Türkiye'de sağlık hi̇zmetleri̇ni̇n tari̇hsel geli̇şi̇mi̇ ve sağlikta dönüşüm programi. *Journal of Health Management*, *1*(1), 48–57. https://dergipark.org.tr/en/pub/saglik/issue/30164/337586

Chevreul, K., Berg Brigham, K., Durand-Zaleski, I., & Hernandez-Quevedo, C. (2015). France: Health system review. *Health Systems in Transition*, *17*(3), 1–128.

Cilliers, L., & Retief, F. P. (2002). The evolution of the hospital from antiquity to the end of the middle ages. *Curationis*, *25*(4), 60–66. https://doi.org/10.4102/curationis.v25i4.806Bleker

EU. (2023). https://cohesiondata.ec.europea.eu, Accessed at 14.07.2024.

German History in Documents and Images (1922). (Vol. 8). https://germanhistorydocs.ghi-dc.org/pdf/eng/429_BismarckWorker's Comp_130.pdf

Ferre, F., de Belvis, A. G., Valerio, L., Longhi, S., Lazzari, A., Fattore, G., Ricciardi, W., & Maresso, A. (2022). Italy: Health system review. *Health Systems in Transition*, *24*(4), 1–203.

Hildreth, M. L. (2018). *Doctors, bureaucrats, and public health in France, 1888–1902*. Garland

Human Development Report. (2023, June 15). *What is human development?* Retrieved May 10, 2023 from https://hdr.undp.org/about/human-development

Human Development Report. (2024, March 13). *Human development summary capturing achievements in the HDI and complementary metrics that take into account gender gaps, inequality, planetary pressures and multidimensional poverty*. Retrieved April 9, 2023 from https://hdr.undp.org/data-center/specific-country-data#/countries/TUR

Kaur, S., Kumar, R., Singh, K., & Huang, Y. L. (2024). Leveraging artificial ıntelligence for enhanced sustainable energy management. *Journal of Sustainable Energy*, *3*(1), 1–20. https://doi.org/10.56578/jse030101

Labisch, A. (2022). From traditional individualism to collective professionalism state, patient, compulsory health insurance, and the panel doctor question in Germany, 1883-1931. In M. Berg & G. Cocks (Eds.), *Medicine and Modernity: Public Health and Medical Care in Nineteenth and Twentieth Century Germany* (pp. 35–54, 1-235). Cambridge University Press, Cambridge, ISBN 0 521564115 (he).

Magri, A., Farrugia, A., Valetta, F., & Grima, S. (2019). An analysis of the risk factors determining motor ınsurance premium in a small ısland state: The case of Malta. *International Journal of Finance, Insurance and Risk Management*, *IX*(1–2), 63–85.

Ministry of Health of Türkiye. (2023). *Republic of Türkiye Ministry of Health*. Retrieved April 5, 2023 from https://www.saglik.gov.tr/EN,15609/ministerial-organization.html

National Library of Medicine. (2018). *Organization and financing of public health services in Europe: Country reports*. Retrieved March 24, 2023, from https://www.ncbi.nlm.nih.gov/books/NBK507320/figure/Ch3-f0001/

Ndekwa, A. G., Kalugendo, E., Sood, K., & Grima, S. (2023). An analysis of agribusiness digitalisation transformation of the sub-Saharan African countries small-scale farmers' production distribution. *Research on World Agricultural Economy*, *4*(3), 63–78.

OECD and IBRD/THE WORLD BANK. (2008). *OECD reviews of health systems* (p. 40). Turkey. ISBN 978-92-64-05108-9.

Paniga, M. (2022). Public health ınstitutions in Italy in the 20th century. *Athens Journal of Mediterranean Studies*, *8*(2), 117–134. https://doi.org/10.30958/ajms.8-2-3

Porter, M. E. & Guth, C. (2012). The German health care system: Overview and historical development (chapter 4). *Redefining German Health Care* (pp. 53–69). DOI 10.1007/978-3-642-10826-6_4, Springer-Verlag Berlin Heidelberg.

Posca, A., Andrea, S., & Walter, R. (2023). *Organization and financing of public health services in Europe: Country reports*. Retrieved April, 5, 2023, from https://www.ncbi.nlm.nih.gov/books/NBK507328/

Rechel, B., Anna, M., Anna, S., Cristina, H.-Q., Gemma, W., Erica, R., Elke, J., & Ellen, N. (Eds.). (2018).*European observatory health policy series*. NCBI. Retrieved March 19, 2023, from https://pubmed.ncbi.nlm.nih.gov/29897704/

Rijal, S., Nursaputra, M. A. C., & Dari, H. U. (2024). Flood susceptibility analysis using Frequency Ratio method in Walanae watershed. *International Journal of Sustainable Development and Planning*, *19*(3), 823–832. https://doi.org/10.18280/ijsdp.190302

SGDS UN. (2023). *Gross National Happiness Index*. Retrieved February 8, 2023, from https://sdgs.un.org/partnerships/gross-national-happiness-index

Statista. (2023). *Germany: Gross domestic product (GDP) per capita in current prices from 1987 to 2029*. Retrieved February 7, 2023, from https://www.statista.com/statistics/295465/germany-gross-domestic-product-per-capita-in-current-prices

Sood, K., & Özen, E. (2024). A systematic review of ESG in the insurance industry: Navigating the path to sustainability. *International Journal of Sustainable Development and Planning*, *19*(3), 807–821. https://doi.org/10.18280/ijsdp.190301

Worldmeters. (2023). *Coronavirus cases*. Retrieved June 14, 2023, from https://www.worldometers.info/coronavirus/#countries

World Health Organization (WHO). (2023a). *Number of COVID-19 cases reported to WHO*. Retrieved February 6, 2023, from https://covid19.who.int/table

World Health Organization (WHO). (2023b). *Number of COVID-19 cases reported to WHO (cumulative total)*. Retrieved February 6, 2023, from https://covid19.who.int

World Health Organization (WHO). (2023c). *WHO Coronavirus (COVID-19) Dashboard*. Retrieved May 4, 2023, from https://portal.who.int/triplebillions/PowerBIDashboards/Countries; https://covid19.who.int/

Yerpude, S., Sood, K., & Grima, S. (2022). Blockchain-augmented digital supply chain management: A way to sustainable business. *Journal of Risk and Financial Management*, *16*(1), 7.

Chapter 4

Culture, Corporate Social Responsibility and Organizational Competitive Performance: Evidence from the Sri Lanka Banking Sector

Narayanage Jayantha Dewasiri[a,d], *Game Kankanange Krishani Kaushalya*[a], *Mananage Shanika Hansini Rathnasiri*[a], *Simbiya Hevage Madu Lakmini Walakumbura*[a], *Kiran Sood*[b,c] *and Jathun Dahanayaka Kaushalyani Ruwandika*[a]

[a]*Faculty of Management Studies, Sabaragamuwa University of Sri Lanka, Sri Lanka*
[b]*Chitkara Business School, Chitkara University, Punjab, India*
[c]*Women Researchers Council (WRC), Azerbaijan State University of Economics (UNEC), Baku, Azerbaijan*
[d]*Adjunct Faculty, University Center for Research and Development (UCRD), Chandigarh University, Punjab, India*

Abstract

Purpose: Focusing on Sri Lanka's banking industry, our study examines the effect of corporate social responsibility (CSR) on organisational competitive performance (OCP) with the moderating role of organisational culture.

Methodology: We conducted a quantitative research study utilising a survey as the research strategy. A standardised, self-administered questionnaire on a 5-point Likert scale was given to 281 banking industry experts who participated in the study.

Findings: The study found a substantial moderating impact of organisational culture on the relationship between corporate social responsibility and organisational competitive performance. Notably, the study found that responsibility to employees, responsibility to suppliers or business

Green Management: A New Paradigm in the World of Business, 51–66

doi:10.1108/978-1-83797-442-920241004

partners, and responsibility to government and regulatory authorities have a positive influence on organizational competitive performance. Nevertheless, our research suggests that in the Sri Lankan context, there is no substantial influence of responsibilities towards customers, shareholders, community, and the environment on the competitive performance of organisations.

Implications of the study: This study's ramifications cover immediate and long-term scenarios. The findings will be helpful for managers in the banking industry, shareholders, and other stakeholders, providing insights into the advantages of implementing CSR principles.

Originality: This study backs the literature by investigating the moderating role of culture on the association between CSR and performance, as the first study to investigate the same in Sri Lanka, to the best of the knowledge.

Keywords: Banking sector; competitive performance; corporate social responsibility; organizational culture; responsibility to employee; responsibility to government, Sri Lanka

JEL Classifications: D22; L21; M14; M51

1. Introduction

A well-known business-reporting concept called corporate social responsibility (CSR) emphasises voluntarily incorporating social and environmental concerns into a company's activities (Dewasiri & Abeysekera, 2022). Companies create CSR policies, which they then include in their annual reports to highlight their CSR initiatives alongside their corporate undertakings. CSR also involves interacting with multinational firms, state governments, and private citizens. Businesses are urged to consider the community's social interests when making choices under the contemporary definition of CSR. Companies are seen as social, political, and economic actors as well as economic ones (Muthusamy et al., 2023). In addition to shareholders, stakeholders affected by their choices include creditors, debtors, employees, and the general public (Centobelli et al., 2020; De Alwis et al., 2023; Sakshi et al., 2020; Shroff et al., 2024).

CSR is becoming more significant in organisations as Sri Lanka's economy grows. The Sri Lankan business sector has undergone a paradigm shift, moving away from simple corporate giving to one that emphasises social responsibility. Organisations understand that creating trust through solid societal connections is just as crucial as profit-making. People have recently become more concerned with how businesses operate, including how well they follow the rules and regulations, manage waste, produce high-quality products, prevent pollution, and care for their employees (Jayawardena et al., 2023; Muttakin, 2014; Srivastava et al., 2023).

Organisational culture is a shared set of values and management philosophies shaped by social conventions and management education. Different national contexts can have different values and views. A company's values, attitudes, and behaviours are shaped by its organisational culture, which fosters a pleasant work environment that affects employee retention, productivity, and engagement. An excellent corporate culture makes achieving objectives, effective teamwork, and overall performance possible (Sood & Özen, 2024; Yerpude et al., 2022).

Internal and external CSR efforts substantially impact the performance of a corporation. Internally, CSR programs raise employee retention, engagement, and morale, which improves productivity and fosters a positive work environment. CSR gives a business a competitive edge by enhancing its reputation, brand image, and customer loyalty externally. CSR also encourages better risk management and stakeholder participation. Comprehensive CSR strategies provide a win–win situation where social and environmental goals are achieved alongside financial success by bringing together business principles and societal demands. CSR adoption as a core company principle can promote long-term success and sustainable growth.

This chapter examines how organisational culture influences the association between internal and external CSR initiatives and the organizational competitive performance of Sri Lanka's banking sector. This research offers valuable insights for firms to improve their CSR strategy and overall performance by examining how CSR practices influence stakeholder interactions and employee engagement and how organisational culture shapes these relationships. Hence, our study contributes to the literature on organisational culture, CSR, and its effects on organizational competitive performance. The knowledge and insights produced by this research will be helpful to academics and researchers who are interested in these subjects. Hence, we aim to clarify the influence of CSR in Sri Lanka's banking industry as it gains importance in the corporate world. The research intends to provide insightful advice for firms looking to improve their CSR practices and overall performance, promoting sustainable development and societal well-being. It does this by examining the function of organisational culture as a moderating element.

2. Literature Review

Research on CSR has gradually expanded, and many studies have focused on the significance of organisations' corporate social responsibility activities. Accordingly, most CSR-related research has examined the positive effect of CSR on an organisation's profits through organisational, social, and economic performance. The researchers have noted the theoretical concepts and empirical findings in this section.

2.1. Theoretical Review

Over the 20th century, the idea of corporate social responsibility (CSR) changed, receiving many definitions and interpretations in the literature. Carroll put up one significant framework in 1979 that divided the range of CSR into four groups: economic, legal, ethical, and discretionary duties (Carroll, 1979).

According to Wood (1991), corporate social responsibility (CSR) coordinates a company's principles, processes, policies, programs, and measurable outcomes on social responsibility regarding its contacts with the larger community. However, the World Business Council for Sustainable Progress (WBCSD, 1991) describes CSR as a firm's continual commitment to moral behaviour, financial progress, and improving the quality of life for employees and society.

According to Turker (2009), CSR involves various parties, including the government, the private sector, the public sector, and employees. Studies have demonstrated that CSR policies can affect employees' feelings about the company, attracting, motivating, and enhancing employee performance. With the aid of various theories, academics have also investigated whether CSR may enhance an organisation's financial success. According to Donaldson and Preston's (1995) description of the stakeholder theory, considering the interests of many stakeholders, including employees, customers, and suppliers, can increase business performance and long-term financial gains (Kaur et al., 2024; Ndekwa et al., 2023; Rijal et al., 2024).

The isomorphism emphasised by the neo-institutional theory concerning CSR is where organisations seek social legitimacy by abiding by moral and ethical standards (Meyer & Rowan, 1977). According to Campbell (2007), CSR is required by governments, civic organisations, and consumers, and businesses use it to establish social legitimacy. According to researchers like Kim (2013) and Campbell (2007), CSR initiatives may be a source of competitive advantage and enhance corporate performance from a strategic standpoint.

The numerous CSR definitions and interpretations illustrate CSR's complexity and importance in defining a company's interactions with society. CSR initiatives boost performance and employee attitudes while benefiting societal well-being. Companies can also obtain long-term economic gains and social legitimacy by strategically implementing CSR activities while considering the interests of many stakeholders.

It is significant to emphasise that the area of CSR is still developing, and firms and researchers are still investigating its effects on corporate operations and societal impact. Understanding CSR's theoretical foundations and practical implications is vital for creating sustainable and morally responsible firms as it becomes a significant component of corporate strategies (Arora et al., 2024; Mittal et al., 2024).

2.2. Empirical Review

Zahid et al. (2021) examined the connection between a firm's CSR activities (CSRA) and financial performance in Pakistan's manufacturing industry. The study also examined how competitive advantages and innovation mediate this association. The study's findings supported the idea because they showed how significantly CSRA affected the firm's financial performance. Furthermore, the findings showed that innovation and competitive advantage were key mediators between CSRA and financial performance. These findings imply that implementing CSR initiatives might positively impact the financial results for Pakistani manufacturing enterprises, with innovation and competitive advantage as crucial mediators of this relationship.

The primary objective of Sharabati's (2018) research was to determine how CSR activities, including social, ecological, and economic responsibility, impact the operating performance of Jordan's pharmaceutical manufacturing (PM) industry. Data from 116 managers representing seven PM firms were gathered through questionnaires as part of the research's quantitative descriptive methodology. The study showed a strong correlation between CSR factors and how they affected corporate success. It was discovered that all three aspects, social responsibility, economic responsibility, and environmental responsibility, had a significant bearing on the JPM industry's financial performance.

Furthermore, Sharabati (2018) hypothesised that these three sub-variables influenced the pharmaceutical manufacturing sector's commercial performance. Interestingly, the results showed that environmental responsibility was more significant than economic and social responsibility in terms of its effect on the financial success of the Pharmaceutical Manufacturing industry. Overall, the study highlights the critical role of CSR programs in enhancing economic performance in the Jordanian pharmaceutical manufacturing industry, focusing on environmental responsibility's considerable contribution to corporate success.

Gu (2023) has conducted a study to examine how CSR is impacted by a company's performance in a particular geographic area. The findings of a sample of 1,557 Chinese firms imply that their surrounding enterprises influence a company's CSR performance. The relationship between firm performance and CSR success is further supported by this study, which further highlights the mediating function of executive and institutional shareholding rates. The genuine relative importance of the spatiotemporal context on CSR is strongly supported empirically, with substantial implications.

Based on a longitudinal survey of Pakistani small- and medium-sized businesses (SMEs), Ikram et al. (2019) conducted a study to examine the effect of CSR activities on firm performance (FP). The findings show a strong correlation between corporate reputation and staff dedication, two factors determining a company's performance. Chung and Yoon (2018) have conducted a study to compare how CSR affects a restaurant company's FP from the perspectives of all stakeholders. The study discovered that operational profitability is adversely affected while external CSR raises a company's market value. Internal corporate social responsibility (CSR) boosts operational profitability but has little impact on the firm's market value.

Laskar and Maji (2016) focused on analysing trends in CSR disclosure and how they relate to firm performance between 2008–2009 and 2013–2014 using content analysis and the global reporting initiative (GRI) methodology in India. According to the survey, the CSR disclosure score has improved. The disclosure score for the CSR components that dealt with society got the highest score (about 89%), followed by those that dealt with people (around 84%) and products (nearly 84%). The regression analysis showed that CSR and its constituent parts significantly and favourably impacted business performance. The study concludes that CSR activities and each of its components have a substantial effect on company performance in India and have been increasing over time.

Investigating the connection between CSR and firm performance in a developing nation setting was the primary goal of Famiyeh's (2017a,b) research. A structural equation modelling survey examined the association among CSR, cost, quality, flexibility, delivery, and overall organisational performance. The results showed a strong correlation between CSR initiatives and the company's competitive performance in delivery, flexibility, cost, and quality. The study also found that cost- and flexibility-related competitive operational capabilities in the Ghanaian business environment considerably impacted total firm performance. In contrast, delivery and quality had less of an effect. According to this study, adopting CSR activities improves operational competitiveness and, as a result, enhances its general performance in the Ghanaian business climate. Ling (2019) investigated the impact of CSR on organisational performance. However, they utilised knowledge management as a moderator instead of the organisational culture. AlAjmi et al. (2023) examined CSR disclosure and banks' performance with the impact of institutional quality as a moderating variable. Choi (2009) investigated the moderating impact of corporate culture in the context of total quality management. However, there has been a notable scarcity of research concerning organisational culture, especially considering culture as a moderating variable (Iddagoda et al., 2021). This research gap is particularly evident within the banking sector, where examining such relationships remains limited globally and within individual countries (Kaur et al., 2021, 2023; Latif, 2015). Despite the significance of CSR in shaping organisational behaviour and values, few studies have explicitly delved into how CSR initiatives impact the broader corporate culture, and even fewer have explored the potential moderating effects of local or national cultures. There is a lack of scientific proof in this field, which necessitates a thorough and detailed examination to understand better the complex interactions among CSR activities, organisational culture, and the moderating influence of culture within the banking industry.

In the Sri Lankan context, Fernando and Danthanarayana (2021) examined the influence of internal corporate social responsibility (CSR) on employees' intention to leave their jobs. However, this lack of study is particularly evident in the Sri Lankan context, as no previous studies have investigated the specific consequences of CSR initiatives on the organisational culture of the banking sector. Therefore, there is a significant opportunity to provide essential and novel insights to the worldwide body of literature by addressing this important lack of empirical evidence. Hence, our study seeks to fill the existing void in the literature by performing a comprehensive and rigorous investigation into the impact of CSR activities on organisational culture within the banking industry. In addition, we examine the possible influence of culture in the specific setting of the banking business in Sri Lanka.

By undertaking this empirical investigation, the research endeavours to generate novel knowledge and contribute to the growing literature concerning CSR, organizational culture, and the interplay with local and national cultures. Subsequently, this study's findings can enrich our understanding of how

CSR initiatives influence organisational dynamics and values, specifically in the banking sector, and how culture can amplify or temper these effects. Ultimately, the study's outcomes are expected to provide valuable implications for banking institutions, policymakers, and academics to make effective decisions about CSR implementation, organisational practices, and culture management. Furthermore, this research will be of broader significance as it addresses the global scarcity of studies in this area, making a noteworthy contribution to organisational behaviour and CSR.

3. Methodology

This study examines the effect of internal and external corporate social responsibility on OP with the moderating impact of culture in Sri Lanka's banking industry. Hence, we utilize the survey strategy to test the hypothetically developed assumptions (Dewasiri et al., 2018). The study employed a convenient sampling approach to collect primary data from 323 banking managers across Sri Lanka. Data acquisition was facilitated through Google Forms. Initially, the questionnaire was distributed to identified bank managers, requesting dissemination among their respective bank colleagues. This phase yielded 93 responses. Subsequently, employing the snowball sampling technique, these respondents were encouraged to forward the questionnaire to their professional networks within the banking sector. This method garnered additional 230 responses. The study amassed 323 responses, comprising the dataset for analysis. The researchers have used responsibility to the employees, customers, suppliers and business partners, community, government, environment, and regulatory authorities, which have been considered independent variables. In contrast, organisational culture and corporate competitive performance were considered moderation and dependent variables. The research adopts a rigorous analytical approach, employing regression and correlation analyses to scrutinise the effects and interconnections between corporate social responsibility (CSR) initiatives and key organisational performance metrics. These analyses are conducted utilising the IBM SPSS 26.0 software package. Moreover, the study investigates the moderating influence of corporate culture on these relationships through hierarchical regression analysis, adding depth to the investigation. Through these statistically robust methodologies, the research aims to illuminate the intricate dynamics among CSR practices, corporate culture, and organisational performance within the banking sector of Sri Lanka.

4. Results and Discussion

4.1. Descriptive Statistics

The fact that the study's standard deviation is between the permitted bounds of +2 and −2 suggests that the data points are close to the mean. As a result, the results in Table 4.1 are more trustworthy and consistent for further analysis, pointing to a modest amount of dispersion and stability in the dataset.

Table 4.1. Descriptive Analysis.

Construct	Minimum	Maximum	Mean	Standard Deviation
Responsibility to employee	2.80	4.60	3.5153	0.36361
Responsibility to customer	3.00	5.00	3.5030	0.40617
Responsibility to suppliers and business partners	2.80	5.00	3.4811	0.50931
Responsibility to shareholders	2.80	4.93	3.8530	0.49306
Responsibility to community	2.63	4.25	3.7131	0.36676
Responsibility to the environment	2.27	4.45	2.9560	0.50024
Responsibility to the government and regulatory authorities	2.50	4.50	3.3354	0.50559
Organisation culture	2.75	4.38	3.5707	0.30882
Competitive performance	2.80	4.70	3.5893	0.39237

Source: Authors' compilation based on the SPSS output.

4.2. Testing for Multivariate Assumptions

4.2.1. Normality Test

For a normal distribution, the acceptable skewness value shall be within the range of −3 and +3, and kurtosis is appropriate from the scope of −10 to +10 (Brown, 2006). Furthermore, the results of skewness and kurtosis tests indicated in Table 4.2 are also within the range of −3 and +3 and −10 to +10. Therefore, the data series for this study's dependent and independent variables are typically distributed.

4.2.2. Multicollinearity Diagnostic Test

Tolerance should be greater than 0.2, and the VIF value should be less than 5 to confirm whether there is no significant multicollinearity in the model. According to Table 4.3, the tolerance for each independent variable included in this study is more important than 0.2, and the VIF value indicates no multicollinearity issue.

4.3. Regression Analysis

We used the regression analysis to investigate the effect of CSR activities on organisational competitive performance in the banking sector.

To determine if the entire model is a significant predictor of the result variable, utilise an ANOVA table. This model's computed P-value (0.000) is less than 0.05, as Table 4.4 illustrates. As a result, it may be said that the fitted regression model extremely significantly predicts the dependent variable ($P < 0.0005$, $F(8,272) = 32.561$).

Table 4.2. The Normality Test.

Construct	Skewness	Kurtosis
Responsibility to employee	1.362	1.539
Responsibility to customer	1.627	3.446
Responsibility to suppliers and business partners	1.095	0.932
Responsibility to shareholders	0.108	−0.206
Responsibility to community	−0.734	0.217
Responsibility to the environment	1.055	0.338
Responsibility to the government and regulatory Authorities	0.508	−0.137
Organisation culture	0.509	0.109
Competitive performance	0.814	0.197

Source: Authors' compilation based on the SPSS output.

Table 4.3. Multicollinearity Test.

Construct	Tolerance	VIF
Responsibility to employee	0.393	2.546
Responsibility to customer	0.364	2.745
Responsibility to suppliers and business partners	0.346	2.894
Responsibility to shareholders	0.429	2.333
Responsibility to community	0.537	1.861
Responsibility to the environment	0.390	2.561
Responsibility to the government and regulatory Authorities	0.503	1.990
Organisation culture	0.586	1.707

Source: Authors' compilation based on the SPSS output.

Table 4.4. ANOVA.

Model	Some of Squares	Df	Mean square	F	Sig.
Regression residual total	21.088	8	2.636	32.561	0.000
	22.020	272	0.081		
	43.108	280			

Source: Authors' compilation based on the SPSS output.

4.3.1. Model Summary

R-square shows the degree of explanation of the dependent variable, which is explained by the independent variables (Chicco, 2021). Table 4.5 shows that 69.9% (R-vsquare = 0.699[a]) of the variation in competitive performance of the banking sector is explained by their internal and external CSR activities. In other words, the developed model can cover 69.9% of the total variability of the dependent variable in the current study. Furthermore, the remaining 30.1% could be due to other exogenous factors that affect the banking sector's competitive performance.

4.3.2. Coefficient Table

The coefficient table represents the level of impact of the independent variables in explaining the model. The coefficient table is given in Table 4.6 according to the multiple linear regression results. As dimensions of CSR activities that impact competitive performance, responsibility to employees, customers, suppliers and business partners, community, government, and the responsibility to organizational culture are statistically significant in this model as its P-values are less than the significance level of 0.05.

Table 4.5. Model Summary.

Model	R	R-Square	Adjusted R-Square	Sth. Error of the Estimate
1	0.699	0.489	0.474	0.284

Source: Authors' compilation based on the SPSS output.

Table 4.6. Coefficient Table.

Model	Unstandardised Coefficients		Standardised Coefficients	*T*	Sig.
	B	Standard error	Beta		
(Constant)	0.073	0.184		0.395	0.693
RTE	0.256	0.069	0.234	3.696	0.000
RTC	0.001	0.064	0.001	0.019	0.985
RTSP	0.172	0.050	0.202	3.408	0.001
RTS	0.054	0.045	0.065	1.210	0.227
RTCM	0.065	0.053	0.064	1.233	0.219
RTEN	−0.052	0.050	−0.058	−1.043	0.298
RTG	0.244	0.045	0.286	5.486	0.000
OC	0.248	0.067	0.183	3.716	0.000

Source: Authors' compilation based on the SPSS output.

Table 4.7. Hierarchical Multiple Linear Regression Analysis.

Model		Unstandardised Coefficients		Sig.
		B	B Std. Error	
1	(Constant)	0.938	0.197	0.000
	CSR	0.762	0.056	0.000
2	(Constant)	0.541	0.233	0.021
	CSR	0.665	0.064	0.000
	OC	0.206	0.067	0.002
3	(Constant)	1.589	0.286	0.000
	CSR OC	0.447	0.071	0.000
	CSR.OC	0.112	0.066	0.088
		0.091	0.061	0.000

Source: Authors' compilation based on the SPSS output.

4.4. Moderator Analysis

In this study, organisational culture has been considered as the moderating variable. The moderation effects were tested using the hierarchical multiple linear regression analysis described by Baron and Kenny (1986). The results are indicated in Table 4.7.

Accordingly, the interaction term of corporate social responsibility and organisational culture is statistically significant at a % confidence level of 90%, as its P-value (0.000) is less than 0.1 at a 10% confidence level. Therefore, it could be concluded that organisational culture significantly moderates the link between CSR activities and competitive performance in the banking sector.

5. Discussion

This study examined whether corporate social responsibility impacts organisational competitive performance with the moderating impact of organisational culture in the banking sector in Sri Lanka. Employing a regression analysis, the researcher found a substantial association between CSR and organisational competitive performance. The findings imply that organisational culture is a moderating variable impacting CSR and organisational competitive performance.

The present research analysis concludes that organisational culture is key in moderating the association between corporate social responsibility initiatives and competitive performance in the banking sector. Empirical research has shown a direct correlation between an organisation's culture and performance (Denison, 1995). This means that an organisation with a strong and consistent culture is more likely to achieve superior performance. This is because a strong culture involves aligning the organisation's strategy, structure, and other resources in a supportive way. A strong culture is characterised by most of the organisation's members adhering to shared values and beliefs promoted by the firm's leaders (Büschgens et al., 2013). Therefore, it excels in performance compared to its competitors in the highly competitive and inventive banking industry. However, limited research studies have been undertaken to ascertain the influence of organisational culture and reveal its significance on a global scale.

Based on the multiple linear regression results provided above, it can be concluded that both responsibility to the environment and responsibility to the shareholders do not substantially impact the organisational competitive performance when considering external CSR activities. Waheed et al. (2021) discovered that the dimension of responsibility to employees has a favourable impact on the competitive performance of organisations. Conversely, the responsibility to the community dimension of CSR had the smallest positive impact on the firm's competitive performance. This is because sustainability is a highly significant capacity for organisations, and this research has verified that CSR and corporate culture are reliable indicators of the organisation's sustainable performance. However, this research revealed that the responsibility to the environment had a negligible effect on corporate culture. The level of environmental disclosure in the banking industry is comparatively lower than in other industries (Abdymomunov, 2020). In Sri Lankan contexts, bankers assert that engaging in environmental-related CSR activities does not affect the competitive performance of the banks. Based on the findings of Waheed et al. (2021), our study indicates that employee responsibility, responsibility to suppliers or business partners, and responsibility to government and regulatory authorities positively influence organizational competitive performance. However, our findings indicate there is no significant impact of responsibility to customers, responsibility to shareholders, responsibility to the community, and responsibility to the environment on the organisation's competitive performance in the Sri Lankan context.

6. Conclusions and Implications to the Practice

This study investigates the relationship between CSR and the competitive performance of firms in the banking sector of Sri Lanka. It also considers the impact of organisational culture as a moderating factor. The findings provide valuable information. The study identified a robust association between CSR practices and organisations' competitive success. Moreover, it underscored the vital importance of organisational culture as a moderating factor influencing this relationship. Empirical research consistently shows a strong link between organisational culture and performance, highlighting the significance of a strong and cohesive culture in achieving outstanding outcomes. Recognising the impact of CSR and how it matches an organisation's culture is crucial. Nevertheless, it is imperative to comprehend that diverse aspects of CSR can yield varied impacts on competitive performance.

The findings of this study have significant practical implications for implementing corporate social responsibility (CSR) and its influence on the competitive performance of organisations in Sri Lanka's banking industry. The study emphasises the significant impact of company culture as a key determinant of how CSR initiatives impact competitive performance. Organisations should recognise the importance of developing a strong, unified culture aligning with their corporate social responsibility goals. Leaders should incorporate corporate social responsibility (CSR) ideas into the fundamental aspects of the organisational culture, connecting them with strategic goals to improve performance results. Furthermore, the precise implications of CSR dimensions in terms of dimensions are essential for directing strategic decisions. Although responsibility towards employees has a notable positive effect on competitive performance, other aspects, such as responsibility towards customers, shareholders, community, and the environment, have less influence in the Sri Lankan banking industry. This necessitates a customised strategy in which organisations identify and prioritise CSR projects based on their stakeholders' distinct requirements and expectations. Organisations may enhance the effectiveness of their CSR initiatives and strengthen their competitive edge by tailoring CSR strategies to align with stakeholders' needs.

The study's results, which indicate that environmental CSR initiatives have little impact on competitive performance, require a comprehensive reevaluation of sustainability programmes in the banking industry of Sri Lanka. Despite the global attention to environmental sustainability, the little effect observed necessitates a revitalised and invigorated strategy. Banking institutions should reassess their environmental activities to integrate sustainability practices more effectively into their operational frameworks using innovative methods. This may involve exploring novel approaches to promote sustainability or enhancing existing initiatives to align with corporate objectives and stakeholder expectations.

Finally, our research emphasises the necessity for additional research and analysis of the industry's prospects. Although the primary focus of this research is on the banking industry in Sri Lanka, doing more extensive studies across various industries and worldwide contexts would enhance comprehension. Examining the intricate interactions of organisational culture and CSR in different industries has the potential to generate comprehensive frameworks that may be used more broadly. These frameworks have the potential to assist organisations globally in efficiently incorporating CSR practices into their cultures, hence promoting long-lasting competitive advantage.

References

Abdymomunov, A. (2020). Corporate social responsibility in developing countries: Evidence from Uzbekistan. *Journal of Open Innovation: Technology, Market, and Complexity*, *6*(4), 125.

AlAjmi, J., Buallay, A., & Saudagaran, S. (2023). Corporate social responsibility disclosure and banks' performance: The role of economic performance and institutional quality. *International Journal of Social Economics*, *50*(3), 359–376.

Arora, M., Gupta, J., Mittal, A., & Prakash, A. (2024). Achieving sustainable development goals (SDGs) through corporate sustainability: a topic modeling-based bibliometric analysis approach. *Kybernetes*.

Baron, R. M., & Kenny, D. A. (1986). The moderator-mediator variable distinction in social psychological research: Conceptual, strategic, and statistical considerations. *Journal of Personality and Social Psychology*, *51*(6), 1173–1182.

Brown, J. D. (2006). *Understanding research in second language learning*. Cambridge University Press.

Büschgens, T., Bausch, A., & Balkin, D. B. (2013). Organisational culture and innovation: A meta-analytic review. *Journal Of Product Innovation Management,30*(4), 763–781.

Campbell, J. L. (2007). Why would corporations behave in socially responsible ways? An institutional theory of corporate social responsibility. *The Academy of Management Review*, *32*(3), 946–967.

Carroll, A. B. (1979). A three-dimensional conceptual model of corporate social performance. *The Academy of Management Review*, *4*(4), 497–505.

Centobelli, P., Cerchione, R., & Shashi, E. E. (2020). Evaluating environmental sustainability strategies in freight transport and logistics industry. *Business Strategy and the Environment*, *29*(3), 1563–1574.

Chicco, D. (2021). Ten quick tips for machine learning in computational biology. *Bio Data Mining*, *14*(1), 1–15.

Choi, J. S., Lee, H. R., & Hong, S. K. (2009). Research notes on the moderating role of organisational culture in the relationship between total quality management and organisational performance. *The TQM Journal*, *21*(5), 509–519.

Chung, S. M., & Yoon, Y. (2018). Corporate social responsibility and firm financial performance: The mediating role of marketing capability. *Sustainability Journal*, *10*(8), 2866–2887.

De Alwis, T., Dewasiri, N. J., & Sood, K. (2023). Persistent fiscal deficit as a determinant of inflation in Sri Lanka: An ARDL approach, In K. Sood, B. Balusamy, & S. Grima (Eds.), *Digital transformation, strategic resilience, cyber security and risk management (contemporary studies in economic and financial analysis* (Vol. 111C, pp. 27–51). Emerald Publishing Limited. https://doi.org/10.1108/S1569-37592023000111C002

Denison, D. R. (1995). What is the difference between organisational culture and organisational climate? A native's point of view on a decade of paradigm wars. *Academy of Management Review*, *21*(3), 619–654.

Dewasiri, N. J., & Abeysekera, N. (2022). Corporate social responsibility and dividend policy in Sri Lankan firms: A data triangulation approach. *Journal of Public Affairs*, *22*(1), e2283.

Dewasiri, N. J., Weerakoon, Y. K. B., & Azeez, A. A. (2018). Mixed methods in finance research: The rationale and research designs. *International Journal of Qualitative Methods*, *17*(1), 1–13.

Donaldson, T., & Preston, L. (1995). The stakeholder theory of the corporation: Concepts, evidence, and implications. Academy of Management Review, *20*, 65–91.

Famiyeh, S. (2017a). Corporate social responsibility and firm's performance: Empirical evidence. *Social Responsibility Journal*, *13*(2), 390–406.

Famiyeh, S. (2017b). Corporate social responsibility and competitive operational performance of firms in Ghana. *International Journal of Business Administration*, *8*(5), 53–60.

Fernando, A. G. N. K., & Danthanarayana, C. P. (2022). Impact of internal corporate social responsibility on employees' turnover intention in the hotel sector: The mediating and moderating roles of job satisfaction and work-life conflict. *South Asian Journal of Tourism and Hospitality,*2(1), 1–29.

Gu, Y. (2023). Corporate social responsibility, performance, and geographic context. *Sustainability Journal*, *15*(4), 1654.

Ikram, M., Anwar, S., Khan, M. M., & Waqar, A. (2019). The impact of corporate social responsibility initiatives on firm performance: An evidence from SMEs of Pakistan. *Academy of Strategic Management Journal*, *18*(6), 1–14.

Iddagoda, A., Dewasiri, N. J., & Keppetipola, M. (2021). Conceptualisation and operationalisation of military organisational culture. *International Journal of Sustainable Economies Management (IJSEM)*, *10*(2), 19–30.

Jayawardena, N. S., Chavali, K., Dewasiri, N. J., Perera, C. H., Koswatte, I., Pereira, V., Gupta, M., & Mardani, A. (2023). Exploring the challenges in developing and managing digital agility among Sri Lankan family business owners during the economic crisis. *Journal of Global Information Management (JGIM), 31*(8), 1–22.

Kim, C. H. H. Y. C. (2013). Corporate social responsibility and corporate financial performance: An empirical analysis. *Accounting and Finance Research, 2*(3), 104–110.

Kaur, B., Kaur, R., Sood, K., & Grıma, S. (2023). Impact of non-performing assets on the profitability of the Indian banking sector. In S. Grima, K. Sood, & E. Øzen (Eds.), *Contemporary studies of risks in emerging technology, Part A (Emerald studies in finance, insurance, and risk management)* (pp. 257–269). Emerald Publishing Limited, Leeds. https://doi.org/10.1108/978-1-80455-562-020231017

Kaur, B., Sood, K., Grima, S., & Rupeika-Apoga, R. (2021). Digital banking in Northern India: The risks on customer satisfaction. *Risks, 9*(11), 209–219.

Kaur, S., Kumar, R., Singh, K., & Huang, Y. L. (2024). Leveraging artificial intelligence for enhanced sustainable energy management. *Journal of Sustainable Energy, 3*(1), 1–20. https://doi.org/10.56578/jse030101

Laskar, N., & Maji, S. G. (2016). Disclosure of corporate social responsibility and firm performance: Evidence from India. *Asia-Pacific Journal of Management Research and Innovation, 12*(2), 145–154.

Ling, Y. H. (2019). Influence of corporate social responsibility on organisational performance: Knowledge management as moderator. *VINE Journal of Information and Knowledge Management Systems, 49*(3), 327–352.

Latif, N. A. (2015). Corporate social responsibility practices in banking sector: Comparative study on its contribution in society and on the performance of the bank. World Journal of Entrepreneurship, *Management and Sustainable Development, 11*(1), 55–72.

Meyer, J. W., & Rowan, B. (1977). Institutionalised organisations: Formal structure as myth and ceremony. *The American Journal of Sociology, 83*(2), 340–363.

Mittal, A., Raheja, K., Raut, R., & Deshpande, A. (2024). Fostering perceived wealth among SMEs through green business: unveiling the mediating influence of consumers' green attitude. *Management of Environmental Quality: An International Journal, 35*(2), 341–357.

Muthusamy, V., Dewasiri, N. J., Lankanatha, K. M. R. C., Sood, K., & Grima, S. (2023). Financial soundness of general insurance industry in Sri Lanka: A CARAMELS approach. In S. Grima, E. Thalassinos, M. Cristea, M. Kadłubek, D. Maditinos, & L. Peiseniece (Eds.), *Digital transformation, strategic resilience, cyber security and risk management (Contemporary studies in economic and financial analysis)* (Vol. 111A, pp. 231–242). Emerald Publishing Limited, Leeds.

Muttakin, M. B. (2014). Corporate social responsibility and firm performance: Evidence from Bangladesh. *Asian Academy of Management Journal of Accounting and Finance, 6*(4), 175–185.

Ndekwa, A. G., Kalugendo, E., Sood, K., & Grima, S. (2023). An analysis of agribusiness digitalisation transformation of the sub-Saharan African countries small-scale farmers' production distribution. *Research on World Agricultural Economy, 4*(3), 63–78.

Rijal, S., Nursaputra, M., Chairil, A., & Dari, H. U. (2024). Flood susceptibility analysis using frequency ratio method in Walanae watershed. *International Journal of Sustainable Development and Planning, 19*(3), 823–832. https://doi.org/10.18280/ijsdp.190302

Sharabati, A. A. (2018). The impact of corporate social responsibility on the financial performance of the Jordanian pharmaceutical manufacturing sector. *International Journal of Business and Management, 7*(5), 73–83.

Sakshi, S., Cerchione, R., & Bansal, H. (2020). Measuring the impact of sustainability policy and practices in tourism and hospitality industry. *Business Strategy and the Environment*, *29*(3), 1109–1126.

Sharabati, A.-A. (2018). Effect of corporate social responsibility on Jordan pharmaceutical industry's business performance. *Social Responsibility Journal*, *14*(3), 566–583.

Shroff, S. J., Paliwal, U. L., & Dewasiri, N. J. (2024). Unravelling the impact of financial literacy on investment decisions in an emerging market. *Business Strategy & Development*, *7*(1), 1–14. https://doi.org/10.1002/bsd2.337

Srivastava, A. P., Yadav, M., Yadav, R., Singh, B., & Dewasiri, N. J. (2023). Exploring digital agility and digital transformation leadership: a mixed method study. *Journal of Global Information Management (JGIM)*, *31*(8), 1–23.

Sood, K., & Özen, E. (2024). A systematic review of ESG in the insurance industry: Navigating the path to sustainability. *International Journal of Sustainable Development and Planning*, *19*(3), 807–821. https://doi.org/10.18280/ijsdp.190301

Yerpude, S., Sood, K., & Grima, S. (2022). Blockchain-augmented digital supply chain management: A way to sustainable business. *Journal of Risk and Financial Management*, *16*(1), 7.

Turker, D. (2009). Measuring corporate social responsibility: A scale development study. *Journal of Business Ethics*, *85*(4), 411–427.

Waheed, A., Zhang, Q., Zafar, A. U., Zameer, H., Ashfaq, M., & Nusrat, A. (2021). Impact of internal and external CSR on organisational performance with the moderating role of culture: empirical evidence from the Chinese banking sector. *International Journal of Bank Marketing*, *39*(4), 499–515. https://doi.org/10.1108/IJBM-04-2020-0215

WBCSD. (1991). Corporate social responsibility: Meeting changing expectations. World Business Council for Sustainable Development. https://growthorientedsustainableentrepreneurship.files.wordpress.com/2016/07/csr-wbcsd-csr-primer.pdf

Wood, D. J. (1991). Corporate social performance revisited. *Academy of Management Review*, *16*(4), 691–718.

Zahid, M., Naeem, H., Aftab, I., & Mughal, S. A. (2021). From corporate social responsibility activities to financial performance: Role of innovation and competitive advantage. *Asia Pacific Journal of Innovation and Entrepreneurship*, *15*(1), 2–13.

Chapter 5

Espousal of Green Energy Sources and Green Initiative for Sustainable Development: A Bibliometric Analysis

Jyotsna Sharma and Nitin Thapar

Department of Management Studies and Commerce, RIMT University, India

Abstract

Purpose: The purpose of the current chapter is to emphasize the importance of renewable energy sources and their impact on society's desire to accept them in light of the substantial energy consumption that determines economic growth and its sustainability.

Need for the study: The ideals of sustainable development are the cornerstones of the green economy. This calls for the creation of new technologies and the adoption of eco-friendly practices that could spur economic growth and boosting efficiency. The chapter tries to measure total efficiency improvement after the adoption of green fuel.

Methodology: This is a qualitative research that uses secondary data sources. It is proposed to include a variety of online databases, e-journals, printed journals, periodicals, newspapers, etc., for the chapter. The scope of the chapter encompasses the discussion about the economic and environmental benefits of green energy resources.

Findings: The results show that the biggest advantages of employing green energy sources are typically acknowledged for their capacity to gradually lower the cost of electricity service, such as the avoided expenses of electricity generation or the avoidance of the need to build new power plants. These advantages may materialize in the short term, the long term, or both.

Green Management: A New Paradigm in the World of Business, 67–81

doi:10.1108/978-1-83797-442-920241005

Practical implications: The result of the chapter implies improvements in life standards and environmental effects. This chapter put forth that renewable energy projects require complicated installation and are sensitive to the local ecology.

Keywords: Green economy; green energy; sustainable development; renewable energy; environment; green energy initiatives; greenhouse effect

JEL Classifications: Q42; Q43; Q44; Q55; Q56

1. Introduction

With an emphasis on the importance of green energy in achieving sustainable development and global stability, the relationships between sustainability based on green energy and stability are examined (Midilli et al., 2007). The idea of green growth has recently gained traction in discussions of international policy that aim to promote economic growth while ensuring the maximum level of environmental protection (Maiti, 2022). By diversifying power supply alternatives, efficient, dependable renewable technologies can make a system less susceptible to market shocks and enhance resilience and energy security (United Nations, n.d.). As a low-carbon substitute for fossil fuels, biofuels are being marketed as a way to lessen greenhouse gas (GHG) emissions and the associated climate change impact of transportation (Feng et al., 2022; Jeswani et al., 2020). Adopting green energy-based fuels is urgently necessary for long-term sustainability given global instability and global stability. The technology for producing renewable energy is a direct replacement for current technologies. By replacing fossil fuels with renewable energy, we can conserve more energy and improve the environment (Dey et al., 2022; Wang & Zhi, 2016). Innovation can dramatically increase the use of renewable energy sources, lower CO_2 emissions, and lessen the effects of climate change. Climate change and environmental degradation can be effectively reduced with green funding (Wang et al., 2022). The concepts of green innovation are impacted by changes in industrial structure, R&D, and economic growth. Sustainable economic transformation, promoting green innovation, and combating climate change all depend on the efficient application of inclusive green finance (Akomea-Frimpong et al., 2021; Irfan et al., 2022). The development of digital finance can positively promote (Wang et al., 2022) the green innovation (Feng et al., 2022). Banks and financial institutions play a relevant role in the promotion of various green initiatives like green securities, green investments, green insurance, green loans, and green infrastructure bonds, which are among the green financial products that banks offer (Akomea-Frimpong et al., 2021). Economic growth and financial development have statistically significant and favorable effects on renewable energy consumption (Erdoğmuş & Çiçek, 2012). Earlier studies have indicated that alternative transport fuels in contrast to conventional fuels have more environmental and economic life cycle effects (Dey et al., 2022; Midilli et al., 2007; Sharma & Strezov, 2017). Furthermore, this paper should be a beneficial source for gaining an understanding of the available techniques and processes for carrying out studies via bibliometric analysis (Donthu et al., 2021).

2. Aim of the Chapter

Energy use has a strong relationship to both climate change and environmental conservation. The excessive amount of CO_2 emissions has escalated into a significant worldwide problem (Bekun et al., 2019). Because environmental issues have increased over the past two to three decades, the use of renewable energy technologies is extremely appropriate for improving environmental circumstances (Dey et al., 2022). Making sure that natural resources continue to offer the resources and environmental services that are essential to our well-being is known as "green growth." Green innovation is a type of technology innovation that focuses on environmental management and includes energy conservation, emission reduction, and environmental management. This bibliometric analysis aims to appraise the prominence and impact of the articles that have been published with the title green energy sources and green initiatives for sustainable development. Advancement of economic growth, increased energy security, improved access to energy sources, and climate change mitigation are the main objectives of the deployment of renewable energy in India (India's Green Energy Potential, IBEF, 2022). The prime motive of this chapter is to provide an overview of the bibliometric approach, with a particular emphasis on its many methodologies, and to provide step-by-step instructions that can be trusted to execute bibliometric analysis rigorously and confidently (Donthu et al., 2021).

3. Literature Review

Climate change and environmental degradation can be effectively reduced with green funding. Sustainable development is primarily driven by the need to hasten the growth of green financing. The relationship between innovation and the energy-environment-climate nexus is moderated by green finance. A higher degree of green finance enhances innovation's beneficial effects on the use of renewable energy (Zhang et al., 2022). A green economy mainstream directs towards environmental issues and social concerns while generating high-paying jobs for the economy (Xing et al., 2022). Very few studies have looked at the function of green finance in reducing carbon emissions, but academics have previously studied the link between financial growth and carbon emissions. There exists a consistent relationship between better green innovation and higher levels of digital finance, which is dependable. A heterogeneity analysis in many regions of China reveals that, while digital finance tends to support green innovation in the country's western and central regions, it has little effect on it in the country's eastern parts (Wang et al., 2022). The key determinants of renewable energy consumption are carbon emissions, energy efficiency, economic growth, and renewable energy generation (Dey et al., 2022). An increasing investment in the production of renewable energy, the energy efficiency industry, and ecologically relevant technology innovation to promote the use of renewable energy is recommended.

Environmental-related technology (EO) innovations are directly impacted by both an increase in CO_2 productivity (CP) and environmental policy strengthening (EPS) (Maiti, 2022). However, there was no statistically significant difference in the supply of renewable energy (RE) and (EO) innovation. Innovations in EO that can make renewable energy more ecologically sustainable for sustainable progress are consequently supported globally (Maiti, 2022). Sustainable economic transformation, promoting green innovation, and combating climate change all depend on the efficient application of inclusive green finance (Irfan et al., 2022). Innovative green technology is supported in large part by financial development. However, it is difficult for traditional finance. An environmental protection sector has garnered a lot of attention as people become more aware of sustainable development (Li et al., 2021). Policymaking and practices for green finance have advanced quickly. By using linkage analysis and input-output theory, this chapter offers a framework for assessing green financing. Growing population and rapid economic developments are factors in India's rising energy demand. The third-highest consumer of final energy in India is the road transport industry, which is virtually entirely dependent on petroleum oil. Almost one-fifth of the nation's import expenditure and more than four out of every five percent of crude petroleum comes from imports (Nouni et al., 2021). Policymakers and scholars have increasingly concentrated on green finance due to increased worldwide concern for environmental protection, climate change, and sustainable development (Akomea-Frimpong et al., 2021). With an eye on the components and determinants of green finance, previous research on the topic has been evaluated The critical evaluation and summarization of pertinent papers have been done using the content analysis technique. Among the important green finance products offered by banks were green securities, green investments, green insurance, green loans, and green infrastructure bonds.

Discovering research trends and opportunities of green finance and energy policy, several industries are pursuing high-profit returns while also taking into account the harmony between people and nature in light of the global promotion of the idea of green growth (Wang et al., 2021). Green energy will play a crucial part in a sustainable energy future. Energy demand is the primary factor that defines the significance of green energy (Malhotra & Thakur, 2020). Countries all over the world have taken steps to develop green energy from renewable sources such as hydropower, solar power, wind, tidal wave, geothermal, biogas, and biomass to meet global energy demand (Aktar et al., 2020).

As a low-carbon substitute for fossil fuels, biofuels are being marketed as a way to lessen greenhouse gas (GHG) emissions and the associated impact of transportation on climate change (Jeswani et al., 2020). The creation of green finance is a holistic system that integrates financial, environmental, and economic operations (Zhang & Wang, 2019). The creation of green credit guarantee schemes (GCGSs) and the repayment to investors of a portion of the tax income are amongst initially produced spillover effect of green energy supply (Taghizadeh-Hesary & Yoshino, 2019). It can, respectively, lower the risk associated with green finance and raise the rate of return for projects utilizing green energy. Furthermore, technical advancements in the field of distributed ledger technology offer the chance to improve the transparency of green investments and financing.

India's use of renewable energy has contributed in economic and financial development of the country (Eren et al., 2019). International and national development banks can be efficiently used as effective intermediary institutions for managing local green bonds (Banga, 2019). Furthermore, local governments must offer guarantees to local green bond issuers that will pay for the transaction costs related to the issuance of green bonds. An additional investment will be needed for both the implementation of the Paris Agreement and the fulfillment of the Sustainable Development Goals (SDGs) (Nassiry, 2018).

The central banks either expressly or implicitly are responsible for financial and macroeconomic stability. It should take a systemic approach to address climate-related and other environmental hazards (Dikau & Volz, 2018). Additionally, central banks are in a strong position to encourage the creation of green finance models and compel financial firms to adequately price environmental and carbon risk due to their regulatory authority over money, credit, and the financial system. Evaluation of the sustainability of alternate transportation fuels is crucial for development (Sharma & Strezov, 2017). The future benefits of Green Energy includes the limited use of fossil fuels and speeding up the transition to green energy-based technologies (Midilli et al., 2007). It is necessary to raise the sustainability ratio based on green energy and lower levels of global unrest. Governments and other authorities can do this through promoting green energy investments and the substitution of fossil fuels with more environmentally friendly fuels.

4. Research Methodology

The data for this chapter have been obtained from Scopus multidisciplinary database available at http://www.scopus.com. The Scopus database is considered a literature database (Sidhu et al., 2020). The association between "Green Energy sources" and "Sustainable Development" was investigated through a bibliometric analysis of research papers produced between 2020 and 2023 (published papers only). The bibliometric analysis is a collection of techniques for quantitative and qualitative chapter of historical research papers (Bhardwaj, 2014). The current methodology evaluates and analyses previously published research articles using a quantitative tool. Such analysis provides a comprehensive overview of the most beneficial contributions made by diverse authors, journals, and research publications. Because of this, authors take into account earlier research works and present qualitative and quantitative insights on any subject of their chapter. Bibliometric analysis is a popular and rigorous method for exploring and analyzing large volumes of scientific data. In one of the important, reliable sources for doing a literature review is the well-known database Scopus, from which the research papers under consideration were gathered (Fan et al., 2020; Iftikhar et al., 2019; Verma et al., 2022). Notably, it was discovered that publications containing "Green Energy sources" and "Sustainable Development" in the title, abstract, and keywords were used. To retrieve the records from the Scopus database following string is used in the title, abstract, and keywords fields (Bhardwaj, 2014; Sweileh, 2020): TITLE-ABS-KEY ("Sustainable Development") OR TITLE-ABS-KEY ("Green Energy sources," "Green Growth," "Green Economy," "Green Initiatives," "Green environment"). The Scopus search terms "Green Economy, Green Energy, Sustainable Development, Renewable Energy, Environment, Green Energy Initiatives" were used to find and choose pertinent papers. Since there is a lot of information available on these topics, we exclusively used published publications to gain a thorough understanding of the topic. VOSviewer 1.6.19 has been used to conduct bibliometric studies. To assess the interactions among various authors, nations, and organizations, network maps were created (Fan et al., 2020). The chapter was further refined by adding filters like language – "English" and a minimum citation number of "5" per paper. As a result, of the total 585 documents, the final sample contains "227" documents which are considered relevant documents for the current chapter.

5. Results and Interpretation

5.1. Top Organization

An analysis of the top organizations across the world is conducted. It has been found that organizations that have a minimum of five documents published are being filtered from the database. With the help of VOSviewer, the data are analyzed. The result indicates that of 1,544 organizations only 4 meet thresholds.

Table 5.1 depicts that the School of Management and Economics, Beijing Institute of Technology, Beijing, China has published a maximum of 8 papers with 175 citations.

Furthermore, it is followed by the Center for Energy and Environmental Policy Research, Beijing Institute of Technology, China with 5 documents cited 106 times, the School of Economics, Quaid-I-Azam University, Islamabad,

Table 5.1. Top Organization with Relevant Documents and Maximum Citations.

Institute	Documents	Citations
Center for Energy and Environmental Policy Research, Beijing Institute of Technology, Beijing, 100081, China	5	106
Department of Economics, University of Insubria, Via Monte Generoso, 71, Varese, 21100, Italy	5	32
School of Economics, Quaid-I-Azam University, Islamabad, Pakistan	5	48
School of Management and Economics, Beijing Institute of Technology, Beijing, 100081, China	8	175

Source: Authors compilation. Calculated using data from Scopus database and analyzed via VOSviewer.

Pakistan with 5 documents with citation 48 and the Department Of Economics, University Of Insubria, Via Monte Generoso, Italy with 5 documents and 32 citations overall.

5.2. Foremost Cited Authors in Green Energy Sources and Sustainable Development

Table 5.2 shows the relevant authors who are cited foremost in the field of Green Energy Sources and Sustainable Development. It also represents the top six authors who have their work published and cited in green energy sources and sustainable development

However, Fig. 5.1 covers the foremost cited authors in Green Energy Sources and Sustainable Development has been analysed in the paper. The results show

Table 5.2. Relevant Authors along with Documents and Citations.

Author	Documents	Citations
Azad R.; Chakraborty S.	3	2
Bhatnagar S.; Sharma D.	2	2
Bowmik C.; Bhowmik S.; Ray A.	2	14
Detemple J.; Kitapbayev Y.	3	21
Ofori I. K.; Gbolonyo E. Y.; Ojong N	2	13
Savin I.; Drews S.; Van Den Bergh J	2	14

Source: Authors compilation. Calculated using VOS viewer.

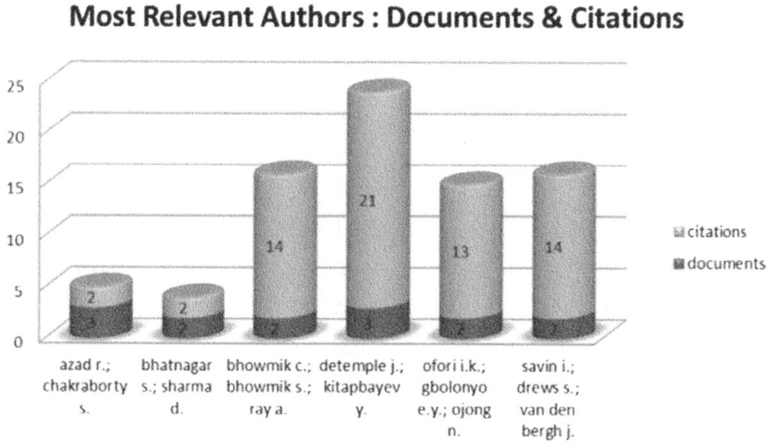

Fig. 5.1. Relevant Authors along with Documents and Citations. *Source*: Authors compilation. Calculated using data from Scopus database and analyzed via VOSviewer.

that of all the published documents from 2020 to 2023, there are only six most relevant authors. The results reveal that Detemple J. and Kitapbayev Y. have been cited a maximum of 21 times and over 3 published papers. Savin I.; Drews S.; Van Den Bergh J.; and Bhowmik C.; Bhowmik S.; Ray A. are the second most important authors cited 14 times each which is followed by Ofori I. K.; Gbolonyo E. Y.; Ojong N. cited 13 times.

5.3. Country-Wise Distribution of Citations

Table 5.3 shows the country wise number of documents published along with citations of the documents. The Country Distribution of Citations analysis shows that in the published papers of countries, 10 countries meet the threshold among 84 countries. A minimum of 25 citations of a country counted over a minimum of 25 documents in the chapter have been considered.

Fig. 5.2 depicts the top countries along with documents published. It also tells about the citations of the published documents too. The different size and color of circles in the figure represents the number of document published and citations across different countries. Bigger circle shows the documents published by countries which has received maximum citations. It is observed that China has a maximum citation of 2,616 with 191 papers, followed by India with 55 papers, and the United States with 53 published papers. The papers published by Pakistan are 50, the United Kingdom is 42 in number, and Italy is 31 only.

In the citation analysis of countries, China has a maximum citation of 2,616 with 191 papers, followed by the United Kingdom with 646, Pakistan with 636 citations, Turkey with 602 citations, and United States with 537 citations.

Table 5.3. Top Countries along with Documents Published and Citations.

Country	**Documents**	**Citations**
China	191	2,616
France	29	368
Germany	25	138
India	55	243
Italy	31	213
Pakistan	50	636
Russian Federation	35	181
Turkey	28	602
United Kingdom	42	646
United States	53	537

Source: Authors compilation. Calculated using data from Scopus database and analyzed via VOSviewer.

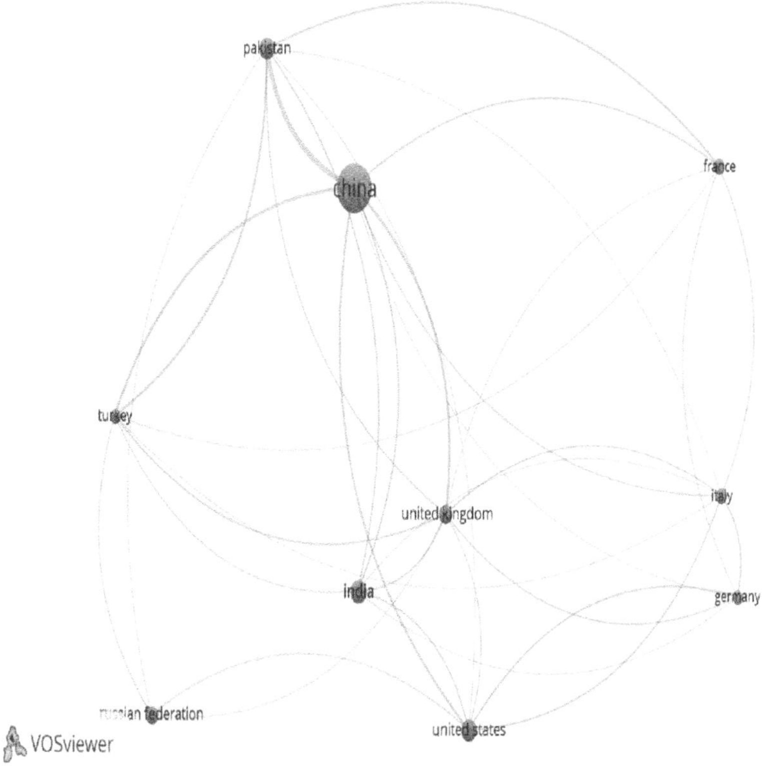

Fig. 5.2. Top Countries along with Documents Published and Citations. *Source*: Authors compilation. Calculated using data from Scopus database and analyzed via VOSviewer.

5.4. Distribution of Citation across Different Sources

The figure reveals the count of citations from different sources (journals). The sources from where a minimum of five documents are published and which are further cited five times selected are analyzed in the chapter. The outcome of the chapter reveals that only 17 journals meet the threshold.

Fig. 5.3 represents the relevant sources from where distribution of citation is analyzed. The various circles in the figure show the different publication sources (journals) worldwide. The size of the circle indicates the quantum, i.e., number of citations (bigger the circle, higher are the citations of the documents published by respective journals). The output shows the *Journal of Cleaner Production* has published documents which has received the maximum number of citations. The figure shows that the important ones are the *Journal of Cleaner Production, Resource Policy, Energy Economics, Economic Research – Ekonomska Istrazivanja, Environment Development & Sustainability*. However, *Ecological Economics, Technological Forecasting & Social Change, Business Strategy and the Environment,*

Fig. 5.3. Distribution of Citation across Different Sources. *Source*: Authors compilation. Calculated using data from Scopus database and analyzed via VOSviewer.

Economic Change & Restructuring, Structural Change & Economic Dynamics International Journal of Energy Economics & Policy are among the top sources that have published more than five papers on green energy initiatives and its role in sustainable development.

5.5. Distribution of Citation across Different Sources

It becomes quite relevant to know the distribution of citations across different sources. Table 5.4 shows distribution of citation across different sources. The output includes maximum papers that are published by a source with a minimum of five citations.

It is found that the *Journal of Cleaner Production* has published a maximum of papers, i.e., 78 with a maximum citation, i.e., 1,101, followed by *Resource Policy*, 42 papers with a citation of 514, and *Energy Economics*, 32 with a citation of 323.

5.6. Keyword Analysis

The increasingly popularized keyword analysis is a useful analytical tool for studying certain marketing or other literature review subjects. A compelling rationale is provided for the content of publications using keyword analysis (Verma et al., 2022). The four analysis methods employed by bibliometrics are co-word association, co-word frequency, coword cluster, and burst word monitoring. Because it

Table 5.4. Distribution of Citation across Different Sources.

Source	Documents	Citations
Business Strategy and the Environment	7	180
Clean Technologies and Environmental Policy	5	35
Ecological Economics	19	483
Economic Analysis and Policy	7	145
Economic Change and Restructuring	9	63
Economic Research-Ekonomska Istrazivanja	23	271
Energy Economics	32	323
Environment, Development, and Sustainability	21	134
Frontiers in Energy Research	20	100
International Journal of Energy Economics and Policy	21	46
International Journal of Energy Sector Management	6	50
Journal of Cleaner Production	78	1,101
Journal of Environmental Management and Tourism	6	6
Resources Policy	42	514
Resources, Conservation, and Recycling	6	64
Structural Change and Economic Dynamics	7	74
Technological Forecasting and Social Change	15	358

Source: Authors compilation. Calculated using data from Scopus database and analyzed via VOSviewer.

was believed to be a valuable technique for addressing research trends on the interaction between Green Energy initiatives and Sustainable Development by examining current articles, keyword cooccurrence evaluation was also carried out in this chapter.

Co-occurrence with all keywords is analyzed with a minimum number of occurrences of keywords 5 times, as displayed in Fig. 5.4. It is noticed that of 3,799 keywords, 213 meet the threshold.

It is crucial to keep in mind that co-word analysis entails examining keywords that appear together. It is an expression of how strongly they are connected. The link strength reflects how frequently two specific keywords happened to appear in the same article. The circles with different color represent the counts of co-words that has appeared together in different publications. The size of circle indicates the volume (number of word count). The total number of times any two keywords were used in a search is represented by the number of these links. Co-occurrence with authors' key keywords is analysed with minimum number of occurrences of keyword 5. It has been observed that of 1,929 keywords, 62 meet the threshold.

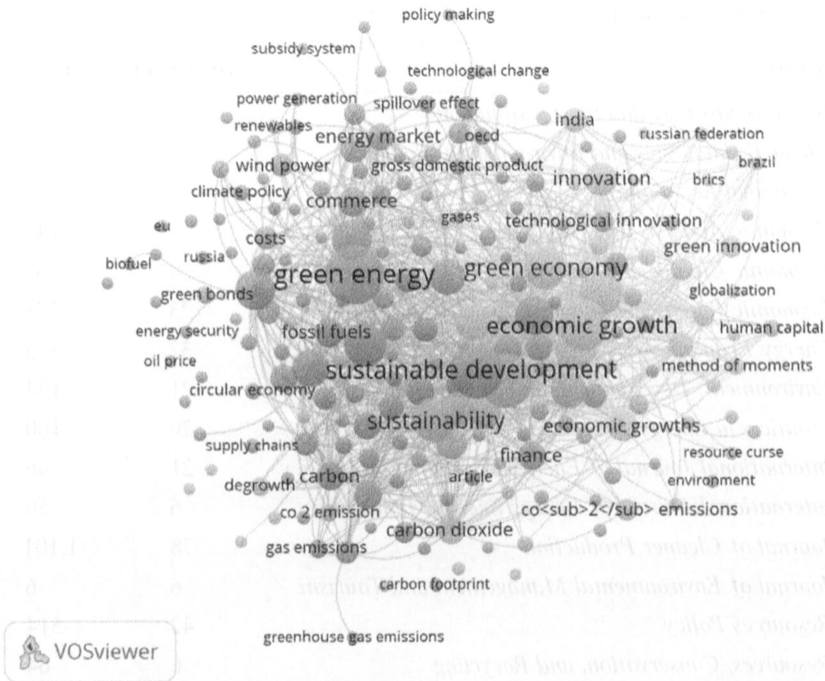

Fig. 5.4. Network Visualization of Keyword Co-Occurrence Extracted from Authors' Compilation. *Source*: Authors compilation. Calculated using data from Scopus database and analyzed via VOSviewer.

As discussed earlier and evident from the keywords cooccurrence analysis, it clearly indicates that green energy has emerged as a strategic method of generating sustainable energy for the entire world. The use of renewable energy is primarily done to advance economic growth, increase energy security, increase access to electricity, lessen carbon emissions, and slow down climate change. By using sustainable energy and guaranteeing that all residents have access to cost-effective, dependable, sustainable, and contemporary energy, energy security, green growth, and sustainable development are made feasible. We can secure a sustainable future for all, coming generations in terms of a green economy, green society, and the environment, by implementing clean, renewable energy sources with the help of various green innovations-based technologies. Together, governments, corporations, and people must hasten the transition to a future with more sustainable energy, which will help to lessen the effects of climate change and provide a better future for all, governments, corporations, and individuals must collaborate.

6. Conclusion

There is no denying the fact that urbanization, resource rent, and economic expansion all contribute to an increase in environmental degradation. The chapter showed that environmental concerns may be reduced through practical means like green finance, the use of renewable energy, and the encouragement of energy innovation (Cai et al., 2022). There is a significant chance that the global transition to sustainability may lead to more conflict and suffering if investments are not done effectively (Khan, 2017). Global efforts are being made to pursue ecological sustainability while reducing the effects of environmental degradation. Governments should support the development of renewable energy technologies and create a more logical and scientific energy system. To lower CO_2 levels globally, government organizations should make an effort to switch from fossil fuels to clean and renewable energy (Wang et al., 2022). The relationship between innovation and the energy-environment-climate nexus is moderated by green finance (Wang et al., 2022). Green energy programs, however, have the potential to spark or exacerbate disputes and tensions, particularly in the world's most vulnerable areas. Green energy efforts have had a positive impact on the environment by reducing carbon dioxide emissions and raising awareness of climate change. Sustainable development is primarily driven by the need to hasten the growth of green financing (Mumtaz & Smith, 2019).

The outcome of the chapter discusses energy security, green growth, and sustainable development which are made possible by utilizing sustainable energy and ensuring that every person has access to affordable, dependable, sustainable, and modern energy. By integrating clean, renewable energy sources with the aid of numerous green innovations-based technologies, we can ensure a sustainable future for all future generations in terms of a green economy, a green society, and the environment. Governments, businesses, and individuals must work together to speed the transition to an energy future that is more sustainable to mitigate the effects of climate change and provide a brighter future for all.

References

Akomea-Frimpong, I., Adeabah, D., Ofosu, D., & Tenakwah, E. J. (2021). A review of studies on green finance of banks, research gaps and future directions. *Journal of Sustainable Finance and Investment*, *12*(4), 1241–1264. https://doi.org/10.1080/20430795.2020.1870202

Aktar, M. A., Harun, M. B., & Alam, M. M. (2020). Green energy and sustainable development. In *Affordable and clean energy. Encyclopedia of the UN sustainable development goals* (pp. 1–11). Springer, Cham. ISBN: 978-3-319- 71057-0. https://doi.org/10.1007/978-3-319-71057-0_47-1

Banga, J. (2019). The green bond market: A potential source of climate finance for developing countries. *Journal of Sustainable Finance and Investment*, *9*(1), 17–32. https://doi.org/10.1080/20430795.2018.1498617

Bekun, F. V., Alola, A. A., & Sarkodie, S. A. (2019). Toward a sustainable environment: Nexus between CO2 emissions, resource rent, renewable and nonrenewable energy in 16-EU countries. *Science of The Total Environment*, *657*, 1023–1029. https://doi.org/10.1016/J.SCITOTENV.2018.12.104

Bhardwaj, R. K. (2014). Dengue research: A scientometric mapping of world publications. *SRELS Journal of Information Management*, *51*(2), 77–86. https://doi.org/10.17821/srels/2014/v51i2/47768

Cai, W., Zhang, C., Zhang, S., Ai, S., Bai, Y., Bao, J., Chen, B., et al. (2021). The 2021 China report of the Lancet Countdown on health and climate change: Seizing the window of opportunity. *The Lancet Public Health*, *6*(12), e932–e947. https://doi.org/10.1016/S2468-2667(21)00209-7

Dey, S., Sreenivasulu, A., Veerendra, G. T. N., Rao, K. V., & Babu, P. S. S. A. (2022). Renewable energy present status and future potentials in India: An overview. *Innovation and Green Development*, *1*(1), 100006. https://doi.org/10.1016/j.igd.2022.100006

Dikau, S., & Volz, U. (2018). Central banking, climate change, and green finance. *Handbook of Green Finance*, *867*, 81–102. https://doi.org/10.1007/978-981-13-0227-5_17

Donthu, N., Kumar, S., Mukherjee, D., Pandey, N., & Lim, W. M. (2021). How to conduct a bibliometric analysis: An overview and guidelines. *Journal of Business Research*, *133*, 285–296. https://doi.org/10.1016/j.jbusres.2021.04.070

Erdoğmuş, İ. E., & Çiçek, M. (2012). The impact of social media marketing on brand loyalty. *Procedia - Social and Behavioral Sciences*, *58*, 1353–1360. https://doi.org/10.1016/j.sbspro.2012.09.1119

Eren, B. M., Taspinar, N., & Gokmenoglu, K. K. (2019). The impact of financial development and economic growth on renewable energy consumption: Empirical analysis of India. *Science of the Total Environment*, *663*, 189–197. https://doi.org/10.1016/j.scitotenv.2019.01.323

Fan, J., Gao, Y., Zhao, N., Dai, R., Zhang, H., Feng, X., Shi, G., Tian, J., Chen, C., Hambly, B. D., & Bao, S. (2020). Bibliometric analysis on COVID-19: A comparison of research between English and Chinese studies. *Frontiers in Public Health*, *8*(August), 477. https://doi.org/10.3389/fpubh.2020.00477

Feng, S., Zhang, R., & Li, G. (2022). Environmental decentralization, digital finance and green technology innovation. *Structural Change and Economic Dynamics*, *61*, 70–83. https://doi.org/10.1016/J.STRUECO.2022.02.008

IBEF. (2022). *India's green energy potential*. IBEF. Retrieved from https://www.ibef.org/blogs/india-s-green-energy-potential

Iftikhar, P. M., Ali, F., Faisaluddin, M., Khayyat, A., De Gouvia De Sa, M., & Rao, T. (2019). A bibliometric analysis of the top 30 most-cited articles in gestational diabetes mellitus literature (1946-2019). *Cureus*, *11*(2), 1–12. https://doi.org/10.7759/cureus.4131

Irfan, M., Razzaq, A., Sharif, A., & Yang, X. (2022). Influence mechanism between green finance and green innovation: Exploring regional policy intervention effects in China. *Technological Forecasting and Social Change*, *182*(July), 121882. https://doi.org/10.1016/J.TECHFORE.2022.121882

Jeswani, H. K., Chilvers, A., & Azapagic, A. (2020). Environmental sustainability of biofuels: a review. *Proceedings of the Royal Society A*, *476*(2243), 1–13. https://doi.org/10.1098/RSPA.2020.0351

Khan, M. I. (2017). Policy options for the sustainable development of natural gas as transportation fuel. *Energy Policy*, *110*(May), 126–136. https://doi.org/10.1016/j.enpol.2017.08.017

Li, L., Wu, W., Zhang, M., & Lin, L. (2021). Article linkage analysis between finance and environmental protection sectors in China: An approach to evaluating green finance. *International Journal of Environmental Research and Public Health*, *18*(5), 1–16. https://doi.org/10.3390/ijerph18052634

Maiti, M. (2022). Does improvement in green growth influence the development of environmental related technology? *Innovation and Green Development*, *1*(2), 100008. https://doi.org/10.1016/j.igd.2022.100008

Malhotra, G., & Thakur, K.. (2020). Evolution of green finance: A bibliometric approach. *Gedrag & Organisatie Review*, *33*(02), 583–594. https://doi.org/10.37896/gor33.02/067

Midilli, A., Dincer, I., & Rosen, M. A. (2007). The role and future benefits of green energy. *International Journal of Green Energy*, *4*(1), 65–87. https://doi.org/10.1080/15435070601015494

Mumtaz, D. M., & Smith, D. Z. (2019). Green finance for sustainable development in Pakistan. *IPRI Journal*, *XIX*(2), 1–34. https://doi.org/10.31945/iprij.190201

Nassiry, D. (2018). *The role of Fintech in unlocking green finance: Policy insights for developing countries Asian development bank institute*. ADBI Working Paper Series, Institute of Sciences, November (Vol. 883, pp. 1–27). Retrieved from https://www.adb.org/publications/role-fintech-unlocking-green-finance

Nouni, M. R., Jha, P., Sarkhel, R., Banerjee, C., Tripathi, A. K., & Manna, J. (2021). Alternative fuels for decarbonisation of road transport sector in India: Options, present status, opportunities, and challenges. *Fuel*, *305*, 121583. https://doi.org/10.1016/J.FUEL.2021.121583

Sharma, A., & Strezov, V. (2017). Life cycle environmental and economic impact assessment of alternative transport fuels and power-train technologies. *Energy*, *133*, 1132–1141. https://doi.org/10.1016/j.energy.2017.04.160

Sidhu, A. K., Singh, H., Virdi, S. S., & Kumar, R. (2020). A bibliometric analysis on job stress using visualizing network. *Journal of Content, Community and Communication*, *12*, 21–29. https://doi.org/10.31620/JCCC.12.20/04

Sweileh, W. M. (2020). Bibliometric analysis of peer-reviewed literature on climate change and human health with an emphasis on infectious diseases. *Globalization and Health*, *16*(1), 1–17. https://doi.org/10.1186/s12992-020-00576-1

Taghizadeh-Hesary, F., & Yoshino, N. (2019). The way to induce private participation in green finance and investment. *Finance Research Letters*, *31*(March), 98–103. https://doi.org/10.1016/j.frl.2019.04.016

United Nations. (n.d.). *Renewable energy – powering a safer future | United Nations*. Retrieved June 27, 2023, from https://www.un.org/en/climatechange/raising-ambition/renewable-energy

Verma, J., Sharma, J., Sharma, A., & Kaur, J. (2022). *Does metaverse a technological revolution in artificial intelligence? A bibliometric analysis* (pp. 425–428) [Conference session]. PDGC 2022 - 2022 7th International Conference on Parallel, Distributed and Grid Computing. https://doi.org/10.1109/PDGC56933.2022.10053102

Wang, M., Li, X., & Wang, S. (2021). Discovering research trends and opportunities of green finance and energy policy: A data-driven scientometric analysis. *Energy Policy*, *154*(Oct 2020), 112295. https://doi.org/10.1016/j.enpol.2021.112295

Wang, Q.-J., Tang, K., & Hu, H.-Q. (2022). The impact of digital finance on green innovation: Evidence from provinces in China. *Innovation and Green Development*, *1*(Oct), 100007. https://doi.org/10.1016/j.igd.2022.100007

Wang, Y., & Zhi, Q. (2016). The role of green finance in environmental protection: Two aspects of market mechanism and policies. *Energy Procedia*, *104*, 311–316. https://doi.org/10.1016/j.egypro.2016.12.053

Xing, L., Li, J., & Yu, Z. (2022). Green finance strategies for the zero-carbon mechanism: Public spending as new determinants of sustainable development. *Frontiers in Environmental Science*, *10*(July), 1–12. https://doi.org/10.3389/fenvs.2022.925678

Zhang, B., & Wang, Y. (2019). The effect of green finance on energy sustainable development: A case study in China. *Emerging Markets Finance and Trade*, *57*(12), 3435–3454. https://doi.org/10.1080/1540496X.2019.1695595

Zhang, K. Q., Chen, H. H., Tang, L. Z., & Qiao, S. (2022). Green finance, innovation and the energy-environment-climate nexus. *Frontiers in Environmental Science*, *10*(5), 1–13. https://doi.org/10.3389/FENVS.2022.879681/BIBTEX

Chapter 6

Artificial Intelligence (AI) and Green Human Resource Management (GHRM) Practices: A Systemic Review

Shuchi Dawra, Vidhi Pathak and Sandhir Sharma

Chitkara Business School, Chitkara University, Punjab, India

Abstract

Introduction: With a rapid increase in the application of artificial intelligence and machine learning, new Artificial Intelligence (AI) technologies are now playing a vital role in evolving green human resource management practices in the sustainable development of organizations. A thorough analysis of the part of AI technologies in Green Human Resource Management (GHRM) is still an ongoing process.

Purpose: This chapter/study aims to provide an overview of the changing paradigm of human resource management practices into Green Human Resource Management Practices and the role of Artificial Intelligence interventions in various aspects of talent management, talent acquisition, and talent retention.

Design/methodology/approach: This study is based on the systemic review of 37 research studies and reports on human resource management practices, green human resource management, artificial intelligence, and talent management strategies.

Findings: The findings below show a change in human resource management practices encouraging new technologies, software solutions, and artificial intelligence. Green management practices are overtaking the traditional mindsets and work environment. This transformation has synergized the adoption of artificial intelligence and G-HRM practices, encouraging innovative and positive work behaviors.

Green Management: A New Paradigm in the World of Business, 83–96

doi:10.1108/978-1-83797-442-920241006

Originality/value: The originality of this study lies in fulfilling the existing gap in the studies of the role of artificial intelligence and its effects on green human resource management. Its value counts in showing the aspects of innovation in HRM with sustainability and advanced technology.

Keywords: Artificial intelligence; green management; green human resource management; talent management; innovation; digital transformation; Technology

JEL Classifications: J24; J28; M14; M51; M52; M53; O14; O15

1. Introduction

The growth of the availability of various technologies, big data, and data on the internet has made Artificial Intelligence (AI) the top priority for organizations. As AI technology develops, which is a new generation's tool, the human intellect of artificial intelligence plays a vital role in organizations' survival and transformation in changing environments to maintain good competence and cope with the world. AI has become a key source of innovating, processing, and achieving an organization's goals. According to McKinsey's Global Survey on AI, businesses have adopted AI two times more in 2022 than in 2017 (Chui et al., 2022). The exposure of AI-based systems in organizations will transform the work dynamics, goals, nature of jobs, competence, and the relationship between technology and people. It is a tool of the human brain. Work with AI will be easier, better, and more personalized. AI is about a quicker way of thinking and processing filled with much knowledge, like a logical human brain. AI optimizes resource usage, business productivity, decision-making, customer service, employee satisfaction, and experience. AI refers to a technology used to do a task requiring some intelligence. It requires human intelligence to perform tasks. AI can be a boom for every sector. In the retail industry, estimators say that this sector could be automated by over 60% in the next 3–4 years; currently, it is 40% automated (Davey, 2022). According to Oracle, in 2019, 77% of workers in China and 78% in India adopted AI, over double the number of workers in France and Japan (Shores, 2019).

Due to the changing environment, pollution in water, and reduction of resources, organizations are adopting Green Human Resource Management (G-HRM). Green HRM is a phenomenon that promotes green initiatives and behaviors (Fawehinmi et al., 2020). Some research works show that organizations are majorly responsible for these environmental issues because they produce carbons and small particles that mix with air, generate harmful gasses, and release factory waste in rivers, affecting animal and human life (Sharma et al., 2023). A force and need to reduce waste and process cleaner production to maintain the environment is making organizations implement the Green HRM (Gupta, 2021). For all this, organizations need to apply G-HRM, and with that comes the responsibility to handle the changing expectations of their customers. AI will support organizations with its advanced technology system, cloud computing, data storing qualities, and innovative analytical decision-making tools (Gupta, 2021). Today, AI has developed a lot, can change humans' work paths, and can help in various fields of business (Kaur et al., 2024; Rijal et al., 2024).

John McCarthy, a father of AI, defines AI as "the science and engineering of making intelligent machines" (Geetha & Reddy, 2018). All founders of AI are John McCarthy, Alan Turing, Marvin Minsky, Allen Newell, and Herbert A. AI is made up to work just like humans. As humans learn things, we modify ourselves, identify the problems, and correct them. AI does tasks in the same manner. The first-ever task done in the field of AI was done by Alan Mathison Turing in 1935. At first, he described computing machines and talked about their limitless memory and scanners, which move back and forth to read the memory. It consists of symbols that it reads and further writes the symbols. An inbuilt program controlled all these actions. We are talking about the first successful AI program, written by Christopher Strachey, which guided him to become the director of the Programming Research Group at the University of Oxford. In 1956 John McCarthy invented artificial intelligence and had the first AI conference. Then, in 1969, a mobile robot named 'Shakey' was built at the Stanford Research Institute. It can do many things at once. A supercomputer named 'Deep Blue' was designed and made by IBM in 1997. It even defeated the world champion chess player (JavaTPoint). AI is a technology that impersonates human intelligence using a computer system. It is designed to meet the expectations and provide favorable outcomes akin to the workforce of any organization that can learn, solve, and make decisions. Under the Global AI Survey 2019 from McKinsey, it was stated that various companies adopting AI had a rise in their revenue, and 44% of them also said that it had reduced their costs (Chui et al., 2022).

This chapter aims to provide an overview of the changing paradigm of human resource management practices into green human resource management practices and the role of artificial intelligence interventions in various aspects of talent management, talent acquisition, and talent retention. This study is based on the systemic review of 37 research studies and reports on human resource management practices, green human resource management, artificial intelligence, and talent management strategies.

1.1. Green Human Resource Management

GHRM is related to HRM functionalities but with environmental management (EM) aspects. With the growing aspects of sustainability, HR tends to adopt green HR activities focusing on reducing the carbon footprint, paperless activities, and waste management (Shoaib et al., 2021). It focuses on the role of HRM in preventing pollution through an organization's operational processes. A theory of the ability-motivation-opportunity (AMO) is used to examine the impact of GHRM. AMO includes enhancing green motivation, developing green competence, and involving employees (Afrin & Ahmed, 2023). Green HRM practices are upgrading and enhancing over time. According to Renwick et al. (2013), three components of GHRM practices could be evolved, which are: developing green ability (recruitment and selection, training and development, job description); motivating green employees (performance management/appraisal; pay and reward system); and providing green opportunities (employee involvement and empowerment, supportive climate/culture, unions' role in EM, organizational learning) (Pham et al., 2020).

1.2. Artificial Intelligence in Human Resource Management

A phenomenon, The Great Resignation (Chugh, 2021), pulled back many companies from practicing their ongoing processes and systems. This happened when many people resigned from their jobs post-COVID pandemic. Managers started facing contagion effects after the pandemic because employees, especially those in their mid-career stage, left their jobs and evaluated their careers. HR teams of different industries faced this problem. Systems need updating to overcome the ongoing talent shortage. Technological advances, like artificial intelligence, can help HR managers gain control over this loss. With beneficial data and insights, AI can architect a better and more convenient future of work.

HR's primary responsibilities are recruitment, administration, compensation and benefits, training and development, employee relations, and performance management (Bhardwaj et al., 2020). A leap forward of AI in business organizations positively impacts management, especially in Human Resources. A section in Eightfold AI's Talent Survey 2022 briefed about priorities over the next 1 to 2 years of more than 250 HR leaders. They believe things can be achieved by combining processes and technologies. Eighty-three percent of those 250 HRs' top priority is recruiting better candidates. Seventy-seven percent of them prioritized speeding up the recruitment process. Seventy-five percent of them want to lower the turnover rate and upskill the current employees (Eightfold AI's Talent Survey, 2022).

HR roles could be divided into three major categories according to the green sustainability process. Fig. 6.1 shows the three classifications.

HR is the art of dealing with complex problems and finding solutions to the human side of the business. AI might clog the humanistic approach of HR, but with brilliant software, various tasks can be redesigned and accomplished. With the rapid change of technologies, many positive benefits can be applied to the workflow and the workforce. AI could help HR with administrative tasks and save time by robotizing repetitive tasks (Pandey & Khaskel, 2019). A report by Harris Interactive and Eightfold AI judged this practice 19% more effective. This report also proves that AI helps improve talent acquisition in less time (Anderson, 2020).

Fig. 6.2 shows a conceptual model of which systems of AI technology could merge with different HRM fields. As we can see in this model, these systems can be converted and used for Green Management under the eye of G-HRM. Factors included in HRM can be done to promote green human resource management.

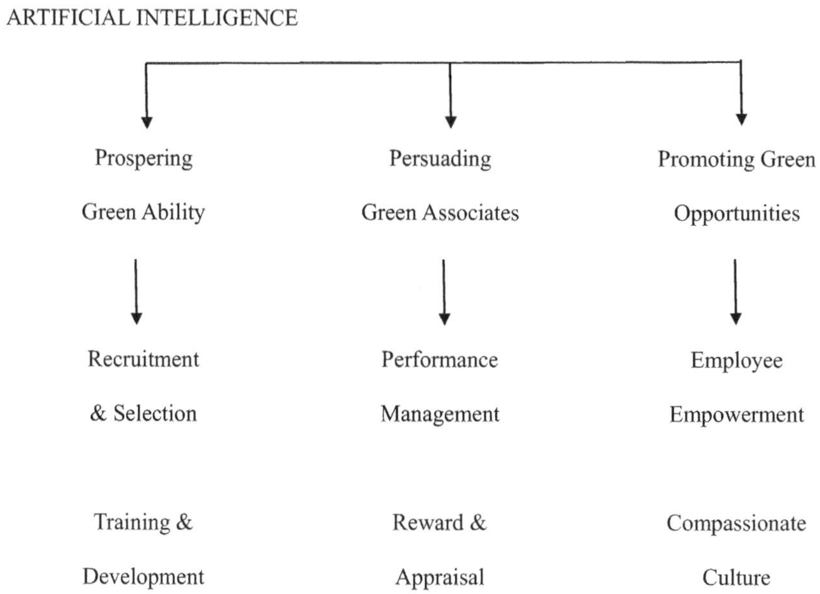

Fig. 6.1. Reproduced from "AI in Green HRM" (Sharma, 2023).

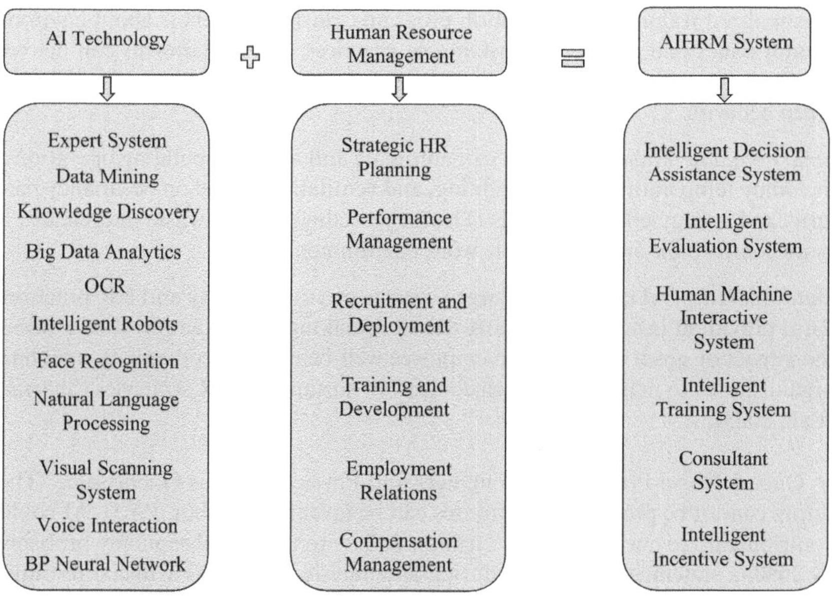

Fig. 6.2. Reproduced from "A conceptual model of AI technology merging with different HRM fields" (Jia et al., 2018).

2. Artificial Intelligence and Green Human Resource Management Practices

Motivating employees to adopt green practices is necessary to conduct good environmental performance. Many companies are trying to upgrade their performance through environmental standards (Garg et al., 2018). Many things and practices can be done using AI in GHRM to help organizations adopt environment-friendly practices. These practices include:

Energy Management: AI can analyze energy consumption patterns within an organization and identify areas where energy is wasted. It can suggest energy-saving measures and optimize the use of resources like lighting, heating, and cooling systems, leading to reduced energy consumption and cost savings.

Waste Management: AI can help manage waste efficiently by analyzing waste generation, disposal, and recycling data. It can identify opportunities for waste reduction, recommend recycling programs, and track waste management performance to ensure compliance with environmental regulations.

Sustainable Supply Chain: AI can assist in creating a sustainable supply chain by optimizing transportation routes to minimize carbon emissions, identifying environmentally friendly suppliers, and promoting using renewable or recycled materials in production processes (Sharma et al., 2023).

Green Training and Education: AI-powered platforms can provide employees with personalized training and education programs, raising awareness about environmental issues and promoting sustainable practices. These platforms can deliver interactive content, quizzes, and simulations to engage employees and encourage green behavior.

Smart Building Management: AI can automate and optimize building operations, including temperature control, lighting, and ventilation, based on occupancy patterns and energy efficiency goals. This helps reduce energy waste and creates a more comfortable and sustainable work environment.

Data Analytics: AI can analyze large volumes of sustainability and HR practices data, providing insights to support decision-making. For example, it can assess the impact of green initiatives on employee well-being and productivity, enabling organizations to make data-driven choices for sustainable HR strategies (Sharma et al., 2023).

Once a Nobel Prize winner, Engineer and Physicist Dennis Gabor said, "The future cannot be predicted, but futures can be invented" (Gabor, 1963). AI could contribute up to a whopping 15.7 trillion dollars to the global economy probably by 2030, a statement PWC gave during an analysis. Using this artificial resource effectively and efficiently could make a boom for everyone and the world. This mindful technology can make a satisfactory and righteous change globally.

3. Artificial Intelligence and Green Human Resource Management: Talent Acquisition

One shines out of the various benefits AI provides to HR, i.e., recruitment. It will be time-adequate, cost-effective, and find the right talent for the proper job position. One of the company's main concerns is recruiting talent. Almost 52% of talent recruiting and acquisition specialists find recruiting talent the most challenging part of the recruitment process. For every single job post, thousands of applications are done, which makes it very difficult to find the right and only single candidate. If the screening step from the recruitment process could be easy, other steps would be done effectively and efficiently (Johansson & Herranen, 2019). Thus, AI for recruitment and hiring is the fusion of AI solutions in the recruitment process. It could free the recruitment managers from their repetitive, exhausting workload. It could shortlist the ideal candidates and streamline the recruitment workflow. One of the most significant advantages of AI indulgence is removing bias (Ahmed, 2018). Every job post will be in the hands of the perfect talent and skills holder, which could further benefit the organization. This will create many opportunities for the applicants. Access will be there for a larger talent pool. As AI uses predictive intelligence, it grasps the details about every candidate. It reads the candidate's knowledge, behavior, and skills quickly. AI can perform better with it; for instance, if AI can make a better user-friendly application form, job applicants would be more likely to finish it. This could lessen the number of abandoned forms. AI-powered algorithms can analyze resumes and job applications to screen candidates based on predefined criteria. There could be three categories of assessment: task-based, video-based, and game-based assessments. Task-based would be written or multiple-choice questionnaires. Video-based would be to record a one-way video response. Furthermore, game-based games would be single-player games (Li et al., 2021). This process will help efficiently identify candidates with relevant skills and qualifications, reducing the time and resources spent on manual screening. AI can contribute to a more sustainable and resource-efficient recruitment process by streamlining the initial selection. AI algorithms can be designed to minimize biases in the recruitment process, ensuring fair and equal opportunities for all candidates. By eliminating human biases and prejudices, AI can help promote diversity and inclusivity, critical aspects of green HRM. AI can utilize historical recruitment data to identify patterns and trends related to successful hires. By analyzing various factors such as experience, education, skills, and performance, AI algorithms can predict a candidate's likelihood of success in a particular role. This predictive capability helps recruiters identify the most suitable candidates, leading to more efficient and effective hiring decisions. AI can analyze employee data, such as performance metrics, engagement surveys, and feedback, to identify patterns contributing to employee turnover.

According to Deloitte's 2019 Global Human Capital Trends Survey, 81% of the respondents believed their firm needed a better recruiting process and stated that the current process was below standards (JavaTPoint). Thus, shifting to AI will help with the better recruitment process. Now, combining HR and AI Technology, smoother recruitment optimization is assumed. The human touch in the recruitment process will be lessened. Nevertheless, it will eliminate human errors, mistakes, and biases. The recruitment process through AI is increasing day by day. Automated smart systems are more refined in recruiting; they even interact with candidates for a better selection process.

Future of Work in 2022 from International Data Corporation predicted that AI will be used by 80% of global 2000 companies to hire, fire, and train workers in jobs. It is named Digital Managers. AI is presently working this way (Carreon & Cruz, 2022). Deloitte uses Mya Systems as a hiring chatbot for the recruiting process. Mya is a guiding tool that guides the candidates through the hiring process until onboarding (Rana, 2018; Rana et al., 2021). Chatbots are quick and intelligent solutions to access daily repeating tasks (Hmoud & Laszlo, 2019). Unilever partnered with two firms of AI technology firms, Pymetrics, and HireVue (Hoque, 2021). They prefer AI when hiring people for their Future Leader's programs worldwide. They hired 800 people and also received almost 2.5 lakh applications. These included extended leadership contact, formal training, and professional development.

AI could uplift the recruitment process and provide many benefits, but with that also come challenges, which will take some time to cure by only processing and updating it frequently. First, adapting the AI system quickly will be a little uncomfortable and difficult. Working on it comfortably will take some time. Initially, it will take much data to understand the whole logic of training and engagement and the patterns of human bias from the existing recruitment process (Johansson & Herranen, 2019). For example, two years back, there was news of Amazon using bots to fire people (Soper, 2021). A machine fired a 63-year-old man. According to the machine, he was not completing and doing his job correctly, as he did not deliver the order. However, the actual case was that nobody was available at the residence where he had to deliver the order. This is how biased behavior will take some time to update in AI. As the delivery man was working there for at least 30 years and due to less information in the AI system, he got fired. Moreover, another challenge would be the decrease in the potential human touch, which would ultimately affect all.

AI in HR can perform various tasks like talent acquisition, online interviews, employee training and development, performance evaluation, employee engagement, and talent prediction. The adoption of AI in HR is the new age of HR. AI plays a huge role in finding, securing, and retaining employees. AI applications will help managers speed up decision-making and their daily tasks.

4. Artificial Intelligence and Green Human Resource Management

4.1. Employee Engagement and Performance Management

Employee disengagement is a whole lot of an issue that has to be cured. Due to lack of time or lack of motivation or appreciation or anything, 67% of employees are not engaged in their work. Founder of Bersin by Deloitte, Josh Bersin, once said, "Turnover is so painful with this job market that companies are realizing – I have got to take better care of my people, or else I cannot grow" (JavaTPoint). Many believe AI practices will make a change in this global issue. However, some HR professionals do not understand strategies that can be used to improve employee experience and so engagement. Employees whom the organizations value stay motivated and provide business growth. AI-powered systems can gather data from various sources, such as employee surveys, performance metrics, and communication platforms, to provide personalized feedback to employees. By analyzing this data, AI can identify individual strengths, areas for improvement, and growth opportunities. This feedback can help employees understand how their work contributes to the organization's green initiatives, fostering a sense of purpose and engagement.

AI-powered virtual assistants and chatbots can provide employees with on-demand access to information and support related to green HRM. These tools can answer questions, provide guidance on sustainable practices, offer suggestions for eco-friendly alternatives, and promote environmentally conscious behaviors within the workplace. By empowering employees with readily available resources, AI enhances engagement and participation in green initiatives.

AI can support gamification techniques to promote sustainable behaviors and engage employees in green initiatives. By incorporating challenges, rewards, and friendly competition, AI-powered gamification platforms can encourage employees to adopt eco-friendly workplace and daily practices. This approach fosters a sense of camaraderie, collaboration, and excitement around sustainability, thereby boosting employee engagement (Ndekwa et al., 2023).

AI can monitor employee performance in real time by analyzing data from various sources, such as project management tools, communication platforms, and performance metrics. This enables managers to provide timely feedback, recognize achievements, and promptly address issues (Aggarwal et al., 2022). By leveraging AI for performance monitoring, employees receive continuous support and guidance, enhancing their engagement in their work and green HRM practices. AI algorithms can assess employees' skills, performance, and interests to provide tailored recommendations for learning and development opportunities. This personalized approach helps employees acquire knowledge and skills that align with green HRM objectives. By offering targeted training and development programs, AI contributes to employee engagement by empowering individuals to enhance their capabilities and contribute meaningfully to sustainability initiatives.

Chatbots are a leading system that can be used to generate performance management. More than 60% of users prefer chatbots because it is way faster than human interaction and mostly provides correct and precise answers (Buck & Morrow, 2018). It can give speedy answers to multiple questions. Starbucks very commonly uses chatbots. For order and delivery processes, they use Facebook Messenger as their chatbot. This will also make employees' communications more collaborative and interactive and help organizations improve performance management (Gautam, 2019).

5. Artificial Intelligence and Green Human Resource Management: Audit and Legal Compliance

AI can do various data analyses. It can process large volumes of data related to various green HRM practices, such as energy consumption, waste management, and employee engagement. It can identify patterns, trends, and anomalies in the data, enabling auditors to assess the effectiveness of green HRM initiatives.

AI can assist auditors in monitoring compliance with environmental regulations and standards. AI can flag discrepancies or non-compliance issues by analyzing data from various sources, including energy usage records and waste management reports, helping auditors identify areas requiring attention. The environmental risks can be assessed through AI algorithms, which will be associated with HRM practices. AI can identify potential risks and recommend mitigation strategies by analyzing data and considering energy consumption, carbon emissions, and sustainability policies. AI can assist auditors in tracking and evaluating the performance of green HRM initiatives. By analyzing relevant metrics, such as energy savings, waste reduction, and carbon footprint, AI can provide real-time updates on the progress of sustainability goals, enabling auditors to assess the effectiveness of the initiatives.

Its benefit is that it makes the auditors work better and faster. It optimizes their time and analyzes a lot of deep data and broad documents. It will make the questioning and interaction process more accessible and crisper.

6. Artificial Intelligence and Green Human Resource Management: Compensation and Benefits

AI could help by generating compensation metrics to reward employees for their efforts to advance organizational goals. In this specific field, AI could help shift only job-oriented toward skill-oriented. An AI compensation system could help recognize employees' obscure skills and talents and recommend paying them more. IBM managers use an in-house system to make better decisions about compensation and counsel about salary increases from high, low, to no increase (Sammer, 2019). Green Incentive Programs can be made. AI can help design and optimize incentive programs that reward employees for adopting environmentally friendly behaviors. AI can determine appropriate incentives and assess their effectiveness by analyzing energy consumption, carbon emissions, or waste reduction data. By considering factors such as flexible work arrangements, remote work options, or eco-friendly commuting benefits, AI can tailor benefits to individual employee needs while aligning with green HRM objectives. Thus, it provides a supportive culture and job satisfaction (Kumar et al., 2021).

AI can assist in establishing performance metrics and benchmarks for Green HRM initiatives. By monitoring and analyzing relevant data, AI can determine when employees or teams have achieved specific sustainability targets and calculate performance-based bonuses accordingly. AI can provide personalized recommendations to employees on green HRM practices. By considering individual work patterns, consumption habits, and preferences, AI can suggest environmentally friendly behaviors, such as energy-saving tips, waste reduction strategies, or eco-friendly commuting options (Sharma et al., 2022).

The only challenge that compensation AI faces is unwanted bias. AI-based compensation systems must be maintained, monitored, managed, and updated frequently and appropriately. If not done so, this system will create ingrained bias and increase it. Even with no intention of discrimination, algorithms can perpetuate inequalities if left unchecked.

7. Artificial Intelligence and Green Human Resource Management: Talent Development and Training

Overall, AI could help in organization's and individual's development. AI uses predictive analysis (Searle & Sty, 2021), which further assists in seamless assessment, instant feedback, better suggestions, personalized learning, intelligent tutoring, and much more. Every AI system used in HR functions is devoted to learning, development, and training. The best part of using AI for this field is that it will be available 24/7 for digital tuition. It performs personalized learning according to every individual (Abdeldayem & Aldulaimi, 2020). Then, identifying the knowledge gap suggests the best and most appropriate content and knowledge for the learner. It provides virtual assistance, which can be the most comfortable and personalized way to adopt a new skill without hesitation.

AI can analyze employee skills, job roles, and learning preferences to develop personalized training paths in green HRM. By considering individual knowledge gaps and career aspirations, AI can recommend specific courses, resources, and development activities to enhance employees' understanding of sustainable practices. Workers choose AI over humans for career advice (Doniger, 2021). AI-powered adaptive learning platforms can dynamically adjust the content and difficulty levels of training materials based on employees' performance and comprehension. This ensures that each employee receives tailored instruction, allowing them to learn at their own pace and focus on areas that require improvement in green HRM. AI can provide real-time access to relevant resources and information at the moment of need. By leveraging natural language processing and machine learning, AI-powered chatbots or virtual assistants can respond to employee inquiries about green HRM practices, regulations, or policies, ensuring timely and accurate guidance.

8. Conclusion

By leveraging AI in Green Human Resource Management, organizations can enhance their environmental performance, reduce costs, and create a more sustainable and eco-friendly workplace for employees.

The best way to utilize AI resources is to use them in recruitment. For the initial stage, it would make tasks for recruiters way easier. AI can help organizations take proactive measures to improve employee satisfaction, well-being, and overall retention by identifying the factors leading to attrition. This focus on employee retention aligns with green HRM principles by reducing turnover-related environmental impacts, such as the need for additional recruitment and training. Overall, updating the AI system properly will make a finer way of recruiting more applicants possible. AI will apply proper human knowledge. Predictive analysis and behavior mapping will analyze employees' interests and attitudes toward their work. They will guide and make tasks accordingly, keeping them more engaged rather than ignoring and disengaging. Human connection, empathy, and communication remain essential for building trust, fostering collaboration, and successfully implementing green HRM strategies. Deep learning and machine learning can help analyze various data and go through vast amounts of data in less time. It can make work better and faster. It is important to note that while AI can significantly enhance auditing processes related to Green HRM, human expertise and judgment remain crucial in interpreting the results, making decisions, and implementing appropriate actions. Rewards make employees satisfied and keep them motivated. Compensation metrics can analyze work done by employees, suggest their rewards, and ensure benefits related to Green HRM, but updating systems frequently will be required to avoid unwanted biases. Again, the system can find the lack of knowledge and skill through predictive analysis and assist the employee with further personalized learning. Overall, being a 24/7 worker, AI could change a lot globally and individually, transforming working professionals' lives to be more efficient.

References

Abdeldayem, M. M., & Aldulaimi, S. H. (2020). Trends and opportunities of artificial intelligence in human resource management: Aspirants for public sector in Bahrain. *International Journal of Scientific & Technology Research*, *9*(1), 3867–3871.

Afrin, K. H., & Ahmed, A. (2023). Green human resource management history: A bibliometrics reflection. *International Journal for Multidisciplinary Research*, *5*(3), 1–11.

Aggarwal, A., Sadhna, P., Gupta, S., Mittal, A., & Rastogi, S. (2022). Gen Z entering the workforce: Restructuring HR policies and practices to foster task performance and organizational commitment. *Journal of Public Affairs*, *22*(3), e2535.

Ahmed, O. (2018). Artificial intelligence in HR. *International Journal of Research and Analytical Reviews*, *5*(4), 971–978.

Anderson, K. (2020, February). *How artificial intelligence is transforming HR*. IHRIM. Retrieved from https://www.ihrim.org/2020/02/how-artificial-intelligence-is-transforming-hr/

Bhardwaj, G., Singh, S. V., & Kumar, V. (2020). *An empirical study of artificial intelligence and its impact on human resource functions* (pp. 47–51). IEEE.

Buck, B., & Morrow, J. (2018). *AI, performance management and engagement: Keeping your best their best* (Vol. 17, pp. 261–262). Emerald Publishing Limited.

Carreon, M., & Cruz, M. D. L. (2022, September 26). *IDC: AI spending will rise over $46 billion by 2026 in Asia/Pacific*. Retrieved from https://www.idc.com/getdoc.jsp?containerId=prAP49721022

Chugh, A. (2021, November 29). *What is 'The Great Resignation'?* Retrieved from https://www.weforum.org/agenda/2021/11/what-is-the-great-resignation-and-what-can-we-learn-from-it/

Chui, M., Hall, B., Mayhew, H., Singla, A., & Sukharevsky, A. (2022, December 6). *The state of AI in 2022 and a half decade in review*. Retrieved from https://www.mckinsey.com/capabilities/quantumblack/our-insights/the-state-of-ai-in-2022-and-a-half-decade-in-review

Davey, J. (2022, December 7). *Why are more retailers using robots?* Retrieved from https://www.weforum.org/agenda/2022/12/retailers-artificial-intelligence-robots/

Doniger, A. (2021, October 10). *In this job market, more workers are choosing AI over humans for career advice*. Retrieved from https://www.cnbc.com/2021/10/26/82percent-of-workers-say-ai-can-support-career-growth-better-than-humans.html

Eightfold AI's Talent Survey. (2022). *The future of work: Intelligent by design*. Retrieved from https://eightfold.ai/wp-content/uploads/2022_Talent_Survey.pdf

Fawehinmi, O., Yusliza, M., Mohamad, Z., Faezah, J. N., & Muhammad, Z. (2020). Assessing the green behavior of academics: The role of green human resource management and environmental knowledge. *International Journal of Manpower*, *41*(7), 879–900.

Gabor, D. (1963). *Inventing the future*. Secker & Warburg. Retrieved May 30, 2023, from http://quoteinvestigator.com/2012/09/27/invent-the-future/

Garg, V., Srivastav S., & Gupta A. (2018). *Application of Artificial Intelligence for Sustaining Green Human Resource Management* (pp. 113–116). IEEE.

Gautam, A. (2019, June 28). *Artificial intelligence and employee engagement: Connecting the dots*. Retrieved from https://blog.shrm.org/sasia/blog/artificial-intelligence-and-employee-engagement-connecting-the-dots

Geetha, R., & Reddy, B. S. (2018). *Recruitment through artificial intelligence: A conceptual study* (Vol. 9(7), pp. 63–70). IAEME Publications.

Gupta, M. (2021). *The role of artificial intelligence in adopting green HRM practices*. CRC Press.

Hmoud, B., & Laszlo, V. (2019). Will artificial intelligence take over human resources recruitment and selection? *Network Intelligence Studies*, *7*(13), 21–30.

Hoque, W. (2021). *Unilever recruitment case study: How IT Works*. Retrieved from https://www.scribd.com/document/506497399/Unilever-Case-Study#

Jia, Q., Guo, Y., Li, R., Li, Y. R., & Chen, Y. W. (2018). A *conceptual artificial intelligence application framework in human resource management* [Conference session]. Proceedings of The 18th International Conference on Electronic Business, pp. 106–114.

Johansson, J., & Herranen, S. (2019). *The application of artificial intelligence (AI) in human resource management: Current state of AI and its impact on the traditional recruitment process* (pp. 7–60). Jonkopin International Business School.

Kumar, S. P., Saha, S., & Anand, A. (2021). A green human resource management approach of participation in decision-making and behavioral outcomes – a moderated mediated model. *International Journal of Organizational Analysis*, *31*(5), 1724–1747.

Kaur, S., Kumar, R., Singh, K., & Huang, Y. L. (2024). Leveraging artificial intelligence for enhanced sustainable energy management. *Journal of Sustainable Energy*, *3*(1), 1–20. https://doi.org/10.56578/jse030101

Li, L., Lassiter, T., Oh, J., & Lee, M. K. (2021). *Algorithmic hiring in practice: Recruiter and HR professional's perspectives on AI use in hiring* [Conference session]. Proceedings of the 2021 AAAI/ACM Conference on AI, Ethics, and Society (AIES'21), pp. 166–176.

Michael, S. (2021, November 18). *IDC FutureScape: Top 10 predictions for the future of work*. Retrieved from https://www.idc.com/getdoc.jsp?containerId=prUS48395221

Ndekwa, A. G., Kalugendo, E., Sood, K., & Grima, S. (2023). An analysis of agribusiness digitalisation transformation of the sub-Saharan African countries small-scale farmers' production distribution. *Research on World Agricultural Economy*, *4*(3), 63–78.

Odugbesan, J. A., Aghazadeh, S., Al Qaralleh, R. E., & Sogeke, O. S. (2023). Green talent management and employees' innovative work behavior: The roles of artificial intelligence and transformational leadership. *Journal of Knowledge Management*, *27*(3), 696–716.

OnPassive. (2021, November 5). *Role of artificial intelligence in human resource management*. Retrieved from https://onpassive.com/blog/role-of-artificial-intelligence-in-human-resource-management\

Pandey, S., & Khaskel, P. (2019). Application of AI in human resource management and Gen Y's Reaction. *Blue Eyes Intelligence Engineering & Sciences Publication*, *8*(4), 10325–10331.

Pham, N. T., Hoang, T. H., & Phan, Q. P. T. (2020). Green human resource management: A comprehensive review and future research agenda. *International Journal of Manpower, 41*(7), 845–878.

Rana, G., Khang, A., Sharma, R., Goel, A. K., & Dubey, A. K. (Eds.) (2021). *Reinventing manufacturing and business processes through artificial intelligence* (pp. 1–18). CRC Press.

Renwick, D., Redman, T., & Maguire, S. (2012). Green human resource management: A review and research agenda. *International Journal of Management Reviews. 15*(1). DOI:10.1111/j.1468-2370.2011.00328.x

Rana, T. (2018). *The future of HR in the presence of AI: A conceptual study*. The Social Science Research Network.

Rijal, S., Nursaputra, M. A. C., & Dari, H. U. (2024). Flood susceptibility analysis using Frequency Ratio method in Walanae watershed. *International Journal of Sustainable Development and Planning, 19*(3), 823–832. https://doi.org/10.18280/ijsdp.190302

Sammer, J. (2019, December 10). *Bringing artificial intelligence into pay decisions*. Retrieved from https://www.shrm.org/resourcesandtools/hr-topics/compensation/pages/bringing-artificial-intelligence-into-pay-decisions.aspx#:~:text=AI%20could%20help%20develop%20compensation,the%2Dminute%20competitive%20pay%20rates.

Searle, B., & Sty, C. (2021, August 2). The role of AI in HR decision making. Retrieved from https://www.myhrfuture.com/blog/2021/7/28/the-role-of-ai-in-hr-decision-making

Sharma, A., Talwar, T., Chauhan, D., & Vasisht, P. (2023). Role of AI in green HRM in pursuit of sustainable development. *European Chemical Bulletin, 5*, 373–379.

Sharma, C., Sakhuja, S., & Nijjer, S. (2022). Recent trends of green human resource management: Text mining and network analysis. *Environmental Science and Pollution Research, 29*(56), 84916–84935.

Shoaib, M., Zamecnik, R., Abbas, Z., Javed, M., & Rehman, A. U. (2021). *Green human resource management and green human capital: A systematic literature review*. 10.3846/cibmee.2021.649

Shores, R. (2019, October 15). *64% of people trust a robot more than their manager*. Retrieved from https://www.oracle.com/corporate/pressrelease/robots-at-work-101519.html

Song, Y., & Wu, R. (2021). *Analyzing human-computer interaction behavior in human resource management systems based on artificial intelligence technology* (pp. 1–10). Taylor & Francis.

Soper, S. (2021, June 28). *Fired by Bot at Amazon: 'It's you against the machine.'* Retrieved from https://finance.yahoo.com/news/fired-bot-amazon-against-machine-100013296.html?guccounter=1&guce_referrer=aHR0cHM6Ly93d3cuYnVzaW5lc3NuZXdzZGFpbHkuY29tLw&guce_referrer_sig=AQAAAA9okMruxG4wYnWvoFaeD-_UHEhSNOsOl-aWlaR4s-7XSpHTn6usAf_HhxmZ1qLI8rwccO8_rkjU8HUD8QsZPgbU6_HHOW4eR5cZIgiu7RGEcwZGYhTjZFoXmaH_nNECFwwx5wBDce-JhAinDX-HivBZ9pJ46pXqciEk_HWHXDl_n

Chapter 7

The Application of the Green Economy Policy of Switzerland to the Karabakh Region of Azerbaijan: A Review and Appraisal

Adalat Muradov and Nargiz Hajiyeva

Azerbaijan State University of Economics (UNEC), Baku, Azerbaijan

Abstract

Introduction: The importance of green economy policies for sustainable development is widely recognized, yet there is a notable gap in literature regarding their application in regions like Karabakh, Azerbaijan. This study addresses this gap by exploring the feasibility of transferring Swiss green economy policies to Karabakh, considering its socio-economic context and aspirations.

Purpose: This study assesses the feasibility and efficacy of applying Switzerland's green economy policies to Karabakh. By evaluating Switzerland's innovation potential and Azerbaijan's renewable energy landscape, it aims to determine the compatibility and potential benefits of implementing Swiss policies in Karabakh.

Methodology: Utilizing a multifaceted approach, the study first analyzes Switzerland's innovation potential using data from the Global Innovation Index. It then employs a mathematical model to assess the shares of renewable energy sources in Karabakh's energy supply from 2020 to 2022, providing insights into its renewable energy landscape and alignment with Swiss policies.

Findings: The study uncovers substantial potential for renewable energy growth in Karabakh, notably in wind and solar power. Hydropower

Green Management: A New Paradigm in the World of Business, 97–119

Published under exclusive licence by Emerald Publishing Limited
doi:10.1108/978-1-83797-442-920241007

maintains its reliability in energy supply, while wind and solar sources gain prominence. Insights from Switzerland's Innovation Index highlight the relevance of Swiss green economy policies for Karabakh's context.

Practical implications: Emulating Switzerland's green economy model can drive sustainable development in Karabakh. Collaboration among Azerbaijan, Switzerland, and the private sector is pivotal for setting global sustainable development goals and enacting policy reforms. Switzerland's dedication to a circular economy provides a compelling framework for revitalizing the Karabakh region.

Keywords: Green economy; green growth; sustainability; Switzerland; Karabakh; Azerbaijan; economic growth

JEL Classifications: O44; Q42; Q56

Introduction

The concept of a "green economy" can be broadly defined as an economic system aligned with robust environmental conditions, operating within ecological limits. This alignment is inherently linked to the principles of sustainability, characterized by development that transcends temporal constraints, meeting current needs without compromising the ability of future generations to fulfill their own requirements (World Commission on Environment and Development, 1987). It is crucial to note that the term "green economy" does not inherently endorse a growth-centric strategy but encapsulates the economic facets of a society transitioning towards sustainability. At a strategic level, various narratives and concepts surround this transition, encompassing fundamental considerations such as perspectives on development, economic advancement, transformation, ecological constraints, the envisioned role of the state, technology, and innovation, and a focus on equity issues and consumption patterns (Fulai et al., 2011).

The concept of a green economy was initially introduced by the renowned economist Pearce, who posited that the environment and economy are inherently interconnected (UNEP, 2011). The United Nations Environment Programme (UNEP) provides a concise definition, describing a green economy as one that prioritizes both human and natural elements while fostering the creation of high-paying jobs (Pearce et al., 1989). In 2011, UNEP expanded the notion of "green" to encompass an economy that is not only efficient but also fair, ensuring a just transition to a low-carbon, resource-efficient, and socially inclusive economy (UNEP, 2011). The relationship between a green economy and clean energy policy is integral, with a focus on practical political applications. National policies explicitly incorporate the real value of environmental services and the actual environmental costs. Notably, renewable energy constitutes the primary sector of the green economy, and the development of such energy sources relies on supportive public policies (Cai et al., 2011). A green economy is characterized by the provision of public goods, where both public and private investments drive income and employment growth (Engel & Kammen, 2009). The global potential for stimulating growth through greening the economy is substantial (Pearce et al., 1989). Additionally, it is emphasized that renewable energy can catalyze employment (Lesser, 2010). In essence, the realization of a green economy necessitates robust support from public policies to integrate environmental considerations into economic frameworks (UNEP, 2008).

Numerous scholars assert that the green economy has a positive influence on employment, contributing to job creation and fostering social equity (Pearce et al., 1989). The implementation of renewable energy initiatives catalyzes employment growth, leading to increased labor demand and a net expansion of job opportunities (Apergis & Payne, 2010). Additionally, a transition to a low-carbon economy can impact the employment structure positively, enhancing the scale of a low-carbon economy. However, it is important to note that the green economy can also have adverse effects on employment, potentially reducing overall employment levels. The creation of one green job may offset another job, and mandated subsidies for renewable generation might have implications for economic well-being (Cai et al., 2011). The employment effects are dynamic and contingent on current policies, and these effects may vary over different periods of the green economy's development (Fulai et al., 2011).

In recent years, Switzerland has embarked on a transformative journey towards a green economy, recognizing the need to address resource consumption, waste management, and overarching environmental impacts. The 2020 report, "Federal Measures for a Resource-Conserving, Future-Proof Switzerland" (Federal Department of the Environment, Transport, Energy and Communications, 2020), outlines a comprehensive action plan targeting three priority areas: consumption and production, waste and raw materials, and cross-cutting instruments (FOEN, 2020). Switzerland's focus on consumption and production acknowledges the environmental impact of product manufacture and consumer behavior. The plan aims to raise consumer awareness and promote environmentally friendly production methods. Collaboration between the government and the private sector is deemed essential to foster resource-conserving production methods and business models. The second priority area tackles the environmental impact of waste generation, raw material extraction, and disposal. Switzerland places a high priority on waste prevention, efficient raw material use, and improved recycling. The recent enactment of the waste ordinance reflects a commitment to prioritize waste prevention, emphasizing that "waste is raw materials in the wrong place." In supporting and developing existing initiatives, the third priority area underscores collaboration with business, science, and society. Given Switzerland's significant environmental impact abroad, international involvement is crucial. The report stresses the need for a consolidated knowledge base and sector-specific approaches, particularly in sustainable finance. Notable achievements include agreements with sectors to reduce peat imports and projects, such as the collaboration with SwissZinc to reclaim zinc residues. Additionally, partnerships with organizations like Reffnet.ch have led to resource efficiency improvements in approximately 170 businesses, showcasing Switzerland's progress in resource conservation. Ongoing work on individual measures continues within the current legal framework and political mandates. A holistic approach is increasingly necessary, especially in sectors with high environmental relevance, such as food and agriculture, housing and construction, and mobility (PwC & WWF, 2020).

Exploring Challenges and Opportunities in Switzerland's Green Growth and National Green Economy Policies

The concept of the "green economy" gained prominence at the Rio+20 Conference in June 2012, emerging as a key tool for sustainable development. The transition to a green economy necessitates shifts in production and consumption patterns, embracing new technologies, in-depth knowledge, innovation, and collaborative experience sharing (Fedlex, 1983). Fundamentally, a green economy embodies an economic system characterized by efficient resource-conserving consumption and production models, designed to be future-proof and mindful of the transient nature of scarce resources and the regenerative capacity of renewables. Switzerland, recognizing the imperative for sustainability, identifies sectors like food and agriculture, housing and construction, and mobility, as contributing to two-thirds of total pollution. Achieving resource-conserving consumption/production models requires active government involvement across federal, cantonal, and municipal levels, involving various sectors, private enterprises, scientific communities, and local communities. The "Federal Measures for a Resource-Conserving, Future-Proof Switzerland – Green Economy" report outlines the current state of resource use, required actions, and government measures from 2016 to 2019 across consumption and production, waste and raw materials, and overarching instruments. Switzerland's report on the implementation of the 2030 Agenda emphasizes the nexus between resource overexploitation and consumption/production patterns (EU4Environment, 2019). The Federal Council's 2018 environmental report delves into the intricate connections between resource consumption and environmental pollution, with a core objective of conserving natural resources and enhancing economic performance and social welfare (FOEN, 2020). The Swiss government, traditionally prioritizing water, air, and soil protection, integrates natural resource preservation into current environmental policy under the Environmental Protection Act (EPA), which includes incentive taxes added over multiple revisions since its enactment nearly four decades ago. The EPA aims to protect people, animals, plants, and their habitats from harmful effects, sustainably preserving the natural foundations of life, particularly biological diversity and soil fertility. For achieving a substantial decrease in resource consumption and associated environmental pollution, there is an increasing recognition of the necessity for a comprehensive approach, particularly in crucial environmental sectors like food, housing, and mobility. On February 27, 2013, the Federal Council decided to extend measures promoting a resource-efficient approach to Switzerland's economic system and consumption, accompanied by amendments to the Environmental Protection Act. The proposed revisions to the EPA align with the priority areas outlined in the Green Economy

Action Plan: (1) consumption and production, (2) waste management and raw materials, (3) cross-cutting instruments, and (4) targeting, monitoring, information, and reporting. This action plan aims to safeguard natural resources, enhance eco-friendly practices, and strengthen the circular economy (FOEN, 2020).

Table 7.1 summarizes Switzerland's key sustainability policies across seven policy areas, including renewable energy, sustainable transport, circular economy, biodiversity conservation, green finance, climate change mitigation, and research and innovation. Each policy area is accompanied by specific measures,

Table 7.1. Key Components of Swiss Green Economy Policy.

No.	Policy Area	Policy Measures	Implementation Timeline	Responsible Agency/Body
1.	Renewable Energy	Increase the share of renewable energy in the energy mix	2020–2030	Federal Office of Energy (FOE)
2.	Sustainable Transport	Promote public transportation, electric vehicles, and cycling	Ongoing	Federal Department of the Environment, Transport, Energy and Communications (DETEC)
3.	Circular Economy	Implement measures to reduce waste and promote recycling	2022–2030	Federal Office for the Environment (FOEN)
4.	Biodiversity Conservation	Protect and enhance biodiversity through conservation measures	Ongoing	Federal Office for the Environment (FOEN)
5.	Green Finance	Encourage sustainable investments and banking practices	Ongoing	Swiss Financial Market Supervisory Authority (FINMA)
6.	Climate Change Mitigation	Set and achieve targets for reducing greenhouse gas emissions	2020–2030	Federal Office for the Environment (FOEN)
7.	Research and Innovation	Support green technology research and innovation	Ongoing	State Secretariat for Education, Research and Innovation (SERI)

Source: Federal Department of Foreign Affairs, Switzerland.

an implementation timeline, and the responsible agency or body overseeing its execution. These policies reflect Switzerland's commitment to promoting environmental protection, resource conservation, and sustainable development practices.

In Switzerland, the collaborative efforts of the ministries overseeing economic and environmental affairs have resulted in the formulation of a governmental action plan focused on the green economy. The Swiss Green Economy Action Plan delineates key areas of action, emphasizing the promotion of clean technologies, enhanced consumer information regarding product environmental impact, and ecological tax reform (FOEN, 2020). The Federal Office for the Environment (FOEN) actively facilitates "green" dialogues among business, science, society, and the public sector, aiming to implement resource-efficient and recyclable production methods. The FOEN is a member of the "Go for Impact" association, fostering collaboration among various stakeholders for resource-conserving and socially acceptable economies aligned with the UN Sustainable Development Goals (SDGs) (FOEN, 2020). Internationally, Switzerland supports the Green Growth Knowledge Platform (GGKP), which gathers and disseminates knowledge about green policies, benefiting policymakers and other stakeholders. The collaboration between UNIDO and the Swiss Government in the IGGE project with Egypt in 2021 exemplifies Switzerland's commitment to green growth and circular economy practices, promoting optimized resource use and creating new markets. Switzerland made history by initiating a ballot on September 25, 2016, to decide whether to adopt a green economy. The ballot aimed to advocate for resource efficiency and the adoption of a circular economy. It sets specific targets to reduce Switzerland's resource consumption to a globally replicable level. Fig. 7.1 indicates substantial positive interest, with 36% of voters supporting the initiative and a 42.5% turnout for sustainable living within the planet's means. Notably, Geneva was the sole canton where the initiative gained majority support, attributed to the active engagement of International Organizations and NGOs in the region. The referendum and the widespread recognition of the necessity for a significant shift in resource usage mark a global historical precedent.

Swiss universities play an active role in advancing green growth and circular economy initiatives at the national level. The Institute of Science, Technology, and Policy at the Swiss Federal Institute of Technology in Zürich (ETH), a globally esteemed institution, engaged in developing a voluntary green economy policy for the "National Research Programme 73: Sustainable Economy: resource-friendly, future-oriented, innovative" (NRP 73) funded by the Swiss National Science Foundation in 2020. Spearheaded by Prof. Dr. Thomas Bernauer and Dennis Kolcava, the project aimed at fostering an ecologically more sustainable economy, emphasizing behavioral changes from both producers and consumers (ETH Zurich, 2020; Swiss National Science Foundation, 2016). The Swiss government actively promotes the involvement of policymakers, experts, and business professionals in programs and symposiums dedicated to the effective implementation of green economy policies. The Swiss Green Economy Symposium (SGES) in Winterthur, held on 5–7 September 2023, served as a comprehensive sustainability business summit, fostering motivation, knowledge transfer, and networking among leaders in various sectors. The symposium, discussing renewable technologies (RES) and raw materials aligning with the United Nations' Sustainable Development Goals (SDGs), is scheduled for a subsequent session in early September 2022 in Winterthur to further enhance green growth measures and actions (Swiss Green Economy Symposium, 2023). The Sustainable Finance report for 2021 by the Swiss Bankers Association (SBA) and Boston Consulting Group highlighted that Switzerland requires 387 billion Swiss francs ($422 billion) in investments to achieve climate neutrality by 2050, equivalent to approximately 2% of the country's annual output (Federal Office for the Environment, 2020). The report underscored that bank loans and the capital market could contribute 91% of the funding, with the government covering the remaining portion, primarily for public services like transportation. To reach its net-zero target by 2050, Switzerland must adopt more sustainable practices, and the country's banks can play a crucial role in facilitating this transition, as emphasized by the Swiss Bankers Association and Boston Consulting Group (Federal Office for the Environment, 2020).

Establishing the Green Economy System in Karabakh: Following the Swiss Model

In response to the climate emergency, Switzerland is undergoing a significant transformation towards a clean and green economy. Following the Fukushima reactor disaster in 2011, the Swiss government, through the Energy Strategy 2050, aims to reduce its carbon footprint and shift away from nuclear energy production. The strategy focuses on minimizing energy demand, enhancing efficiency, promoting renewable energy use, and gradually phasing out nuclear power plants. To fund these initiatives, Swiss electricity customers have been contributing to a grid surcharge since 2018, supporting various renewable energy projects. The country plans to shut down nuclear power plants at the end of their safe operating life, emphasizing the importance of investing in alternative, sustainable energy sources. This approach not only aligns with environmental goals but also stimulates job creation and local investment (FOEN, 2020).

Switzerland's commitment to renewable energy is evident in projects like the hydroelectric power station in the Swiss Alps, utilizing pumped-storage technology for quick energy response and excess energy storage. The country boasts 200 pumped-storage hydroelectricity stations in the Alps, showcasing a dedication to harnessing clean and versatile power generation. While hydropower remains a significant contributor, the International Energy Agency (IEA) suggests that "new" renewables, including solar, wood, biomass, wind, geothermal energy, and ambient heat, will play an increasingly vital role in Switzerland's energy landscape. However, the IEA report highlights a potential slowdown in hydropower growth due to insufficient government policies. Despite this, Switzerland's emphasis on diversifying its renewable energy sources demonstrates a commitment to sustainable energy practices. The country's strategic focus on renewables not only addresses environmental concerns but also positions Switzerland as a leader in the global transition to cleaner, more resilient energy systems (Ndekwa et al., 2023; Sood & Özen, 2024; Yerpude et al., 2022).

Switzerland's dedication to promoting an eco-conscious economy extends globally through active engagement in international initiatives targeting environmental impacts related to mineral resources. Collaborating with entities like UNEP, OECD, and UNECE, Switzerland advocates for bolstering international standards and guidelines within the commodities sector, particularly regarding mineral extraction and trade. Meanwhile, SBB, the national railway company, spearheads Switzerland's sustainable travel efforts, leveraging its expansive network to facilitate over 11,000 daily train journeys. Through participation in the "Swisstainable" program, SBB underscores its commitment to ongoing corporate sustainability endeavors. Switzerland's recent renewable energy breakthrough, the Nant de Drance water battery, signifies another stride in its green energy journey (Swissinfo, 2021). This pumped storage hydropower plant, operational since last month, boasts a storage capacity equivalent to 400,000 electric car batteries. This innovation aligns with Switzerland's broader sustainability objectives and showcases its prowess in renewable energy technology. In Karabakh, where substantial hydropower resources exist, the application of similar water batteries could offer a sustainable approach to reserve water resources. By implementing these giant batteries, Karabakh can harness its hydroelectric potential effectively, ensuring long-term water resource management while advancing its renewable energy agenda. This approach not only fosters sustainable development but also enhances energy security and resilience in the region.

Over the past 30 years of occupation, Karabakh and its surrounding regions have experienced significant environmental challenges due to the impact of hazardous chemical and biological weapons. Following the Second Karabakh War, the Azerbaijani government has implemented crucial measures for the reconstruction and revitalization of the liberated territories. A pivotal initiative outlined in the "Action Plan for the Formation of a Green Energy Zone in the Recovered Areas for 2022–2026," approved by the Cabinet of Ministers, involves the creation of production and service zones dedicated to green technologies in the liberated territories. According to the Action Plan, the Ministry of Economy, in collaboration with the Ministry of Energy, is tasked with establishing green technology products and service areas in the liberated territories of Azerbaijan between 2022 and 2026 (Azerbaijan Ministry of Energy, 2024).

The establishment of a "green energy" zone, particularly in Karabakh and surrounding areas, holds strategic significance for Azerbaijan. The Azerbaijani government, recognizing the importance of a "green energy" zone, issued a decree in 2021 for its establishment after the liberation of these territories from Armenian occupation during the Second Karabakh War. A pivotal agreement between the Ministry of Energy of Azerbaijan and the Japanese company TEPSCO was signed to facilitate the formation of the "green energy" zone in the liberated territories (TEPSCO, 2021). The project focuses on the development of energy-saving technologies, employing modern energy management approaches to harness the renewable energy potential in the liberated territories, including wind, solar, hydro, geothermal, and bioenergy. Green energy is poised to serve as a backbone for the establishment of a green economy and the fostering of green growth in the region. To achieve this, the implementation of a robust Research and Development (R&D) strategy in Karabakh and its neighboring districts is imperative.

This strategy aims to comprehensively investigate the evolving landscape, climate, soil structure, and natural resources of the region. Leveraging its expertise in green economic models, Switzerland stands as a potential collaborator in ensuring the effective utilization of renewable energy resources in the newly liberated territories of Azerbaijan (Azerbaijan Ministry of Energy, 2024).

Table 7.2 outlines the diverse renewable energy potential in the Karabakh region. It underscores the significant but underutilized hydropower resources, with notable hydroelectric plants like Tartar already liberated. Solar and wind

Table 7.2. The Green Energy Potential of Karabakh and its Nearby Districts.

Energy Source	Description	Potential	Status
Hydropower	Karabakh boasts significant water resources, generating approximately 25% of Azerbaijan's local water annually.	High	Significant potential remains untapped
	Three large hydroelectric power plants existed in occupied territories, including the Tartar Hydroelectric Plant.	50 MW (Tartar Hydroelectric Plant)	Currently already liberated; maintenance needed
	Projects like Khudafarin and Giz Galasi Hydroelectric Plants are in progress, but their construction is hindered.	50 MW (Khudafarin), 40 MW (Giz Galasi)	Affected by occupation; construction ongoing by Iran
Solar Energy	The southern plains of Garabagh receive significant solar radiation, ranking second after Nakhichevan AR.	3,000–4,000 MW	Potential to be assessed post-liberation
Wind Energy	Mountainous areas of Karabakh experience average annual wind speeds of 7–10 m/s, suitable for wind energy projects.	300–500 MW	Potential to be assessed post-liberation
Geothermal Energy	Thermal waters present in Kalbajar and Shusha districts offer potential for geothermal energy utilization.	–	Potential to be studied post-liberation
Coal Reserves	Chardagli village in Tartar district hosts significant coal reserves, estimated at 8.5 million tons.	–	Resource available

Source: Ministry of Energy of the Republic of Azerbaijan 2020 and Azerbaijan Renewable Energy Agency under the Ministry of Energy of the Republic of Azerbaijan (2022).

energy offer substantial capacity post-liberation, with the southern plains and mountainous areas presenting prime locations. Geothermal energy and coal reserves provide additional opportunities for sustainable energy development. However, their utilization awaits post-liberation study. Despite hindered progress due to geopolitical challenges, projects such as Khudafarin and Giz Galasi Hydroelectric Plants are ongoing. Solar energy presents immense opportunities, particularly in the southern plains of Garabagh (Azerbaijan Ministry of Energy, 2024). Wind energy, favored by mountainous terrain, and geothermal energy from thermal waters in Kalbajar and Shusha districts also hold promise. Additionally, coal reserves in Chardagli village offer another energy source. However, full realization depends on resolving geopolitical constraints and post-liberation assessment (Azerbaijan Ministry of Energy, 2024). Another significant step in this direction involves the development of Master Urban Design and Green Territorial planning for the liberated Gubadli and Zangilan districts of Azerbaijan, both of which were awarded to Sa_partners (Azernews, 2022), a Swiss Urban Planning and Architecture Company based in Zurich, Switzerland. Having secured victory in both tender projects initiated by the Azerbaijani government, Sa_partners is slated to deliver the master plan by the end of the year 2022. For Gubadli, the Swiss company introduced the innovative "Sponge" urban concept as part of the Master Plan (Azerbaijan Ministry of Energy, 2024). This concept is specifically tailored for rational water resource management, aligning with the local context of Gubadli. The proposal aims to optimize the use of water reserves, showcasing a forward-thinking urban development strategy (Air Center, 2024). The sa_partners' initiatives for these cities underscore a holistic and context-specific urban planning approach, considering environmental sustainability, health tourism potential, and innovative water resource management (Azernews, 2022). Furthermore, the European Union-funded EU Environment Program has been actively supporting Azerbaijan since 2019, along with five other Eastern Partner countries, in their journey toward green transformation. This collaborative effort focuses on safeguarding natural resources, enhancing environmental well-being, endorsing ecological measures, and identifying mechanisms for more effective management of environmental risks and impacts. By paving the way for greener growth opportunities, this initiative aligns with the broader vision of promoting sustainable practices and green development in the region. Given the aforementioned considerations, the applicability of the Swiss green economy model to the liberated territories, including Karabakh and its seven adjacent areas, can be strategically assessed through a series of priority measures and actions (Azerbaijan Ministry of Energy, 2024).

Fig. 7.1 outlines specific aspects of the Swiss model and assesses their feasibility and relevance to the Karabakh region.

The Swiss emphasis on minimizing energy demand, enhancing efficiency, and promoting renewable energy aligns with Karabakh's goal of establishing a "green energy" zone. The focus on wind, solar, hydro, geothermal, and bioenergy sources applies to the region's energy potential. Its commitment to sustainable urban planning, biodiversity conservation, and eco-friendly practices resonates with Karabakh's post-war reconstruction efforts. The creation of green zones and

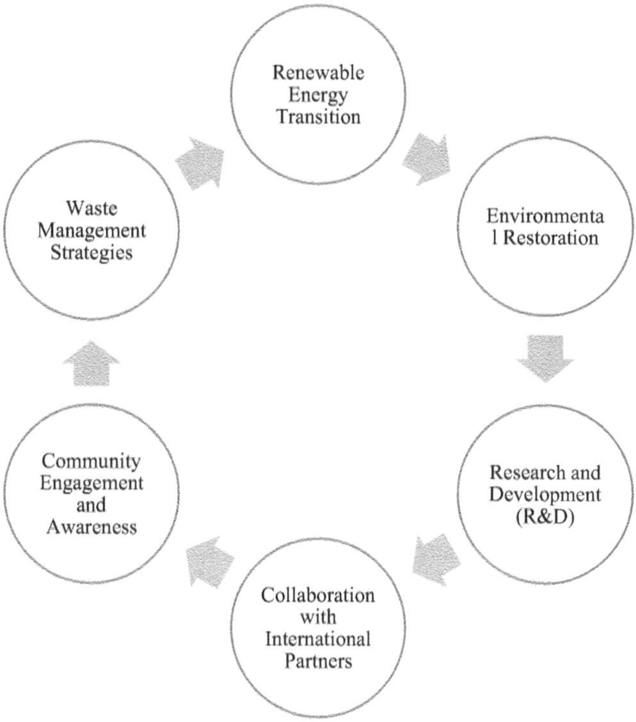

Fig. 7.1. Assessment of the Swiss Model's Feasibility and Relevance to the Karabakh Region. *Source*: Swiss Federal Department, Presidential Administration of Azerbaijan.

spaces can contribute to environmental rehabilitation. Switzerland's investment in R&D for climate, soil, and natural resource studies is crucial for Karabakh's understanding of its evolving landscape. Collaborative R&D initiatives with Swiss expertise can enhance local insights. The country's collaborations with countries known for successful green policies can be emulated by Karabakh. Establishing ties with Switzerland, Sweden, Iceland, Denmark, and others can facilitate knowledge exchange and best practices of the "green" policy (Kaur et al., 2024; Rijal et al., 2024).

Recent collaborations, such as those with British Petroleum (BP) and Masdar (Azerbaijan Ministry of Energy, 2024), highlight the nation's commitment to green energy. Masdar's involvement in projects like the 240 MW solar power plant in Jabrayil district and plans for utility-scale solar and wind projects underscore Azerbaijan's strides in renewable energy. Simultaneously, the Azerbaijani government is currently progressing with the construction of two hydropower plants situated along the Aras River in the Jabrayil region. These plants, collectively generating 140 MW of power, consist of the "Khudaferin" plant with a capacity of 100 MW and the "Giz Galası" plant with a capacity of 40 MW. Additionally, efforts are underway to establish a wind power plant in Lachin/Kalbajar, projected to yield 100 MW of electricity, further bolstering the development of a "green energy zone" within the liberated territories. Moreover, on June 3, 2021, the Ministry of Energy of the Republic of Azerbaijan and bp inked an Implementation Agreement aimed at assessing and executing a project to erect a 240 MW solar power plant in the Zangilan/Jabrayil region (Hajiyeva & Karimli, 2021). Similarly, ACWA Power's interest in hydrogen production and renewable projects signifies growing foreign investment (Ministry of Energy, 2024). Enactment of laws such as Law No. 339-VIQ in May 2021 underscores the nation's commitment to fostering the growth of its renewable energy sector, as articulated in strategic documents like "Azerbaijan 2030: National Priorities for Socio-economic Development" (Azerbaijan Ministry of Energy, 2024), which emphasizes climate change mitigation and renewable energy adoption across all sectors in line with UN Sustainable Development Goals. In addition to its efforts in renewable energy, Azerbaijan is poised to host COP29, showcasing its commitment to addressing climate change despite its heavy reliance on oil and gas (Air Center, 2024). This November 2024 summit reflects Azerbaijan's constructive approach towards environmental sustainability. Azerbaijan's commitment to sustainable development is evident in the establishment of a Green Energy Zone in liberated territories, supported by international cooperation and investments. Efforts to develop offshore wind energy, establish utility-scale solar and wind projects, and explore green hydrogen production underscore the nation's progressive approach to clean energy transition. By leveraging innovative strategies and international partnerships, Azerbaijan seeks to transform Karabakh into a hub of green innovation and economic prosperity, showcasing its dedication to a sustainable future.

Methodology

To evaluate the application of Switzerland's green growth policy to the Karabakh region of Azerbaijan, it is essential to assess both the Swiss potential in innovation and the green energy or renewable energy sources (RES) potential of Azerbaijan. This evaluation helps determine the feasibility and success of implementing the Swiss model in the Karabakh region. The methodology employed in this study involves a multifaceted approach to evaluate the application of Switzerland's green economy policies to the Karabakh region of Azerbaijan. This approach combines two key components: an analysis of Switzerland's innovation potential using data from the Global Innovation Index (WIPO, 2023) and a mathematical model to calculate the shares of renewable energy sources in the total energy supply in Karabakh. The shares of renewable energy sources in the total energy supply *(SRi)* for the last three years (2020, 2021, and 2022) after the liberation of Karabakh and Azerbaijani territories *(i)* are calculated using the following formulas:

$$SR_i = \frac{E_i}{TE_i} \times 100$$

where

- SR_i represents the share of the specific renewable energy source (hydropower, biomass and waste, wind power, solar power) or the total renewable energy supply (total renewable energy) in the total energy supply.
- E_i represents the energy production from the specific renewable energy source or the total renewable energy supply for the given year.
- TE_i represents the total energy supply for the given year.

We will utilize the data provided by the State Statistical Committee for the years 2020, 2021, and 2022 to implement the mathematical model. This data includes the total energy supply and the shares of different renewable energy sources, such as hydropower, biomass and waste, wind power, and solar (photovoltaic) power, expressed as percentages of the total energy consumption. Additionally, we have a share of the total renewable energy supply in total energy consumption for each of these years. It is important to note that a limitation of our study is the unavailability of data for the year 2023, as it has not yet been provided by the State Statistical Committee. Therefore, our analysis will be based on the available data up to the year 2022, presented in Table 7.3.

Table 7.3. Renewable Energy Supply, Azerbaijan, last updated on 26 July 2023.

	2020	**2021**	**2022**
Total energy supply	**16,642.8**	**17,566.6**	**18,655.4**
of which:			
Hydropower	92.0	109.8	137.2
Share of hydropower in total energy consumption, in %	0.5	0.6	0.7
Biomass and waste	108.4	102.6	96.1
Share of biomass and waste in total energy consumption, in %	0.7	0.6	0.5
Wind power	8.3	7.9	7.2
Share of wind power in total energy consumption, in %	0.1	0.1	0.1
Solar (photovoltaic) power	4.0	4.8	5.2
Share of solar power (photovoltaic) in total energy consumption, in %	0.0	0.0	0.0
Total renewable energy supply	212.7	225.1	245.9
Share of total renewable energy supply in total energy consumption, in %	1.3	1.3	1.3

Source: State Statistical Committee of the Republic of Azerbaijan (2023).

Following the methodology outlined in the combined mathematical model, we formulated specific equations to calculate the percentage shares of each renewable energy source and the total renewable energy supply in the total energy supply. These equations were applied to the available data for three years from 2020 to 2022, enabling us to derive the following results:

Hydropower share (%):

$$SRHP_{2020} = \frac{134.6}{16642.8} \times 100 \approx 0.81\%$$

$$SRHP_{2021} = \frac{92.0}{17566.6} \times 100 \approx 0.52\%$$

$$SRHP_{2022} = \frac{137.2}{18655.4} \times 100 \approx 0.73\%$$

Biomass and Waste Share (%):

$$SRBW_{2020} = \frac{115.9}{16642.8} \times 100 \approx 0.70\%$$

$$SRBW_{2021} = \frac{108.4}{17566.6} \times 100 \approx 0.62\%$$

$$SRBW_{2022} = \frac{102.6}{18655.4} \times 100 \approx 0.55\%$$

Wind Power share (%):

$$SRWP_{2020} = \frac{9.1}{16642.8} \times 100 \approx 0.05\%$$

$$SRWP_{2021} = \frac{8.3}{17566.6} \times 100 \approx 0.05\%$$

$$SRWP_{2022} = \frac{7.9}{18655.4} \times 100 \approx 0.04\%$$

Solar (Photovoltaic) Power share (%):

$$SRSP_{2020} = \frac{4.0}{16642.8} \times 100 \approx 0.02\%$$

$$SRSP_{2021} = \frac{4.8}{17566.6} \times 100 \approx 0.03\%$$

$$\text{SRSP}_{2022} = \frac{5.2}{18655.6} \times 100 \approx 0.03\%$$

The total renewable energy supply share (%) is following:

$$\text{SRRE}_{2020} = \frac{263.4}{16642.8} \times 100 \approx 1.58\%$$

$$\text{SRRE}_{2021} = \frac{212.7}{17566.6} \times 100 \approx 1.21\%$$

$$\text{SRRE}_{2022} = \frac{225.1}{18655.4} \times 100 \approx 1.21\%$$

These calculations were performed using the provided total energy supply and renewable energy source data for the years 2020, 2021, and 2022, following the liberation of Karabakh and Azerbaijani territories. The total renewable energy supply share was calculated as approximately 1.58%, 1.21%, and 1.21% for the respective years. These calculations provide insights into the contribution of renewable energy sources to the overall energy landscape in the Karabakh region, facilitating the assessment of the feasibility and potential impact of implementing Swiss green economy policies. By applying these equations to the available data, we gained insights into the contribution of renewable energy to the overall energy landscape. These findings are instrumental in guiding sustainable development strategies in the Karabakh region and Azerbaijan, emphasizing the importance of renewable energy in achieving environmental and economic goals.

Subsequently, the second methodology involves evaluating the Swiss innovation policy. The Innovation Index for Switzerland is a comprehensive assessment that considers various dimensions crucial for measuring a country's innovation potential. The index is calculated based on several key categories, each comprising sub-categories with assigned weights reflecting their relative importance. In this analysis, we delve into six main categories: Institutions, Human Capital and Research, Infrastructure, Market Sophistication, Business Sophistication, and Creative Outputs. The methodology involves assigning weights to sub-categories within each main category and calculating weighted averages. These weights are determined based on the perceived significance of each sub-category in contributing to the overall innovation landscape. The resulting scores are then averaged to derive the final Innovation Index for Switzerland. According to the main categories of Switzerland in the Global Innovation Index 2023, the provided Innovation Index scores are derived through a weighted average method. The sub-categories within each main category contribute to the overall score, with their weights reflecting their perceived importance in the assessment. The formula for the weighted average takes into account the weight assigned to each sub-category multiplied by its corresponding score. This methodology provides an evaluation of Switzerland's innovation performance by considering various factors within distinct categories. The weighted averages offer insights into the country's strengths and weaknesses across different dimensions, facilitating a comprehensive understanding of its innovation landscape (WIPO, 2023).

The formula used for the weighted average is

$$\text{Weighted Average} = \sum_{i=1}^{n} (\text{Weight}_i \times \text{Score}_i)$$

where:

Weight_i is the weight assigned to the *i*th sub-category,
Score_i is the score of the *i*th sub-category,
n is the total number of sub-categories.

The weights used in these calculations are based on the perceived importance of each sub-category within its main category (WIPO, 2023).

Institutions:

$$(0.2 \times 87.3) + (0.2 \times 85.3) + (0.1 \times 77.8) + (0.2 \times 92.8) + (0.2 \times 92.8) + (0.1 \times 87.1) + (0.1 \times 92.7) + (0.1 \times 10.1)$$

Human Capital and Research:

$$(0.2 \times 59.8) + (0.2 \times 61.9) + (0.2 \times 45.6) + (0.2 \times 71.8)$$

Infrastructure:

$$(0.2 \times 64.3) + (0.2 \times 83.7) + (0.1 \times 50.5) + (0.1 \times 90.9) + (0.1 \times 69.8)$$

Market Sophistication:

$$(0.2 \times 64.4) + (0.2 \times 70.1) + (0.2 \times 59.5) + (0.1 \times 63.7) + (0.1 \times 76.8)$$

Business Sophistication:

$$(0.2 \times 65.5) + (0.2 \times 67.1) + (0.2 \times 76.8)$$

Creative Outputs:

$$(0.2 \times 68.5) + (0.2 \times 67.5) + (0.1 \times 53.0) + (0.1 \times 86.1)$$

Now, we can calculate the final Innovation Index for Switzerland by averaging the scores from each main category.

$$\text{Final Innovation Index for Switzerland} = \frac{\text{Six main categories}}{6}$$

Substituting the calculated values:

$$\text{Final II for CH} = \frac{66.806 + 57.775 + 73.26 + 65.195 + 69.113 + 66.226}{6}$$

$$= \frac{398.369}{6} \approx 66.395$$

As seen from the result, the final Innovation Index for Switzerland, based on the provided data and calculations, is approximately 66.395. Adapting the Swiss Innovation System to evaluate the Karabakh region involves a contextual assessment of the region's innovation landscape. By aligning the key categories—*Institutions, Human Capital and Research, Infrastructure, Market Sophistication, Business Sophistication, and Creative Outputs* (WIPO, 2023) with the specific characteristics and socio-economic dynamics of Karabakh, we can gauge its innovation potential. Assigning relevant weights to each sub-category based on their perceived importance in the regional context, we can calculate a modified Innovation Index for Karabakh.

Findings

The Karabakh region, characterized by its diverse topography and climatic conditions, offers favorable conditions for wind and solar power generation. Wind farms and solar photovoltaic installations can be deployed in suitable locations to harness renewable energy potential. These projects can contribute to energy diversification, reduce reliance on imported fuels, and enhance energy independence. The results derived from the mathematical model demonstrate the significant contribution of renewable energy sources to the total energy supply in Azerbaijan, including the Karabakh region. The model indicates that hydropower accounts for a consistent share of total energy consumption over the years, ranging from approximately 0.81% to 1.55%. This highlights the reliability and stability of hydropower generation in Azerbaijan, making it a viable option for meeting energy demands in Karabakh. Investing in hydropower projects can capitalize on this renewable resource, providing a reliable source of clean energy while creating employment opportunities and supporting local economies. By harnessing the potential of rivers and streams, Azerbaijan can increase its energy production capacity while minimizing environmental impact. In the country, biomass and waste contribute consistently to the total energy supply, with a share ranging from approximately 0.52% to 0.70%. This underscores the potential of biomass and waste-to-energy projects in Karabakh, utilizing agricultural residues, industrial by-products, and municipal waste to generate electricity and heat. Implementing such projects can address waste management challenges, reduce emissions, and promote sustainable development in the region.

While the shares of wind power and solar power in total energy consumption are relatively small in the initial years, the model reveals a significant increase in their contributions over time. Wind power shows a gradual rise from approximately 0.04% to 0.05%, while solar power demonstrates a more substantial growth from approximately 0.02% to 0.03%. These trends indicate the growing importance of wind and solar energy in Azerbaijan's energy mix, presenting opportunities for expansion in Karabakh. Investing in wind and solar projects can capitalize on the region's renewable energy potential, diversify the energy portfolio, and enhance energy security. By incorporating the insights from the mathematical model, policymakers and stakeholders can justify the importance of renewable energy in Karabakh's economic development and advocate for policies and investments that promote green growth. The model results serve as empirical evidence of the feasibility and effectiveness of renewable energy solutions, providing a strong foundation for the formulation and implementation of green growth strategies in the region.

Furthermore, the analysis of Switzerland's Innovation Index, with its score of approximately 66.395, offers a valuable reference point for assessing the potential application of Swiss green economy policies to the Karabakh region of Azerbaijan. By aligning the categories of the Innovation Index with the unique characteristics of Karabakh, we can develop a tailored framework that addresses the specific challenges and opportunities present in the region. This approach enables policymakers to leverage Switzerland's proven strategies to promote sustainable development, capitalize on renewable energy sources identified in our previous mathematical model, and ultimately foster economic resilience and social well-being in Karabakh.

As seen from Table 7.4, the Swiss Green Economy Policy's application in the Karabakh region of Azerbaijan involves various initiatives across renewable energy, energy efficiency, waste management, water management, sustainable agriculture, biodiversity conservation, green transport, and environmental education. These efforts aim to reduce dependency on fossil fuels, minimize waste generation, conserve water resources, promote sustainable agriculture, protect biodiversity, improve transportation, and raise awareness about environmental issues. Implementation of these measures is crucial for fostering sustainability and resilience in the Karabakh region's development.

Table 7.4. The Application of Swiss Green Economy Policies in the Karabakh Region of Azerbaijan.

Aspect	Swiss Green Economy Policy Application in Karabakh region of Azerbaijan
Renewable Energy	Implementation of solar and wind energy projects to reduce dependency on fossil fuels and promote sustainability. For example, establishing solar farms and wind turbines in suitable locations within the Karabakh region.
Energy Efficiency	Introduction of energy-efficient technologies and practices in infrastructure development and renovation. This includes promoting energy-efficient building designs, implementing energy-saving measures in public facilities, and encouraging the use of energy-efficient appliances and vehicles.

Table 7.4. (*Continued*)

Aspect	Swiss Green Economy Policy Application in Karabakh region of Azerbaijan
Waste Management	Implementation of comprehensive waste management systems to minimize landfill waste and promote recycling and composting. This involves establishing recycling facilities, promoting community recycling programs, and implementing policies to reduce single-use plastics and packaging.
Water Management	Implementation of sustainable water management practices to conserve water resources and mitigate the impact of droughts and water scarcity. This includes promoting water-saving technologies in agriculture, implementing water conservation measures in urban areas, and enhancing water infrastructure for efficient distribution and utilization.
Sustainable Agriculture	Promotion of sustainable agricultural practices to improve productivity while minimizing environmental impact. This involves supporting organic farming methods, promoting agroforestry and permaculture techniques, and providing training and resources to farmers for sustainable land management.
Biodiversity Conservation	Implementation of measures to protect and preserve biodiversity in the Karabakh region's ecosystems. This includes establishing protected areas, promoting habitat restoration initiatives, and implementing wildlife conservation programs to safeguard endangered species and ecosystems.
Green Transport	Promotion of green transportation alternatives to reduce emissions and traffic congestion. This involves investing in public transportation infrastructure, promoting the use of electric vehicles, implementing bike-sharing programs, and creating pedestrian-friendly urban spaces in the Karabakh region.
Environmental Education and Awareness	Implementation of educational programs and campaigns to raise awareness about environmental issues and promote sustainable behavior change. This includes integrating environmental education into school curricula, organizing community outreach events, and providing resources for environmental awareness campaigns in the Karabakh region.

Source: Composed by authors based on the analysis of the chosen study. Data collected from Ministry of Energy of the Republic of Azerbaijan, FOEN, Switzerland.

The government of Azerbaijan, in collaboration with international partners and private investors, can prioritize investments in renewable energy infrastructure in the Karabakh region. This includes the development of hydropower plants, biomass and waste-to-energy facilities, wind farms, and solar photovoltaic installations. The implementation of supportive policies and incentives, such as feed-in tariffs, tax credits, and subsidies, can stimulate private sector investment in renewable energy projects. Clear regulatory frameworks and streamlined permitting processes can facilitate the development of green energy projects in Karabakh. Referring to this, building local capacity in renewable energy technologies through training programs, education initiatives, and knowledge transfer activities can strengthen the skills and expertise necessary for green growth in Karabakh. Collaborating with international partners can facilitate technology transfer and knowledge sharing. To conclude, integrating renewable energy into the national energy strategy of Azerbaijan, with a specific focus on the Karabakh region, can ensure alignment with broader development objectives and sustainability goals. This involves setting targets for renewable energy deployment, establishing regulatory frameworks, and promoting energy efficiency measures.

Conclusions

Overall, the findings underscore the potential for integrating Swiss green economy policies into the Karabakh region's development strategy, highlighting the importance of leveraging renewable energy sources and innovative approaches to foster sustainable growth and resilience. By adapting Switzerland's successful green economy model to the Karabakh context, policymakers can address key challenges such as energy security, environmental sustainability, and socioeconomic development. By aligning the categories of the Innovation Index with the unique characteristics of Karabakh, we can develop a tailored framework that addresses the specific challenges and opportunities present in the region. This approach enables policymakers to leverage Switzerland's proven strategies to promote sustainable development, capitalize on renewable energy sources identified in our previous mathematical model, and ultimately foster economic resilience and social well-being in Karabakh.

Emulating the Swiss green economy model becomes pivotal in fostering sustainable and balanced progress in the Karabakh region. This necessitates essential adjustments in legislation and governance at various levels to address new and intricate concerns. Collaboration between Azerbaijan and Switzerland, along with the private sector, should culminate in the establishment of global sustainable development goals. These goals will guide policy reforms at the national and international levels, aligning with a "bottom-up" approach for comprehensive economic, technical, and social transformation toward sustainable development. Switzerland, as a progressive country with a successful green growth model, serves as an exemplary guide in the regeneration of the Karabakh region. The Swiss commitment to a circular economy and sustainable solutions provides a blueprint for fostering green economies. By leveraging the Swiss model, Azerbaijan can enhance the well-being of its citizens and preserve the natural systems essential for current and future needs. Switzerland's innovative economic policies align with the shared mission of achieving sustainable development in the Karabakh area. The bottom-up approach emphasized by Switzerland, involving civil society in resource-conserving practices, is relevant to Karabakh. Building connections between businesses, academia, and civil society can enhance green awareness. Switzerland's waste management strategies, prioritizing product reuse, can inspire Karabakh's initiatives. Implementing efficient waste management practices aligns with sustainable development goals. This collaboration will not only contribute to the region's long-term growth but also position Azerbaijan as an influential player on the global stage. In conclusion, this study endeavors to bridge the existing gap in the literature by exploring the potential application of Switzerland's green economy policies to the Karabakh region of Azerbaijan. Despite the dearth of prior research in this area, our investigation sheds light on the importance of this topic and its relevance to sustainable development efforts in Karabakh. The absence of scholarly inquiry into this subject underscore the novelty and significance of our study, as it addresses a critical knowledge gap in the field of sustainable development and green economy strategies in the case of Karabakh region. The application of Swiss green growth policies in Karabakh represents a transformative opportunity to foster long-term prosperity, environmental sustainability, and social well-being in the region, aligning with the objectives of the 2030 Agenda for Sustainable Development. Thus, the Swiss green economy model presents a comprehensive framework that can be strategically applied to Karabakh. While certain adaptations are needed to address regional complexities, the fundamental principles of renewable energy, environmental restoration, collaborative research, international partnerships, community engagement, and efficient waste management are highly relevant.

References

Air Center. (2024). Azerbaijan speeds up the green transition by hosting the COP29 UN climate change conference. Retrieved March 01, 2024, from https://aircenter.az/en/single/azerbaijan-speeds-up-the-green-transition-by-hosting-the-cop29-un-climate-change-conference-1393

Apergis, N., & Payne, J. E. (2010). Renewable energy consumption and economic growth: Evidence from a panel of OECD countries. *Energy Policy, 38*(1), 656–660.

Azernews. (2022). *Swiss company interested in deepening co-op with Azerbaijan in liberated territories*. Retrieved December 05, 2022, from https://report.az/en/karabakh/swiss-company-interested-in-deepening-co-op-with-azerbaijan-in-liberated-territories/

Cai, C., Li, L., Tan, Z., Wang, J., Xu, J., & Hou, Y., et al. (2011). Green economy and green jobs: Myth or reality? The case of China's power generation sector. *General Information, 36*(10), 5994–6003.

Engel, D., & Kammen, D. M. (2009). *Green jobs and the clean energy economy*. Copenhagen Climate Council.

ETH Zurich. (2020). Department of Humanities, Social and Political Sciences (D-GESS), Center for Comparative and International Studies (CIS, from 1997), Institute of Science, Technology and Policy (ISTP, from 2015), Institute for Environmental Decisions (IED, until 2014; Geistes-, Sozial- und Staatswissenschaften D-GESS ETH Zürich). Retrieved October 21, 2022, from https://www.ethz.ch/en/the-eth-zurich/portrait/departments-and-institutes/department-d-gess.html

EU4Environment. (2019). *Towards a green economy in Azerbaijan, work in progress – 2019–20*. Retrieved March 03, 2023, from https://www.eu4environment.org/app/uploads/2021/05/Azerbaijan-country-profile-2020-21-second-edition.pdf

Federal Department of the Environment, Transport, Energy and Communications (DETEC). (2020). *Energy strategy 2050*. Retrieved November 30, 2022, from Energy Strategy 2050 - DETEC (admin.ch)

Federal Office for the Environment. (2020). *Green economy action plan*. Retrieved August 07, 2022, from Green Economy Action Plan: priority areas (admin.ch)

Fedlex. (1983). *Federal act on the protection of the environment (Environmental Protection Act, EPA)*. Retrieved June 14, 2023, from SR 814.01 – Federal Act of 7 October 1983 on the Protection of the Environment (Environmental Protection Act, EPA) (admin.ch)

FOEN. (2020). *Political mandate for a green economy*. Retrieved September 25, 2022, from Political mandate for a green economy (admin.ch)

Fulai, S., Flomenhoft, G., Downs, T. J., Grande-Ortiz, M., Graef, D., Scholtens, B., Mol, A. P. J., Sonnenfeld, D. A., Spaargaren, G., Goel, R. K., Hsieh, E. W. H., Scrieciu, S., Steurer, R., Polzin, C., Kostka, G., Ancev, T., Pirgmaier, E., Boons, F., Robèrt, K.-H., ... Hermann, S. (2011). Is the concept of a green economy a useful way of framing policy discussions and policymaking to promote sustainable development? *Natural Resources Forum*, *35*(1), 63–72.

Hajiyeva, N., & Karimli, A. (2021). Economic evaluation of "Green Energy" potential in Nagorno-Karabakh and neighboring regions. *Modern Applied Science*, *15*(3). https://news.unec.edu.az/images/news/2021/elmi_meqale_310521.pdf

Kaur, S., Kumar, R., Singh, K., & Huang, Y. L. (2024). Leveraging artificial intelligence for enhanced sustainable energy management. *Journal of Sustainable Energy, 3*(1), 1–20. https://doi.org/10.56578/jse030101

Lesser, J. A. (2010). Renewable energy and the fallacy of 'green' jobs. *Electricity Journal*, *23*(7), 45–53.

Ministry of Energy. (2021). *The meeting was held with Japanese company TEPSCO*. Retrieved September 05, 2022, from https://minenergy.gov.az/en/xeberler-arxivi/yaponiyanin-tepsco-sirketi-ile-gorus-kecirilib

Ministry of Energy of the Republic of Azerbaijan. (2022). *Memorandums of understanding*. Retrieved February 26, 2023, from https://minenergy.gov.az/en/beynelxalq-muqavileler/anlasma-memorandumlari

Azerbaijan Ministry of Energy. (2024.). Utilization of renewable energy sources in Azerbaijan. Retrieved from https://minenergy.gov.az/en/alternativ-ve-berpa-olunan-enerji/azerbaycanda-berpa-olunan-enerji-menbelerinden-istifade

Ndekwa, A. G., Kalugendo, E., Sood, K., & Grima, S. (2023). An analysis of agribusiness digitalisation transformation of the sub-Saharan African countries small-scale farmers' production distribution. *Research on World Agricultural Economy*, *4*(3), 63–78.

Pearce, D. W., Markandya, A., &Barbier, E. (Eds.). (1989). *Blueprint for a green economy* (Vol. 1). Earthscan.

PwC & WWF. (2020). *Circularity as the new normal future fitting Swiss businesses*. Retrieved March 16, 2023, from Circularity-as-the-new-normal_whitepaper-EN.pdf (wwf.ch)

Rijal, S., Nursaputra, M. A. C., & Dari, H. U. (2024). Flood susceptibility analysis using Frequency Ratio method in Walanae watershed. *International Journal of Sustainable Development and Planning*, *19*(3), 823–832. https://doi.org/10.18280/ijsdp.190302

Sood, K., & Özen, E. (2024). A systematic review of ESG in the insurance industry: Navigating the path to sustainability. *International Journal of Sustainable Development and Planning*, *19*(3), 807–821. https://doi.org/10.18280/ijsdp.190301

State Statistical Committee of the Republic of Azerbaijan. (2023). *Energy*, Retrieved from https://www.stat.gov.az/source/balance_fuel/?lang=en

Swiss Green Economy Symposium (SGES). (2023). Retrieved from Swiss Green Economy Symposium 2023, https://sges.ch/

Swiss National Science Foundation. (2016). *Energy Transition in Switzerland: Challenges and Opportunities*. Retrieved from https://www.snf.ch/en

Swissinfo. (2021). *Giant water battery plant inaugurated in Switzerland*. Retrieved June 20, 2022, from https://www.swissinfo.ch/eng/sci-tech/giant-water-battery-plant-inaugurated-in-switzerland/47888682

TEPSCO. (2021). *The Republic of Azerbaijan electric power development master plan for the green energy zone (GEZ) project contract execution*. Retrieved October 04, 2022, from http://www.tepsco.co.jp/english/topic/etopic_20210517.html

UNEP. (2008). *Green jobs: Towards decent work in a sustainable, low-carbon world*. UNEP, Geneva.

UNEP. (2011). *Towards a green economy: Pathways to sustainable development and poverty eradication – A synthesis for policymakers*. Report, UNEP, Nairobi, Kenya.

WIPO. (2023). *Global innovation index 2023, Innovation in the face of uncertainty*. Retrieved December 11, 2023, from https://www.wipo.int/edocs/pubdocs/en/wipo-pub-2000-2023-en-main-report-global-innovation-index-2023-16th-edition.pdf

World Commission on Environment and Development. (1987). Brundtland report. Switzerland federal office for spatial development ARE. Retrieved July, 7, 2023, from https://www.are.admin.ch/are/en/home/media/publications/sustainable-development/brundtland-report.html

Yerpude, S., Sood, K., & Grima, S. (2022). Blockchain-augmented digital supply chain management: A way to sustainable business. *Journal of Risk and Financial Management*, *16*(1), 7.

Chapter 8

An In-depth Examination of Green Practices in Human Resource Management: Integrating Ecological Responsibility into Human Resource Management

Preeti Sharma and Pawan Kumar

Department of Commerce, University School of Business, Chandigarh University, India

Abstract

Purpose: With a focus on its foundations, significance, applications, and results, this chapter attempts to investigate the idea of Green HRM, or Green Human Resources Management, in the context of changing business environments.

Need for the study: The growing focus on environmental sustainability is a challenge for HR professionals in terms of successfully integrating eco-friendly practices into HR initiatives. The benefits and ramifications of implementing Green HRM are discussed in this paper, which also highlights the growing significance of incorporating environmental issues into HRM processes.

Methodology: The chapter investigates the principles and results of Green HRM by conducting a thorough analysis of the body of existing literature and empirical investigations. The influence of eco-friendly HRM on work-related attitudes, productivity, resource efficiency, waste reduction, work–life balance, cost savings, and employee performance and retention is examined using a qualitative approach.

Findings: The results indicate that implementing Green HRM has a favorable impact on a number of organizational functioning elements. In addition to encouraging resource efficiency and waste reduction, it improves

Green Management: A New Paradigm in the World of Business, 121–135

doi:10.1108/978-1-83797-442-920241008

staff attitudes, productivity, and retention. Green HRM also helps to create workplaces that are socially and environmentally conscious.

Practical implications: The study provides useful insights for HR practitioners by highlighting the core components of Green HRM that enhance conventional HRM methods. Organizations can develop sustainable workplaces that meet environmental goals while improving overall performance and employee well-being by integrating eco-friendly activities into HR strategies.

Keywords: Business climate; HR practitioners; green HRM; ecological responsibility; HR strategies; employee performance; sustainability

JEL Classifications: Q56; M12; O32; Q01

1. Introduction

Global environmental concerns force businesses to transition to eco-friendly policies and environmentally conscious operations. According to international guidelines for preserving and protecting the environment, businesses must create ecologically friendly strategies. With everyone becoming more environmentally conscious, including consumers, employees, and investors, "green human resource management (also known as green HRM or GHRM)" is becoming a major field in behavioral sciences (Mehta & Chugan, 2015). Many companies now utilize green HRM strategies when conducting business abroad (Arunrajah et al., 2015). Businesses must undertake formal environmental procedures due to developing international environmental standards and growing global awareness (Ndekwa et al., 2023; Sood & Özen, 2024; Yerpude et al., 2022).

The need to address environmental sustainability has become more pressing in recent years, and this has forced organizations worldwide to reconsider their methods and adopt eco-friendly strategies in various fields. Of these domains, human resource management (HRM) is one of the most important ones for incorporating ecological responsibility into business plans. The concept of green human resource management (Green HRM), which emphasizes integrating environmentally sustainable practices into HRM strategies, was born out of the convergence of environmental concerns and HRM principles (Renwick et al., 2013). In the face of businesses' challenges in navigating the complex landscape of Sustainability, green human resource management (GRRM) becomes a strategic priority that unites environmental stewardship and human capital management to build organizational resilience and competitiveness.

The need for environmental Sustainability has grown in importance in today's business environment, pushing companies in all industries to include eco-friendly practices in their operational plans. Integrating ecological responsibility into organizational practices is an important domain of human resource management

(HRM) in light of the paradigm shift towards sustainability. The concept of green human resource management (Green HRM) emerged from the convergence of environmental concerns with HRM concepts. Its main focus is on incorporating environmentally friendly practices into HRM strategies (Rijal et al., 2024; Kaur et al., 2024).

The increased acknowledgment of environmental sustainability as a strategic objective for enterprises highlights the importance of incorporating ecological responsibility into HRM processes. Studies show that environmental sustainability improves organizational resilience and competitiveness while reducing the risks of resource depletion and climate change (Bansal, 2005). Green HRM helps achieve this goal by encouraging employees to act in an environmentally responsible manner, making the best use of available resources, and lowering the carbon footprint of businesses.

Adopting Green HRM has several benefits for companies that are dedicated to Sustainability, but there are drawbacks as well (Renwick et al., 2013). Overcoming resistance to change is one of the main problems since stakeholders in the business, and employees may be reluctant to adopt eco-friendly practices that are outside of the norm. Furthermore, a lack of knowledge about the advantages of Green HRM and budget limitations may prevent its wider adoption. Nevertheless, these difficulties offer chances for businesses to promote creativity and develop an eco-friendly culture.

Given this context, this research article aims to present a thorough analysis of green practices in HRM, emphasizing incorporating ecological responsibility into HRM tactics.

The study is directed by the following goals:

- to clarify the basic ideas and precepts that underpin green human resource management;
- to investigate the opportunities and difficulties related to implementing Green HRM practices;
- to investigate the possible advantages and results of incorporating ecological responsibility into human resource management tactics; and
- to find best practices and useful information for businesses looking to start green HRM projects.

According to several research findings (Jackson et al., 2011), a business's ability to run efficiently depends on its use of environmental practices, and HRM practices strengthen this relationship. Lee (2009) defines "green management" as the process through which businesses design an environmental management plan to manage their environmental impact. Researchers like Brio et al. (2007) argue that we must incorporate green human resource management (HRM) methods into our daily and professional lives. According to research by Rashid et al. (2006), workers' moral principles are positively impacted when actively participating in environmental management systems. Furthermore, it encourages individuals to adopt environmentally sensitive attitudes and behaviors in their daily lives.

In conclusion, by thoroughly examining the concepts, difficulties, and consequences of green human resource management for organizational sustainability, this research study hopes to add to the growing body of knowledge on the subject (Renwick et al., 2013). This study intends to inform practice and policy in ways that promote environmental stewardship and boost organizational resilience in the face of global environmental concerns by analyzing the integration of ecological responsibility into HRM strategies.

2. Literature Review

The repository of knowledge on green human resource management, or "green HRM," has grown dramatically in recent years as environmental sustainability is becoming increasingly acknowledged as a crucial requirement for businesses all over the world. Academics have looked into several facets of green human resource management (HRM), including its theoretical foundations, applications, and possible advantages for long-term organizational viability. The conceptualization of the frameworks and guiding concepts that support environmentally friendly HR practices is a fundamental component of the literature on green HRM. Renwick et al. (2013) provide an early conceptual framework for Green HRM and outline its main components: employee involvement, environmental awareness, and green performance management. Expanding upon this concept, offer an integrated model of Green HRM that highlights how HRM processes should be in line with environmental goals. It also highlights how employee involvement, leadership, and culture play a key part in advancing sustainability activities within businesses.

Empirical research has looked at the application and results of Green HRM practices in various organizational situations in addition to conceptual frameworks. The adoption of environmentally friendly HR practices in the manufacturing sector is examined by research by Rehman et al. (2017), emphasizing the function of organizational culture and leadership in supporting green initiatives. Similarly, Ahmad et al. (2018) investigate how Green HRM affects organizational performance and discover links between green practices and profitable outcomes like market share and profitability.

Moreover, the literature on green human resource management emphasizes the significance of company culture and employee participation in promoting environmental sustainability. Research by Delmas and Pekovic (2018) and Raimi-Abraham et al. (2020) highlights the importance of top-down support and communication in driving environmental activities. These studies also look at leadership's function in encouraging employees' green practices. Furthermore, research by Robertson and Carleton (2019) indicates that an effective environmental ethos can encourage the adoption of green practices at all organizational levels by highlighting the influence of organizational culture on employees' attitudes and behaviors toward Sustainability.

Scholars have investigated institutional pressures and external variables that influence the adoption of Green HRM practices, in addition to organizational issues. Research by Jabbour et al. (2021) highlights the significance of institutional context in influencing the adoption and application of green practices by examining the impact of stakeholder pressures and regulatory frameworks on firms' sustainability initiatives. Similar to this, research by Sroufe et al. (2023) and Jabbour et al. (2022) examines how supply chain sustainability influences Green HRM practices, highlighting the significance of partnerships and teamwork in advancing eco-friendly efforts across value chains.

Future studies should address the noticeable gap in Green Human resource management literature, which is primarily Western-centric, given the significance of Asian economic growth in environmental management (Renwick et al., 2013, p. 3). According to Fayyazia et al. (2015), incorporating environmental management into human resource management (HRM) is desirable, vital, and extremely important. A corporation must put more effort into its HRM practices to properly manage its environment.

Regarding HR sustainability, many HR directors indicate they want to see their companies become environmentally conscious. Several empirical studies using different measures demonstrate how environmental management techniques affect the performance of organizations (Yang et al., 2010). A good environmental management system integrates environmental goals and tactics with a company's strategic growth objectives, according to Haden et al. (2009). Since implementing green practices has been demonstrated to boost earnings, Daily and Huang (2001) stress the necessity for enterprises to create a balance between environmental preservation and industrial expansion (Murari & Bhandari, 2011). A company can successfully implement an environmental management system (EMS) by skillfully integrating environmental goals and objectives into a comprehensive strategic development plan (Haden et al., 2009). Researchers have confirmed that human resource management (HRM) methods help build human capital (Boselie et al., 2001).

The chapter focuses on GHRM, which is composed of two primary elements, as Dutta (2012) delineates: the conservation of investment for learning and the adoption of ecologically sustainable HR practices. According to Mandip (2012), "green human resources" refers to utilizing workforce contacts to advance endeavors, strengthen employee commitment, and increase public understanding of sustainability issues. Integrating environmental responsibility into an organization's corporate mission statement is primarily the duty of the HR department. Given that workers may carry over these consumption patterns into their personal lives, green human resource management (HRM) focuses on how employees behave environmentally both inside and outside of the office (Muster & Schrader, 2011).

When all factors are considered, the literature on green human resource management (HRM) offers insightful information about how to include ecological responsibility into HRM strategies, outlining both the advantages and disadvantages of implementing green practices in businesses. Scholars have increased our understanding of the mechanisms by which Green HRM contributes to organizational Sustainability by combining theoretical frameworks and empirical evidence (Sharma et al., 2024). This has practical consequences for both HR practitioners and policymakers. Nevertheless, future studies must examine the long-term impacts of green human resource management (HRM) on worker satisfaction, company culture, and environmental performance. They also need to investigate how technology and innovation contribute to advancing sustainable HRM practices in the digital era.

3. Objectives

The chapter aims to clarify the tenets, policies, and practices of GHRM. To accomplish this, the study is organized into four main categories. First, an overview of GHRM research is done. The primary Green HRM initiatives are then determined based on the knowledge gained from this literature analysis. Secondly, suggestions are made for areas that HR professionals engaged in Green HRM practices should focus on. Finally, the study seeks to identify particular topics within the Green HRM domain worthy of additional research, providing a foundation for future studies.

3.1. Justification of the Study

Incorporating green management principles into HR strategy is the basic idea behind the recently popularized "green HRM" notion. Growing awareness of environmental management and sustainable development has led to the emergence of green human resource management (Green HRM) as a separate topic of study. Examining the fundamentals, importance, uses, and outcomes of Green HRM is the main aim of this chapter, which also aims to further knowledge in this field.

There are several uses for this research. Its primary goal is to assist HR employees in embracing and implementing Green HR practices. Second, it aims to support laborers and unions in implementing GHRM procedures and guidelines that protect and improve the health and welfare of employees. Thirdly, academics will gain a broader comprehension of green management, including human resource management. Finally, the chapter aims to participate in the continuing investigation and advancement of the subject by laying the groundwork for future research projects.

3.2. Methodology

The foundation of this qualitative study is a thorough analysis of the corpus of prior research on green HRM. A literature review is essential since it makes organizing research findings easier and helps build a trustworthy body of knowledge in this sector (Tranfield et al., 2003). The research employed an archival methodology, carrying out a methodical examination of the literature with a particular objective.

In order to do this, papers found in databases including Sage, Taylor and Francis Online, SpringerLink, ScienceDirect, JSTOR, Wiley Online Library, and Emerald were carefully examined utilizing a methodological strategy specifically designed to meet the goals of this investigation. Apart from these databases, additional data sources included books, journals, e-papers, and websites. Through the use of a variety of scholarly and informative sources, this holistic approach guarantees a thorough investigation of the topic.

3.3. Defining "Green"

According to The Oxford Paperback Dictionary (1979), "green" is described as being between blue and yellow, evocative of growing grass, and connected to developing, unripe, inexperienced, and pale qualities. As a result, the term "green" has several meanings, most of which are associated with the natural world. "Green" is a phrase frequently used to refer to eco-friendliness in the context of the environment.

3.3.1. Green HRM

According to Deshwal (2015), "green human resources management" or "green HRM" refers to the use of human resource management (HRM) rules to promote the sustainable use of resources within enterprises. It includes all practices, guidelines, and laws designed to make workers conscious of environmental issues for the company's good, the environment, society, and each person (Opatha & Arulrajah, 2014).

Green HRM aims to develop, support, and maintain environmentally conscious behavior in each employee so they can fully participate in four roles: preservationist, conservationist, non-polluter, and creative (Sharma et al., 2023). Therefore, environmental movements inside businesses view it as a tactical method to guarantee environmental preservation (Shaikh, 2012).

Greening or aligning with business environmental goals requires identifying green human resource needs. Green talents, green attitudes, green actions, and green results are the four categories into which these needs are divided. These five main areas of green human requirements can be handled separately, even though they are interconnected. This highlights the whole approach of green HRM in supporting environmental stewardship and organizational Sustainability. These specifications and pertinent measurements are depicted in Fig. 8.1.

Green behavior refers to the acts and practices that employees engage in that are ecologically friendly and demonstrate their dedication to sustainable practices. "Green abilities" describe the knowledge, skills, and abilities that allow workers to support organizational environmental goals effectively. Green attitudes are the ideas and beliefs that employees hold that are environmentally conscientious and that impact how they approach their work and make decisions that align with green goals, see Fig. 8.2.

3.4. Critical Role of Green HRM

In the past, meeting shareholders' expectations and achieving high economic performance were the main markers of business success. Nevertheless, modern standards have moved beyond material and financial success. Nowadays, businesses must reduce their environmental impact and consider social and environmental

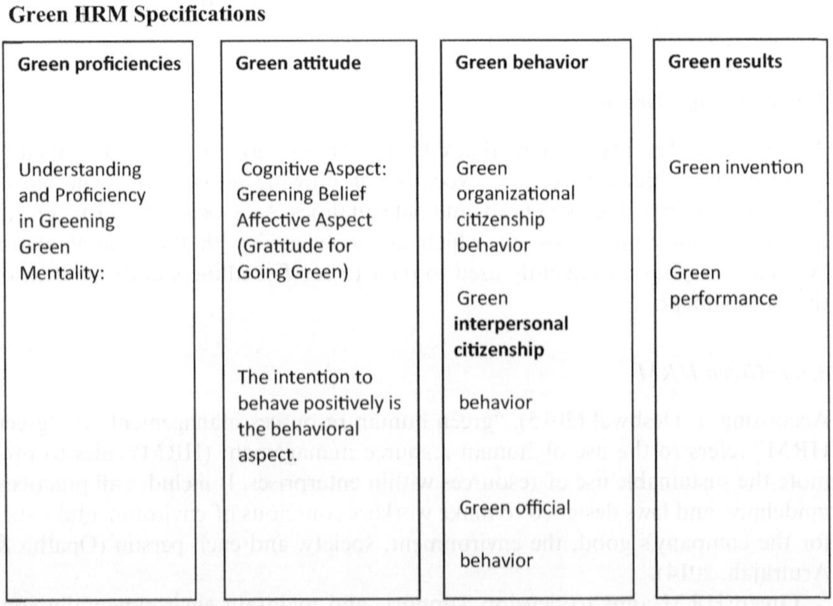

Fig. 8.1. Green Human Resource Requirements. *Source*: Opatha and Arulrajah (2014).

issues in addition to their financial objectives (Sudin, 2011). This change paved the way for corporate environmentalism, also known as green management, which became a global phenomenon in the 2000s and a strategic focus in the 1990s (Lee, 2009).

Daily and Huang (2001) state that organizations must balance protecting and improving natural habitats and promoting industrial progress. Because implementing ecologically sustainable practices has been shown to provide benefits, the idea of being "green and competitive" has gained traction (Molina-Azorin et al., 2009; Wagner, 2007).

Using green practices has been linked to several benefits for businesses. These include enhancing organizational culture, encouraging teamwork, improving operational performance, and lowering total costs (Jackson et al., 2011). Managing environmental systems is believed to improve synchronization with other

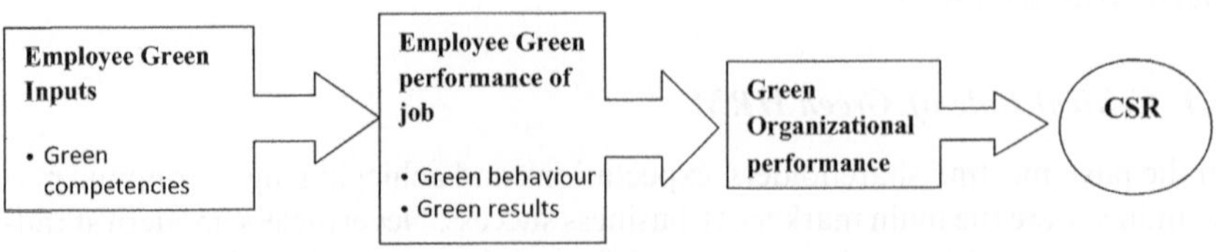

Fig. 8.2. Employee Green Inputs and Employee Green Performance of Job. *Source*: Opatha and Arulrajha (2014).

business management techniques (Wagner, 2007). Scholars stress that integrating environmental practices into HRM practices and organizational well-being are mutually exclusive

According to Pawar (2016), implementing green HRM in the workplace can have several positive effects on people and businesses, such as higher employee retention rates, better public perception, the capacity to draw in more qualified applicants, higher productivity, sustainable resource use, a decrease in environmentally harmful behaviour, lower utility costs, a reduction in environmental impact, and possible tax benefits and rebates. Businesses adopting green HRM practices also benefit from increased commercial opportunities provided by this strategy (Khanna & Sharma, 2024).

3.4.1. Green HRM Process

The human resource department is essential to implementing green policies and developing a sustainable organizational culture. Thus, green process are essential to achieving environmental objectives at every stage of human resource management, from recruiting to hiring. According to Cherian and Jacob's (2012) research, particular elements have a marked influence on how employees adopt green practices. Several elements, including hiring policies, educational efforts, incentives, and green remuneration and benefits, influence the organization's ability to achieve desired employee green performance and input. This section of the article provides an overview of the green HRM process, including green hiring, employee relations, performance management and assessment, training, and development (Fig. 8.3).

A range of green practices are included in each HRM job, some of which are widely accepted as standard. For every green HRM function, there are summaries of novel and current approaches in the next area.

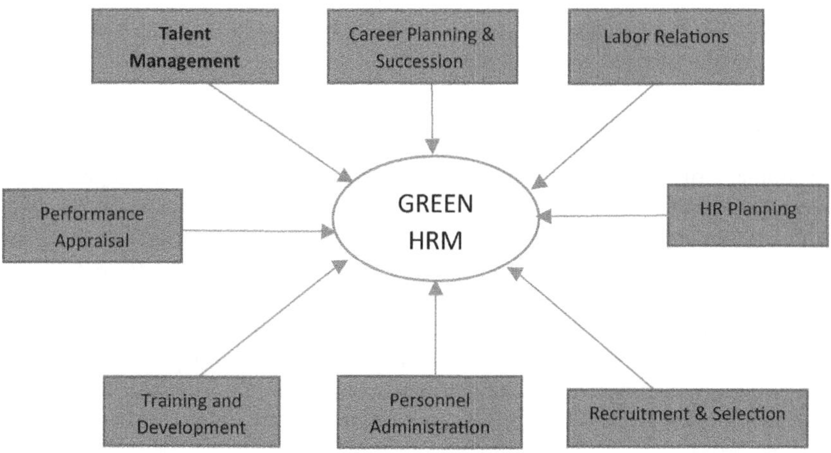

Fig. 8.3. Process of Green HRM. *Source*: Deshwal (2015).

3.4.2. Green HR Planning

Many companies estimate the number of employees – of all different kinds – required to carry out corporate environmental management initiatives. Projects, plans, and guidelines like ISO 14001, cleaner production, responsible care, and others could be a part of these activities.

3.4.3. Green Recruitment

The process of locating and employing new personnel with a thorough awareness of environmental systems, conservation terminology, and sustainable practices is known as "green recruitment." Ensuring new personnel are knowledgeable about environmental systems and green practices helps the firm manage its environmental impact effectively (Wehrmeyer, 1996). Improving recruitment potential and obtaining top-notch staff are major difficulties in the talent war to draw in the most creative and innovative people (Renwick et al., 2013). Companies must also understand how to recruit new talent successfully.

3.4.4. Green Induction

New hire orientation programs should be created to ease their transition into an eco-friendly workplace culture. A company's induction programs must prioritize green factors such as worker health and safety and environmentally friendly workspaces (Deshwal, 2015).

3.4.5. Green Training and Development

Green training and development aims to teach employees how to work more productively, save energy, use resources sensibly, and lessen their environmental effects. This strategy offers a chance to involve employees in tackling environmental issues (Zoogah, 2011). Perron et al. (2006) conducted a study that utilized a multiple case study methodology to determine how green training and development contribute to increased corporate value.

3.4.6. Green Performance Appraisal

Attainment of the organization's environmental objectives is contingent upon executing GHRM. In order to help a business accomplish its strategic goals, performance management – a continuous communication process between an employee's supervisor and the organization throughout the year – is essential.

It protects environmental management efforts from harm by incorporating environmental management into a performance management system. Since it directs employee performance toward the environmental performance that the company requires, green performance management is especially important for the long-term success of green management initiatives (Jabbour & Santos, 2008).

3.4.7. Green Learning and Development

Training, development, and learning initiatives should include programs, seminars, and workshops to provide staff members with knowledge and abilities linked to environmental management, green practices, and attitudes. Rotations through green duties in the workplace should be a segment of future career development plans for skilled green managers. Materials development is necessary to improve employees' environmental management skills and knowledge.

3.4.8. Green Compensation and Reward Management

It is important for incentive and compensation schemes to appropriately recognize contributions to green management. Pay plans should be tailored to staff members' accomplishments and their pursuit of green skills (Deshwal, 2015). Rewards for employees who implement eco-friendly practices can take several forms, such as cash, non-cash, or recognition-based incentives.

3.4.9. Green Employee Relations

When employees actively participate in green projects, the possibility of improved green management increases when employee objectives, abilities, motivations, and perceptions are met. Research indicates that integrating workers into environmental management (EM) can enhance EM systems through waste reduction, resource optimization, and workplace pollution reduction. Employee studies show that empowerment of the individual develops self-discipline, independent thinking, and problem-solving skills, which in turn improves output and performance (Wee & Quazi, 2005).

4. Research Gap and Scope for Further Research

The material that has already been published was thoroughly examined in order to undertake this investigation. The author has tried to provide interested readers, researchers, and academics with a methodical organization of the concepts, procedures, specifications, and challenges aligned with GHRM. These shortcomings include a thorough summary of the breadth and scope of new literature, a clearly stated research goal, and a process model. More theoretical and empirical study is required to fill these gaps and broaden our understanding of green human resource management. In-depth qualitative and quantitative research is encouraged by researchers and authors interested in Green HRM to further this discipline.

5. Conclusion

The advent of green HRM is a recent development in the field of human resource management (HRM), posing new difficulties for HR professionals. This study used information from a thorough literature analysis to investigate the fundamentals, importance, practices, specifications, and difficulties related to green human resource management. Ensuring the subject was thoroughly examined was the goal.

> HR professionals need to consider the environment when creating HR strategies and putting into practice HR policies and procedures that align with environmental management. Adopting improved HR policies is more likely if HR professionals thoroughly investigate and assess HR practices that align with environmental management, even with the extra obstacles presented by green HRM.

> The study's goal is to direct researchers in identifying particular domains where the notion of GHRM might not be fully integrated or applied.

Managerial Implications:

The research results on green human resource management (GHRM) have important managerial ramifications for companies looking to include eco-friendly practices in their HR plans. First, HR professionals need to change how they think about GHRM practices because they are crucial to their acceptance and execution. When creating HR policies and processes, managers should prioritize the environment and ensure that they support the organization's larger objectives of sustainability and eco-consciousness.

The necessity of having a thorough awareness of green HRM practices across all HR functions is one important managerial aspect. Every HR domain should incorporate eco-friendly procedures, including hiring, performance reviews, training, and employee relations. Green HR planning is essential to guarantee a trained and informed staff for environmental projects and activities.

Organizations should also spend money on green hiring techniques to attract candidates who understand sustainable practices and environmental systems. Green induction programs ought to be created to make it easier for new workers to fit in with an environmentally conscious corporate culture. This includes eco-friendly training and development programs that enable staff members to operate in more sustainable ways, encouraging an ongoing culture of learning and advancement.

Environmental goals must be incorporated into performance appraisal systems, connecting individual employee ambitions with the organization's larger sustainability agenda. Pay and reward management should also acknowledge and reward employees who contribute to green projects, matching their financial rewards to their environmental responsibility. Enhancing employee engagement, improving company culture, and having a beneficial environmental impact are all possible outcomes of successfully implementing green HRM practices.

Finally, the study's management implications highlight how crucial it is for HR professionals to adopt and use GHRM techniques on a proactive basis. In an increasingly environmentally sensitive global landscape, by doing this, firms may build a workplace that supports environmental goals and enhances employee satisfaction, retention, and overall economic performance.

References

Abbott, R., Abbott, T. D., Abraham, S., Acernese, F., Ackley, K., Adams, C., & Bruno, G. I. O. V. A. N. N. I. (2020). GW190521: A binary black hole merger with a total mass of 150 M☉. *Physical Review Letters*, *125*(10), 101102.

Ahmad, N., Ahuja, S. D., Akkerman, O. W., Alffenaar, J. W. C., Anderson, L. F., Baghaei, P., & Menzies, D. (2018). Treatment correlates of successful outcomes in pulmonary multidrug-resistant tuberculosis: An individual patient data meta-analysis. *The Lancet*, *392*(10150), 821–834.

Arunrajah, A. A., Opatha, H. H. D. N. P., & Nawaratne, N. N. J. (2015). Green human resource management practices: A review. *Sri Lankan Journal of Human Resource Management*, *5*(1), 1–16.

Arulrajah, A. A., Opatha, H. H. D. N. P., & Nawaratne, N. N. J. (2016). Employee green performance of job: A systematic attempt towards measurement. *Sri Lankan Journal of Human Resource Management*, *6*(1).

Bansal, P. (2005). Evolving sustainably: A longitudinal study of corporate sustainable development. *Strategic Management Journal*, *26*(3), 197–218.

Boselie, P., Paauwe, J., & Jansen, P. (2001). Human resource management and performance: Lessons from the Netherlands. *International Journal of Human Resource Management*, *12*(7), 1107–1125.

Cherian, J. (2015). Emergence of digital publishing–a great challenge to the print publications. *Procedia Economics and Finance*, *23*, 576–586.

Daily, B., & Huang, S. (2001). Achieving sustainability through attention to human resource factors in environmental management. *International. Journal of Operations & Production Management*, *21*(12), 1539–1552. https://doi.org/10.1108/01443570110410892

Del Brío, J. Á., Fernandez, E., & Junquera, B. (2007). Management and employee involvement in achieving an environmental action-based competitive advantage: An empirical study. *The International Journal of Human Resource Management*, *18*(4), 491–522.

Delmas, M. A., & Pekovic, S. (2018). Corporate sustainable innovation and employee behavior. *Journal of Business Ethics*, 150, 1071–1088.

Deshwal, P. (2015). Green HRM: An organizational strategy of greening people. *International Journal of Applied Research*, *1*(13), 176–181.

Dutta, S. (2012). Greening people: A strategic dimension. *ZENITH: International Journal of Business Economics & Management Research*, *2*, 143–148.

Fayyazia, M., Shahbazmoradib, S., Afsharc, Z., & Shahbazmoradic, M. R. (2015). Investigating the barriers of the green human resource management implementation in oil industry. *Management Science Letters*, *5*, 101–108.

Jabbour, C. J. C., & Santos, F. C. A. (2008). The central role of human resource management in the search for sustainable organizations. *The International Journal of Human Resource Management*, 19(12), 2133–2154.

Kaur, S., Kumar, R., Singh, K., & Huang, Y. L. (2024). Leveraging artificial intelligence for enhanced sustainable energy management. *Journal of Sustainable Energy*, *3*(1), 1–20. https://doi.org/10.56578/jse030101

Khanna, K., & Sharma, V. (2024). Business decision-making with an analytical approach: A new leadership pattern. Global Financial Analytics and Business Forecasting.

https://www.scopus.com/inward/record.uri?eid=2-s2.0-85184428077&partnerID=40&md5=f70a811294cc3df9d00cfd4cf25735f3

Lee, K. H. (2009). Why and how to adopt green management into business organizations: The case study of Korean SMEs in manufacturing industry. *Management Decision*, *47*(7), 1101–1121.

Mandip, G. (2012). Green HRM: People management commitment to environmental sustainability. *Research Journal of Recent Sciences*, ISSN, 2277, 2502.

McNally, R. J., & Frueh, B. C. (2012). Why we should worry about malingering in the VA system: Comment on Jackson et al.(2011). *Journal of Traumatic Stress*, *25*(4), 454–456.

Mehta, K., & Chugan, K. P. (2015). Green HRM in pursuit of environmentally sustainable business. *Universal Journal of Industrial and Business Management*, *3*(3), 74–81. https://doi.org/10.13189/ujibm.2015.030302

Molina-Azorin, J. F., Claver-Cortés, E., López-Gamero, M. D., & Tarí, J. J. (2009). Green management and financial performance. A literature review. *Management Decision*, *47*(7), 1080–1100. https://doi.org/10.1108/00251740910978313

Murari, K., & Bhandari, M. (2011). Green HR: Going green with pride. *Journal of Social Welfare and Management*, *3*, 107–110.

Muster, V., & Schrader, U. (2011). Green work-life balance: A new perspective for Green HRM. *Zeitschrift Fur Personalforschung*, *25*, 140–156.

Ndekwa, A. G., Kalugendo, E., Sood, K., & Grima, S. (2023). An analysis of agribusiness digitalisation transformation of the sub-Saharan African countries small-scale farmers' production distribution. *Research on World Agricultural Economy*, *4*(3), 63–78.

Pawar, B. S. (2016). Workplace spirituality and employee well-being: An empirical examination. *Employee Relations*, *38*(6), 975–994.

Rashid, A., Hollington, P. A., Harris, D., & Khan, P. (2006). On-farm seed priming for barley on normal, saline and saline -sodic soils in North West Frontier Province, Pakistan. *European Journal of Agronomy*, *24*(3), 276–281.

Rijal, S., Nursaputra, M. A. C., & Dari, H. U. (2024). Flood susceptibility analysis using frequency ratio method in Walanae watershed. *International Journal of Sustainable Development and Planning*, *19*(3), 823–832. https://doi.org/10.18280/ijsdp.190302

Renwick, D. W., Redman, T., & Maguire, S. (2013). Green human resource management: A review and research agenda. *International Journal of Management Reviews*, 15(1), 1–14.

Robertson, J. L., & Carleton, E. (2018). Uncovering how and when environmental leadership affects employees' voluntary pro-environmental behavior. *Journal of Leadership & Organizational Studies*, *25*(2), 197–210.

Sharma, V., Gupta, M., & Jangir, K. (2024). Exploring the impact of risk factors on profitability in commercial banking in India: A PLS-SEM analysis approach. In N. Kumar, K. Sood, E. Özen, & S. Grima (Eds.), *The framework for resilient industry: A holistic approach for developing economies* (pp. 89–107). Emerald Publishing Limited. https://doi.org/10.1108/978-1-83753-734-120241007

Sharma, V., Taneja, S., Gupta, M., & Ozen, E. (2023). Impact of service quality on behavioural intention to use fin tech payment services: An extension of SERVEQUAL model. *Asia Pacific Journal of Information Systems*, *33*(4), 1093–1117.

Sood, K., & Özen, E. (2024). A systematic review of ESG in the insurance industry: Navigating the path to sustainability. *International Journal of Sustainable Development and Planning*, *19*(3), 807–821. https://doi.org/10.18280/ijsdp.190301

de Sousa Jabbour, A. B. L., Jabbour, C. J. C., Choi, T. M., & Latan, H. (2022). 'Better together': Evidence on the joint adoption of circular economy and industry 4.0 technologies. *International Journal of Production Economics*, 252, 108581.

Sudin, S. (2011). Fairness of and satisfaction with performance appraisal process. *Journal of Global Management*, 2(1), 66–83.

Tranfield, D., Denyer, D., & Smart, P. (2003). Towards a methodology for developing evidence-informed management knowledge by means of systematic review. *British Journal of Management*, *14*(3), 207–222.

Wagner, M. (2007). Integration of environmental management with other managerial functions of the firm. Empirical effects on drivers of economic performance. *Long Range Planning*, *40*(6), 611–628. https://doi.org/10.1016/j.lrp.2007.08.001

Waite, M. (Ed.). (2012). *Paperback Oxxford English Dictionary*. Oxford University Press, USA.

Wee, Y. S., & Quazi, H. A. (2005). Development and validation of critical factors of environmental management. *Industrial Management & Data Systems*, *105*, 96–114.

Wehrmeyer, W. (1996). *Greening people: Human resources and environmental management*. Routledge.

Yang, C., Lin, S., Chan, Y., & Sheu, C. (2010). Mediated effect of environmental management on manufacturing competitiveness: An empirical study. *International Journal of Production Economics*, *123*, 210–220. https://doi.org/10.1016/j.ijpe.2009.08.017

Yerpude, S., Sood, K., & Grima, S. (2022). Blockchain-augmented digital supply chain management: A way to sustainable business. *Journal of Risk and Financial Management*, *16*(1), 7.

Zoogah, D. (2011). The dynamics of Green HRM behaviors: A cognitive social information processing approach. *Zeitschrift fur Personalforschung*, *25*, 117–139.

Chapter 9

The Role of Energy in Human Well-being: A Case from Jordan

Mohammad M. Jaber and Tekla Szép

University of Miskolc, Hungary

Abstract

Purpose: This study explores the relationship between energy use and human development, specifically focusing on Jordan's household sector. The purpose is to understand the implications for achieving the UN's Sustainable Development Goal 7 (Affordable and clean energy).

Need for the study: Given the global challenge of achieving sustainable development, it is crucial to investigate the dynamics between energy use and human development. Understanding the factors influencing this relationship is essential for formulating effective strategies and policies.

Methodology: This study focuses on Jordan and analyzes data from 2008 and 2017 using the theory of energy ladder and energy stacking. It examines the effects of household energy use on human well-being through socio-economic and environmental factors such as income, health, and education expenditure.

Findings: The results indicate a strong association between household energy expenditure and the human development index in Jordan. However, this relationship is likely to be indirect, with household energy use influencing welfare through its effects on income, health, and education expenditure. Improving the quality of education, increasing access to universal health services, and promoting income growth are key factors for enhancing human well-being.

Practical implications: The findings highlight the importance of considering social, economic, and environmental factors in achieving a sustainable and equitable energy transition. Policy recommendations are formulated

Green Management: A New Paradigm in the World of Business, 137–156

Published under exclusive licence by Emerald Publishing Limited
doi:10.1108/978-1-83797-442-920241009

based on the study's insights, aiming to address the specific challenges and opportunities in Jordan and facilitate the realization of SDG7.

Keywords: Energy transition; justice; energy consumption; human development index; path analysis; Jordan

JEL Classifications: C21; O13; Q01; Q43

Introduction

On 21 October 2015, the United Nations General Assembly adopted a new integrated framework for sustainable development ('Transforming our world: the 2030 Agenda for Sustainable Development'), also known as Agenda 2030 (UN, 2015). Agenda 2030 sets out the Sustainable Development Goals (SDGs), which continue the Millennium Development Goals. The 17 goals are intended to end poverty, protect the Earth's environmental system, and ensure development for all by 2030 (Sightsavers, 2017). No national targets have been set, but UN member states have pledged to do their utmost to meet the goals (by integrating them into their national programs and policies).

From a climate and energy perspective, the most important are Sustainable Development Goals 7 and 13 (SDG7 and SDG13). SDG7 ('Affordable and clean energy') is based on the assumption that the world's energy use is unsustainable in its current form. It aims to improve energy efficiency and increase the share of renewable energy sources while ensuring universal access to affordable, reliable, sustainable, and modern energy. The sub-goals include energy justice, reducing poverty, and transitioning to low-carbon energy systems. SDG13 ('Action against climate change') emphasizes urgent action to combat climate change and its impacts. Reducing greenhouse gas emissions is the basis of the objective, but spillover effects are also considered.

To tackle our global problems, all countries have to take responsibility. In implementing the SDGs, countries in the Global South face different challenges than developed countries. It also means that plans for the energy transition cannot come at the expense of energy market stability, energy security, or equitable development in the Global South (World Economic Forum, 2023). The effect of energy price changes is more damaging in the countries of the Global South, where the resilience is lower, and a significant share of the population is vulnerable and highly exposed to price growth.

This chapter presents the connection between energy consumption and human development, utilizing the concepts of the energy ladder and energy stacking. Through a case study, we analyze the relationship between household energy expenditures and the human development index in Jordan for the years 2008 and 2017 to measure the direct and indirect effects among the variables included in the study. Path analysis is used along with some descriptive statistics. Additionally, we outline the critical indicators of Sustainable Development Goal 7 (SDG7) in

Jordan and offer policy recommendations to facilitate the sustainable, fair, and just energy transition.

To understand better the connections and pathways of energy relationships in Jordan, this chapter asks the following questions:

(1) Can a substantial relationship between household energy use and HDI be identified in Jordan?
(2) Does increasing residential energy consumption, and in line with that, the growth of energy expenditures, positively affect HDI?
(3) What major socio-economic factors influence Jordan's human well-being?

In the rest of the chapter, Section 2 (Theoretical background) presents the energy ladder and energy stacking theory and summarizes the main research results on the relationship between energy use and human development. Section 3 provides a case study of Jordan, including a description of the applied data, methodology, and results. Section 4 proposes, among other policy recommendations, that enhancing the quality of education and ensuring universal access to health services, coupled with income growth, would significantly elevate human well-being in Jordan.

Theoretical Background

The Energy Ladder and Energy Stacking Theories

The energy ladder is a concept that illustrates the dominant sources of household energy at different levels of income. It suggests that as people's incomes increase, they move up the 'ladder' to more efficient and cleaner energy sources (Roser, 2021). According to this model, households will behave as utility-maximizing neoclassical consumers, which means that when their income rises, they will switch to more advanced energy sources (van der Kroon et al., 2013).

During the 1990s, the energy ladder theory emerged as a conceptual framework to illustrate the sequential movement of household fuel preferences in developing nations (Baldwin, 1987; Hosier & Dowd, 1987; Leach, 1992). Subsequently, a considerable volume of existing scholarship has concentrated on investigating the factors influencing this energy transition process and its underlying mechanisms. Despite accounting for demographic patterns, infrastructural development, and economic attributes, a body of research has consistently demonstrated that the energy ladder model adheres to a linear and unidirectional trajectory, wherein households progress from traditional biomass fuels to modern alternatives as their income levels rise (Han et al., 2018).

Hiemstra-van der Horst and Hovorka (2008) presented three observations regarding the relationship between economic growth, the use of modern fuels, and the energy transition. First, a positive correlation was found between economic growth and the use of modern fuels when comparing countries. This suggests that as countries become more industrialized, their dependence on petroleum and electricity increases while biomass use decreases. Second, research in Asia indicated that the transition to modern fuel use is due to urbanization and development trends that increase access to modern fuels and household income. Finally, while transitioning to modern fuel use in sub-Saharan Africa was hypothetical, differences in energy use among income groups and the urban-rural divide indicated that a widespread shift away from traditional biomass fuels would be a fundamental feature of economic growth, urbanization, and industrialization.

According to Heltberg (2004), the energy ladder model provides three distinct phases. A general dependence on biomass characterizes the first phase. The second phase of fuel switching assumes households switch to 'transitional fuels' such as kerosene, coal, and charcoal in response to higher incomes, urbanization, and biomass scarcity. The third and final phase of fuel switching is households switching to LPG, natural gas, or electricity for cooking. The constituents of the classical 4A paradigm, namely, availability, affordability, accessibility, and acceptability, hold significant influence in the selection of fuel sources. As individuals ascend the energy ladder, their overall well-being also experiences a corresponding enhancement. This correlation is closely intertwined with the theory of consumption, which posits that as income levels rise, households consume more goods and opt for higher-quality commodities. This theory assumes that households utilize a singular fuel type for each household activity (Szép et al., 2023). Moreover, as an integral component of the broader energy system discourse, the 5D model, proposed by Wagner and Götz (2021), delineates five fundamental dimensions crucial to transforming energy systems. These dimensions encompass decarbonization, digitalization, decentralization, democratization, and the diversification of service orientation, collectively defining the critical pillars of the energy transition.

In a study by Leach (1992) on energy transition in developing countries, it is stated that the transition towards sustainable energy sources is not primarily motivated by a growing demand for modern fuels but rather by socioeconomic changes that alleviate the barriers to their broader adoption, particularly for low-income households relying on traditional biomass. The most significant of these changes are enhancements in the distribution of sustainable fuels, spanning urban and rural areas, and the ability to afford modern fuel technologies, facilitated either by financial means or favorable market conditions that reduce appliance costs.

However, some studies suggest that the 'energy ladder' concept is a theoretical myth, and the reality of household energy use is more complex (Szép et al., 2023). Masera et al. (2000) criticize the energy ladder theory because it cannot adequately describe the dynamics of household fuel consumption. Instead, they note that fuel stacking is common in developing countries' urban and rural areas. Fuel stacking corresponds to multiple uses of fuels, with households choosing a combination of fuels from the lower and upper rungs of the ladder. Modern fuels can replace traditional fuels only partially but not fully (Muller & Yan, 2018). Fuel stacking is prevalent in households at the beginning and mid-way in their ascension up the energy ladder, where households cannot fully let go of their traditional energy sources (Yadav et al., 2021). The energy ladder model may help predict trends in energy use in the household sector in many developing countries; however, it may not fully explain the dynamics of fuel used in households. Fig. 9.1 shows the energy ladder and stack models.

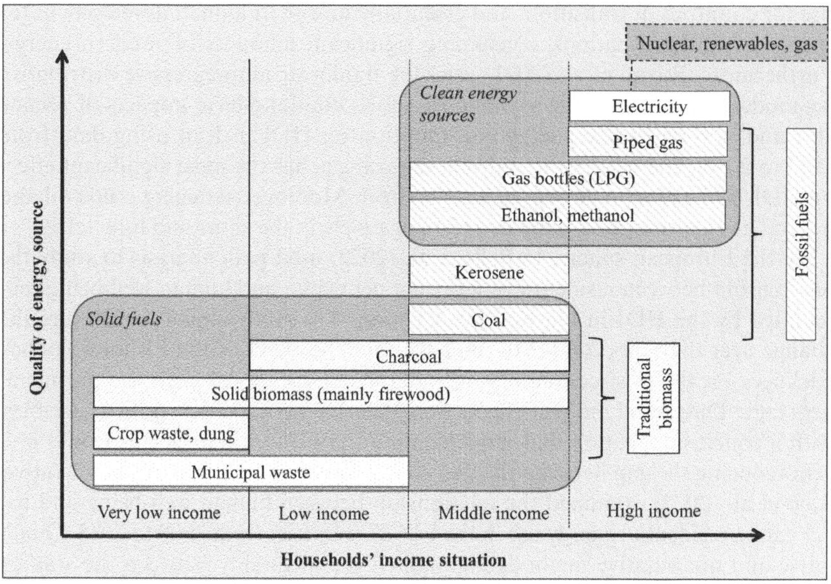

Fig. 9.1. The Energy Ladder and Energy Stack Models. *Source*: Authors' compilation.

Unlike the energy ladder, the stacking model expands upon the analysis above and provides a more comprehensive understanding of energy transition by portraying it as a multifaceted process wherein households do not strictly follow a linear progression toward cleaner fuels. Instead, they combine concurrent fuel sources to fulfill their daily energy needs. With an improvement in their socioeconomic status, households reduce their reliance on primitive fuels while simultaneously increasing their utilization of modern fuels as part of the transition process (Waleed & Mirza, 2023). The simultaneous consumption of various fuels is contingent upon the specific nature of household tasks and the range of technologies accessible to households. The factors influencing household decisions regarding stove and fuel selection are complex and multifaceted, encompassing a range of socio-economic and cultural considerations and aspects related to the availability and accessibility of clean cookstoves and fuels. Additionally, socio-political and environmental influences play a significant role. One crucial determinant is the household's income level and the associated costs of acquiring and utilizing devices and fuels, including upfront and recurring expenses (Shankar et al., 2020).

Energy Use and Human Well-being

Martínez and Ebenhack (2008) studied the correlation between the Human Development Index (HDI) and energy consumption in 120 nations. The results showed a strong correlation in most parts of the world. The results also showed three main pathways where three regions are isolated: a sharp rise in human development relative to energy consumption for energy-poor nations, a moderate rise for countries in transition, and essentially no rise in human development for energy-advantaged nations, consuming significant amounts of modern energy. Furthermore, Razmi et al. (2021) used the nonlinear autoregressive distributive lag model to investigate the asymmetric short- and long-term impacts of renewable and non-renewable energy consumption on HDI in Iran using data from 1990 to 2018. The results showed that natural gas has the most significant effect on HDI, while renewable energy has no effect. Moreover, reducing crude oil and natural gas consumption impacts HDI negatively in the short and long term.

In the European sphere, LaBelle et al. (2022) used path analysis to study the relationship between residential energy use per capita and human well-being represented by the HDI in the European Union. The study aimed to measure the change over the years 2000–2018 and examine the effect of the Fit for 55 policy packages on the post-communist member states compared with the old member states. Direct and indirect effects were detected between the studied variables, with a conclusion stating that implementing the Fit for 55 packages would prevent reducing the gap between the two country groups. In a concurrent narrative, Szép et al. (2022) examined the relationship between human well-being and the per capita residential energy use in the EU-27 countries from 2000 to 2018. Qualitative and quantitative methods highlighted the inequality between the studied countries. The results showed that residential energy use per capita has a moderate positive relationship with human development. Moreover, the results indicated that while the delinking process became dominant in the EU in 2018 and 19, the classification of the EU countries needs to be redefined.

On the southern horizon, Musakwa and Odhiambo (2022) used the autoregressive distributed lag method to investigate the impact of oil products, electricity, renewable energy, natural gas, coal, lignite, and overall energy consumption on the HDI for 1990–2019 in South Africa. The results indicated that renewable energy has a positive impact on HDI. On the other hand, oil products, natural gas, and total energy hurt in the short run. In the upper levels of human development, Kaewnern et al. (2023) investigated the impact of economic growth, research and development expenditure, renewable energy consumption, and total natural resource rents on the HDI in the top ten human development countries. The study used the Driscoll-Kraay, feasible generalized least square (FGLS), and generalized method of moments (GMM) on a time series from 1996 to 2007. The results showed that all the used variables tested positive on the HDI, while the Dumitrescu-Hurlin panel causality tests showed a bidirectional relationship between economic growth and HDI. Moreover, the results revealed that causality runs from HDI towards renewable energy consumption and research and development expenditure. Finally, Kashour (2023) studied the influence of the HDI on residential energy consumption inequality in the EU-27 countries. The study used the Gini coefficient and the least squares dummy variables (LSDV) on data from 2010 to 2018. It also analyzed the HDI's three components: life expectancy, education, and gross national income on residential energy use. The results showed that life expectancy hurt energy use, education had no effect, and GNI had a positive effect. In addition, energy efficiency significantly impacted the HDI for all the countries.

Case Study for Jordan

Since 2015, when the United Nations (UN) launched the Agenda 2030 and set the SDGs, the SDG7 is most closely related to energy transition. It has five targets, which are to ensure universal access to affordable, reliable, and modern energy services, increase substantially the share of renewable energy in the global energy mix, double the global rate of improvement in energy efficiency, enhance international cooperation to facilitate access to clean energy research and technology, including renewable energy, energy efficiency and advanced and cleaner fossil-fuel technology, and promote investment in energy infrastructure and clean energy technology, and expand infrastructure and upgrade technology for supplying modern and sustainable energy services for all in developing countries, in particular least developed countries, small island developing states, and land-locked developing countries, by their respective programs of support. Table 9.1 shows the critical achievements of SDG7 in Jordan in 2019 and 2020.

Achieving the SDGs is still in progress, mainly with the primary objective of not leaving anyone behind. Not leaving anyone behind means that developed and developing countries should get their chance of achieving those goals. A mission that may call for improving equality and ensuring a safer system transition. Developed countries certainly have better energy capabilities, but they still must think about making a safe transition to more clean and efficient resources in the sense of an environmentally friendly transition that does not contribute to environmental problems such as climate change. Those ideas related to energy governance and poverty were discussed by O'Brien et al. (2007), and the paper concluded with three points. First, energy and poverty are interrelated; solving one problem means considering the other. Second, developed countries did not benefit from top-down approaches. Third, the importance of international agreements cannot be overstated. For the last point, international agreements are not

Table 9.1. Jordan's SDG 7 Statistics in 2019 and 2020.

SDG number	Indicator	Data (%)
7.1.1.	Share of the population with access to electricity	99.9
7.1.2.	Share of the population with access to clean fuels for cooking	99.9
7.2.1.	Share of final energy use that comes from renewable sources	8.17
7.3.1.	Energy intensity (MJ/USD)	3.80
7.A.1.	International finance received for clean energy (million USD)	73.76
7.B.1.	Renewable electricity-generating capacity per person (W)	186.5

Source: Authors' compilation based on *Goal 7: Affordable and Clean Energy – SDG Tracker* (2023).

binding to those countries who sign them, making it easy for those who want to withdraw after a while (Newberry, 2017). Furthermore, pursuing environmental economics and attaining sustainable development goals (SDGs) pose increasingly formidable challenges, particularly for developing nations. These challenges stem from multifaceted constraints, encompassing inadequate financial resources, limited access to advanced technologies, a dearth of specialized knowledge, and insufficient public awareness regarding the significance of engaging in economically sustainable practices (Setioningtyas et al., 2022).

Similarly to other countries in the Global South (particularly regarding the Middle East), Jordan's position is challenging regarding energy prices and regulations. Before 2003, Jordan purchased oil from Iraq below market rates, and the government subsequently transferred some of these cost advantages to consumers. After 2003, Jordan lost this affordable oil source, and the rise in global prices followed. While global food prices doubled between 2002 and 2008, global energy prices increased more than threefold (Atamanov et al., 2017). Although the government was compelled to raise prices in 2005 and again in 2006, it kept them below levels elsewhere. As a result, government spending on petroleum subsidies alone accounted for 5.8% of GDP in 2005 (Coady et al., 2006). In February 2008, the government abolished oil price subsidies, except for liquefied petroleum gas (LPG), and concurrently established an automatic fuel pricing mechanism (Ajlouni & Alodat, 2021). This innovative mechanism allowed monthly price revisions to mirror the actual production costs more accurately. However, by the close of 2010, when oil prices escalated to US$90 per barrel, the government ceased the monthly petroleum price adjustments and reinstated petroleum subsidies (Ajlouni & Alodat, 2021). In December 2012, due to escalating fiscal pressures, the Government of Jordan (GoJ) was compelled to recommence monthly price adjustments, exempting only LPG (Ajlouni & Alodat, 2021).

After Palestine, Jordan has the second-highest fuel and electricity prices in the Arab world, attributed to price liberalization initiatives in recent years and a fixed tax on oil derivatives (Jordan News, 2022). A new electricity tariff was introduced in the first third of 2022 and targeted Jordanian families, holders of permanent Jordanian passports, and Gazans will also benefit, as well as subscription service meters for households (The Jordan Times, 2021). The subsidized tariffs are divided into three categories: consumers who use between 1 and 300 kWh of electricity pay approximately 65.28 Euro cents per kWh, those who use between 301 and 600 kWh pay approximately 130.57 Euro cents per kWh, and those who use more than 600 kWh pay approximately 261.14 Euro cents per kWh (The Jordan Times, 2021).

The liberalization process has many advantages. It can stimulate competition in the energy market, potentially driving down prices and fostering innovation. Additionally, it can lead to efficiency improvements as firms are incentivized to invest in cost-reducing and innovative technologies. Transparent pricing is another benefit, with prices being determined by market forces of supply and demand rather than government regulation (Pepermans, 2019). Furthermore, liberalization can facilitate the diversification of energy sources, enhancing energy security (Halkos & Tsirivis, 2023). Additionally, it encourages renewable energy investments and energy efficiency improvements, reducing the payback periods and stimulating energy savings (Markard et al., 2004; Pepermans, 2019). The process can also lead to increased competition, potentially driving down prices and leading to more innovative solutions in the energy sector.

However, energy price liberalization also has its drawbacks. It can result in market instability and price volatility, negatively impacting consumers. Inequality is another concern, as the benefits of liberalization often disproportionately favor large consumers (mainly industrial users), while the benefits for domestic consumers compared to a public monopoly or a regulated private monopoly are questionable (Pepermans, 2019). In some instances, liberalization has led to the exit of several electricity retailers from the market, as observed in Singapore (Bojnec & Križaj, 2021). These points underscore the need for careful management of the liberalization process to maximize benefits and minimize potential downsides. Furthermore, higher residential energy prices push more people into energy poverty and further increase the share of energy expenditures in total expenditures (Lu & Ren, 2023). The liberalization process can also lead to market instability and price volatility, negatively impacting consumers.

Data and Methodology

Path analysis uses multiple regression to formulate causal models explicitly. Causality cannot be established using this method; it can examine the pattern of relationships between three or more variables, but it can neither confirm nor reject the hypothetical causal imagery. This type of analysis aims to provide quantitative estimates of the causal connections between sets of variables (Bryman, 2004). Path analysis was conducted to estimate the direct and indirect effects influencing the HDI in Jordan. Direct, or zero-path, assesses the linear relationship between the primary explanatory variable and the dependent variable. On the other hand, the indirect or secondary path determines those effects through a set of secondary explanatory variables. Fig. 9.2 shows the path diagrams of the factors that were included in this paper.

The model is measured based on the specific factor analytic with the assumption that the explanatory variable influences the outcome variable:

$$Y = \beta Y + \gamma X + \varepsilon \tag{1}$$

where Y is the vector of observable dependent variables, X is the vector of observable independent variables, ε is the vector of errors, and β and γ are coefficient matrices.

The multiple linear regression is

$$y_i = \beta_0 + \beta_1 x1_{1,i} + \beta_2 x1_{2,i} + \cdots + \beta_k x1_{k,i} + \varepsilon_i \tag{2}$$

where k is the number of explanatory variables.

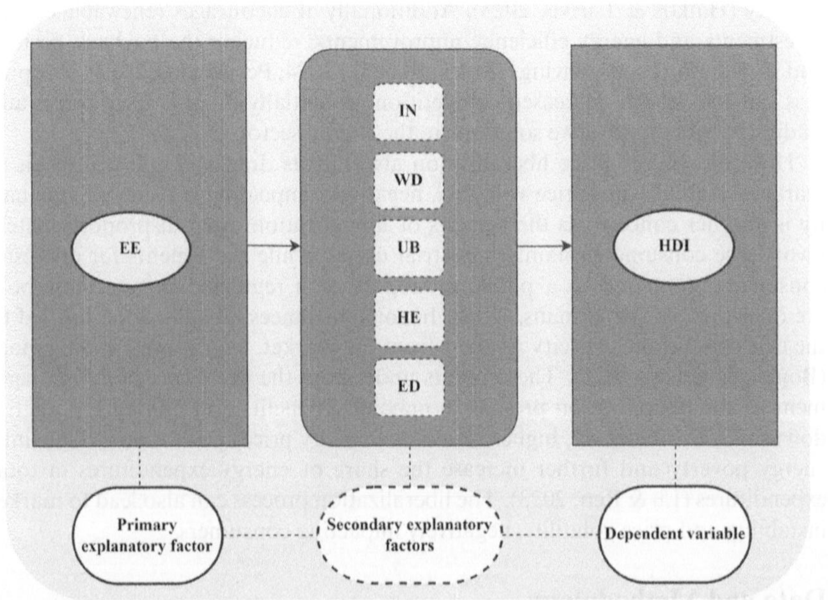

Fig. 9.2. Path Diagram of the Explanatory Variables. *Source*: Authors' compilation.

In their research, LaBelle et al. (2022) summarize the path analysis in five steps:

1. Identifying the primary and secondary influencing factors taking into consideration multicollinearity where applicable.
2. Running a simple multivariate linear regression, including the primary and secondary variables, to estimate the impact of these factors on the dependent variable.
3. Estimating the bivariate regression model to analyze the relationship between the primary explanatory factor and the dependent variable.
4. Determining the path's strengths. On the one hand, indirect paths may cross over secondary variables; at this point, all paths from the start to the dependent variable must be added together, and the correct path segments must be multiplied together, i.e., regardless of significance. The consequences of the relevant indicators and the revealed paths are next examined.
5. The fourth step is determining the primary factor's direct and indirect effect on the dependent variable by breaking down the β coefficients of the binary linear regression.

Thus, the model performs a chain of simple linear regressions to best interpret the relationships between the explanatory factors and the targeted (dependent variable). This method is simple and can reveal the desired relationships between the variables under study (Jaber, 2022). Fig. 9.2 shows the constructed path diagram of the explanatory variables.

Data

To better understand the relationship between energy poverty and other topics, this paper applies the traditional path analysis on cross-sectional data collected from two household expenditure and income surveys conducted in 2008 and 2017. Unfortunately, because of data availability issues, the latest data available from Jordan is 2017. While data availability may limit the ability to perform complex analysis, the data retrieved from the surveys will provide insight into geographical differences between Jordanian governorates regarding income, energy, health, education expenditures, urbanization, and the use of wood for heating. These variables will be evaluated concerning human well-being, as measured by the HDI. Table 9.2 lists all the indicators used to build the path model and their respective sources.

Table 9.2. Indicators Used to Build the Path Model.

Abbreviation	Indicator	Source
EE	Annual energy expenditure	Jordanian Department of Statistics
IN	Average annual total income	Jordanian Department of Statistics
WD	Percentage of households that use wood/coal/jift as a primary source of heating	Jordanian Department of Statistics
UB	Urbanization level	Jordanian Department of Statistics
HE	Average annual household expenditure on health	Jordanian Department of Statistics
ED	Average annual household expenditure on education	Jordanian Department of Statistics
HDI	Human development index in every governorate	Global Data Lab

Source: Authors' compilation.

IV. Results and Discussion

In Jordan, fossil fuel is the primary source of energy. The country's energy consumption in 2021 is dominated by the transport sector (around 40%), followed by the residential sector (around 25%). By source, oil products followed by electricity are the dominant ones. Net energy imports in Jordan reached 378.9 TJ by 2019 (IEA, 2022), which accounts for nearly 94% of Jordan's total energy in Jordan. In addition, the energy sector suffers from several challenges, such as increasing demand, limited domestic energy resources, the unstable political situation in the surrounding countries, and the resulting security/prices issues, poor planning, and losses in the sector (Albezuirat et al., 2018).

Fig. 9.3 compares energy imports vs. final energy consumption in each sector in Jordan. Over the years, while the energy demand has increased, the local energy sources need to contribute more to the system. Even with the country's ambitious goals to increase the share of renewable energy, the storage problem still exists.

Path analysis is used in this section to study the main primary and secondary causes of HDI in the Jordanian governorates. Factors examine the relationship between household annual energy expenditure and HDI in 2008 and 2017. The analysis directly assesses the primary explanatory factor's effect on the independent variable or through other intermediate (secondary explanatory) factors (Jaber, 2022; LaBelle et al., 2022). Path analysis uses a set of ordinary least squares (OLS) built on one another.

The selected factors included in the path analysis are a proxy for energy consumption represented by average annual energy expenditure in each governorate and HDI on the governorate level, among other factors, as mentioned in the previous section. The initial number of variables was filtered and excluded from part of the list to eliminate the multicollinearity issues. The path analysis compares the geographical differences between the Jordanian governorates regarding energy expenditure relationship to HDI directly and indirectly. The cross-sectional data used are based on the Expenditure and Income Survey conducted by the Department of Statistics in 2008 and 2017.

The application of simple multivariate linear regression, including all the variables' results, is listed in Table 9.3. HDI is used as the dependent variable in this step.

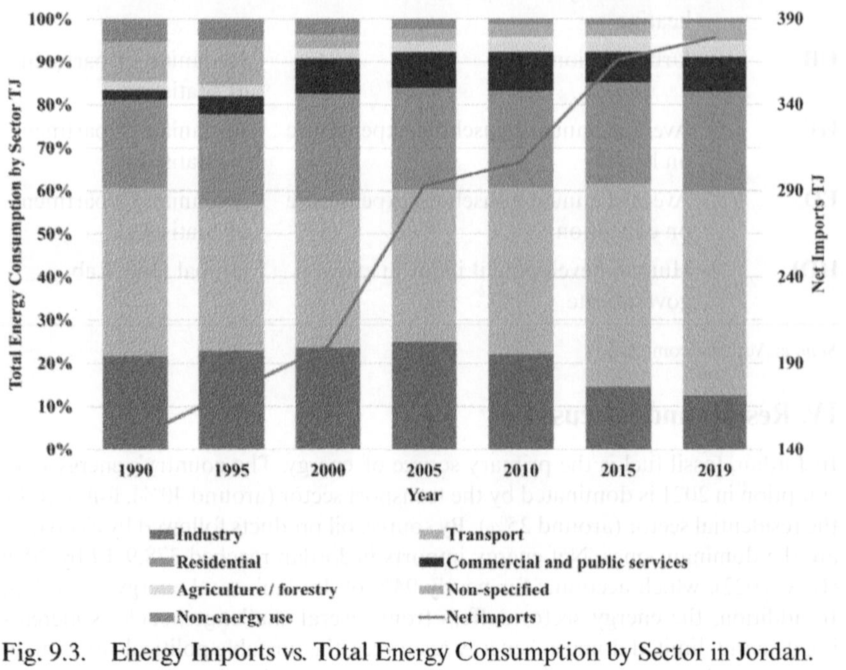

Fig. 9.3. Energy Imports vs. Total Energy Consumption by Sector in Jordan. *Source*: Authors' compilation.

The variables included in the analysis explain that the regional ratio of HDI with R^2 in the two-year analysis is slightly the same. Changes in the weights of the variables show a significant change through the years. In 2008, urbanization had the most significant effect on HDI, while in 2017, energy expenditure and income were the significant factors. Regardless of significance, it is noted that the coefficient values changed between the two years.

The regression analysis results between energy expenditure and HDI are listed in Table 9.4. The findings indicate that energy expenditure explains itself in 30% and 10% of the variances of the HDI. Energy expenditure plays a vital role in the distribution of the dependent variable. It is also noticed that the relationship between the variables in 2017 is insignificant, and the coefficient value has decreased compared with 2008, showing a slightly significant effect. The positive values indicate that energy expenditure motivates HDI, enhancing human well-being. On the contrary, declining energy expenditure hinders human well-being.

Indirect paths should be constructed to understand how energy expenditure influences secondary explanatory factors (step 4). In 2008, energy expenditure significantly affected income, urbanization, health, and education expenditures. On the other hand, in 2017, energy expenditure significantly affected income, health, and education expenditures. Figs. 9.4 and 9.5 show the constructed path results for the years under study. The results show that using wood for heating has no significant relationship with energy expenditure in the two years and that when a household chooses to spend more on energy services, the tendency to use wood for heating decreases. In general, in the model, energy expenditure alone did not influence HDI in Jordan in 2008 but only in 2017. It is also noted that increasing the expenditure on energy affects HDI negatively.

Regarding the secondary explanatory variable effect on the dependent variable, in 2008, urbanization was the most significant effect on HDI, while in 2017, average annual income significantly affected HDI. The shift from urbanization to income indicates that in Jordan, while the urbanization level stabilized in

Table 9.3. Regression Results for the Primary and the Secondary Indicators Against HDI.

Coefficients	Variable	HDI, 2008	Std. Error	HDI, 2017	Std. Error
β_1	EE	−0.016	0.000	−0.789*	0.000
β_2	IN	−0.285	0.000	1.072*	0.000
β_3	WD	−0.243	0.000	0.428	0.000
β_4	UB	0.731**	0.029	0.303	0.038
β_5	HE	−0.316	0.000	−0.126	0.000
β_6	ED	0.664	0.000	0.562	0.000
R^2		0.814		0.813	

Note: *10% significance level, **5% significance level, and ***1% significance level.
Source: Authors' calculations.

Table 9.4. Binary Regression Results between EE and HDI.

Coefficients	HDI, 2008	Std. Error	HDI, 2017	Std. Error
β	0.527*	0.000	0.316	0.000
R^2	0.278		0.100	

Note: * 10% significance level, ** 5% significance level, and *** 1% significance level.
Source: Authors' calculations.

recent years, income became more vital in determining the value of HDI. Energy expenditure only had a significant effect on HDI in 2017.

Direct and Indirect Impacts on HDI

In the previous section, the strength of the paths was identified. In this step, the territorial impacts of energy expenditure are identified. Here, the reason behind identifying the paths' strengths is to understand whether energy expenditure directly or indirectly (through the secondary explanatory variables) impacts

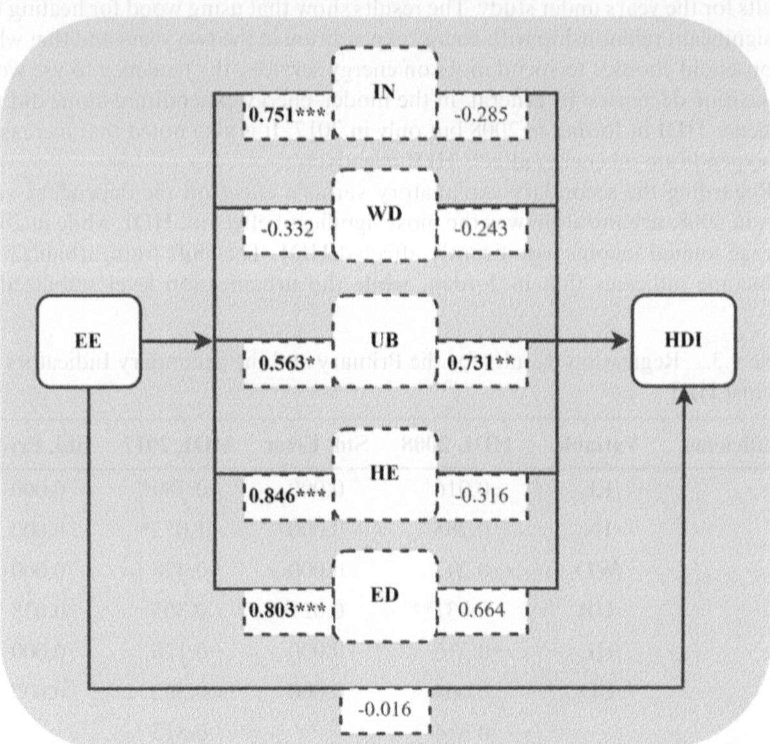

Fig. 9.4. Role of EE in Explaining HDI in Jordan in 2008. *Note*: Significant values are bold. *Source*: Authors' calculations.

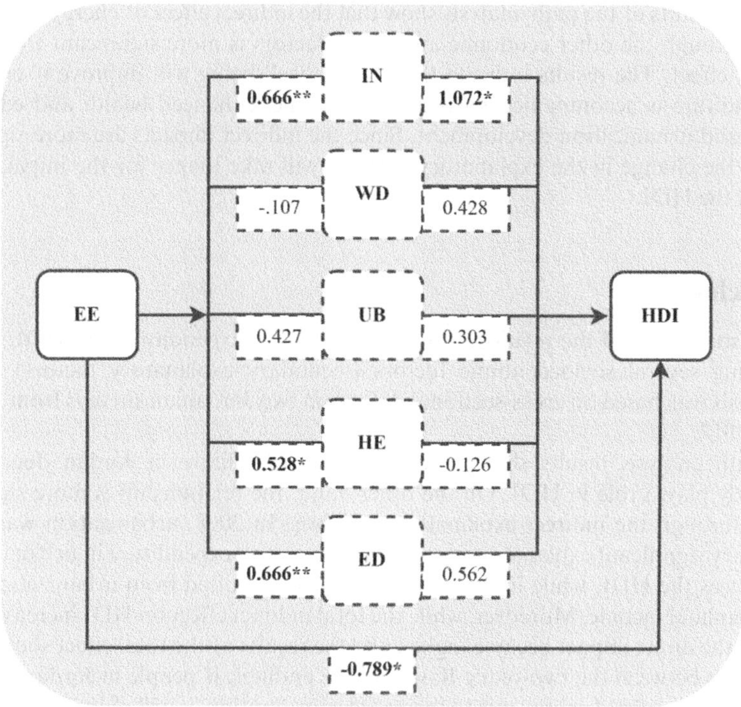

Fig. 9.5. Role of EE in Explaining HDI in Jordan in 2017. *Note*: Significant values are bold. *Source*: Authors' calculations.

human well-being. β coefficient values of the binary regression are broken into two parts (direct and indirect). Table 9.5 lists the results.

The direct effect of energy expenditure on HDI over the two years is negative. While appropriate path parts are multiplied, indirect paths may pass across the primary and secondary variables, combined from the beginning to the dependent variable (irrespective of significance). In 2008, the indirect effect was calculated as follows: (0.751* − 0.214) + (−0.332* − 0.243) + (0.563*0.731) + (0.846* − 0.316) + (0.803*0.664) = 0.543. On the other hand, in 2017 is calculated as follows: (0.666*1.072) + (−0.107*0.428) + (0.427*0.303) + (0.528* − 0.126) + (0.666*0.562) = 1.105.

Table 9.5. The Roles of the Direct and Indirect Paths in Explaining the HDI.

	HDI, 2008	HDI, 2017
Indirect	0.543	1.105
Direct	−0.016	−0.789
Total	0.527	0.316

Source: Authors' calculations.

The results of the path analysis show that the indirect effect of energy expenditure through the other economic and social factors is more significant than the direct effect. The results indicate that human well-being will improve if energy expenditure is accompanied by increased income, enhanced health and education, and urbanization development. Since the indirect impacts are more significant, the change in the explanatory variable will take longer for the impacts to affect the HDI.

Conclusions

This study studied the relationships between energy expenditure and HDI, considering several socioeconomic factors (secondary explanatory factors). The analysis was based on cross-sectional data from two Jordanian surveys from 2008 and 2017.

Path analysis results showed that energy expenditure in Jordan does not directly play a role in HDI. On the other hand, the relationship is more significant through the indirect explanatory variables. In 2008, urbanization was the primary significant explanatory variable where energy expenditure in urban areas enhances the HDI, while in 2017, this relationship shifted from urbanization to total annual income. Moreover, while the total indirect effect on HDI increased in 2017, the direct impact became higher, and the results of the total effect showed a decrease between the two years. Based on the findings, if people in Jordan spend more on household energy due to increased consumption, it will reduce their well-being because it has a negative relationship with the Human Development Index (HDI). However, combining energy expenditure with other factors like income, health, and education expenditure will have a positive effect in the long term. Still, it will take longer to see the results. Improving the quality of education and universal health services alongside growth in income levels would enhance the level of human well-being in Jordan.

Policy Recommendations

Based on the results of this study, the following policy recommendations are concluded:

1. Consider Household Energy Needs and Practices: The study found a direct inverse relationship between residential energy expenditure and human well-being, indicating a discrepancy between household energy needs and practices and what is optimal for Jordanian households. Policymakers should consider this when designing energy policies and strive to align household energy practices with their needs.
2. Promote Energy Efficiency: Improving energy efficiency in the residential sector should be a key objective of future energy plans. This can be achieved by promoting energy-efficient appliances, improving building insulation, and encouraging behavioral changes towards energy conservation.

3. Incorporate User Perspectives: The end-users perspective is crucial in formulating effective energy policies. Policymakers should engage with residents to understand their energy needs, consumption patterns, and challenges and incorporate these insights into policy design.
4. Account for Population Growth and Regional Variations: Future energy strategies should also consider demographic trends and regional differences in energy consumption. As the population grows, energy demand will increase, and policies should be designed to meet this demand without compromising sustainability or equity.
5. Invest in Renewable Energy: Given Jordan's abundant solar and wind resources, renewable energy generation has a significant potential. Investing in renewable energy infrastructure can help diversify the energy mix, reduce dependence on fossil fuels, and contribute to environmental sustainability.

In conclusion, a comprehensive and inclusive approach to energy policymaking, considering regional disparities, household energy needs and practices, user perspectives, demographic trends, and renewable energy potential, can help ensure Jordan's sustainable and equitable energy future. These recommendations are based on our current understanding of the situation and should be revisited as new data and insights become available.

Acknowledgments

The authors would like to acknowledge that the chapter is based on a Ph.D. dissertation prepared by the lead author – Jaber, M., Towards Better Understanding of Energy Poverty in Jordan: A Multidimensional Phenomenon, 2024, University of Miskolc, Ph.D. degree. This paper was supported by the János Bolyai Research Scholarship of the Hungarian Academy of Sciences.

References

Ajlouni, S. A., & Alodat, M. T. (2021). Gaussian process regression for forecasting gasoline prices in Jordan. *International Journal of Energy Economics and Policy*, *11*(3), 502–509. https://doi.org/10.32479/ijeep.11032

Albezuirat, M., Iqbal Hussain, M., Al-saraireh, F., & Ahmad, R. (2018). Jordan energy sector choices and challenges. *Jordan Energy Sector Choices and Challenges*. *1*, 22. https://doi.org/10.5281/zenodo.1452373

Atamanov, A., Jellema, J., & Serajuddin, U. (2017). Energy subsidies reform in Jordan: Welfare implications of different scenarios. In *The quest for subsidy reforms in the middle East and North Africa region* (pp. 179–206). World Bank. https://doi.org/10.1007/978-3-319-52926-4_7

Baldwin, S. F. (1987). *Biomass stoves: Engineering design, development, and dissemination*. Volunteers in Technical Assistance. Princeton University.

Bojnec, Š., & Križaj, A. (2021). Electricity markets during the liberalization: The case of a European union country. *Energies*, *14*(14), 4317. https://doi.org/10.3390/en14144317

Bryman, A. (2004). *Quantitative data analysis with SPSS 12 and 13: A guide for social scientists* (1st ed.). Routledge. https://doi.org/10.4324/9780203498187

Coady, D., El-Said, M., Gillingham, R., Kpodar, K., Medas, P., & Newhouse, D. (2006). *The magnitude and distribution of fuel subsidies: Evidence from Bolivia,* Ghana, Jordan, Mali, *and Sri Lanka*. IMF Working Paper WP/06/247. https://www.imf.org/external/pubs/ft/wp/2006/wp06247.pdf

SDG Tracker. Goal 7: Affordable and *clean energy* – SDG Tracker. (2023). *Our World in Data*. https://sdg-tracker.org/energy

Halkos, G. E., & Tsirivis, A. S. (2023). Sustainable development of the European electricity sector: Investigating the impact of electricity price, market liberalization and energy taxation on RES deployment. *Energies*, *16*(14), 5567. https://doi.org/10.3390/en16145567

Han, H., Wu, S., & Zhang, Z. (2018). Factors underlying rural household energy transition: A case study of China. *Energy Policy*, *114*, 234–244. https://doi.org/10.1016/j.enpol.2017.11.052

Heltberg, R. (2004). Fuel switching: Evidence from eight developing countries. *Energy Economics*, *26*(5), 869–887. https://doi.org/10.1016/j.eneco.2004.04.018

Hiemstra-van der Horst, G., & Hovorka, A. J. (2008). Reassessing the "energy ladder": Household energy use in Maun, Botswana. *Energy Policy*, *36*(9), 3333–3344. https://doi.org/10.1016/j.enpol.2008.05.006

Hosier, R. H., & Dowd, J. (1987). Household fuel choice in Zimbabwe: An empirical test of the energy ladder hypothesis. *Resources and Energy*, *9*(4), 347–361. https://doi.org/10.1016/0165-0572(87)90003-X

IEA. (2022). *Jordan—countries & regions*. IEA. https://www.iea.org/countries/jordan

Jaber, M. M. (2022). Analysis of selected economic factor impacts on CO_2 emissions intensity: A case study from Jordan, 1990-2015. *Regional Statistics*, *12*(1), 193–208. https://doi.org/10.15196/RS120101

Jordan News. (2022, November 21). Gas is optimal fuel for winter heating in Jordan – Expert–Jordan News | Latest News from Jordan, MENA. *Jordan News|Latest News from Jordan, MENA*. https://www.jordannews.jo/Section-113/All/Gas-is-optimal-fuel-for-winter-heating-in-Jordan-expert-24821

Kaewnern, H., Wangkumharn, S., Deeyaonarn, W., Yousaf, A. U., & Kongbuamai, N. (2023). Investigating the role of research development and renewable energy on human development: An insight from the top ten human development index countries. *Energy*, *262*, 125540. https://doi.org/10.1016/j.energy.2022.125540

Kashour, M. (2023). Interlinkages between human development, residential energy consumption, and energy efficiency for the EU-27 Member States, 2010-2018. *Regional Statistics*, *13*(1), 36–54. https://doi.org/10.15196/RS130102

LaBelle, M. C., Tóth, G., & Szép, T. (2022). Not fit for 55: Prioritizing human well-being in residential energy consumption in the European union. *Energies*, *15*(18), 18. https://doi.org/10.3390/en15186687

Leach, G. (1992). The energy transition. *Energy Policy*, *20*(2), 116–123. https://doi.org/10.1016/0301-4215(92)90105-B

Lu, S., & Ren, J. (2023). A comprehensive review on energy poverty: Definition, measurement, socioeconomic impact and its alleviation for carbon neutrality. *Environment, Development and Sustainability*. *Published Online*. https://doi.org/10.1007/s10668-023-04143-7

Markard, J., Truffer, B., & Imboden, D. M. (2004). The impacts of market liberalization on innovation processes in the electricity sector. *Energy & Environment*, *15*(2), 201–214. https://doi.org/10.1260/095830504323153405

Martínez, D. M., & Ebenhack, B. W. (2008). Understanding the role of energy consumption in human development through the use of saturation phenomena. *Energy Policy*, *36*(4), 1430–1435. https://doi.org/10.1016/j.enpol.2007.12.016

Masera, O. R., Saatkamp, B. D., & Kammen, D. M. (2000). From linear fuel switching to multiple cooking strategies: A critique and alternative to the energy ladder model. *World Development*, *28*(12), 2083–2103. https://doi.org/10.1016/S0305-750X(00)00076-0

Muller, C., & Yan, H. (2018). Household fuel use in developing countries: Review of theory and evidence. *Energy Economics*, *70*, 429–439. https://doi.org/10.1016/j.eneco.2018.01.024

Musakwa, M. T., & Odhiambo, N. M. (2022). Energy consumption and human development in South Africa: Empirical evidence from disaggregated data. *Studia Universitatis "Vasile Goldis" Arad – Economics Series*, *32*(2), 1–23. https://doi.org/10.2478/sues-2022-0006

Newberry, J. (2017). U.S. Withdrawal from the Paris Agreement. *International Journal of Environmental Sciences & Natural Resources*, *3*, 555618. https://doi.org/10.19080/IJESNR.2017.03.555618

O'Brien, G., O'Keefe, P., & Rose, J. (2007). Energy, poverty and governance. *International Journal of Environmental Studies*, *64*(5), 605–616. https://doi.org/10.1080/00207230600841385

Pepermans, G. (2019). European energy market liberalization: Experiences and challenges. *International Journal of Economic Policy Studies*, *13*(1), 3–26. https://doi.org/10.1007/s42495-018-0009-0

Razmi, S. F., Arabamiry, S., Torki, L., & Khodaparast, M. (2021). *Asymmetric effects of consumption of renewable and nonrenewable energies on human development index*. SSRN Scholarly Paper 3927014. https://doi.org/10.2139/ssrn.3927014

Roser, M. (2021). *The 'Energy Ladder': What energy sources do people on different incomes rely on?* Our World in Data. https://ourworldindata.org/energy-ladder

Setioningtyas, W. P., Illés, C. B., Dunay, A., Hadi, A., & Wibowo, T. S. (2022). Environmental economics and the SDGs: A review of their relationships and barriers. *Sustainability*, *14*(12), 12. https://doi.org/10.3390/su14127513

Shankar, A. V., Quinn, A. K., Dickinson, K. L., Williams, K. N., Masera, O., Charron, D., Jack, D., Hyman, J., Pillarisetti, A., Bailis, R., Kumar, P., Ruiz-Mercado, I., & Rosenthal, J. P. (2020). Everybody stacks: Lessons from household energy case studies to inform design principles for clean energy transitions. *Energy Policy*, *141*, 111468. https://doi.org/10.1016/j.enpol.2020.111468

Sightsavers. (2017, September 25). *Global goals|Policy and advocacy*. Sightsavers. https://www.sightsavers.org/policy-and-advocacy/global-goals/

Szép, T., Pálvölgyi, T., & Kármán-Tamus, É. (2023). "Landscape" of energy burden: Role of solid fuels in Central and Eastern European residential heating. *International Journal of Sustainable Energy Planning and Management*, *37*, 61–74. https://doi.org/10.54337/ijsepm.7503

Szép, T., Tóth, G., & LaBelle, M. C. (2022). Farewell to the European Union's east-west divide: Decoupling energy lifts the well-being of households, 2000–2018. *Regional Statistics*, *12*(3), 159–190. https://doi.org/10.15196/RS120307

The Jordan Times. (2021). *Reduced electricity tariff will take effect in first-third of 2022*. EMRC. https://jordantimes.com/news/local/reduced-electricity-tariff-will-take-effect-first-third-2022-%E2%80%94-emrc

UN. (2015). *Transforming our world: The 2030 agenda for sustainable development*. https://documents-dds-ny.un.org/doc/UNDOC/GEN/N15/291/89/PDF/N1529189.pdf?OpenElement

van der Kroon, B., Brouwer, R., & van Beukering, P. J. H. (2013). The energy ladder: Theoretical myth or empirical truth? Results from a meta-analysis. *Renewable and Sustainable Energy Reviews*, *20*, 504–513. https://doi.org/10.1016/j.rser.2012.11.045

Wagner, O., & Götz, T. (2021). Presentation of the 5Ds in energy policy: A policy paper to show how germany can regain its role as a pioneer in energy policy. *Energies*, *14*(20), 20. https://doi.org/10.3390/en14206799

Waleed, K., & Mirza, F. M. (2023). Examining fuel choice patterns through household energy transition index: An alternative to traditional energy ladder and stacking models. *Environment, Development and Sustainability*, *25*(7), 6449–6501. https://doi.org/10.1007/s10668-022-02312-8

World Economic Forum. (2023, November 15). *Why the energy transition must include the Global South*. World Economic Forum. https://www.weforum.org/agenda/2023/11/energy-transition-global-south-cop28/

Yadav, P., Davies, P. J., & Asumadu-Sarkodie, S. (2021). Fuel choice and tradition: Why fuel stacking and the energy ladder are out of step? *Solar Energy*, *214*, 491–501. https://doi.org/10.1016/j.solener.2020.11.077

Chapter 10

Green Public Procurement: The Implementation in Asian Countries

Phung Thu Ha, Cu Hoang Lam Vu, Nguyen Hoang Oanh and Le Nguyen Ngoc Dung

Academy of Finance, Ha Noi, Vietnam

Abstract

Introduction: Public procurement is the most substantial national expenditure in many countries worldwide. Public procurement can contribute to the nation's sustainable development. In developed countries, green public procurement is not unfamiliar, as the green public financing framework has been operational for over two decades.

Purpose: In developing nations, however, green public procurement is relatively recent. Green public procurement has the potential to serve as a beneficial tool in promoting sustainable development, particularly in light of the growing responsibility of governments to account for the environmental impacts of their acquisitions in light of climate change.

Methodology: The government will take the initiative to promote sustainable economic development by increasing the market share of companies that exhibit an unwavering commitment to environmental preservation by adopting green public procurement practices.

Findings: This document aims to present a thorough depiction of how green public procurement is being implemented in the Philippines, Japan, Korea, Thailand, Malaysia, and Indonesia. Following this, the authors propose several recommendations for advancing green public procurement in developing nations such as Vietnam.

Green Management: A New Paradigm in the World of Business, 157–181

Published under exclusive licence by Emerald Publishing Limited
doi:10.1108/978-1-83797-442-920241010

Keywords: Green public procurement; Asian countries; public procurement; sustainable finance; climate change; product lifecycle; transparency; value in money

JEL Classifications: E60; E65; H50; H72

Introduction

A government use of public procurement to accomplish their development objectives is a potent tool. An anticipated $11 trillion, or 12% of the worldwide gross domestic product, is the value of public procurement on a global scale (World Bank, 2021). The government is frequently the most significant purchaser of a wide range of products and services in numerous developing countries. Green public procurement is an approach that leverages the public sector's purchasing power to accomplish sustainable development goals. The European Commission has undertaken multiple initiatives and undertakings to encourage member states to adopt green public procurement, including the development of production and consumption standards, the dissemination of policies, and the execution of research and projects (European Union, 2016). Several federal green procurement programs in the United States were designed to establish and enforce green public procurement. These programs mandate that authorities evaluate a product's environmental impacts, expense, and additional relevant factors before reaching a purchasing determination.

Several Asian nations have adopted green public procurement policies to promote sustainable development. This chapter will provide an overview of green public procurement practices in Asian countries, focusing on the practical implementation of green public procurement in Japan and Korea as case studies. Then, we compare the green public procurement policy practices of four Southeast Asian nations concerning implementing green public procurement. In conclusion, we offer suggestions to assist developing countries such as Vietnam in effectively promoting green public procurement (Ndekwa et al., 2023; Sood & Ozen, 2024; Yerpude et al., 2022).

Literature Review

The Definition of Green Public Procurement

Sustainable public procurement is defined as "a procedure by which governmental entities procure goods, services, works, and utilities in a manner that maximises cost-effectiveness throughout the entire life cycle, benefiting not only the institution but also society and the economy while minimising environmental harm" (United Nations Environment Programme, 2011). Sustainable public procurement shifts the focus of procurement endeavours from exclusively pursuing the most economical option to achieving the most excellent value for money. Employing strategic purchasing functions ensures that policy objectives about sustainable development's economic, environmental, and social dimensions are consistently met. Frequently, the objectives of sustainable public procurement systems include the promotion of green growth, environmental protection, the development of small- and medium-sized businesses, the advancement of enterprises owned by women and minorities, innovation, ethical business practices, and broader industrial policy goals.

According to the research conducted by Bugge and Voigt (2008), green public procurement can be further described as how public institutions procure services and commodities to encourage sustainable consumption and production while considering environmental costs and benefits throughout the product's life cycle. The product life cycle includes extracting primary materials, manufacturing and production, packaging, distribution, use, and disposal. Externalities manifest throughout the product's life cycle and are not factored into its present purchase price. Other indirect supply chain costs and environmental externalities are not factored into purchase prices. In its most comprehensive form, life-cycle costing attempts to quantify and assign a value to these externalities. By employing life-cycle costing tools, green public procurement aims to operate as an effective instrument for environmental regulation and an alternative form of environmental governance that transcends the conventional public law paradigm. By facilitating the establishment of public and private markets for more environmentally friendly products and bridging the divide between traditional ecological law and private environmental governance, green public procurement establishes a model for environmental progress by enabling public institutions to develop public and private markets.

Green public procurement, which leverages public sector purchasing to attain environmental policy objectives, is a component of sustainable public procurement. Green public procurement is "a process whereby public authorities seek to procure goods and services and work with a reduced environmental impact throughout their life-cycle compared to goods and services and works with the same primary function that would otherwise be procured" (European Union, 2016).

State agencies engage in green public procurement when they acquire goods and services with a reduced environmental footprint over their valuable lives relative to alternative products and services serving the same function. Public sector procurement activities are considered critical undertakings within this framework and constitute a significant portion of the state budget's overall expenditure. In a broader sense, sustainable procurement evaluates equitable contracts' employment and societal effects to incorporate their social dimension (Kaur et al., 2024; Rijal et al., 2024).

The Content of Green Public Procurement

Before making purchasing decisions, green public procurement requires organisations, businesses, and individuals to contemplate the environmental ramifications of the product or service throughout its entire life cycle and the necessity of procurement. Three fundamental considerations should be taken into account when designating priority products, services, and operational areas in green public procurement, as stated by the European Union (2011):

- Environmental Implications: Opt for services or products (e.g., janitorial services) that substantially influence the environment throughout their life cycle.
- Budgetary significance entails directing endeavours towards domains that incur substantial expenditures within the government.
- Market Influence Potential: Concentrating efforts on regions where market impact is most probable. This could be determined by the magnitude and scope of the contract or by the value that suppliers place on public sector clients.

The Principles of Green Public Procurement

Each nation's government must adhere to specific principles when implementing green public procurement. This ensures that these activities align with the country's fiscal management regulations while achieving environmental protection objectives.

Principle of Necessity: As an initial step in public procurement, diligently assess the essentiality of the product or service. Prioritise repair or modification of existing products where feasible. Additionally, explore tax incentives or leasing options as alternatives to the outright purchase of new products, ensuring quantities strictly align with operational requirements (International Green Purchasing Network, 2010).

Principle of Product Lifecycle: Products proposed for government procurement necessitate meticulous scrutiny throughout their constituent materials and production processes. As a significant purchaser, the government holds leverage to influence manufacturer behaviour, incentivising the development of environmentally sustainable products. Procurement decisions must encompass comprehensive environmental impact assessments spanning the entirety of a product's lifecycle, from raw material acquisition to eventual disposal. Following the International Green Purchasing Network (2010), consideration should be given to the following characteristics:

- Hazardous Substance Minimisation: Consumers play a role in reducing pollutants by opting for environmentally conscious products with minimal toxic content. This compels producers to eliminate the incorporation of substances detrimental to the environment and human health in their manufacturing practices.
- Resource and Energy Efficiency: Promote consumer preference for products designed to conserve resources and minimise energy consumption.
- Sustainable Natural Resource Utilization: Consumers should prioritise products that sustainably employ renewable natural resources to minimise adverse environmental effects.
- Durability Enhancement: Select products engineered for longevity. Furthermore, consumers are advised to evaluate components' replaceability, repairability, and maintenance requirements before purchase. Frequent component replacement should be avoided.
- Design for Reuse: Consumers should prioritise products designed for repeated use without the need for remanufacturing within the same application context. This approach significantly lessens environmental strain.

- Design for Recycling: Recycling presents an optimal solution when a product ends. Consumers should factor in established collection and recycling infrastructure when making procurement decisions.
- Recycled Content: Products containing recycled materials or reusable components promote resource conservation and waste reduction
- Disposability: Consumers should favour options that facilitate ease of handling and disposal for products unsuited for reuse or recycling to minimise detrimental environmental impacts.

Principle of Value for Money: Goods and services procured by the government utilising taxpayer funds necessitate an assurance that their value justifies the expenditure. Optimal value assessment transcends cost considerations, encompassing quality, efficacy, and alignment with intended objectives. Environmental protection may be incorporated as a critical criterion, ensuring equitable consideration within the context of procurement contract awards (European Union, 2016).

Principle of Equity: Adherence to internal market principles and national legislation must govern green public procurement activities. Vendor selection and the execution of procurement contracts shall be based on established national green public procurement standards, ensuring the absence of any discriminatory practices among bidders (European Union, 2016).

Principle of Transparency: Green public procurement program information must be disseminated clearly and transparently through various media channels such as legal documents, websites, news programs, etc. This open access to information grants producers adhering to environmentally conscientious practices the opportunity to engage with the government as suppliers. Transparent decision-making processes within procurement activities deter any potential for bias or arbitrary actions by contracting authorities. Furthermore, contracting agencies should inform unsuccessful bidders of the rationale behind proposal rejections – the process of green public procurement (European Union, 2016).

Institutional frameworks hold a decisive influence over the development of green public procurement practices. These institutions shape the formal (e.g., legislation) and informal (e.g., cultural norms, customs, beliefs) rules and regulations that establish behavioural parameters for organisations and individuals within government agencies. This regulatory environment must encompass environmental considerations throughout all public procurement processes, from initial planning to selection, tendering, implementation, and project oversight.

Fig. 10.1 illustrates the crucial role played by governments in enacting policies and mechanisms that directly and indirectly influence the behaviours of both consumers and producers within the broader marketplace, thereby fostering the emergence of a green market (Kyu Woong Ko, 2015).

- The enactment of mandatory regulations or incentives targeting consumers is in both public and private domains, prioritising eco-friendly procurement practices and reshaping consumer behaviour and lifestyles. By establishing ecologically conscious procurement standards, downstream alterations in manufacturing

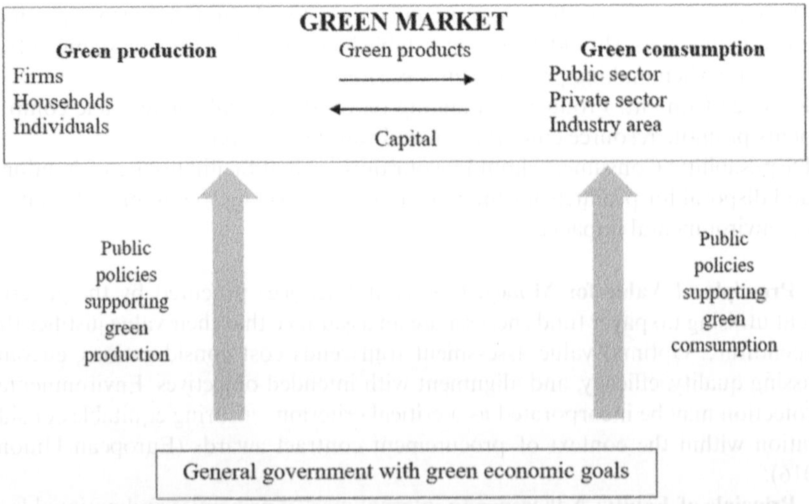

Fig. 10.1. Institutional Framework for the Establishment of a Green Market. *Source*: Illustrated by authors.

practices are induced, resulting in the development of environmentally sustainable products.

- Green public procurement represents a conditional form of public procurement. When the state, acting as a consumer, imposes stipulations, suppliers of public goods must adapt their production methods and potentially reorient product offerings to align with consumer demands.
- Green public procurement regulations necessitate governmental agencies to incorporate environmental considerations, such as ecological friendliness, minimal emissions, and reduced energy intensity, into their procurement evaluations and supplier requirements.
- Moreover, the demands of the green market and mandatory production standards compel manufacturers and supply chain partners to innovate technologies and develop environmentally responsible products. This leads to an intrinsic market transformation and a green market paradigm.

Successful implementation of green public procurement necessitates adherence to a defined process. Typically, the core stages of a green public procurement process are (i) procurement planning, (ii) tender specification development, (iii) supplier selection, (iv) procurement contract finalisation, (v) contract execution, and (vi) contract management and oversight (see Fig. 10.2).

Green Public Procurement in Japan

Japan has emerged as a notable Asian country in establishing a robust public procurement framework prioritising environmental sustainability. In the late 1980s, the inception of the green procurement movement in Japan commenced. The government launched the Eco Mark Programme, a Type I environmental

Fig. 10.2. Green Public Procurement Process. *Source*: Vietnamese Ministry of Natural Resources and Environment (2017).

labelling scheme, in 1989. In 1994, a local government organisation implemented green procurement practices throughout its facilities. The promotion of container and packaging material recycling in Japan has been facilitated by the 1995 Containers/Packaging Recycling Act. In Japan, containers and packaging materials comprise as much as 60% of domestic waste (International Green Purchasing Network, 2010). Additionally, this legislation requires that end-users segregate materials before their collection by local governments and transfer them to designated recycling organisations. The Ministry of Environment effectively launched the green purchasing network in Japan in February 1996, capitalising significantly on its prior efforts to promote green purchasing domestically. The principal aim of the green purchasing network is to enhance green procurement in Japan by providing all-encompassing guidance and information regarding green public procurement practices. The green purchasing network has implemented numerous green public procurement initiatives, such as organising green exhibitions and conferences, bestowing "Green Purchasing" awards, and creating a product information database.

Law on Promoting Green Purchasing

The Japanese government enacted the Act on Promoting Green Purchasing, alternatively titled the Act on Promotion of Procurement of Eco-Friendly Goods and Services by the State and Other Entities, in 2001 to augment the market presence of environmentally sustainable products. The Law on Promoting Green Purchasing was implemented in Japan starting in 2001. This legislation mandated that the central government of Japan actively enhance and improve green purchasing policies, as well as execute procurement plans that adhere to a catalogue of environmentally friendly products. The Law on Promoting Green Purchasing also seeks to reduce society's environmental impact while fostering sustainability. The law mandates that all government agencies and organisations procure goods using green public procurement practices. It is the responsibility of the Ministry of the Environment to establish the fundamental policies of the law, which include evaluation criteria for all designated procurement categories. Numerical values must be integrated into these criteria to guarantee objectivity. Ensuring evaluation standards, product value, quality, and performance is imperative. The following are the characteristics of the evaluation criteria of the Law on Promoting Green Purchasing (Japanese Ministry of Environment, 2016): (i) Define evaluation standards for specific procurement categories; (ii) take into account the quantity of environmentally friendly public procurement in addition to environmental concerns; (iii) solicit deliberation at committee meetings before seeking Cabinet approval, taking into account public opinion; and (iv) absence of a specialised certification programme. Before 2007, green purchasing was practised by 68% of 700 local governments and cities, all ministries of the central government, 47 prefectural governments, and 12 specified cities in Japan. The proportion of green products in the overall purchases of the selected categories was 95%. To provide direction for government procurement, the Japanese government established a green purchasing programme that predominantly employed product criteria derived from the Energy Star and Ecomareco-labelling programmes (94 and 37 per cent, respectively), in addition to a set of criteria and database designed exclusively for the government green purchasing programme (International Green Purchasing Network, 2010).

The Ministry of Environment, per the Law on Green Purchasing, has instituted environmental review guidelines for suppliers to verify the accuracy and reliability of information about environmentally friendly products. The protocols for establishing credibility encompass methodologies for information preparation and verification. Suppliers ought to collect the requisite data from other suppliers within the supply chain to ascertain whether their products and services satisfy the evaluation criteria of the primary policy. Additionally, they must keep compliance documentation readily available to purchasers. The environmental performance indicator guidance delineates the methodology for showcasing suitable ecological adherence and performance. This directive is contingent upon the self-assessed compliance claims of each organisation with ISO14021 Type II (Japanese Ministry of Environment, 2016).

The implementation of green public procurement by central government agencies is regulated by the Green Purchasing Promotion Act, which establishes specific procurement categories and their corresponding evaluation criteria. On the other hand, the Eco Mark Programme is administered by the Japan Environmental Association. It uses certification criteria established independently from the government to assist consumers and suppliers in green purchasing. The Act generally establishes evaluation standards that consider the green and environmentally friendly public procurement volume. Concurrently, the Eco Mark Programme establishes certification criteria to develop technologies and lead the market, irrespective of the volume of green public procurement by communities and government agencies. Significantly, when third-party certifiers, such as the Eco Mark Programme, are by the Act, they are deemed to satisfy its assessment criteria. These can be identified through the procurement activities of government agencies that procure environmentally sustainable products that meet the assessment criteria outlined in the Act (Japanese Ministry of Environment, 2016).

All ministries and government agencies must implement green procurement policies per this legislation. Public green procurement law is intended to encourage the government to acquire environmentally friendly goods and services at both the state and local levels. Through the implementation of this legislation, customer education regarding ecologically friendly products and services is additionally fortified. The central government establishes and declares an annual procurement policy containing targets for product categories and services through green procurement. Additionally, recycling packaging and packaging materials is governed by Japanese policy (Japanese Ministry of Environment, 2016).

The Japanese government implemented green public procurement for 189 out of 199 designated procurement categories, or 95% of the total, by established criteria, according to a 2013 survey by the Ministry of the Environment. This starkly contrasts with their performance of 44% in 2001 (Japanese Ministry of Environment, 2016). This indicates that since the law's promulgation, the government has actively promoted green procurement activities. Furthermore, according to survey results, the market share of environmentally friendly products in the reviewed categories has increased since the law's implementation. There is neither a certification programme nor a label established by the Law on Promoting Green Purchasing to identify products that satisfy evaluation criteria. Instead, suppliers may self-certify that their products fulfil the evaluation criteria outlined in the fundamental policy.

Law on Green Contract

The Green Contract Law, which governs the promotion of contracts by the government and other entities to reduce greenhouse gas emissions, was also enacted in 2007. The provisions of this legislation concern the green contracting responsibilities that government agencies and public institutions must uphold when acquiring contracts for automobiles, electricity, and energy service company projects. The Green Contract Law is a supplementary legislation to the Act on Promoting Green Purchasing in Japan, as it establishes the legal framework for green public procurement (International Green Purchasing Network, 2010). Its primary focus is on the greenhouse gas reduction aspect of specific products and services.

Act on Promoting Green Purchasing

The year 2016 marked the Japanese government's enactment of the Act on Promoting Green Purchasing. In addition, the Act on Promoting Green Purchasing seeks to create a society in which environmentally sustainable footprints are diminished. The Act (Fig. 10.3) requires all public institutions and government agencies to utilise green public procurement (GPP) for specific procurement items. The Ministry of the Environment is responsible for developing the Act's foundational policy, including item-specific evaluation criteria for procurement purposes. By fundamental policy, every public institution and government agency must establish its procurement policy and objective. An annual report detailing the agency's progress shall be submitted to the Minister of the Environment (Fig. 10.4).

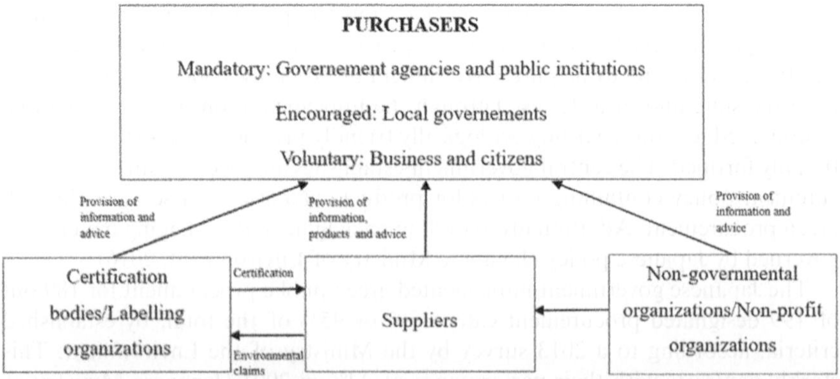

Fig. 10.3. Roles of Stakeholders in Green Purchasing in Japan. *Source*: Japanese Ministry of Environment (2016).

The Ministry of the Environment will annually revise the fundamental green public procurement policy in conjunction with other specialised ministries. However, the Ministry of Environment will be primarily responsible for devising the necessary forms to review the evaluation criteria and other pertinent subjects. Academicians comprise the Reviewing Committee, whereas industry associations and other specialised stakeholders comprise the technical committees.

The Japanese government evaluates the environmental impact of 19 out of 270 product categories through standardised metrics. To identify a "typical" green product for each category, the minimum green specifications specified in the green public procurement policy are applied. The quantification of environmental advantages is done in CO_2 equivalents, which signify the decreases in emissions of greenhouse gases. Emission estimates for energy-consuming or energy-influencing products are calculated using the energy consumption factor of the utilised energy source and product attributes in conjunction with energy consumption over a specified number of years during the use phase. The environmental specifications of energy-efficient products, including textiles and stationery, are converted to CO_2-equivalent emissions estimates. The advantages are subsequently ascertained by comparing the market share of environmentally friendly products in 2000, as sourced from industry data preceding the current period. The implementation of the legislation at that time required the participation of green public procurement officials (Japanese Ministry of Environment, 2016). The delineation of this is detailed below in Table 10.1.

The Japanese government's implementation of the green public procurement programme substantially aided the green market's expansion. For example, public buyers in Japan significantly contributed to the expansion of the electric vehicle industry. Nissan debuted the Leaf, the initial mass-produced electric vehicle, in 2010. In the early stages of production, most units were acquired by local administrations (UNESCAP, 2012). In the year after the introduction of the vehicle, approximately half of the 619 charging stations were situated on municipal property. The remaining charging stations were located on the property of organisations promoting electric vehicles. Nissan successfully developed an expedited

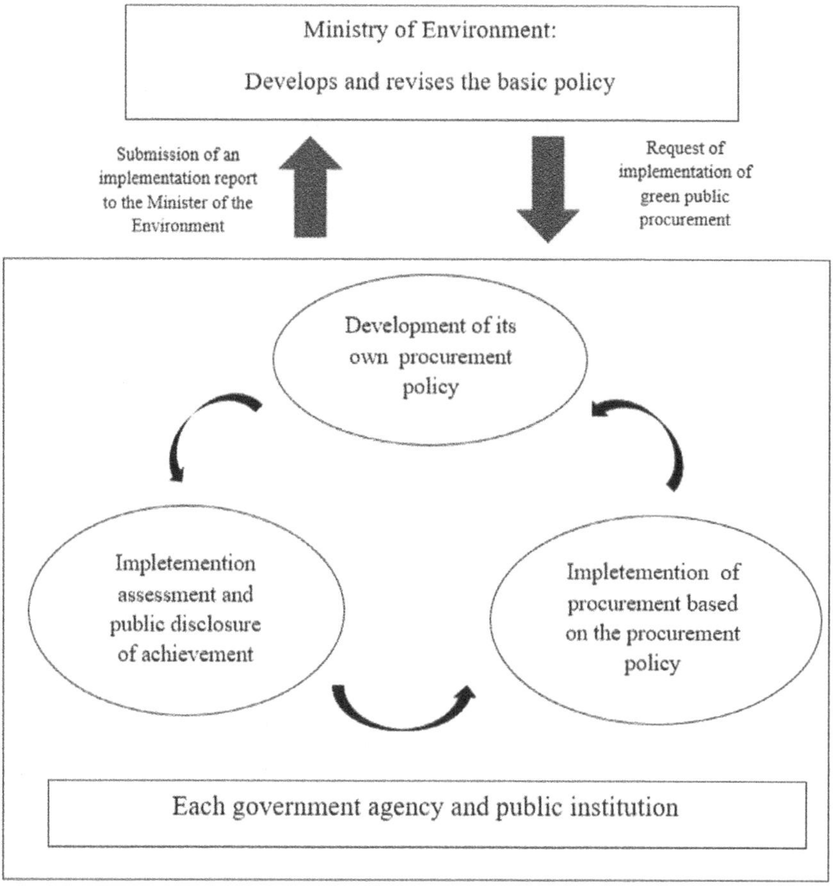

Fig. 10.4. Implementation of Green Public Procurement in Japan.
Source: Japanese Ministry of Environment (2016).

charging unit that was more compact, economical, and user-friendly due to the early support provided by the government. Nissan deployed these cutting-edge recharge stations in diverse areas across Japan. Recurring customer sales increased significantly. Local administrations allocate one fast-charging station every 15 km nationwide (UNESCAP, 2012).

Green Public Procurement in Korea

In Korea, green public procurement is crucial for advancing sustainable development. The Korean government has enacted many policies and regulations to promote the procurement of more sustainable products and services by private enterprises and public organisations. Korea, similar to Japan, has swiftly adopted and enforced green public procurement policies. Korea has adopted Sustainable Production and Consumption (SPC) policies since the 1990s to promote

Table 10.1. List of Categories for Designated Procurement Items as of February 2016.

1	Paper	8	Home electronic appliances (TVs, microwave ovens, etc.)	15	Interior fixtures and bedding (carpets, curtains, etc.)
2	Stationery	9	Air conditioners, etc.	16	Work gloves
3	Office furniture, etc.	10	Water heaters, etc. (electric water supply system, gas water heaters, etc.)	17	Other fiber products
4	Imaging equipment, etc.	11	Lighting (lamps, LEDs, etc.)	18	Facilities (solar panels, solar thermal appliances, etc.)
5	Computers, etc.	12	Vehicles, etc. (vehicles, tityresengine oil)	19	Stockpiles for disaster
6	Office equipment, etc.	13	Fire extinguishers	20	Public works projects
7	Mobile telephones, etc.	14	Uniforms and work clothes	21	Services (printing, transportation, delivery, etc.)

Source: Japanese Ministry of Environment (2016).

resource-conserving and sustainable production practices. The establishment of green public procurement in Korea occurred concurrently with the implementation of the Korea Eco-label, which was mandated by the Act on Development and Support of Environmental Technology 1994. Government agencies were recommended to prioritise acquiring products that possessed the Korea Eco-label. On the contrary, the lack of labelled products and the absence of a surveillance mechanism rendered this recommendation futile (OECD, 2015).

The notion of green public procurement became more precise following the Ministry of Environment's enactment of the Act on Promoting the Purchase of Green Products in 2005 (hereafter referred to as the 2005 Act). Public organisations – central and, per the 2005 Act, local governments and public agencies – are required to submit to the Ministry of Environment, at the start of each year, an annual green public procurement implementation plan and a record of implementation from the previous year. Numerous consultations were conducted to ascertain the precise details of the 2005 Act, encompassing ministries, public organisations, experts, and industries. As a result of these dialogues, it was determined that green public procurement ought to be standardised based on labelling schemes already in place, namely, the Recycled Oil and Korea Eco-labels. The objective of this strategy was to decrease the administrative expenses linked to the establishment of distinct green procurement criteria for every ministry.

The government establishes no quantitative targets for green public procurement. Nonetheless, each public organisation must establish and report its voluntary objectives to the Ministry of Environment (e.g., the projected volume of green procurement and the proportion of green purchases to the total procurement amount annually). According to the Ministry of Environment projections, the green public procurement market is expected to experience a 1.5-fold expansion over 15 years, or from 2012 to 2015.

(i) Products and services that meet the criteria for green public procurement are those that the Korea Eco-Label endorses or meet its fundamental standards, as defined by the 2005 Law. (ii) Products that are certified or satisfy the Good Recycled Mark quality certificate criteria. (iii) Products adhere to additional environmental standards established by the Ministry of Environment in consultation with the respective ministry chiefs.

The 2005 Law mandates that government agencies give precedence to procuring environmentally friendly products and services that meet social responsibility standards. The 2005 Law was adhered to by around 30,000 subordinate organisations and 870 sponsoring organisations in 2012 (OECD, 2015). Two approaches exist for implementing green procurement. Organisations may acquire environmentally sustainable products and services on an individual basis. The Korea Public Procurement Service will manage the procurement, the central public procurement agency, should the total procurement exceed a predetermined threshold. In contrast, by including green technical specifications or special conditions in the contract, each organisation may require contractors to procure environmentally friendly products in exchange for their services (e.g., construction, maintenance, repair, and operation). Local administrations and public institutions in the Republic of Korea can receive annual performance incentives to comply with green public procurement practices (United Nations Environment Programme and Korea Environmental Industry and Technology Institute, 2019).

The "Green Market," an e-commerce marketplace, has been operational since 2009. It furnishes a streamlined tool for public procurers across Korea to execute low-volume green procurement activities without formal tendering. The automatic monitoring of these transactions reduces the reporting burden for procurers regarding green public procurement (United Nations Environment Programme and Korea Environmental Industry and Technology Institute, 2019).

The information regarding green public procurement is conveniently published on the websites of the Green Products Information Systems and the Ministry of Environment, enabling the general public to examine and compare the data. Furthermore, prominent media organisations in the Republic of Korea frequently report the findings after disclosing the data. This phenomenon fosters competition among public entities. According to the OECD (2015), the submission rate for government agencies' procurement plans and implementation records was 96.4% in 2013. Similarly, the reporting rate for organisation implementation records stood at 97.7%. Since its inception, the total quantity of green public procurement has increased substantially since the enactment of the 2005 Act, and this upward trend has continued. In addition, to inform the public of the advantages, the Korea Environmental Industry and Technology Institute computes the yearly economic, environmental, and social ramifications of green public procurement. The reduction in CO_2 emissions is estimated to be the equivalent of 3.1 million tonnes, resulting in 54.5 billion KRW in economic savings (Kyu Woong Ko, 2015).

By capitalising on public demand, the passage of the 2005 Act has accelerated the development of eco-labelled products in terms of both quantity and quality. Since 2004, when it was 254.9 billion won, the government budget for green procurement activities has increased by more than threefold, from 787 billion won in 2005 to 1,727 billion won in 2012. From 2004 to 2012, the number of products that obtained certification from the Korea Eco-Labeling Agency experienced a 3.8-fold increase (Kyu Woong Ko, 2015).

The assessment of the training needs of contracting authorities was the subject of a survey conducted by the Korea Environmental Industry and Technology Institute (Korea Environmental Industry and Technology Institute (KEITI), 2018). The survey encompassed enquiries regarding green public procurement awareness, the motivations behind the procurement of green products, and the elements that would promote green public procurement. According to the survey results, the principal driver was the government's enforcement of mandatory green procurement and supervision of implementation. Furthermore, procurers expressed satisfaction with the e-procurement system's ability to streamline selecting authorised green products. Moreover, they insisted that local green product catalogues and stores be established. The most frequently expressed concerns regarding requests for training sessions were clarifications regarding the economic and environmental benefits of green products, the exchange of insights regarding optimal methods, and assistance with utilising the online platform and e-procurement tools.

Green Public Procurement in South East Asia

Green public procurement is one of the crucial methods to promote sustainability and reduce the negative impact of business activities on the environment. Southeast Asian countries increasingly focus on green public procurement activities to achieve sustainability goals and reduce environmental pollution. This chapter analyses the status of green public procurement in four Southeast Asian nations: Thailand, Indonesia, Malaysia, and the Philippines. These countries share many similarities in terms of culture and economic development levels. Additionally, the governments of these four countries are implementing numerous reforms and innovations in public financial management to promote the expansion of green public procurement programs.

Green Public Procurement in Thailand

Since 2005, the Royal Thai Government has implemented a range of strategies, plans, and policies to guide Thailand's development towards sustainability. That same year, the Pollution Control Department, operating under the Ministry of Natural Resources and Environment, initiated green public procurement in Thailand. Two Green Public Procurement Promotion Plans were established in 2008 to propel and implement green public procurement initiatives (as below).

The Pollution Control Department has spearheaded green public procurement implementation within the public sector, and various initiatives have been pursued by the plan, such as conducting workshops and training seminars for procurement staff and establishing a voluntary monitoring system to evaluate advancements towards the objectives of green public procurement policy. Thailand has made significant strides in developing goals and metrics associated with its Green Public Procurement Promotion Plans concerning training workshops and other crucial aspects of its green public procurement program.

The primary goal of the Green Public Procurement Promotion Plan (2008–2011) was to raise the government's spending on environmentally friendly products and services through practical tools. The product criteria for the Thai green public procurement program were derived primarily from the Thai Green Label Scheme (82%), supplemented by the Energy Efficiency Label (6%), and additional criteria (6%). The Pollution Control Department is implementing many proactive promotional measures to facilitate and promote green public procurement implementation. These initiatives include devising green procurement guidelines, conducting training courses for government procurement officials, and operating a dedicated generic gateway protocol website. An electronic reporting system is implemented to oversee performance and provide semi-annual updates on dedicated generic gateway protocol results (International Green Purchasing Network, 2010).

The Second Green Public Procurement Promotion Plan (2013–2016) broadened the target groups to include local authorities, private sector enterprises, and the general public (International Green Purchasing Network, 2010). In 2012, the plan was drafted to expand the scope of green public procurement from the central government to local authorities and the private and public sectors. The National Environmental Agency approved the second plan and is awaiting cabinet approval. Nevertheless, the Pollution Control Department has initiated green public procurement initiatives as outlined in the plan. The Second Green Public Procurement Promotion Plan aims to incentivise government agencies to participate in green public procurement and to assist the private sector in adopting green production practices. Additionally, it seeks to enhance the availability of green products in the market, thereby fostering sustainable consumption (Korea Environmental Industry and Technology Institute, 2019).

Besides, under the Thailand Environment Institute, the Thai Green Label Committee is the primary organisation responsible for the green labelling program. The Thailand Environment Institute Board of Directors manages the Thai Green Label Scheme, while a technical sub-committee shoulders the responsibility of developing product criteria and testing methods. Overall, selecting product categories for the Thai Green Label program hinges on stakeholder needs. Green Label criteria encompass a product's entire life cycle. The Board of Directors approves product selection, whereas the technical sub-committee drafts criteria for selected product categories. By 2014, criteria for green public procurement had been established for 17 products and five services under the program (Korea Environmental Industry and Technology Institute, 2019). A database of certified products/services was created to streamline procurement decision-making for bidders, containing pertinent information on product categories and criteria accessible on the Pollution Control Department website.

To sum up, green public procurement in Thailand can be described in Table 10.2.

Green Public Procurement in Indonesia

Activities of Green Public Procurement for the period 2016–2018 focused on developing criteria and programs for environmentally friendly goods and services: Achievements of green public procurement in the tasks of the green public procurement Technical Working Group in 2016; establishment of criteria, programs/eco-labelling schemes in Ministries/Sectors; development of criteria and programs for environmentally friendly Goods and Services; drafting of the regulation of the Minister of Ministry of Environment and Forestry on green public procurement. Following the issuance of Decision No. 5/2019 of the Ministry of Environment and Forestry Minister, information on the commencement of green public procurement implementation for relevant ministries/sectors was disseminated. Green public procurement Achievements in 2019: Decision No. 5/2019 of the Ministry of Environment and Forestry Minister on the Procedures for Conducting Eco-labeling for green public procurement; introduction of green public procurement implementation in Indonesia issued on July 11, 2019 (Asia Pacific Roundtable for Cleaner Production and SWITCH-Asia (APRSCP, 2022a)).

Due to the COVID-19 pandemic, green public procurement-related activities in 2020 were mainly conducted online (video conferences). Green public procurement achievements in 2020 (APRSCP, 2022a): implementation of Market Readiness Research in cooperation with GIZ and SWITCH-Asia; piloting green public procurement for two groups of environmentally friendly goods and services, namely, printing paper and indoor furniture; Launch of green public procurement public information in December 2020 as following:

- ☐ Information System for Environmentally Friendly Goods and Services for Green Public Procurement;
- ☐ Video on green public procurement implementation in Indonesia;
- ☐ Green Public Procurement Handbook;
- ☐ Dissemination of the next phase of green public procurement sustainable public procurement implementation in December 2020.

The Indonesian government has issued a List of Environmentally Friendly Products for Green Public Procurement (Appendix to Decision No. P.5/2019 of the Minister of Ministry of Environment and Forestry and Appendix to Decision No. SK 1207/Menlhk/Setjen/Kum.1/12/2021 of the Minister of MoEF), which includes several product groups such as paper, plastic, wood, medical waste treatment equipment, air conditioners, and building materials. Outcomes and agreements from the coordination meet with the program owner and the Association of Furniture Manufacturers with Forest Legality Verification System certification (APRSCP, 2022a).

Table 10.2. The Comparison of Green Public Procurement Policy among Thailand, Indonesia, Malaysia, and the Philippines.

Criteria	Thailand	Indonesia	Malaysia	Philippines
Standards and Regulations	- Issue-specific regulations on green public procurement in industry, agriculture, and services - Set specific targets for increasing the use of environmental products and services in procurement processes	- Have specific standards and regulations for green public procurement but lack a legal framework and detailed guidance on green public procurement - Promulate the process of providing information on the initial implementation of Good Pharmacy Practices to relevant agencies since 2019	Have green public procurement standards and regulations, but not used wildly and effectively	There are several standards and guidelines on green public procurement, but they do not complete the legal framework and specific standards.
Legal Framework	- Strengths: Establish a relatively comprehensive and robust legal framework for green public procurement, including specific regulations and government guidelines - Weaknesses: Enforcement and compliance with regulations still face several challenges, including monitoring and control issues	- Strengths: Developing regulations and guidelines for green public procurement, with detailed instructions from government agencies - Weaknesses: The remaining limits on the legal framework, such as not being widely implemented	- Strengths: Having a relatively comprehensive and solid legal foundation for green public procurement - Weaknesses: Having issues with monitoring and control to ensure the effectiveness of the policies	- Strengths: Regulations and guidelines related to green public procurement should be included, along with legal documents and instructions from government agencies. - Weaknesses: Facing several challenges when implementing and complying with the regulations on green public procurement policy

(Continued)

Table 10.2. (continued)

Criteria	Thailand	Indonesia	Malaysia	Philippines
Incentives and Promotions	- Provide incentives and preferential treatment for Organizations and Government Agencies to Conduct Green Public Procurement; - Develop green public procurement criteria for 17 products and five services for the green public procurement program	Consider using incentives and preferential treatment to encourage green public procurement, but these are not yet widely implemented	- Green Investment Tax Allowance for Green Assets or Green Projects provides a 100% tax allowance (credit for buyers of qualified systems and equipment). This allowance is offset against taxable income over a maximum of 5 years - Green Income Tax Exemption for 100% tax exemption on services provided for a maximum of 5 years from 2013 to 2020 for eligible service providers	Encourage the implementation of green public procurement through incentives and promotions, but the level of implementation is still low.
Achievements of the Green Public Procurement Policy	Accelerate the shift towards green public procurement within government agencies and organisations; Significant environmental benefits from green public procurement projects include reduced waste and energy consumption	Not yet	Public green procurement can achieve some environmental benefits, but expanding and strengthening these projects is necessary	Reduce waste and energy consumption.

Source: Summarized by authors.

Green Public Procurement Malaysia

The Malaysian Government adopts a decentralised procurement approach aligned with the principle of "empowering the manager." This approach aims to enhance efficiency and transparency in the government's procurement process. Therefore, funds are allocated to the respective Controlling Officers. Each Ministry is authorised to conduct procurement activities based on the approved budget. The objectives of decentralisation are to stimulate economic growth, expedite project implementation, and facilitate faster payment processes. However, although the procurement responsibility has been authorised to the relevant agencies, the Ministry of Finance still formulates central government procurement rules and procedures, which all agencies must follow. It is important to note that several items are procured under centralised contracts, which can only be purchased through the Ministry of Finance. This is about specialised postal services that provide express delivery, envelopes, high-density polyethylene accessories, fire extinguishers, Microsoft software, A4 paper, small arms, and fireworks equipment. Because A4 paper is a sustainable buying priority product for government agencies, the central agreement has facilitated the purchase of green products in this category. The decentralised nature of acquisition is why a dedicated generic gateway protocol bureau has been set up at each ministry level and agency, and a dedicated generic gateway protocol coordinator has been appointed. The first step in a total acquisition process cycle is planning, and the Green Procurement Plan is several tasks of the annual procurement plan. Agencies must submit yearly procurement plans including green purchasing to the Ministry of Finance before January 15. The Green Procurement Plan provides information on particular green contracts to be implemented in the coming year. The information introduced in the green public procurement plan includes green procurement titles and banners, type of acquisition (supplies, services, works, or consultancy), green public procurement production group, estimated procurement value by production group, and the predicted value of green public procurement by product group (APRSCP, 2022b).

The Instructions for Government Inspectors (issued in July 2014 to support those implementing green public procurement) outline the steps for integrating green public procurement into actual policies. The guidelines contribute helpful information, such as the influence of managing the demand for purchasing goods and services and how to combine environmental criteria into each stage of the procurement process, including identifying needs, preparing technical blueprints, evaluating bids, selecting suppliers, and managing contracts. In addition, a tool has been promoted to support procurers in considering life cycle costs so that life cycle cost results can be used to inform procurement decisions. The Ministry of Finance has schemes to improve the electronic procurement system as a future program to capture green public procurement data. This part of the Government Transformation Program is expected to be undertaken early. Nevertheless, since the "NextGen e-procurement" system will combine various factors, including green public procurements, into a consolidated procurement system, the final timetable for enrichment is still anonymous (APRSCP, 2022b).

The text discusses green public procurement in Malaysia and mentions the role of the Malaysian government in promoting it: Several research studies show that recognition of green public procurement among administrators in Malaysian state-owned enterprises is good. Initiatives promoted by the Malaysian government have generated a knowledge base to stimulate action among all industry players. For instance, the Malaysian government has implemented short- and long-term action plans to promote the implementation of green public procurement. These initiatives include the MyHijau Program under the Ministry of Science, Technology, and Innovation and the Malaysian Green Technology and Climate Change Centre. These programs are efficacious platforms to promote green public procurement. Malaysian Green Technology and Climate Change Centre offers training programs to all government agencies over time, which builds capacity for understanding green public procurement guidelines on processes and reports. Malaysian Green Technology and Climate Change Centre also conducts green public procurement audits for the private sector to understand green public procurement requirements. This increases awareness among private entities participating in green public procurement (APRSCP, 2022b).

The Malaysian government has implemented the Green Technology Grant Program and the Green Technology Incentive Program. These initiatives aim to promote the development of green technology and encourage green investment. The document also mentions the tax incentives for green technology (Green Income Tax Exemption). Companies that meet the requirements can be exempted from 100% of their corporate income tax for up to 5 years (from 2013 to 2020) (APRSCP, 2022b).

Green Public Procurement in the Philippines

The implementation of green public procurement (GPP) in the Philippines is incorporated into the government's procurement procedures, overseen by the Government Procurement Policy Board (GPPB). It is primarily based on competitive bidding from qualified suppliers or contractors, based on technical specifications, as well as eligibility criteria set by the GPPB. These criteria include economic standing, past performance regarding reliability and comfortability with service, and value for money. Transparency, fairness, and promoting a level playing field are the core principles of government procurement. These principles are applied to both conventional government procurement and green public procurement (APRSCP, 2022c).

The criteria used to select the product list were based on the experience and practices of other countries and were adapted to the local context based on their relevance. The following criteria were identified by the Budget and Management Bureau and the Government Procurement Policy Board: Market Availability, Environmental Impact, Cost Significance, Feasibility, Support for Government Environmental Goals, and Ort for the Local Economy. Based on the cumulative scoring matrix, the 10 most commonly used supplies and equipment for green procurement were identified through consultative processes in collaboration with the SWITCH-Asia team. Specifically, these are multi-copy paper, toilet paper, notebooks, cleaning agents, chairs, disinfectant spray, trash bags, liquid, hand soap, laundry detergent, and light emitting diode (LED) light bulbs (APRSCP, 2022c).

It references a Provincial Procurement Service Report dated December 31, 2020. Six out of ten Considered Supplies and Equipment with green specifications were implemented. These include notebooks, toilet paper, disinfectant spray, LED lights, detergent, and cleaning agents (the proportion of these products procured from 2017 to 2022 as Fig. 10.5). Four of 10 non-common source equipment products with green specifications were also procured. These include computer monitors, vehicles, copiers, and air conditioners. (The proportion of these products procured between 2017 and 2020 is Fig. 10.6.) The total spending on common source equipment products amounted to PhP 147,547,681.85 (USD 7 billion), while spending on non-common source equipment products totalled PhP 3,134,074,204.35 (USD 150 billion) from 2017 to 2020. This information is based on a report by Ruiz (2021).

Following the Asia Pacific Roundtable for Cleaner Production and SWITCH-Asia (2022c) for the period of fiscal year 2018–2020, below are the agency procurement compliance performance indicator reports from the sample of 407 Procuring Units:

- ☐ There are 68 purchasing units have consistently applied green specifications in procuring non-common equipment and equipment items.

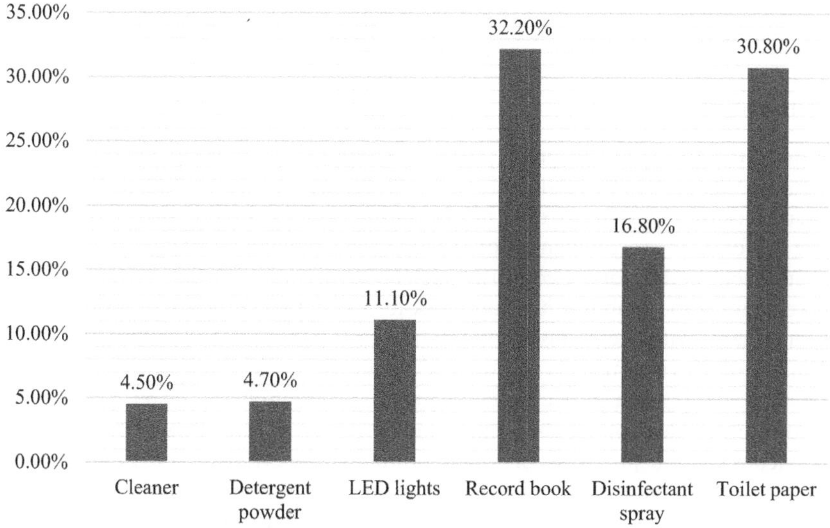

Fig. 10.5. Percentage Contribution of Common Source Equipment Products Procured between 2017 and 2022. *Source*: Ruiz (2021)

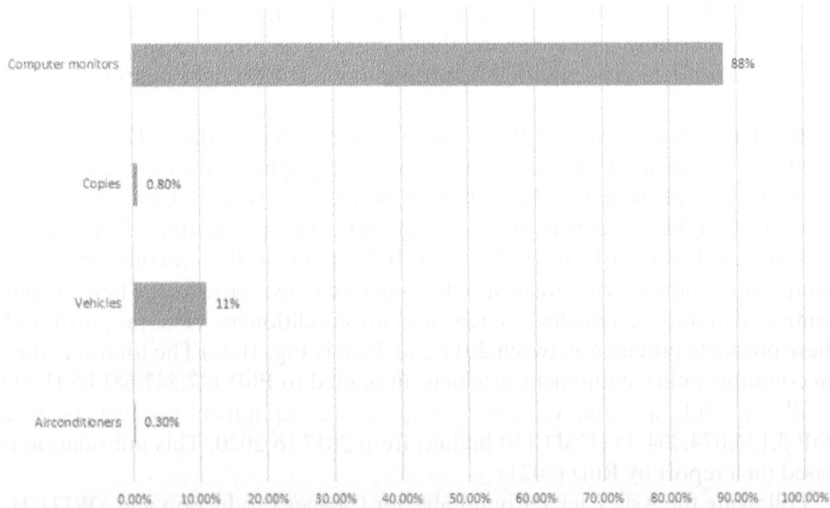

Fig. 10.6. Percentage Contribution of Non-common Source Equipment Products Procured between 2017 and 2020. *Source*: Ruiz (2021)

- ☐ Two hundred and twenty-eight purchasing units have inconsistently applied green specifications in procuring non-common equipment and equipment items.
- ☐ There are 38 purchasing units have not consistently applied green specifications in procuring non-common equipment and equipment items.

In summary, we would like to compare green public procurement policies in four Southeast Asian countries, as shown in Table 10.2.

Conclusion

Drawing insights from the green public procurement endeavours of four Southeast Asian nations (Thailand, Indonesia, Malaysia, and the Philippines) and the experiences of Japan and Korea in promoting such initiatives, the authors propose the following recommendations to aid in the implementation of green public procurement in developing countries such as Vietnam:

To begin with, establish the framework for the implementation of green public procurement, with the Ministry of Environment assuming the central role: The Ministry of Environment is responsible for drafting the legislation and regulations governing green public procurement in the Republic of Korea and Japan, in addition to developing the impact indicators used to evaluate this practice. To encourage the purchase of green products, the Ministry of Environment will formulate a comprehensive strategy delineating a range of policies that will promote green manufacturing, distribution, and consumption. Additionally, the expansion of the green market has been fueled by the introduction of eco-friendly products that incorporate technological advances to satisfy national environmental goals or standards. Subsequently, these policies are executed across various ecological domains, encompassing refuse, air, and water. Above all else, policy objectives encompass social benefits alongside economic and environmental benefits. Periodically, the policy on green public procurement should be reevaluated to account for the most recent research on technological developments, legislation, and standards. This procedure uses evaluation criteria to determine the number of prioritised product and service categories.

Subsequently, it is imperative to devise the inventory of commodities and services mandatory for the green public procurement initiative. Initiate national eco-labels and certification programmes in Vietnam. Public sector entities may establish ecolabels, including standards authorities or ministries, industry associations, or third parties. A transparent and unambiguous examination of the products and services is necessary to ascertain their compliance with the criteria for green production. The government may evaluate and revise the public procurement process by the list above to support sustainable development. Eco-labels enable purchasers to distinguish environmentally friendly products or services without assess their environmental impact or implementing ecological criteria.

Furthermore, it is recommended that green public procurement initiatives be initiated as a means to support and streamline the business community's shift towards environmentally sustainable practices. The endeavours above seek to expand the market's supply and diversity of ecologically sustainable goods and services while discouraging and, in certain instances, proscribing commercial strategies with adverse environmental consequences. Enhanced competition stimulates innovation and reduces costs, thereby expanding the accessibility of environmentally sustainable business practices. The market will be developed through public procurement of green products, bringing market share closer to a tipping point where prices become competitive and significant consumer preference exists. Governments can facilitate the growth of green markets by providing information, capacity building, financing, fiscal incentives, and regulatory oversight of business operations.

Fourth, it elicits the support of stakeholders for green public procurement reforms, as well as stakeholders' resistance and underlying motivations. Stakeholders comprise all entities and individuals that could be affected by the enforcement of green public procurement reforms. This typically includes civil society organisations, government policymakers, procurement professionals, suppliers and contractors from the private sector, households, and management and staff of procuring entities. Leaders of green public procurement reforms will better comprehend the stakeholder landscape, enabling them to recognise potential opportunities, anticipate opposition, and formulate appropriate responses. Stakeholder interests, values, and perceptions can be determined via consultative groups, online surveys, and interviews. Conducting focus groups with specific stakeholders allows one to examine their perceptions and concerns thoroughly. Potential dedicated generic gateway protocol champions who are motivated, able, and authorised to effect a change in procurement culture can be identified through stakeholder mapping.

References

Asia Pacific Roundtable on Sustainable Consumption & Production and SWITCH-Asia (APRSCP). (2022a). *Indonesia current status of green public procurement (GPP)* (pp. 12–35). Retrieved February 23, 2024, from https://www.switch-asia.eu/site/assets/files/3400/indonesia_country_report.pdf

Asia Pacific Roundtable on Sustainable Consumption & Production and SWITCH-Asia (APRSCP). (2022b). *Malaysia current status of green public procurement (GPP)* (pp. 4–20). Retrieved February 23, 2024, from https://www.switch-asia.eu/site/assets/files/3401/malaysia_country_report.pdf

Asia Pacific Roundtable on Sustainable Consumption & Production and SWITCH-Asia (APRSCP). (2022c). *The Philippines current status of green public procurement (GPP)* (pp 10–53). Retrieved February 23, 2024, from https://www.switch-asia.eu/site/assets/files/3402/philippines_country_report_13_july_2022.pdf

Bugge, H. S., & Voigt, C. (2008). Sustainable development in national and international law. In *The Avosetta Series*. Europa Law Publishing.

European Union. (2011), *Buying green: A handbook on green public procurement*, 2nd ed. European Union.

European Union. (2016), *Buying green: A handbook on green public procurement*, 3rd ed. European Union.

International Green Purchasing Network. (2010), Green purchasing: The new growth frontier: Policies and programs to enhance green business growth in Asia, Europe and the United States. *Cosmos Aoyama*, *5*, 53–67. Retrieved March 11, 2024, from http://www.igpn.org/DL/Green_Purchasing_The_New_Growth_Frontier.pdf.

Japanese Ministry of Environment. (2016). *Introduction to green purchasing legislation in Japan*. Retrieved June 22, 2022, from https://www.env.go.jp/content/000064788.pdf

Kaur, S., Kumar, R., Singh, K., & Huang, Y. L. (2024). Leveraging artificial intelligence for enhanced sustainable energy management. *Journal Sustainable Energy*, *3*(1), 1–20. https://doi.org/10.56578/jse030101

Korea Environmental Industry and Technology Institute (KEITI). (2018). *The survey results on green public procurement by public authorities*. Korea Environmental Industry and Technology Institute, Seoul. Retrieved June, 22, 2022, from https://publicadministration.un.org/unpsa/Portals/0/UNPSA_Submitted_Docs/2019/373639f9-df3c-4a81-95ea-0f6239a596dc/2020%20UNPSA_Korea%20Green%20Public%20Procurement_Stakeholder%20Evaluation_27112019_065809_382df38c-3004-4182-8dff-9e87a42e68b5.pdf?ver=1441-03-30-065809-907

Korea Environmental Industry and Technology Institute (KEITI). (2019). Recommendations for green public procurement incentive mechanisms: Thailand. In *Asia Pacific green public procurement partnership project*. Korea Environmental Industry and Technology Institute, Seoul. Retrieved June 22, 2022, from https://www.oneplanetnetwork.org/sites/default/files/from-crm/asia-pacific_green_public_procurement_partnership_project_in_thailand_recommendations_for_gpp_incentive_mechnisms2018.pdf

Kyu Woong Ko (2015), *Korea's green public procurement & lessons learnt*. Retrieved June 22, 2022, from https://www.oneplanetnetwork.org/sites/default/files/koreas_green_public_procurement_lessons_learned.pdf

Ndekwa, A. G., Kalugendo, E., Sood, K., & Grima, S. (2023). An analysis of agribusiness digitalisation transformation of the sub-Saharan African countries small-scale farmers' production distribution. *Research on World Agricultural Economy*, *4*(3), 63–78.

Organization for Economic Cooperation and Development (OECD). (2015). *Going green: Best practices for sustainable procurement*. Retrieved June 22, 2022, from https://www.oecd.org/gov/public-procurement/Going_Green_Best_Practices_for_Sustainable_Procurement.pdf

Rijal, S., Nursaputra, M. A. C., & Dari, H. U. (2024). Flood susceptibility analysis using frequency ratio method in Walanae watershed. *International Journal of Sustainable Development and Planning*, *19*(3), 823–832. https://doi.org/10.18280/ijsdp.190302

Ruiz, R. C. M. (2021). *Green public procurement in the Philippines*. Retrieved from https://wedocs.unep.org/20.500.11822/37011

Sood, K., & Özen, E. (2024). A systematic review of ESG in the insurance industry: Navigating the path to sustainability. *International Journal of Sustainable Development and Planning*, *19*(3), 807–821. https://doi.org/10.18280/ijsdp.190301

UN Economic and Social Commission for Asia and the Pacific (UNESCAP). (2012). *Green public procurement. Low carbon green growth roadmap for Asia and the Pacific: Fact sheet*. UNESCAP, Bangkok. Retrieved June 22, 2022, from https://repository.unescap.org/bitstream/handle/20.500.12870/301/ESCAP-2012-RP-Low-carbon-green-growth-roadmap-Asia-Pacific.pdf?sequence=1&isAllowed=y

United Nations Environment Programme. (2011). Annual Report. Retrived from https://wedocs.unep.org/bitstream/handle/20.500.11822/8053/-UNEP%202011%20Annual%20Report-20121086.pdf?sequence=5&amp%3BisAllowed=y%2C%20French%7C%7Chttps%3A//wedocs.unep.org/bitstream/handle/20.500.11822/8053/-UNEP%202011%20Annual%20Report-20121086-french.pdf%3Fsequence%3D6&amp%3BisA=

United Nations Environment Programme and Korea Environmental Industry and Technology Institute (UNEP and KEITI). (2019). *Green public procurement in the Republic of Korea: A decade of progress and lessons learned*. United Nations Environment Programme, Nairobi. Retrieved June 22, 2022, from https://wedocs.unep.org/bitstream/handle/20.500.11822/32535/GPPK.pdf?sequence=1&isAllowed=y

Vietnamese Ministry of Natural Resources and Environment. (2017). *Approach and implementation of sustainable procurement, project to promote consumption and production of green products through sustainable public procurement and eco-labels (SPPEL)*.

World Bank. (2021). *Green public procurement: An overview of green reforms in country procurement systems*. Retrieved June 22, 2022, from https://documents1.worldbank.org/curated/en/157141636056129273/pdf/Green-Public-Procurement-An-Overview-of-Green-Reforms-in-Country-Procurement-Systems.pdf

Yerpude, S., Sood, K., & Grima, S. (2022). Blockchain-augmented digital supply chain management: A way to sustainable business. *Journal of Risk and Financial Management*, *16*(1), 7.

Chapter 11

Green Credit in Vietnam: Policies and Practices

Ngo Duc Tien

Academy of Finance, Hanoi, Vietnam

Abstract

Introduction: To facilitate the effective operation of green credit, every nation should establish a framework of green credit policies. The banking system, particularly commercial banks, has implemented several regulations to encourage green credit and financial activities in general. The State Bank of Vietnam also emphasizes the development of green credit by utilizing management documents issued by the Government and the State Bank.

Purpose: The chapter focuses on statistical analysis and policy recommendations for green credit implementation in Vietnam, employing practical implications to support the development of macro-management policies that promote sustainable development.

Methodology: We use analysis methods, statistics, comparison, and synthesis of data on green credit at Vietnamese commercial banks to analyze the current situation.

Findings: Challenges arise during the execution phase due to the need for more legal documentation about management concerning risk assessment, standards, and subjects bestowed with green credit.

Practical implications: The government should build a solid legal framework with detailed guidance for all stakeholders relating to the green credit process. Commercial banks in Vietnam should develop various products and services related to green credit with attractive content to promote this kind of credit.

Green Management: A New Paradigm in the World of Business, 183–207

doi:10.1108/978-1-83797-442-920241011

Keywords: Green credit; green banking; commercial bank; Vietnamese commercial banks; national green growth; sustainable finance; sustainable development

JEL Classifications: G21; E51; E81

Introduction

Since the 1990s, many investors have begun to find businesses that can control the impact of production activities on the environment and build a sustainable economy (Keane, 2009). The United Nations has officially declared 17 sustainable development goals since 2015. These goals prioritize the eradication of poverty, combating AIDS, addressing gender-based discrimination, and safeguarding the environment. The interconnection of these 17 sustainable development goals fosters sustainability in a nation's progress, analogous to the three pillars of sustainability identified by Elkington (1999): economy, environment, and society. Furthermore, green credit is regarded as an initiative in numerous nations to assist countries in achieving sustainable development goals.

Amid the escalating depletion of natural resources, climate change accompanied by numerous severe adverse effects, and escalating air pollution, among other challenges, countries progressively realize that green credit will serve as a preeminent instrument for implementing development strategies. Green credit is a form of credit implemented in numerous nations worldwide to promote sustainable development on a global scale and balance economic growth with environmental preservation. Green credit can be any financial action or planned financial activity, a product or service, to protect the environment (World Economic Forum, 2020). To encourage the use of green credit, governments and central banks of both developed and developing nations have issued policies and regulations.

Vietnam is one of the five nations most vulnerable to the impacts of climate change (World Bank Group and the Asian Development Bank, 2020). In response to this situation, the Vietnamese government has implemented some measures, with green credit regarded as the most crucial. The Vietnamese government has resolved to devise a system to encourage green investment and ensure the sustainable development of the entire nation (Communist Party of Vietnam, 2013). Regulations pertaining to managing environmental and social hazards problems and green credit in credit-granting activities and promoting credit growth are also employed (State Bank of Vietnam, 2015a). The directive's content makes it abundantly clear that the banking industry's credit-granting activities must prioritize human health and environmental protection to promote sustainable development. Subsequently, the Green Bank Development Project was approved in Vietnam; this project outlined objectives and proposed remedies for credit institutions to enhance their social responsibility and consciousness regarding environmental protection, climate change mitigation, the progressive transition of banking operations to green practices, and the active promotion of sustainable development and growth (State Bank of Vietnam, 2018a).

In contrast, the implementation of green credits in Vietnam has progressed sluggishly, comprising less than 5% of the total credit amount, according to a report by the SBV. This chapter will, therefore, provide an overview of green credit in Vietnam, an emerging nation that is making significant efforts to innovate its financial market to address the challenges posed by climate change and achieve sustainable development goals.

Literature Review

The Definition of Green Credit

Green credit is one of the solutions that the financial industry applies to deal with the world's environmental and social challenges through financial tools (Aizawa & Yang, 2010). According to Jin and Mengqi (2011), green credit, also called sustainable finance, primarily seeks sustainable development by modifying the financial industry's operational procedures, management policies, and business philosophies. Furthermore, Wang et al. (2019) propose that the implementation of green credit will prompt financial institutions to modify their credit strategies concerning environmentally polluting companies. This may involve implementing regulations on the structure of long- and short-term credit ratios. This will impact companies' investment structure and efficacy, significantly contributing to environmental pollution. Additionally, this cohort of researchers affirms that a primary objective of green credit is to assist enterprises in mitigating energy consumption throughout their operational activities. He et al. (2019) argue that green credit is a mechanism through which governmental bodies and financial institutions exert macroeconomic control. Furthermore, green credit is the primary funding source for initiatives to reduce industrial pollution, conserve energy, and protect the environment. Green credit influences the degree of investment in renewable energy directly by directing consumption and investment decisions and allocating credit resources.

Under the green loan principles published by the Asian Pacific Loan Market Association and the Loan Market Association (2018), green credit can be defined as any loan extended specifically to finance or refinance new or existing green initiatives that meet the eligibility requirements. The categories of green sectors include renewable energy, energy efficiency, green transportation, environmentally friendly and economically adapted products and production technologies, sustainable water management and wastewater treatment, green buildings, sustainable agriculture and forestry, and pollution prevention and control (Ndekwa et al., 2023; Sood & Özen, 2024; Yerpude et al., 2022).

Hence, as a check standard during the lending process, the bank considers information about the business and project applying for the green credit before making a lending decision (Yao et al., 2021). Green credit can be defined as financial support for business and production initiatives that pose minimal or no environmental risk. Its purpose is to contribute to the overall protection of the environment and serves as a tangible example of financing that supports sustainable development.

The Structure of the Green Credit System

The green credit system of a country will be built from green banking credit and green non-banking credit, as shown in Fig. 11.1.

The nature of credit is a borrowing relationship based on the principle of repayment and interest. Understanding the precise movement of capital within the Green Credit ecosystem is crucial for elucidating how funds are sourced, allocated, and deployed towards environmentally sustainable projects. This analysis delves into the specific pathways through which capital flows from capital owners to green banking credit institutions, green non-banking credit entities, and ultimately to capital mobilizers for green projects (Fig. 11.1).

Capital owners: Capital owners comprise various entities such as commercial banks, institutional investors, governmental bodies, and private investors. Capital owners initially provide the financial resources necessary for investment in green projects.

Green banking credit: Green credit from banks can be determined as green banking credit. Financial institutions extend Green banking credit for environmental protection or low-risk initiatives. In essence, green banking credit encompasses various credit granting methods, including loans, grants, and others, that incorporate considerations of environmental conservation and environmental impacts. Through financing pollution-reducing initiatives and green technology, green banking credit will contribute to the overall reduction of external carbon emissions and internal carbon footprint (Rahman & Barua, 2016). Green credit enables banks to safeguard the environment indirectly. Financial institutions or governing bodies establish various criteria to determine whether a project protects the environment (Julia & Kassim, 2021).

The banks will fulfill three requirements as part of the introduction of the green credit program. To begin with, green banking credit programs must provide suitable credit policies or instruments—such as loans, terms, interest rates, and amounts—to support energy-efficient and environmentally sustainable enterprises or plans. Furthermore, financial institutions must implement stringent penalties for enterprises and projects that contravene energy conservation

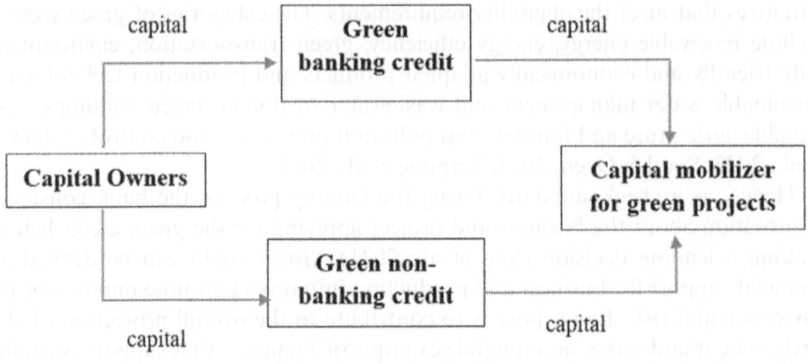

Fig. 11.1. The Structure of the Green Credit System. *Source*: Author's work.

and environmental protection laws and regulations. These penalties may include credit recovery, suspension, or delayed credit issuance. Under credit policies, banks should also supervise and advise debtors regarding environmental risks and incorporate social responsibility practices to mitigate credit risks.

Green non-banking credit: Green credit can be provided by governmental organizations, non-governmental organizations, and private enterprises to support green projects.

The extrabudgetary fund is one of the governmental organizations that can provide green credit for individuals or companies to conduct green investments. The extrabudgetary fund is often called the "Environmental Protection Fund." The government establishes and administers the fund. Loans are extended to support risk-free business and production endeavors that safeguard society and the environment. Funds can mobilize capital from governments, organizations, or individuals to finance loans designated for particular initiatives. Furthermore, these funds offer supplementary services to their clients, including but not limited to equity investments, loan guarantees, and interest rate support. In particular, the purpose of interest rate subsidies is to decrease the cost of borrowing.

In addition, non-governmental organizations such as the Environment Fund of the United Nations or the OECD Clean Energy Finance and Investment Mobilisation can provide green non-banking credit. These organizations are dedicated to promoting sustainable economic development on a global scale. Funds, such as these primarily support the public sector in its efforts to foster a favorable environment, facilitate public-private partnerships regarding financial mechanisms like green bonds, and bolster the microcredit capabilities of community enterprises, among other initiatives.

Capital Mobilizer for Green Projects: Capital Mobilizer for Green Projects, including green investment funds, public-private partnerships, and specialized financial institutions focused on sustainable development, plays a pivotal role in aggregating and deploying capital towards green projects. These entities receive capital from capital owners and green non-banking credit entities, consolidating funds through investment vehicles and financial instruments tailored to support environmental sustainability. Capital mobilizers deploy the aggregated capital towards green projects through various channels, including project financing, equity investments, and development loans, aiming to maximize the impact of investments on environmental outcomes.

Legal Framework on Green Credit

International Legal Framework on Green Credit

UNEP FI action plan: developed by the United Nations, The United Nations Environment Program's Financial Initiative (UNEP FI) action plan was released in 1992 by the United Nations to strengthen the financial sector's role in global sustainable development.

With a focus on the banking industry, the United Nations Environment Program serves as the standard for UN action and offers a particular platform for banks to support sustainability concerns. The UNEP FI Guidelines on Banking and Sustainability were created with three main goals to accomplish this shared objective: (i) give UNEP FI's banking member institutions a clear understanding of how to apply the UNEP FI Declaration and know how to comply with this Declaration in each specific banking activity; (ii) provide an initial benchmark to all banks preparing to pursue or further sustainability goals; and (iii) accelerate the realization of UNEP FI's and its signatory organizations' vision for the banking and sustainability roadmap to a broader community of stakeholders (United Nations Environment Program – Finance Initiative, 2016).

In addition to a number of additional partners, UNEP FI works together with about two hundred dedicated financial institutions to strengthen the link between sustainable development and economic performance. Through its network and training programs, UNEP FI seeks to find, promote, and acknowledge best practices in sustainable development and environmental protection across all levels of financial institution operations. This is a perfect example of how the global financial sector is beginning to recognize the importance of sustainable development. Furthermore, UNEP FI works closely on vital projects that advance sustainable development and increase awareness with the UN and other organizations. UNEP FI mandates that its members adhere to 19 core obligations, which are categorized into three categories: The following are five pledges made: (i) sustainable development, (ii) sustainable governance, and (iii) public awareness and information sharing (United Nations Environment Program – Finance Initiative, 2016).

Operational standards of the International Financial Corporation: For clients of its member financial institutions, the International Finance Corporation has established the following eight operating requirements on social and environmental sustainability: First, there is risk assessment, management, and social environment impacts; second, labor and working conditions; third, efficient resource use and pollution prevention; fourth, community health, safety, and security; fifth, land purchase and forced relocation; sixth, preserve ecological diversity and manage living natural resources sustainably; seventh, do not affect indigenous people or ethnic minorities; and eighth, cultural heritage. All projects that include risks or influence the social environment must adhere to Standard (1). Standards (2)–(8) may be used concurrently, depending on the particulars of each project. Performance requirements ought to be cross-referenced and referred to collectively when needed. In addition to fulfilling the requirements as mentioned earlier, customers must certify to compliance with all applicable laws of the host country, including its international laws (International Finance Corporation, 2012).

Equator Principles: The Equator Principles are a collection of voluntary benchmarks the financial services sector can employ to identify, evaluate, and control environmental and social risks in initiatives methodically and continuously. These principles have been formulated considering established standards and financial investors' requirements. Financial institutions employ these principles to guarantee that the projects they endorse and counsel will be executed by sustainable environmental management and social responsibility stipulations while yielding favorable economic outcomes. By establishing a partnership between grantees and the affected local communities, donors, consultants, grantees, and regional stakeholders will benefit from adhering to and respecting the Equator Principles (Equator Principles Association, 2024).

COP 21 International obligations and the Paris Agreement on climate change mitigation: Two worldwide challenges that are becoming increasingly prominent are the acceleration of global warming and environmental concerns. The fight against climate change has been a long-running international endeavor. The 195 countries that comprised the Paris Agreement-COP 21 aimed to prevent global warming reached a consensus on December 12, 2015, following 20 years of negotiations. After nearly two decades of persistent talks to achieve a consensus on a sustainable Earth-saving resolution, this development is regarded as a significant milestone. Consequently, a novel legal framework has emerged on a global scale, which imposes obligations on nations to engage in endeavors aimed at diminishing emissions. Simultaneously, it affords developing countries that emit minimal greenhouse gases but are profoundly impacted by climate change the chance to implement mitigation strategies (United Nations, 2015).

In addition to recognizing countries' pledges to reduce emissions from the use of fossil fuels, the Paris Agreement establishes a regulatory framework to support and monitor the implementation of those pledges – assistance in the form of funds and expertise to developing nations. Consequently, member nations agreed to restrict the worldwide temperature surge to a maximum of 2 °C relative to the temperature levels observed during the pre-industrial revolution era. About the financial dimension, the Paris Agreement stipulates the necessity of modifying financial flows in alignment with the roadmap for climate-resilient, low-emission development. It is the responsibility of developed nations to mobilize and furnish financial resources in support of developing countries. The objective is for developed nations to amass a minimum of USD 100 billion annually by 2020 to facilitate developing countries' transition to clean energy sources and aid them in mitigating the effects of climate change (United Nations, 2015).

Therefore, the Paris Agreement functions as a foundation for global collaboration in the efficient execution of measures to address climate change, thereby aiding in the preservation of our shared planet, which present and future generations will inhabit. Furthermore, this accord aids in the resolution of national, regional, and international security concerns that arise from tensions, conflicts, and terrorism instigated by climate change (Kaur et al., 2024; Rijal et al., 2024).

Vietnamese Legal Framework on Green Credit

Vietnamese Government's Strategies and Action Plan for Sustainable Development

Decision No. 160/2013/QD-TTg, dated November 12, 2013, issued the sustainable development action plan for 2013–2025, whereas Decision No. 432/2012/QD-TTg, dated April 16, 2012, issued the Vietnam Sustainable Development Strategy. It lays out the top priorities for sustainable development from 2011 to 2025 with an eye toward 2020: "Maintaining sustainable economic growth, gradually implementing green growth, developing clean and renewable energy." In particular, create and implement a green growth strategy to ensure low-carbon economic development; use energy resources wisely and effectively; create clean and renewable energy sources to guarantee national energy security; progressively raise the share of clean and renewable energy sources in Vietnam's overall energy consumption (Vietnamese Prime Minister, 2012a, 2013).

Three tasks are outlined in Vietnam's national green growth strategy for 2011–2020 toward 2050, which was released along with Decision No. 1393/2012/QD-TTg on September 25, 2012. (i) encouraging the use of clean, renewable energy sources and lowering the intensity of development that produces greenhouse gases; (ii) greening production (Vietnamese Prime Minister, 2012b). The strategy stipulates the responsibility for mobilizing resources to implement green growth with main contents including:

- promulgate mechanisms and policies to encourage financial institutions and businesses, small and medium-sized enterprises, in particular, to implement production and business activities by green growth criteria;
- use a financial, credit, and market tools system to encourage and support the development of green economy and products;
- moving toward building a management and transaction system for greenhouse gas emissions, taxes, and carbon fees.

Decision No. 403/2014/QD-TTg, dated March 20, 2014, was released together with a national action plan on green growth for 2014–2020. The plan has 66 activities, comprising 12 activity categories, 66 particular action tasks, and 04 significant issues. In order to oversee action No. 37, "Improving institution and strengthening the financial and credit operational capacity of commercial banks to serve green growth in 2013–2020," the State Bank of Vietnam works in tandem with the Ministry of Finance and the State Treasury (Vietnamese Prime Minister, 2014). Accordingly, the duties of the State Bank of Vietnam are as follows:

(i) examine, modify, and enhance financial and credit organizations to meet objectives for green growth;
(ii) arrange for coaching and training to increase commercial banks and other financial institutions capability in financial and credit activities;
(iii) create and expand banking and financial services to assist companies in achieving green growth.

On October 28, 2016, the Prime Minister signed Decision No. 2053/QD-TTg, approving the Plan for implementing the Paris Agreement on climate change. In order to further the development and application of financial instruments, such as green credit, green bonds, and green investment funds, by a predetermined set of criteria, this decision creates a cooperative effort between the State Bank, Ministry of Finance, Ministry of Planning and Investment, and State Capital and Investment Corporation (Vietnamese Prime Minister, 2016).

The Prime Minister adopted Decision No. 986/QD-TTg on August 8, 2018, which sets forth the goals of the Vietnam Banking Industry Development Strategy through 2025, with a particular emphasis on 2030. Vietnam aims to accomplish the following by the conclusion of 2025:

> Increase the proportion of bank credit capital invested in renewable energy, clean energy, and low-carbon production and consumption industries; promote the development of "green credit" and "green banking" to aid in the transformation of the economy towards green growth, low carbon emissions, and adaptation to climate change; and enhance the efficiency of credit capital allocation to meet socio-economic development requirements. Incorporate discourse about green growth, sustainable development, and climate change into credit loan initiatives and programs. (Vietnamese Prime Minister, 2018)

Guidance Documents Issued by the State Bank of Vietnam

On March 2, 2015, the State Bank of Vietnam released Directive No. 03/CT-NHNN, the first step in putting the National Green Growth Action Plan into action. Vietnamese commercial banks must abide by this regulation, which calls for them to support environmentally friendly corporate practices and green loans for initiatives with specific environmental protection objectives (State Bank of Vietnam, 2015a).

On August 6, 2015, the State Bank of Vietnam Governor issued Decision No. 1552/QD-NHNN, allowing the Banking Industry Action Plan to be published until 2020 to carry out the National Strategy on Green Growth. The purpose of this decision is to increase public awareness of the banking sector's expertise, function, and ability to lend money to green economic sectors and to create goods and services that help companies adopt green growth (State Bank of Vietnam, 2015b).

The Governor of the State Bank of Vietnam issued Circular No. 39/2016/TT-NHNN on December 30, 2016, to govern lending to clients by credit institutions and foreign bank branches. The circular specified guidelines on customer loans made by credit institutions and overseas bank branches. Financial firms' lending policies to their customers must abide by environmental protection laws (State Bank of Vietnam, 2016).

On August 7, 2018, Decision No. 1604/QD-NHNN was issued by the Governor of the State Bank of Vietnam, granting authorization for the Green Bank Development Project in Vietnam. Using this decision, the intention is to direct credit capital flows to finance environmentally sustainable projects. To aid in advancing sustainable development in Vietnam, the decision's overarching aim is to enhance the banking sector's accountability and consciousness concerning climate change and environmental protection. Credit resources will be allocated to green production, services, eco-friendly projects, programs, and clean and renewable energy (State Bank of Vietnam, 2018a).

The Banking sector's action plan to implement the 2030 Agenda for Sustainable Development issued together with Decision No. 1731/QD-NHNN dated August 31, 2018, of the Governor of the State Bank of Vietnam sets out several tasks; Related solutions include: (i) Encourage credit institutions to design and deploy programs, credit products, and banking services suitable to the characteristics of all types of businesses, minimal and medium-sized businesses. Medium-sized, micro-enterprises, businesses using environmentally friendly technology; (ii) Credit institutions develop banking products and services that take into account environmental benefits; Give top priority to creating goods that raise money and provide credit to companies or initiatives working in the clean energy, low-carbon production, and renewable energy sectors. This will help protect the environment and increase the efficiency with which resources and energy are used (State Bank of Vietnam, 2018b).

The State Bank of Vietnam issued Decision No. 34/QD-NHNN on January 7, 2019, to establish the Banking Industry Action Program to carry out the Vietnam Banking Industry Development Strategy until 2025. The following are mentioned by 2030:

> enhancing the ability of credit institutions to create products to mobilize and lend credit capital for renewable energy, clean energy, low-carbon production and consumption sectors to contribute to environmental protection and improve efficiency use of resources and energy; implementing green banking activities through increasing awareness and responsibility for the social environment of the banking industry in business. (State Bank of Vietnam, 2019)

Law on Environmental Protection

The most important national legal framework for environmental protection is the Law on Environmental Protection. Its goals are to protect and improve the environment, uphold ecological balance, responsibly harvest and use natural resources, and encourage ecologically friendly business and production methods. In Vietnam, green credit is defined as credit given to the following investment projects by Article 149 of the Law on Environmental Protection No. 72/2020/QH14, which was passed by the XIV National Assembly on November 17, 2020: Utilizing natural resources efficiently, addressing climate change, managing waste, treating pollution and enhancing environmental quality, restoring natural ecosystems, conserving nature and biodiversity, and generating additional environmental benefits are just a few of the things that need to be done (Vietnamese National Assembly, 2020).

Green Credit Implementation in Vietnam

Green Outstanding Credit at Commercial Banks in Vietnam

Overall, Vietnam's and many other nations' green outstanding credit has increased in recent years due to promotional policies implemented by the governments of different countries. As presented in Fig. 11.2, the value of green outstanding credit in Vietnam has experienced substantial growth from over VND 70 trillion after 2015 to VND 317.6 trillion in 2019, reflecting an approximately 4.5-fold increase compared to 2015. Due to the COVID-19 pandemic and social distancing measures, Vietnam's outstanding green credit experienced a marginal decline in 2020, amounting to a mere VND 290 trillion. This decline can be attributed to the inability to execute numerous projects. Once the epidemic situation has been progressively managed by 2021, there will be a resurgence in green outstanding credit debt. Green outstanding credit in Vietnam will have accumulated to VND 474.9 trillion by 2022 (Fig. 11.2).

While there is a yearly upward trend in the amount of outstanding green credit in Vietnam, this proportion remains relatively minor compared to the overall exceptional credit of the banking system. Indeed, it is anticipated that the percentage of extraordinary green credit relative to the total outstanding credit in Vietnam will further escalate in the years to come, from 1.5% in 2015 to 5.3% in 2022 (Fig. 11.3).

Regarding the term-wise composition of outstanding credit, it is observed that medium- and long-term outstanding credit constitutes 76% of the overall green outstanding credit by the conclusion of 2022. The annual interest rates on short-term loans in green sectors range from 5% to 8%, while those on medium and long-term loans are between 9% and 12%.

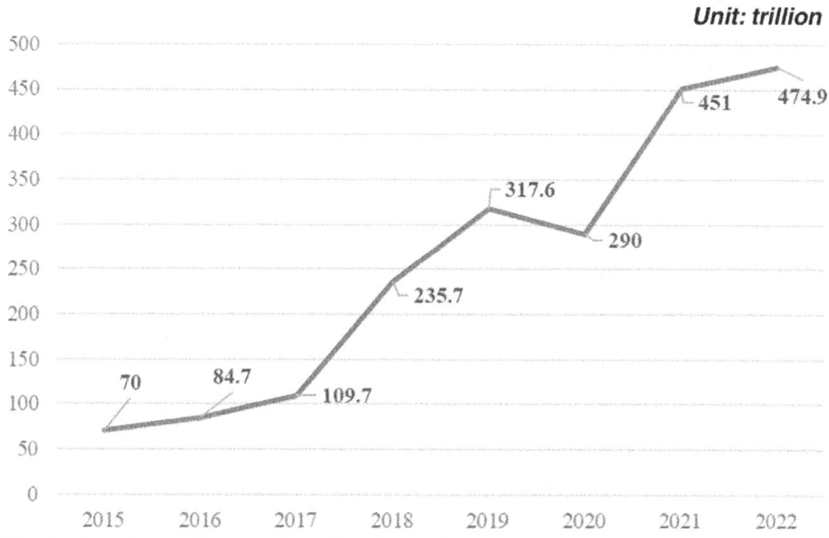

Fig. 11.2. Green Outstanding Credit in Vietnam from 2015 to 2022.
Source: Credit for Economic Sector – State Bank of Vietnam (2023).

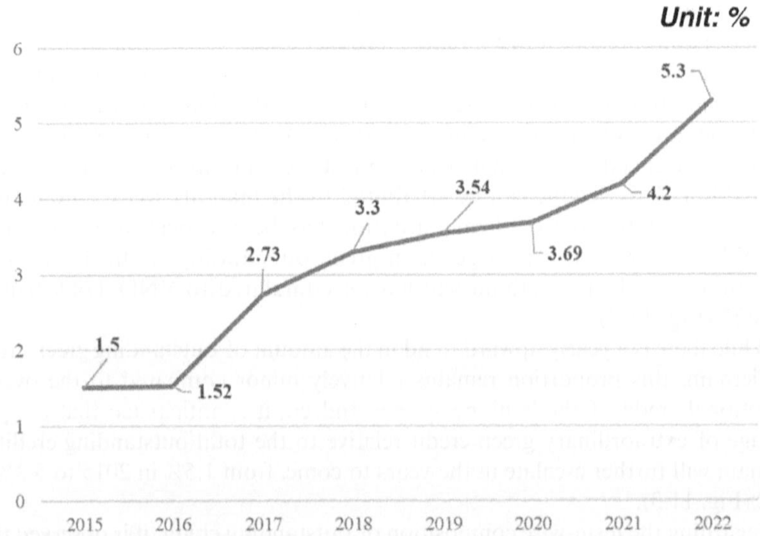

Fig. 11.3. The Proportion of Green Outstanding Credit in Vietnam from 2015 to 2022. *Source*: Credit for Economic Sector – State Bank of Vietnam (2023).

Credit Policy for Green Credit at Vietnamese Commercial Banks

When determining loan policies, Vietnamese commercial banks consider a combination of non-financial and financial factors, including consumer reputation, the viability of plans and projects, and balancing future cash flows resulting from projects. Green credit policies must align with individual projects' unique attributes and characteristics while also adhering to the principles of green credit established by the Credit Market Association and the United Nations Sustainable Development Goals.

A wide range of credit facilities are available, encompassing project loans, bond investments, structured products, guarantees, letters of credit, and more. Green credit policies are flexible about collateral assets, accepting assets generated by the initiative. Commercial banks prioritize expedited processing and document optimization for green projects over conventional credit, mainly when offering incentive packages that include reduced insurance premiums and interest rates. Several financial institutions impose interest rate caps on loans to the agricultural sector. Many banks offer lower interest rates on high-tech agricultural projects than standard business and production loans. Short-term loans for these projects carry interest rates of 4% to 5% per annum (Vietnam dong) or 2% per annum (USD), with extended repayment periods (Credit for Economic Sector – State Bank of Vietnam, 2023). On request, green credit initiatives owned by women-owned enterprises will be eligible for preferential interest rates, payment services, cash flow management, trade finance, and additional services. The bank may provide consulting services to clients in certain circumstances, including financial restructuring, partner introduction, and trade promotion.

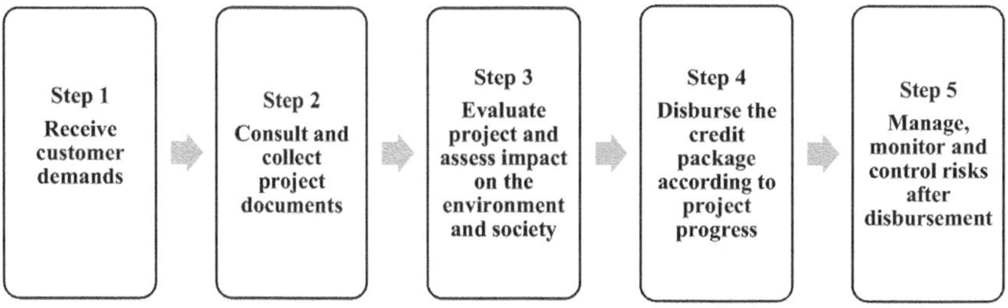

Fig. 11.4. Green Credit Appraisal Process at Vietnamese Commercial Banks. *Source*: Author's work.

Green Credit Procedures in Vietnamese Commercial Banks

The green credit appraisal procedure at commercial banks in Vietnam consists essentially of the subsequent stages, as mentioned in Fig. 11.4.

To mitigate risks and assist credit officers at commercial banks in evaluating green loan applications, green finance specialists may help in certain phases of the evaluation process for green credit initiatives. The appraisal officer must ascertain whether each project falls into one of the three categories below for each project: (i) Project devoid of significant environmental and social risks; (ii) project accompanied by such risks; and (iii) project entailing substantial environmental and social risks.

The regulation of green credit projects in Vietnam is presently well-defined, facilitating the categorization of projects and the evaluation of risks for commercial banks. The following categorization of green finance initiatives illustrated in Fig. 11.5 is mandated for commercial bank loan evaluations:

Green Credit Programs in Vietnamese Commercial Bank System

The Vietnam Bank for Agriculture and Rural Development (Agribank)

The State Bank of Vietnam's Directive 03/CT-NHNN, dated March 24, 2015, is now being implemented by Agribank. As soon as the latter was released, the Prime Minister approved the National Strategy on Green expansion, promoted the expansion of green credit, and managed environmental and social risks in credit granting activities, respectively, with Decision No. 1393/QD-TTg, dated September 25, 2012. Issuing papers encouraging the expansion of green finance, as well as managing social and environmental risks while extending credit, are examples of specific initiatives. Agribank's credit handbook consistently links project appraisal and loan plans with ecological concerns during the credit operations process. Projects must have an environmental impact assessment report that the appropriate authorities have duly approved in compliance with the law. Credit is unequivocally denied for endeavors that possess the capacity to significantly and adversely affect both the environment and society.

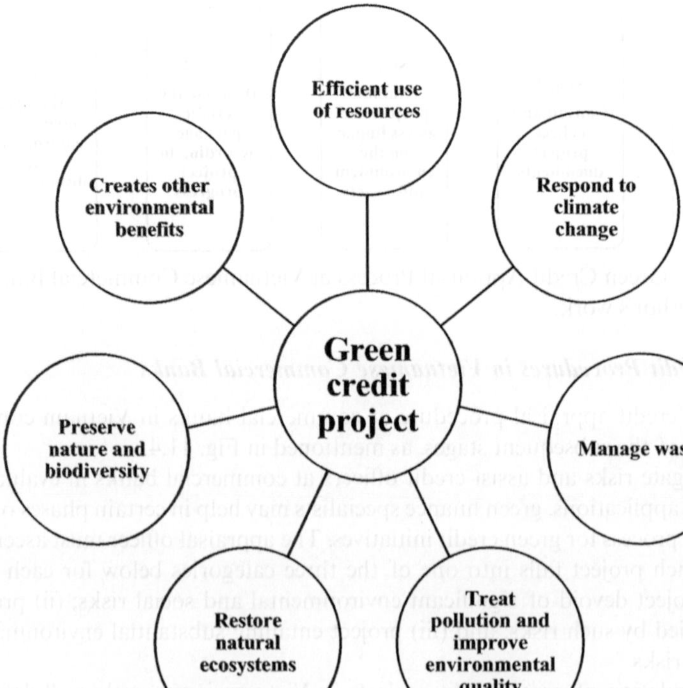

Fig. 11.5. Green Credit Projects of Commercial Banks. *Source*: Article 149, Law on Environment Protection 2020.

In anticipation of the "wave" of investments in agricultural development utilizing clean agriculture and advanced technology, Agribank has instituted a preferential credit program with a minimum scale of VND 50,000 billion to support clean agriculture for export beginning in November 2016 (Agribank, 2016). The program's borrowers comprise enterprises, cooperatives, cooperative unions, and farm proprietors engaged in every secure, large-scale agricultural product production chain phase. In contrast to the preferential interest rates that the State Bank of Vietnam and Agribank currently offer loans to the rural agricultural sector, loan interest rates for this program have been reduced from 0.5% per annum to 1.5% per annum. Outstanding credit in this sector remained stable at 5,221 billion VND by the end of September 2019, and loan turnover for this program surpassed 20,000 billion VND (Agribank, 2018). Agribank also sponsors the national television channel VTV1's "Clean Agriculture" program, a joint effort between Vietnam Television and the Ministry of Agriculture and Rural Development. Agribank intends to contribute to this initiative. The gradual formation of secure agricultural production models across the nation has altered consumer perceptions regarding the safety and quality of agricultural products in Vietnam. Indeed, numerous large-scale agricultural production models have been established throughout the country and its regions with the assistance of Agribank capital and the application of cutting-edge technology. These include the flower growing model in Lam Dong, large sample fields in Can Though, pangasius in An Giang, pig farming in Ha Nam, sugarcane in Khanh Hoa, and corn in Son La. The widespread agreement among individuals and organizations regarding these models acknowledges Agribank's contributions to agricultural development by applying cutting-edge technology and sustainable agriculture.

Agribank has implemented the following green credit products: loans secured by investments in hydroelectric construction projects; loans designated for rubber development; loans supporting rural agricultural projects; loans financing tourism services; projects aimed at enhancing the quality and safety of agricultural products; projects developing biogas programs; and activities related to water supply, waste, and wastewater management and treatment. Furthermore, Agribank has actively engaged in numerous environmental protection initiatives supported by financial institutions and the World Bank. These include the following: Developing a biogas program to enhance the quality and safety of agricultural products; Creating a project involving coastal resources to advance sustainable development; controlling the chance of natural calamities; advocating for low-carbon farming; supplying the Red River Delta with clean water and rural sanitation; promoting wind energy; additionally Putting loan capital to use (Agribank, 2022).

The leading commercial bank for funding in rural and agricultural areas is Agribank. Agribank is well aware of the risks facing Vietnamese agriculture as it works through several difficult roadblocks and difficulties as part of its economic development and integration, such as environmental contamination, climate change, and food safety and hygiene. Because of this, Agribank is steadfast in its resolve to lead the State Bank of Vietnam's directions about growing green credit and controlling the social and environmental risks related to its operations, acknowledging in the process of creating a safe and enduring agriculture system.

Vietnam Joint Stock Commercial Bank for Industry and Trade (Vietinbank)

VietinBank, which has played a pioneering and pivotal role in effectively implementing the policies and guidelines of the State Bank of Vietnam and the Government, has concurrently and successfully implemented policies to assist and resolve capital challenges for agricultural businesses and farmers, focusing on green enterprises.

In addition to preparing technical infrastructure and human resources, VietinBank has promoted activities to secure global preferential capital for the financing of green fields since 2015. The collaboration agreement signed between the International Finance Corporation and VietinBank is particularly noteworthy. The agreement furnishes VietinBank with the means to execute preferential policies and imparts the bank's expertise and understanding in financing and executing green credit initiatives in Vietnam. VietinBank has also agreed to prioritize green credit for initiatives that promote energy conservation and the reduction of CO_2 emissions, as stated in this agreement.

VietinBank has provided credit to businesses during the program's implementation to finance investments in machinery and equipment and to increase working capital to support the production and operational endeavors of environmentally friendly products and equipment that protect consumer health and prevent pollution of the environment.

To facilitate the flow of environmentally friendly credit capital to its clientele, VietinBank expeditiously implemented initiatives in line with the State Bank's and the government's directives. These initiatives included loans for supporting industrial loans, high-tech clean agriculture, and loans for rural agriculture. At the same time, VietinBank applies proactively preferential policies to clients operating in the green sector via the following credit products and programs:

- When accompanying corporate clients, VietinBank provides SME Stronger preferential packages that include the following subjects: development by implementing preferential policies regarding interest rates and fees, enhancing operational efficiency, optimizing capital use efficiency, and expanding production and business;
- Demonstrate a readiness to embrace innovation by offering incentives that are contingent upon industry attributes, business domains, and business affiliations within the supply and distribution chain;
- Extend efforts to establish connections on a global scale, thereby expanding operating markets, fostering business collaboration, and facilitating connections with customers both domestically and internationally.

In addition to developing green credit products proactively, VietinBank offers insurance and incentive packages for rooftop solar power projects and guidelines for extending investment credit for wind power and agricultural solar energy projects (solar farms). VietinBank develops credit products specifically for each specialized industry, including unsecured loans secured by export contract cash flow management. Export Factoring, the Agricultural Chain seeks to provide quick-processing financial assistance to organizations, individuals, and businesses that are one or more links in the agricultural value chain; collateral consists of businesses' or individuals' recurring receivables or goods. The crop loan policy explicitly targets companies and individuals who cultivate and maintain livestock and seasonal crops that coincide with the year's production cycle and original trees and industrial crops harvested annually.

Over the years, VietinBank's outstanding loans to the green sector have increased due to implementation actions; the proportion of exceptional loans devoted to green projects has risen from 1.47% in 2018 to 6.05% in 2022 (VietinBank, 2022). The proportion of customers engaged in credit contracts with a renewable energy sector exceeding one thousand is the total number of customers.

Following the conclusion of the COP28 (28th Conference of the Parties to the United Nations Framework Convention on Climate Change), VietinBank introduced the GREEN UP–green financial package, which features preferential fees and interest rates for projects and plans that generate social and environmental advantages. VietinBank allocates VND 5,000 billion between

January 5, 2024, and December 31, 2024, to provide preferential capital for plans and projects that generate social and environmental benefits in the following sectors: green construction, green energy, green exports (including textiles, footwear, coffee, rice, wood, and seafood), and green energy. The GREEN UP Green Financial Package carries an interest rate of no more than 5.8% per annum on short-term loans and 6.2% per annum on medium- and long-term loans (VietinBank, 2024). Participation in this program is open to businesses of any scale that adhere to sustainable development certifications and standards, including those from VFCS Sustainable Forest Management Certification, EDGE Gold Green Building Certification, GRS Global Recycling Standards, and OEKO Standards.

Joint Stock Commercial Bank for Investment and Development of Vietnam (BIDV)

BIDV and the Ministry of Natural Resources and Environment have entered into a Memorandum of Understanding, marking BIDV's inaugural involvement in collaborative endeavors to foster sustainable green financial development in Vietnam. To facilitate the implementation of the COP26 commitment of the Vietnamese Government, BIDV establishes a Sustainable Finance Project Management Board, perfects internal processes for green credit, and consistently improves institutional capacity. The bank engages in knowledge exchange and adoption of insights from international organizations and partners regarding implementing sustainable financial objectives and applying ESG management to every facet of operations. Concurrently, BIDV has consistently demonstrated transparency and openness regarding its sustainable development obligations through implementing sustainable development reports by GRI standards since 2017. These reports unequivocally outline the bank's commitment to establishing BIDV as a "Net-Zero Bank" beginning with its day-to-day operations. In 2018, BIDV became the first domestic bank to release an Environmental and Social Risk Management Framework that applied to projects and customers receiving international capital, and it encouraged projects to borrow funds carried out by BIDV.

Several projects in which BIDV served as the wholesaler bank are detailed below:

- Da Phuoc Solid Waste Treatment Complex Project: In collaboration with VWS Company, BIDV contributed ninety million US dollars to the Ho Chi Minh City Da Phuoc Solid Waste Treatment Complex project. The project, which has an initial investment capital of 450 million USD, is structured into four distinct phases, with phase 1 requiring 211 million USD in investment capital (BIDV, 2022).
- Project on sustainable agricultural transformation: Through applying sustainable farming methods and ongoing improvement of the value chains for two commodity industries – rice, coffee, and paddy – this project seeks to support the Vietnamese government in reorganizing the agricultural sector. The total investment capital for the project is 301 million USD, of which 196 million

USD (or roughly 65.1%) is non-credit capital and 105 million USD (or 34.9%) is loan capital (BIDV, 2022).
- Project Vietnam Energy Saving Project for Industries: BIDV has been chosen as one of two banks by the World Bank and the Government to re-lend USD 100 million as part of the Energy Saving Project. This initiative aims to increase energy efficiency in the industrial sector and support the government's objectives of reducing greenhouse gas emissions and conserving energy (BIDV, 2022).

With 1,718 projects and a green outstanding credit of $2.7 billion by the end of 2022, BIDV maintains its leadership position in green financing. This represents 4.3% of BIDV's overall outstanding credit and 13% of the green exceptional credit in the economy. The first bank to announce a Sustainable Loan Framework was BIDV in February 2023. The framework enables the bank to offer ecological, social, and sustainable loan products exclusively to domestic business clients. In May 2023, BIDV issued Regulations on Environmental Risk Management in credit granting activities by Circular 17/2022 of the State Bank of Vietnam. By leveraging its existing capabilities and expertise, which are consistently augmented and refined, in conjunction with the backing of the preeminent development financial institutions globally, BIDV guarantees the ability to furnish project owners and businesses with technical assistance in green finance and sustainable economic activities through international standards (BIDV, 2022).

Ho Chi Minh City Development Joint Stock Commercial Bank (HDBank)

HDBank has implemented resource-augmentation solutions to foster green finance and credit growth since 2018. HDBank operates by this development-oriented stance, diligently monitoring the Government's resolute dedication and objectives regarding implementing mechanisms mandated by the Paris Agreement to attain carbon neutrality by 2050.

In recent years, HDBank has received significant capital support and in-depth advice through green credit from reputable international financial institutions, such as the International Finance Corporation, the Development Fund of the German KFW Reconstruction Bank (DEG), the French Development Finance Organization, the Asian Development Bank (ADB), and the World Bank (WB). Reaffirming HDBank's standing and position in the market, as well as its commitment to the future implementation of the sustainable development strategy and community duty, is the ongoing expansion of this joint venture coupled with increased funding limits.

With a decade of uninterrupted growth, HDBank's financial capacity and operational efficiency have steadily enhanced; Basel III regulations have been thoroughly implemented. Through its robust financial capacity, the support of resources from the world's largest financial institutions, and adherence to international operational standards, HDBank has emerged as a prominent commercial bank in Vietnam specializing in promoting green credit resources.

The bank guarantees two criteria before extending green credit to businesses: business credit assurance and green criteria. HDBank has collaborated with established financial institutions to implement the ESG (environmental, social, and governance) system by global benchmarks, utilizing green criteria. As of 2022, HDBank has allocated more than 11,000 billion VND towards high-tech agricultural initiatives and green transformation (HDBank, 2022). The bank places emphasis not only on providing financial products and capital resources to small and medium-sized enterprises (SMEs) but also on prioritizing disbursements to SME businesses that are owned by women.

Joint Stock Commercial Bank for Foreign Trade of Vietnam (Vietcombank)

With a focus on waste treatment and pollution prevention projects, renewable energy and clean energy initiatives, green agriculture and industry projects, and green construction initiatives, Vietcombank has actively promoted green credit growth and environmental and social risk management in credit granting activities over its six decades of construction and development. The ultimate goal of becoming a green bank that fosters sustainable development for the community is to become a green bank.

Vietcombank experienced substantial growth in its overall green credit balance from 2018 to 2021. By the conclusion of 2021, the balance had decreased from over VND 7,890 billion in 2018 to an approximate amount of VND 18,400 billion. Indeed, it was noteworthy in 2021, despite being significantly affected by the COVID-19 pandemic, that Vietcombank maintained a favorable green credit growth rate of 28% during the corresponding period in 2019–2020. Additionally, Vietcombank was a pioneer in implementing the policies of the State Bank and Government regarding the waiver and reduction of interest and customer support fees to mitigate the more than 10,000 billion VND in damages caused by the COVID-19 pandemic (Vietcombank, 2021).

Green project-related outstanding loans at Vietcombank will surpass 4% of the bank's total outstanding loans by the end of 2022. In particular, funding is allocated as follows (see Fig. 11.6): 87.3% for renewable energy and clean energy projects, 3.1% for sustainable water management projects, 1.3% for projects involving the recycling and reuse of natural resources, 1.3% for waste treatment and pollution prevention, 1% for green industry, 1% for green agriculture, 1% for sustainable construction, and 1% for sustainable transportation (Vietcombank, 2022). Medium- and long-term capital financing activities for clean energy and renewable energy initiatives increased by nearly 350% in 2022, demonstrating Vietcombank's commitment to credit orientation for sustainable development (Vietcombank, 2022).

Vietcombank and Japan Bank for International Cooperation (JBIC) executed a capital financing agreement worth 300 million USD on March 29, 2023, to finance renewable energy initiatives. The loan will support Vietnam's renewable energy and environmental protection initiatives.

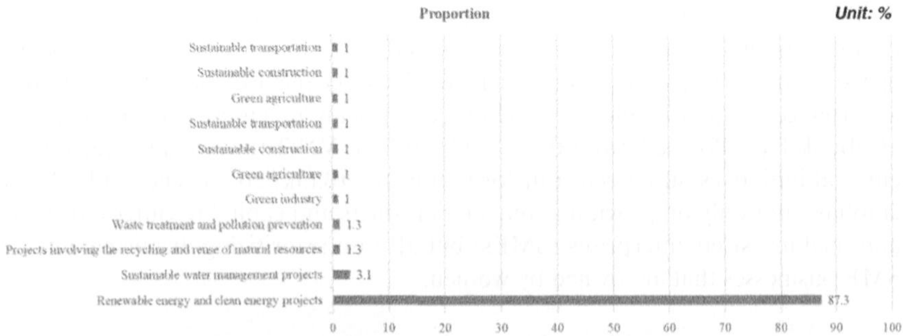

Fig. 11.6. The Proportion of Green Outstanding Credit of Vietcombank in 2022. *Source*: Vietcombank (2022).

Military Commercial Joint Stock Bank (MB)

MB has significantly increased its focus on community and social activities since 2017. MB has investigated and refined the credit policy mechanism associated with environmental and social management in pursuit of green banking and green credit. Furthermore, MB successfully implemented credit capital allocation strategies that supported socio-economic progress, advocated for the advancement of green credit and banking to aid in the transition to green growth, and augmented the share of bank credit allocated to renewable and clean energy. Specifically, MB has pledged to implement the ESG strategy methodically by international measurement standards beginning in 2023. This statement serves as a foundation for MB's sustainable development initiatives and signifies the emergence of a forthcoming "green" generation of MB employees.

MB is still the industry leader in lending to renewable energy projects worldwide, even with the significant resources needed for appraisal, evaluation, and post-loan inspection and supervision (wind power, solar power). MB led in lending to projects in this industry from 2017 to 2018. In order to make sure that these initiatives have a good impact on society and the environment, MB assesses them through research and expert collaboration. The business also believes in its capacity to control risks and devote resources to them. With a combined value of over 70,000 billion VND, MB finances more than thirty solar and wind power projects, helping investors produce 3,600 MW of renewable energy and assisting in expanding clean energy sources to meet the demands of sustainable economic growth. Contributions from credit lines arranged and provided by MB are being made to renewable energy initiatives in the South Central, Central Highlands, and Southwest regions that involve reputable and brand-name investors.

Compared to 2020, the percentage of outstanding loans designated for green initiatives at MB multiplied by 2.5 by the conclusion of 2022. More than 90% of the funding is allocated to clean energy and renewable energy initiatives, with the vast majority comprising medium- and long-term loans. This signifies MB's shift in credit orientation towards sustainability. Additionally, the bank has imposed particular regulations on the Fund about managing environmental risks in its credit activities. During the same period in December 2022, the bank extended green credit to 2,829 customers, resulting in a cumulative credit balance of 44.1 trillion VND, representing a growth of 6.5% (MB, 2020).

Tien Phong Commercial Joint Stock Bank (Tpbank)

As the preeminent financial institution in 2017, TPBank actively promoted transactions that contributed to climate change mitigation (TPBank, 2017). This is assessed according to criteria that include using renewable energy, energy-efficient alternatives, and emissions reduction throughout operation. Through the green credit development action program, TPBank entered into a long-term agreement with the Global Climate Cooperation Fund – The Global Climate Partnership Fund (GCPF) for a green credit loan valued at 20 million USD (approximately 465 billion VND) to be repaid over three years. In particular, rooftop solar power projects, production strategies, and business plans that reduce CO_2 greenhouse gas emissions are environmentally beginning to possess energy-saving attributes. They are eligible for capital at preferential interest rates.

The relevant stakeholders of the project are corporate clients seeking loans for operational and managerial objectives, all while adhering to green growth principles. It is mandatory for clients to explicitly specify that the loan is intended to fund business plans and projects that incorporate CO_2 reduction factors, with a specific focus on rooftop solar power projects. Compared to conventional loan interest rates, this program offers a 0.2% reduction in interest. The exact duration of the loan is project-specific and may extend up to ten years. In addition to adhering to TPBank's credit orientation and lending regulations, borrowers must satisfy the following criteria:

- a minimum of one year of operational experience in the borrower's primary industry;
- absence of debt originating from group 2 at the time of loan request;
- no debt incurred from group 3 to group 5 within 36 months before loan approval.

TPBank ensures that the conditions under which it extends credit to enterprises engaged in various sectors, including solar power, high-tech agriculture, sustainable agriculture, and rooftop electricity, are as favorable as possible. Furthermore, support subjects encompass well-functioning enterprises that are interested in expanding their operations or initiating new ventures that utilize clean agriculture and advanced technology (e.g., hybrid technology), plant varieties, transitioning to the improved rice-intensive farming (SRI) model for rice production, and constructing biogas tanks for the livestock industry.

TPBank supports 11 solar power construction projects in Tay Ninh through green credit capital. These projects include Tensa Joint Stock Company, Truong Thanh Joint Stock Company, Vietnam Solar Power Joint Stock Company, Vietnam Trade and Services Investment Joint Stock Company, and others. TPBank has provided sponsorship for an additional twelve sustainable agricultural initiatives.

Conclusion

Even though recent years have witnessed positive developments in the green credit market in Vietnam as a result of government, agency, branch, and international financial organization support. Nonetheless, the development of green credit activities continues to face obstacles. To commence, a comprehensive set of regulations and definitions about green fields and categories has yet to be consolidated for nationwide implementation. This complicates commercial banks' selection, appraisal, evaluation, and monitoring processes when they extend green credit. Simultaneously, the green sector needs a legal framework and evaluation criteria for environmental impact measurement instruments that would facilitate the creation of policies and products for developing green credits. Furthermore, business strategies must adhere to stringent environmental protection requirements and complex loan procedures. Without interest rate support or other preferential mechanisms, clients will have minimal incentive to utilize the bank's green credit products due to the requirements above. Furthermore, despite recent efforts to support the growth of green credit through policy measures, the issue of securing capital for commercial institutions that are implementing green credit still needs to be solved. Most long-term and medium-term capital invested in green industries and sectors has a lengthy payback period, whereas credit institutions mobilize primarily short-term capital. In the meantime, capital invested in environmentally beneficial sectors and fields, particularly renewable energy, energy conservation, and efficiency, frequently incurs substantial investment costs, lengthy payback periods, and high market risks in Vietnam; therefore, loan terms and cost incentives are required.

Hence, to promote green credit in Vietnam, the government should build a solid legal framework with detailed guidance for all stakeholders relating to the green credit process. Commercial banks in Vietnam should develop various products and services related to green credit with attractive content to promote this kind of credit. Finally, banks must routinely and periodically inspect and monitor the management of social and environmental risks associated with green credit extended to customers. Credit granting for projects that adversely affect the environment and society must be subject to stringent control measures beginning with the appraisal phase. Concurrently, routine credit monitoring will aid in mitigating environmental and social risks. Furthermore, periodic inspection motivates businesses and individuals to operate more securely and efficiently, ensuring their operations are carried out with the intended purpose.

References

Agribank. (2016). *Annual report 2016*. https://cms.my.na/assets/documents/p1btuhpk3r-1reb1nejijrnml1fu64.pdf

Agribank. (2018). *Annual report 2018*. https://cms.my.na/assets/documents/p1d2a-1891f2681aferkr5okk0e1.pdf

Agribank. (2022). *Annual report 2022*. https://cms.my.na/assets/documents/p1hr-0mo59odr71qf11k3t1e2317sc4.pdf

Aizawa, M., & Yang, C. (2010). Green credit, green stimulus, green revolution? China's mobilization of banks for environmental cleanup. *The Journal of Environment & Development*, *19*(2), 119–144.

Asian Pacific Loan Market Association & the Loan Market Association. (2018). *Guidance on green loan principles (GLP)*. https://www.lsta.org/content/guidance-on-green-loan-principles-glp

BIDV. (2022). *Annual report 2022*. https://bidv.com.vn/wps/wcm/connect/52ab7924-1010-42e8-8416-eddad6e6cbc8/BIDV+Annual+Report+2022.pdf?MOD=AJPERES&CACHEID=ROOTWORKSPACE-52ab7924-1010-42e8-8416-eddad6e6cbc8-ozo8.T

Communist Party of Vietnam. (2013). *Resolution No. 24-NQ/TW dated June 3, 2013* [Conference session]. The 7th Central Conference, Session XI on Combating Climate Change, Resource Management, Environmental Protection, Green Growth Orientation, and Green Credit, Hanoi, Vietnam.

Credit for Economic Sector – State Bank of Vietnam. (2023). *Report on green credit in Vietnam from 2015 to 2022*.

Duan, J., & Mengqi, N. (2011). The paradox of green credit in China. *Energy Procedia*, *5*, 1979–1986.

Elkington, J. (1999). *Cannibals with Forks: Triple Bottom Line of 21st Century Business*. Capstone Publishing, Oxford.

Equator Principles Association. (2024). *The equator principles*. Retrieved March 15, 2024, from https://equator-principles.com/about-the-equator-principles/

HDBank. (2022). *Annual report 2022, Hanoi, Vietnam*. Retrieved from https://cdn.hdbank.com.vn/hdbank-file/investor/editor/1AH99t9l1iRq6V1jIyUl20230526171736/HDBAR2022All2605202327MB2_1685096346200.pdf?_gl=1*fl9e91*_gcl_au*OTgwMjAwOTMwLjE3MjEzNzkxNDc.*_ga*MTA4NjgyMzc5My4xNzIxMzc5MTQ2*_ga_L6TMDVXKWJ*MTcyMTM3OTE0Ny4xLjAuMTcyMTM3OTE0Ny42MC4wLjA

International Finance Corporation. (2012). *IFC performance standards on environmental and social sustainability*. Retrieved March 15, 2024, from https://www.ifc.org/content/dam/ifc/doc/mgrt/ifc-performance-standards.pdf

Julia, T., & Kassim, S. (2021). *Green banking*. https://www.researchgate.net/publication/349239027_Green_Banking

Kaur, S., Kumar, R., Singh, K., & Huang, Y. L. (2024). Leveraging artificial intelligence for enhanced sustainable energy management. *Journal of Sustainable Energy*, *3*(1), 1–20. https://doi.org/10.56578/jse030101

Keane. (2009). The life and death of democracy. Simon and Schuster, London.

MBbank. (2022). *Annual report 2022, Hanoi, Vietnam*. Retrieved from https://www.mbbank.com.vn/resources/files/Ve-MB/BAO-CAO-THUONG-NIEN/2022/bao-cao-thuong-nien-mb-2022.pdf

Lingyun, H., Zhang, L., Zhong, Z., Wang, D., & Feng, J. (2019). Green credit, renewable energy investment, and green economy development: Empirical analysis based on 150 listed companies of China. *Journal of Cleaner Production*, *208*, 363–372.

Ndekwa, A. G., Kalugendo, E., Sood, K., & Grima, S. (2023). An analysis of agribusiness digitalisation transformation of the sub-Saharan African countries small-scale farmers' production distribution. *Research on World Agricultural Economy*, *4*(3), 63–78.

Rahman, M., & Barua, S. (2016). The design and adoption of green banking framework for environment protection: Lessons from Bangladesh. *Australian Journal of Sustainable Business and Society*, *2*(1), 1–19.

Rijal, S., Nursaputra, M. A. C., & Dari, H. U. (2024). Flood susceptibility analysis using Frequency Ratio method in Walanae watershed. *International Journal of Sustainable Development and Planning*, *19*(3), 823–832. https://doi.org/10.18280/ijsdp.190302

Sood, K., & Özen, E. (2024). A systematic review of ESG in the insurance industry: Navigating the path to sustainability. *International Journal of Sustainable Development and Planning*, *19*(3), 807–821. https://doi.org/10.18280/ijsdp.190301

State Bank of Vietnam. (2015a). *Directive 03/CT-NHNN, dated March 24, 2015, managing environmental and social hazards problem and green credit in credit-granting activities and promoting credit growth*. https://chinhphu.vn/default.aspx?pageid=27160&docid=8721

State Bank of Vietnam. (2015b). *Decision 1552/QD0NHNN on introducing the action plan of the banking sector for implementation of the national strategy for green growth by 2020, dated 06 August 2015*. https://thuvienphapluat.vn/van-ban/Thuong-mai/Quyet-dinh-1552-QD-NHNN-2015-Chien-luoc-quoc-gia-ve-tang-truong-xanh-nganh-ngan-hang-287408.aspx

State Bank of Vietnam. (2016). *Circular No. 39/2016/TT-NHNN on prescribing lending transactions of credit institutions and/or foreign bank branches with customers, dated 30 December, 2016*. https://thuvienphapluat.vn/van-ban/Tien-te-Ngan-hang/Thong-tu-39-2016-TT-NHNN-hoat-dong-cho-vay-cua-to-chuc-tin-dung-chi-nhanh-ngan-hang-nuoc-ngoai-338877.aspx

State Bank of Vietnam. (2018a). *Decision No. 1604/QD-NHNN, dated August 07, 2018, approving the scheme for green banking growth in Vietnam*. https://thuvienphapluat.vn/van-ban/Tien-te-Ngan-hang/Quyet-dinh-1604-QD-NHNN-2018-phe-duyet-De-an-phat-trien-ngan-hang-xanh-tai-Viet-Nam-411378.aspx

State Bank of Vietnam. (2018b). *Decision 1731/QD-NHNN on introducing the action plan of the banking sector for implementation of the 2030 agenda for sustainable development*. https://thuvienphapluat.vn/van-ban/Tien-te-Ngan-hang/Quyet-dinh-1731-QD-NHNN-2018-Ke-hoach-hanh-dong-thuc-hien-Chuong-trinh-Nghi-su-2030-427403.aspx

State Bank of Vietnam. (2019). *Decision No. 34/QD-NHNN promulgating the banking action program for implementation of the strategy for developing the vietnam's banking industry by 2025 with vision towards 2030*. https://thuvienphapluat.vn/van-ban/Tien-te-Ngan-hang/Quyet-dinh-34-QD-NHNN-2019-Chien-luoc-phat-trien-nganh-Ngan-hang-Viet-Nam-411368.aspx

TPBank. (2017). *Annual report 2017*, Hanoi, Vietnam. Retrieved from https://tpb.vn/wps/wcm/connect/12d51115-a7af-4827-a6d2-2dd2a483e182/Anr_2017_TV.pdf?MOD=AJPERES&CONVERT_TO=url&CACHEID=ROOTWORKSPACE-12d51115-a7af-4827-a6d2-2dd2a483e182-mi8mOhs

United Nation. (2015). *UN climate change conference – Paris agreement*. Retrieved March 15, 2024, from https://unfccc.int/sites/default/files/english_paris_agreement.pdf

United Nations Environment Program – Finance Initiative. (2016). *Guide to banking & sustainability*. United Nations Environment Programme

Vietcombank. (2021). *Annual report 2021, Hanoi, Vietnam*. https://portal.vietcombank.com.vn/content/en-us/Investors/Investors/Annual%20Reports/Year%202021/20220906_BCTN2021_Maquette_English.pdf

Vietcombank. (2022). *Annual report 2022, Hanoi, Vietnam*. https://digital.lapphuong.com/vcb/ar2022/final/en/

VietinBank. (2022). *Annual report 2022, Hanoi, Vietnam* Retrieved from https://investor.vietinbank.vn/Handlers/DownloadReport.ashx?ReportID=1102.

VietinBank. (2024). *VietinBank launches GREEN UP green financial package to promote sustainable development of businesses, Dated 16 March 2024*. https://www.vietinbank.vn/ss/Satellite;jsessionid=wgAj6Af4sKT4vDtJEFnZxM-eiwObxmYdQ5766-qNk54sIOvfTJq8!-407324805?c=NoiDung&cid=1481569346212&pagename=vietinbank.vn%2FNoiDung%2FChiTietTinBaiLayout&rendermode=preview

Vietnamese National Assembly. (2020). *Law No. 72/2020/QH14 on environmental protection, dated 17 November, 2020*. https://thuvienphapluat.vn/van-ban/Tai-nguyen-Moi-truong/Luat-so-72-2020-QH14-Bao-ve-moi-truong-2020-431147.aspx

Vietnamese Prime Minister. (2012a). *Decision No. 432/QD-TTg on approval of sustainable development strategy of Vietnam period 2011-2020, dated 12 April, 2012*. https://vanban.chinhphu.vn/default.aspx?pageid=27160&docid=157753

Vietnamese Prime Minister. (2012b). *Decision No. 1393/2012/QD-TTg on approving national strategy on green growth period 2011-2020, dated 25 September, 2012*. https://vanban.chinhphu.vn/default.aspx?pageid=27160&docid=163886

Vietnamese Prime Minister. (2013). *Decision No. 160/QD-TTg on approval of sustainable development action plan for the period 2013-2025, dated 15 Jan, 2013*. https://vanban.chinhphu.vn/default.aspx?pageid=27160&docid=165426

Vietnamese Prime Minister. (2014). *Decision No. 403/QD-TTg approval of National action plan on green growth period 2014-2020, dated 20 March 2014*. https://vanban.chinhphu.vn/default.aspx?pageid=27160&docid=172886

Vietnamese Prime Minister. (2016). *Decision No. 2053/QD-TTg on approval of National action plan on green growth period 2014-2020, dated 20 March 2014*. Retrieved October 28, 2016, from https://thuvienphapluat.vn/van-ban/Tai-nguyen-Moi-truong/Quyet-dinh-2053-QD-TTg-ke-hoach-thuc-hien-thoa-thuan-Paris-bien-doi-khi-hau-2016-328065.aspx

Vietnamese Prime Minister. (2018). *Decision No. 986/QD-TTg on approving development strategy of Vietnam banking sector by 2025 and vision to 2030*. https://chinhphu.vn/?pageid=27160&docid=194426&tagid=6&type=1

Wang, E., Liu, X., Wu, J., & Cai, D. (2019). Green credit, debt maturity, and corporate investment - Evidence from China. *Sustainability*, *11*(3), 583. https://doi.org/10.3390/su11030583

World Economic Forum. (2020). *What is green finance, and why is it important?* Retrieved March 15, 2024, from https://www.weforum.org/agenda/2020/11/what-is-green-finance

World Bank Group and the Asian Development Bank. (2020). *Climate risk country profile: Vietnam*. Retrieved March 15, 2024, from https://www.adb.org/sites/default/files/publication/653596/climate-risk-country-profile-viet-nam.pdf

Yao, S., Pan, Y., Sensoy, A., Uddin, G. S., & Cheng, F. (2021). Green credit policy and firm performance: What we learn from China. *Energy Economics*, *101*, 105415. https://doi.org/10.1016/j.eneco.2021.105415

Yerpude, S., Sood, K., & Grima, S. (2022). Blockchain-augmented digital supply chain management: A way to sustainable business. *Journal of Risk and Financial Management*, *16*(1), 7.

Chapter 12

Sustainable Development in the Management and Accounting of Healthcare Facilities: The Experience of Medical Reform in Ukraine

Mariya Shygun[a],* *Liubov Gutsalenko*[b] *and Uliana Marchuk*[a]

[a]*Kyiv National Economic University named after Vadym Hetman, Kyiv, Ukraine*
[b]*National University of Life and Environmental Sciences of Ukraine, Kyiv, Ukraine*

Abstract

Introduction: Today, with uncertainty and negative environmental and human health changes, achieving the global goals of sustainable development is becoming extremely important. The experience of reforming the medical sector in Ukraine can be helpful to the countries that are developing and implementing reform processes in the medical field to achieve the goals of sustainable development.

Purpose: Reformation processes are caused by changes in the medical sector financing model due to the introduction of state solidarity health insurance.

Methodology: The research shows changes in the role of the state and local authorities in the healthcare system. It also reveals how the medical reform creates conditions for attracting private investments, stimulating the financing of primary healthcare, and opening a self-financing secondary healthcare sector. Special features of the reform in Ukraine are the transformation healthcare facility management's accounting and information support system and the transition from accounting and reporting standards for the public sector to accounting standards for the private sector.

Findings: The authors describe how introducing a two-tier electronic healthcare system (eHealth), which functions as a state central database

*Corresponding Author

Green Management: A New Paradigm in the World of Business, 209–229

doi:10.1108/978-1-83797-442-920241012

and solutions of the medical information system, can provide comprehensive informatization of healthcare facilities and automation of medical and administrative workplaces.

Practical implications: The innovations introduced in Ukraine should create an environment for rationalizing medical healthcare and promote the effective functioning of public and private healthcare facilities.

Keywords: Medical reform; global goals; healthcare facility; accounting standards; reporting standards; medical information system; health insurance

JEL Classifications: I18; M10; M41; M48

Introduction

The modern world is radically changing the conditions of social and economic life and marks the transition in decision-making processes from conditions of risk to conditions of uncertainty. Human impact on the environment has become critically negative, so the conflict between the biosphere and the techno sphere has intensified, the state of ecosystems has deteriorated, soils and mineral resources have been depleted, and people's health has fallen. World Health Organization (WHO) is constantly working to implement urgent measures to improve the healthcare system in the world, taking into account the achievement of global goals of sustainable development.

According to Biermann (2022), in 2015, the United Nations adopted 17 Sustainable Development Goals, which have created a central normative framework to uphold the principles of sustainable development in the world. However, in the author's opinion, the effectiveness of management based on global goals remains uncertain, there are still no comprehensive meta-studies that would reflect the political influence of the global objectives in different countries and at the world level.

People in low- and middle-income countries do not have adequate access to high-quality health services (Ndekwa et al., 2023; Sood & Özen, 2024; Yerpude et al., 2022).

One of the global goals is "Strong health and well-being." It reflects the great importance of health problems for humanity. Despite the incredible improvements in the health of the global population since 1950, mediated by significant scientific advances and the discovery of new methods of treatments for many diseases, many problems still need to be addressed urgently.

In turn, countries around the world adapt global goals to better achieve their national social and economic characteristics. Ukraine is one of the largest countries in Europe, and its total population as of 01.01.2022 is 41167 million people (The National Health Service of Ukraine (NHSU), 2022). However, the average life expectancy of the population of Ukraine (World health statistics, 2020) is relatively lower than in most European countries, and it is 72.5 years, in particular, for men – 67.6 years, and for women – 77.1 years. The current cost of healthcare per capita is 141 US dollars. The European average rate is 1990 US dollars (Kaur et al., 2024; Rijal et al., 2024).

A feature of Ukraine's economic and social development is the post-Soviet past and the 30 year period of independence, which has not yet allowed bringing the healthcare system to world quality standards. Ukraine is gradually taking the first steps in transforming the health sector according to global sustainable development goals and trying to improve healthcare through health reform.

Ukraine's experience can be valuable for the countries that are developing and implementing reform processes in the medical field to achieve the goals of sustainable development.

The concept of sustainable development continues to influence all areas of human life and the discourse on development science. As Mensah observes, practically everything a person does or plans to do on earth has consequences for the environment, and it may cause economic changes or social shifts, which generally determine the future existence and well-being of the human race (Mensah, 2019).

In today's conditions, Ukrainian medicine characterizes by a hierarchical and territorial administration system with an unreasonably large number of beds in medical facilities as a basis for financing their activities. In Ukraine, healthcare financing remains ineffective, and the distribution and use of available funds for medical needs is unproductive. Even though Ukrainians annually pay about 3 billion UAH in taxes for healthcare, every year 640,000 Ukrainian families face personal bankruptcy due to illness, and they have to pay for expensive treatment at their own expense (Fionik, 2017).

One of the factors that negatively affected the efficiency of financial resources in the healthcare system of Ukraine was and still is the distribution of funds between different budgets (state, regional, district, and city budgets), as well as the distribution of responsibilities for financing treatment and prevention facilities of different levels. The main consequence of such a distribution is poor coordination and insufficient funding for primary and specialized care. In turn, medical institutions, being subordinated to the authorities of different levels, do not have adequate incentives to coordinate their activities in the interests of patients.

Materials and Methods

The study used the following methods of cognition: induction and deduction, grouping, retrospective analysis, comparison and generalization, scientific knowledge, etc., which revealed vital reform processes based on changing the model of financing the health sector through the introduction of state solidarity health insurance. The use of these methods allowed to show changes in the principles of subordination of the bodies of the Ministry of Health of Ukraine, the creation of new state and public services, and the transformation of healthcare facilities into municipal non-profit enterprises with the granting of independent status.

Ensuring a healthy life and promoting well-being at any age are priority tasks for sustainable development.

According to Cerin, sustainable development based on the principles of achieving the global goals of human development, but at the same time it must preserve the ability of natural systems to provide natural resources and ecosystem services used by the economy and society (Cerin, 2006).

The research shows how the role of the state in the healthcare system and the role of local authorities in determining the needs of the number of medical facilities in the region and the quality of medical services, taking into account the mandatory condition – concluding agreements with the National Health Service of Ukraine (NHSU).

By analytical assessment and monitoring of the number of declarations concluded between the population of Ukraine and doctors by specialties (pediatricians, family doctors, therapists, etc.), the universality of the profile of the family doctor is singled out. After the reform, the family doctor provided general family medicine practice and specialized multidisciplinary training. He can provide primary healthcare to all family members of all ages and genders, and his salary depends on the workload and number of patients. The opening of the secondary healthcare sector can now attract funding independently.

Empirical studies of regulatory and legal support of accounting in state medical institutions of Ukraine and relevant accounting systems in developed countries have revealed the features of the reformed system of accounting and information support of healthcare facilities (HCF) management in Ukraine and its transformation from accounting and reporting standards for the public sector to private sector standards.

Information and communication technologies allowed us to show the possibilities of using the implemented two-level electronic healthcare system (eHealth), which can provide comprehensive informatization of HCF and automation of medical and administrative workplaces as a state central database.

The innovations introduced in Ukraine should create an environment for streamlining the provision of medical care, promote the effective functioning of public and private HCF on the principles of independence, open new opportunities to increase the types, and improve the quality of medical services.

Discussions

Healthcare is one of the economy sectors that protects the population in terms of affordable and quality healthcare. Each country formulates its public health policy as a basis for national security.

Wu et al. (2020), Huang et al. (2020), Yackee (2009), Ramlogan (2008), Harrison (2002), Danzon (1994), Born et al. (2009), D'Arcy (1986), Born et al. (2017), Yang et al. (2020), Petrushka (2017), and Suprun (2019) studied theoretical and practical aspects of health sector reformation. According to Petrushka (2017), for the effective implementation of the state policy, the country chooses a model of the organization of the healthcare system based on various mechanisms of financing medical services – at the expense of state and/or local budgets (Beveridge concept, municipal concept), funds of state insurance funds (budget insurance or Bismarck concept), and funds of citizens or business entities (private insurance or market concept).

Features of Medical Reform in Ukraine

In today's globalized economy, the main factor supporting countries on the path to faster growth and achieving higher population welfare is the introduction of economic reforms. The healthcare sector in Ukraine has begun to change dramatically in recent years with the introduction of healthcare reform to change the concept of healthcare financing and the transition from a Beveridge concept to a mixed one that combines public and private funding.

Therefore, in 2016, the Cabinet of Ministers of Ukraine approved the Concept of healthcare financing reform dated November 30, 2016 No. 1013-r (Zakon, 2016), which proposed a model of state solidarity health insurance presenting the best modern practices of the healthcare system and the experience of its transformation in Central and Eastern Europe.

The implementation of the Concept took place in three stages: the preparatory stage (2017), the implementation stage (2018–2019), and the integration stage (2020). Since then, the Ministry of Health of Ukraine has begun to promote public and private partnership models to improve service delivery and stimulate investments in the sector.

The state's role in the healthcare system should change within reform and provide for the pay of medical services directly to medical facilities. The role of local authorities has to be modified to determine the need for the number of medical institutions in the region and the quality of medical services. These tasks are to be performed independently of the decisions made by the public health authorities. They base on the principles of ownership and community needs for health services (Özen & Grima, 2018).

According to the initiators of the reform, these changes should strengthen the provision, stimulate the financing of primary medical and sanitary care, and open a secondary healthcare sector that can attract its funding.

Gils et al. (2020), Shygun (2019), Kvitka et al. (2019), Batsenko et al. (2018), and Nagorny (2018) conducted the studies on the distribution and use of budget funds in medical institutions of Ukraine.

Evaluating the results of various development programs implemented in Ukraine and other countries is an analytical basis for creating further strategies, and it is a reliable prerequisite for ensuring further progress (Fernando et al., 2023; Pajic et al., 2023; Skliar et al., 2020).

The medical reform of 2017–2020 resulted in changes in the principles of subordination of the Ministry of Health of Ukraine, the creation of new state and public services, and the transformation of healthcare facilities into municipal non-profit enterprises with independent status. Fig. 12.1 shows the model of relations between state, public, and private health authorities in Ukraine.

The National Health Service of Ukraine (NHSU) (2022) was established after a medical reform. It became a central body of executive power that ensures the implementation of state policy in the field of state financial guarantees for healthcare.

In general, the Cabinet of Ministers of Ukraine coordinates the activities of the NHSU through the Minister of Health. The tasks of the NHSU are as follows:

Fig. 12.1. Model of Relations between State, Public, and Private Health Authorities in Ukraine. *Source*: Prepared by authors.

(1) implementation of the state policy in the field of state financial guarantees of medical care under the program of state guarantees of medical care (a program of medical guarantee);
(2) performance of functions of the customer of medical services and medicines under the program of medical guarantees;
(3) submission of proposals to ensure the formation of state policy in the field of state financial guarantees of medical care for consideration by the Minister of Health.

According to Batsenko (2018), the Public Control Council formed at the NHSU consists of 15 representatives from public organizations and aims to perform the following tasks:

- public control over the activities of the NHSU;
- promoting the interaction of the NHSU with public associations, as well as other institutions of civil society in the field of providing medical care;
- ensuring the transparency of the NHSU activities;
- informing the NHSU about the existing public opinion, which reflects the level of formation and implementation of state policy in the field of state financial guarantees for medical care and relevant state programs.

The role of the private sector in the model of interrelations between different healthcare bodies in Ukraine realizes through local non-profit enterprises in Ukraine and private commercial enterprises of Ukraine, which directly provide medical services to the population. Insufficient investments in private medical facilities and constant underfunding of former state medical institutions in general created conditions for providing medical services of low quality and limited profile.

The introduction of a guaranteed Healthcare package: content and approach to healthcare contracting (2020) of medical services is an attempt by Ukraine to streamline the provision of medical care to the population, to ensure their proper financial protection and access to medical services, as well as certain additional services for specific age groups. The corresponding launch of the NHSU "medical guarantee program" forms a list and scope of medical services and medicines guaranteed to the population and paid for from the state budget based on uniform national tariffs.

Prioritization is the principle of developing the program of medical guarantees of NHSU in healthcare packages: content and approach to healthcare contracting (2020). The Ministry of Health of Ukraine approved the Order "On Priority Areas of Healthcare for 2020–2022," which defines the following strategic domains that determine the content of the program of medical guarantees:

(1) prevention, primary healing care, and outpatient treatment;
(2) improving the quality of care for patients in emergencies;
(3) increasing the level of availability of medicines.

Transforming the Management System of Medical Facilities of Ukraine and their Financing

Ukrainian medical facilities operated before reforming as budget institutions with vertical management, financed according to the principles of budget legislation. Heads of budgetary institutions did not have freedom of decisions and had to be guided by Orders of Ukraine's Ministry of Health. Reorganization of medical facilities into communal non-profit enterprises should solve the problem of rationalization of medical care to the population, increase the independence of medical institutions in economic and administrative processes, stimulate economic efficiency of existing assets, and improve the quality of medical services.

The changes in the status of medical facilities have created the preconditions for modifying the management system in them using the modern practice of developed countries and the EU (The European Union). In particular, until January 1, 2019, all administrative functions, including economic management and medical management in HCF, were assigned to one person – the Chief Physician.

It is a great deal of work, which provides medical and economic activity; in many developed countries, two specialists – the CEO – Chief executive officer (who deals with administrative and economic issues) and the medical director (responsible for the organization and coordination of medical processes) perform it.

Accordingly, another important step in healthcare reform is *the Handbook of Qualification Characteristics of Workers' Professions* (2018), namely, the transformation of the classifier of occupations, ensured the introduction of several new positions – CEO (director)/chief (head) of HCF, Deputy General Director, Medical Director of HCF, Chief (Head, Leader) of the structural unit of HCF.

The positions of chief physicians of the treatment and prevention institution have been excluded from the classifier of professions; regional, central city, city, central district, and district hospitals; Deputy Chief Physician of a regional, central city, central district, and district hospitals; Deputy Chief Medical Officer.

Chief Physicians who have concluded employment contracts before the order comes into force (January 1, 2019) will work according to the old model with the management of both administrative and medical processes only until expiring a term specified in the employment contract. Upon expiring a contract, such Chief Physicians can pass the competition for the positions of General Director and Medical Director of an HCF.

Fig. 12.2 shows the post-reform approach to the division of responsibilities between the General Director and the Medical Director of the HCF.

The medical reform carried out in Ukraine has radically changed the approach to financing the activities of medical institutions. From now on, the NHSU funds HCF by the tariff for primary healthcare for each patient who has signed a declaration with the doctor of this facility.

According to the Law of Ukraine "About the state financial guarantee of medical service for the population" from 19.10.2017 No. 2168-VIII (Zakon, 2017), payment for medical services of institutions for the provision of primary healthcare to the population is based on the principle of pay per patient using the capital rate under contracts about medical care population. Thus, the main source of income of the primary healthcare provider is payments under the contract with the NHSU. The amount of these payments will depend on the number and age

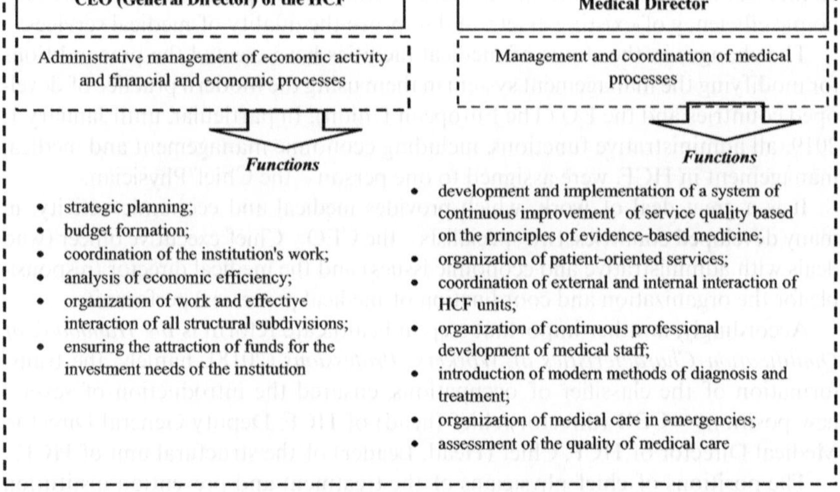

Fig. 12.2. Division of Functions between the General and Medical Directors of the HCF. *Source*: Adapted by authors from Amendments to the Handbook of Qualification Characteristics of Workers' Professions (2018) (Health Care, 1977).

structure of patients who have submitted a declaration about the choice of a doctor working in such a facility. Thus, the principle of "money follows the patient" is implemented at the primary level.

The funding provided by the National Health Service of Ukraine (NHSU) bases on the transfer of funds to the HCF for the future provision of medical services. According to the agreements concluded with the NHSU, primary care facilities provide medical services, receiving advance payment. However, there is no requirement for these funds in terms of the obligations of the HCF to adhere to their intended use and to submit specialized reports, similar to the recipients of budget funds. Primary healthcare facilities are free to use the funds received from the NHSU, subject to compliance with the main requirement of the agreement – the provision of medical healthcare to the population in full, determined by the procedure for providing primary healthcare.

Existing surplus funds can be used for the development of HCF, staff training, equipment upgrades, and other cost items by the approved financial plan agreed with the HCF owner. At the same time, the funds of local programs sent to the HCF as recipients of budget funds should also be included in the financial plan of the institution.

Fig. 12.3 shows a comparative model of changing the order of financing of the HCF of Ukraine before and after the medical reform of 2016–2020.

As evidenced by the change in the model of financing the activities of Ukrainian HCF, in general, due to the medical reform of 2017–2020, the number of financial resources management entities has decreased, which adjusts the focus of goal setting and distribution of funds. There have also been changes in the structure of funding sources, which have become more transparent and open, increasing the possibility of their accountability and taxability.

Data analysis on the number of funds allocated to financing the healthcare sector in Ukraine shows that the resources are limited, especially in comparison with economically developed countries. In particular, according to the *Law of Ukraine on the State Budget for 2020* (2020) (Annex 3 with changes made following the Laws No. 436-IX of 14.01.2020, No. 553-IX of 13.04.2020), total expenditures on healthcare in Ukraine as of 01.01.2020 amount to 114,550,207.7 billion UAH or 2.6% of GDP.

Table 12.1 presents the results of comparing indicators on healthcare financing in Ukraine and economically developed countries.

Analyzing the data in Table 12.1, it should take into account that in the countries of Central and Southern Europe – EU members, the vast majority of social schemes are used, especially social insurance, which depends not on the fact of residence, but on the place of work and the number of contributions paid. Such contributions cover the medical expenses of the insured persons.

Emergencies such as COVID-19 pose a global risk and demonstrate the critical need for healthcare industry preparedness to respond to such challenges. The United Nations Development Programme has highlighted the existence of significant differences in the ability of countries to overcome the crisis phenomena arising from COVID-19 and to recover from it. As stated by the UN, the pandemic has become a turning point for assessing the facilities of countries in case

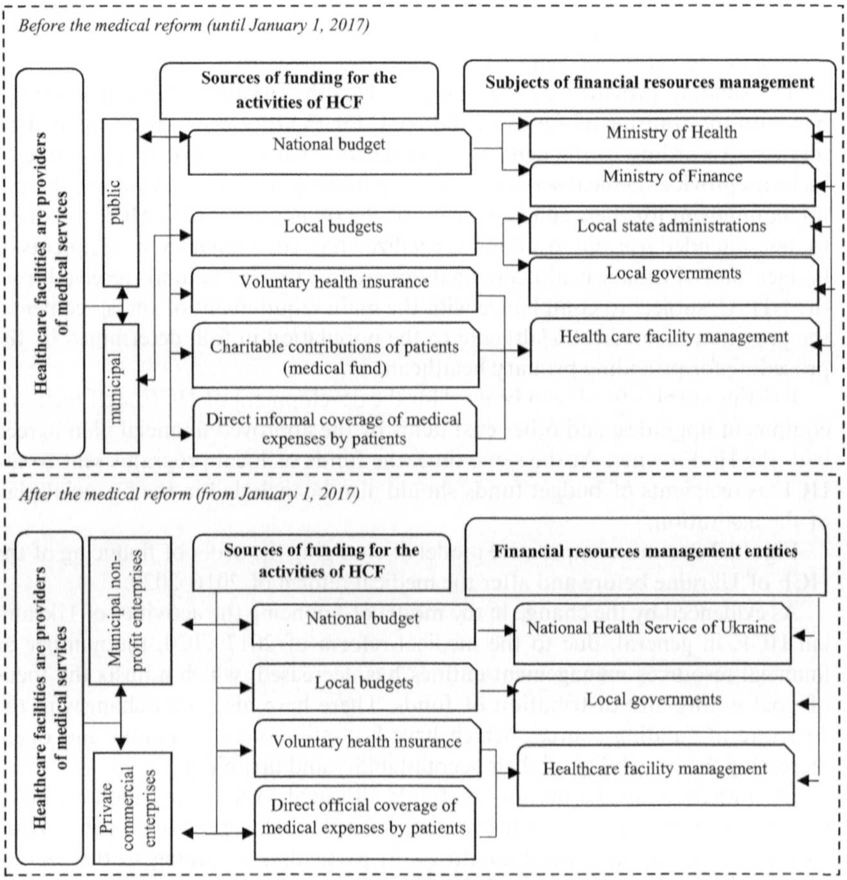

Fig. 12.3. The Procedure for Financing the HCF of Ukraine Before and After the Medical Reform of 2017–2020. *Source*: Prepared by authors.

of emergencies in the field of healthcare, and it provided grounds for increased attention and investment in critical public services of the 21st century (Sustainable Development Goals, 2022).

Within the framework of medical reform in Ukraine, it took some organizational measures and introduced normative and legal support for changes. The autonomy of HCF became the next important step in the transformation that started in 2019 and should be implemented by the heads of medical facilities as a prerequisite for concluding agreements with the NHSU. Thus, according to Suprun (2019), as of November 1, 2019, 70% of facilities in Ukraine that provide specialized medical care are autonomous. These facilities were located mainly in Poltava – 97.89%, Vinnytsia – 96.9%, and Kharkiv – 91.8%.

As of May 1, 2020, *The National Health Service of Ukraine* (2020) noted the key results that have already taken place during the transformation of the

Table 12.1. Financing of Healthcare in the Countries of the World and Ukraine as of January 1, 2020.

Indicator	**Countries**							
	Ukraine	**EU**	**Germany**	**France**	**Netherlands**	**Italy**	**Finland**	**USA**
Population, million people	43.73	447.70	83.78	65.27	17.13	60.46	5.40	331.00
Health care costs,% of GDP	2.6	9.8	11.7	11.2	10.0	8.7	9.1	18.0
Practitioners per 10,000 people	35.4	34.0	38.9	32.0	39.0	37.6	29.1	25.9
Life expectancy:								
• Women	77	82	83	85	83	84	84	81
• Men	68	75	78	80	80	80	78	77

Source: Adapted from the Population of selected European countries in 2020 (Statista, 2020).

healthcare system indicate that 98.9% of medical facilities have joined the provision of primary healthcare, 24,5 thousand doctors connected to the Electronic healthcare system. They signed declarations to provide services to the population. According to the official statistics of the NHSU *Electronic Map of Places of primary healthcare* (2020), as of May 1, 2020, 29,845 thousand people signed declarations on the provision of healthcare support with 22,824 first-rate physicians in contracted 1,619 facilities of various forms of ownership.

Data on the status of the concluded declarations between the population of Ukraine and doctors in terms of age groups and sex of patients on May 1, 2020, are given in Table 12.2.

According to the data of Table 12.2, persons aged 40–64 years (of them: women – 34.55%; men – 33.99%) are the largest share of patients. The total number of doctors of all specialties in Ukraine is 185,675, the number of nurses – 345,364 people. Analytical assessment of degrees of doctors, whose declarations were signed, among which there are mainly pediatricians, family doctors, and therapists, allows us to state that the profession of family doctor is currently in the lead in Ukraine. In particular, the number of declarations concluded with family doctors is 22 million (12.4 million female patients, 9.6 million male patients).

4.3 million people (2.5 million women and 1.8 million men) made declarations with therapists. Declared pediatric patients were 3.1 million people (including 1.5 million women and 1.6 million men). These statistics emphasize the universality of the profile of the family doctor, who provides general practice of family medicine and has specialized multidisciplinary training. Such a doctor can provide primary healthcare to all family members of any age and sex, and his pay depends on the workload and the number of patients.

Important analytical data present the results of the analysis of indicators regarding the declarations concluded between patients and doctors in terms of forms of ownership of healthcare facilities. These results are registered in the Electronic Healthcare System (EHCS) and have signed at least one declaration (Table 12.3).

According to Table 12.3, there is almost no official information on state-owned healthcare facilities. This fact is primarily due to granting autonomy to hospitals and transforming healthcare facilities from budget institutions into municipal non-profit enterprises (Ministry of Health of Ukraine, 2018).

According to the NHSU, in 2019, 99% of payments under the declarations were obtained by municipal healthcare facilities, private institutions, and individual entrepreneurs who have only 1% of pay for the same year. These indicators clearly show the established habits and traditions of Ukrainians to use medical services of public health facilities, which for many years were provided free of charge under state guarantees, and low attention to the work of private institutions, whose services are paid and often unavailable due to their high value for most citizens.

Table 12.2. Detailing of the Concluded Declarations with Doctors by Age Groups of Patients in Ukraine as of May 01, 2020.

Age Groups, Years	Gender of Patients				Total, Persons
	Women		Men		
	Persons	%	Persons	%	
0–5	973,697	5.87	1,013,036	7.65	1,986,733
06–17	2,212,511	13.33	2,302,041	17.38	4,514,552
18–39	4,072,503	24.54	3,612,696	27.27	7,685,199
40–64	5,734,074	34.55	4,503,222	33.99	10,237,296
65+	3,605,182	21.72	1,816,399	13.71	5,421,581
Total	**16,597,967**	**100.00**	**13,247,394**	**100.00**	**29,845,361**

Source: Adapted from Electronic map of places of primary care (National Health Service of Ukraine, 2020).

Table 12.3. Detailing of the Concluded Declarations by Forms of Ownership of Healthcare Institutions of Ukraine for 2019.

Ownership	**Gender of patients**		**Total Patients**	**Number of Facilities**	**Payments on Declarations, UAH**	**Share of Pays,%**
	Women	**Men**				
State	669	503	1,172	–	–	–
Communal	16,121,880	12,828,792	28,950,672	1,082	16,581,818,501	99.00
Private	172,231	139,907	312,138	212	89,788,825	0.54
Individual entrepreneur	154,048	121,887	275,935	325	78,463,241	0.47
Total	**16,448,828**	**13,091,089**	**29,539,917**	**1,619**	**16,750,070,568**	**100.00**

Source: Adapted from Vendor payments medical assistance program medical safeguards (National Health Service of Ukraine, 2020).

Changes in the System of Accounting and Information Support of the HCF Management in Ukraine

A separate area of organizational and managerial changes in HCF, due to the medical reform of 2017–2020, is associated with a radical transformation of the accounting and information system of healthcare management. The main reason for these transformations is due to the transfer of HCF from the category of budgetary institutions, which have their system of methodological and organizational principles of accounting and reporting, to the category of municipal companies working on private sector approaches, for which accounting and reporting methods are based on its standards, different from accounting standards for the public sector.

Ukraine took steps to create an effective system of information support for HCF managers on the results of economic activity. Thus, the methodology of accounting of HCF changed. The cause is the result of changes in the ownership form, which causes the transition to some other accounting principles and the formation of financial statements. Now, the role in the accounting of medical institutions is given to the formation of accounting policies and the emergence of new objects of accounting (financial and non-financial assets, capital, liabilities, income, expenses, and financial results), which are uncharacteristic of the budget sector and need research and solutions.

Research by scientists from around the world is of great value for reforming the information support of HCF management on the issues of formation of the latest types of reporting, organization, and methods of accounting for the financing of healthcare facilities: Born et al. (2017), ElDahshan (2020), Marchuk (2016), Gutsalenko et al. (2018), and Lyashenko (2018). Despite the available publications, there is little research on the organization and methods of accounting for new objects of accounting, which arose as a result of transformation processes in the health sector of Ukraine and aimed by the government to ensure equal access to quality medical services and comprehensive development of health systems focused on the patient.

As a result of the medical reform of 2017–2020, as *the Method of recommendation on the transformation of healthcare facilities from budgetary institutions into municipal non-profit enterprises* (Ministry of Health of Ukraine, 2018), most healthcare facilities in Ukraine have already been transformed or are in the process of transformation from municipal budget institutions to municipal non-profit enterprises.

According to Nagorny (2018), the main consequence of such a transformation for the HCF was that before re-registering, the HCF was considered a manager of budget funds; after re-registration as a municipal non-profit enterprise, it lost this status. The accounting and reporting system of such HCF should also change and move from the National Accounting Standards for the public sector and the Chart of Accounts approved by Order of the Ministry of Finance dated 31.12.13 No. 1203 on the National Accounting Standards for the private sector, as well as to the Chart of Accounts, approved by Order of the Ministry of Finance dated 30.11.99 No. 291 (1999), which follows from Article 56 of the Budget Code of Ukraine, Article 1 of the Law of 16.07.99 No. 996-XIV.

The methodology of accounting and reporting in HCF has its characteristics due to the specifics of its activities. Accordingly, changes in organizing accounting in such facilities are due to the need to move to another package of regulations that provide complete and reliable information about the institution's activities, its property status, the efficiency of state financial resources, and received income from economic activities.

According to Article 8 of Ukraine's Law on Accounting and Financial Reporting in Ukraine, as the authorized body, the owner or manager is responsible for the organization of the accounting system at the enterprise. Due to the reorganization of the HCF, first of all, the possibilities in using the form of accounting organization have changed. Thus, before the reform, the HCF could use only one form to create an accounting department.

After the reform, the HCF could use other forms of accounting provided by the Law *On Accounting and Financial Reporting in Ukraine* No. 996 (Zakon, 1999). It is also possible to use (1) the services of an accounting specialist registered as an entrepreneur carrying out business activities without creating a legal entity, (2) under the relevant agreement, or accounting on a contractual basis in the form of accounting outsourcing (centralized accounting, business entity, conducting activities in the field of accounting or auditing and auditing services). The choice of a form of accounting organization is carried out by HCF General Director, proceeding from features of activity of the medical facility.

Management of activities in market conditions requires a powerful information system that meets modern requirements for management decisions. The state enterprise "Electronic Health" and the IT Ukraine Association signed a Memorandum of Cooperation to address this issue on August 25, 2019. The purpose of this Memorandum is to assist the parties in healthcare informatization through the introduction of the centralized eHealth database. Accordingly, introducing the e-health system was another step of the Ukrainian Parliament in the medical reform of 2017–2020.

A tool for implementing changes to the information support of the HCS was a two-tier Electronic Healthcare System (eHealth), which functions as a state-central database and solutions of the *Medical Information System (MIS)* (Ministry of Health of Ukraine, 2020). MIS is specialized software for comprehensive informatization of healthcare facilities and automation of the work of their medical and administrative staff. According to its structure, MIS has a set of modules filled with different functionalities (Fig. 12.4).

In the presented information system, it must have an independent accounting module that allows the linking of data from different functional modules and includes them in a system of accounts and reporting, as well as link accounting data with warehouse data (warehouse module), which provides a basis for reconciliations of physical and cost indicators to control them.

The functionality of MIS lets accounting quickly and efficiently obtain data from other departments, generate financial, tax, and internal reports, and integrate information of different compositions and quality.

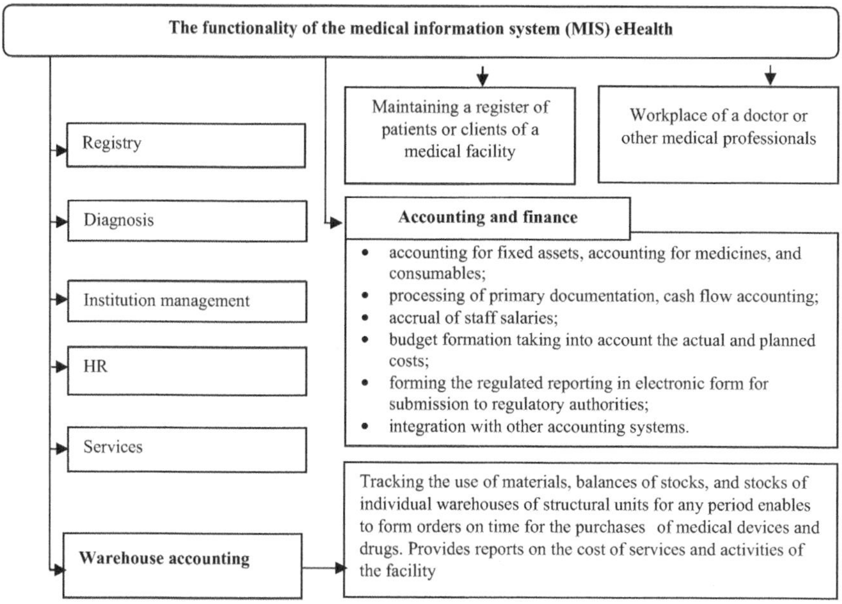

Fig. 12.4. Functionality of the Medical Information System (MIS). *Source*: Adapted by authors from How should a medical institution approach the choice of a medical information system (MIS)? (Ministry of Health of Ukraine, 2020).

Conclusions

Thus, achieving sustainable development goals requires a broad commitment of people, and the concept is to be implemented mainly through increased public participation. The medical reform carried out in Ukraine in 2017–2020 introduced significant changes in the HCS of the country and contributed to the following transformations in management and accounting in healthcare facilities:

(1) change in the model of financing the medical sector based on the introduction of state solidarity medical insurance;
(2) modification of the role of the state in the HCS and the role of local authorities in determining the needs for the number of medical institutions in the region and the quality of medical services;
(3) change the principles of macro-management of the healthcare sector and the transition to the basic principles of ownership and the needs of communities in health services;
(4) creating the preconditions for attracting private investment in the health sector, strengthening the provision and incentives for the financing of primary medical and sanitary aid, and opening a secondary healthcare sector that can attract funding independently;

(5) change of principles of subordination of bodies of the Ministry of Health of Ukraine, creation of a new state (National Health Service of Ukraine (NHSU)) and public services (Public Control Council), and transformation of healthcare facilities into municipal non-profit enterprises with independent status;
(6) change of statuses of medical facilities and their reorganization from budget organizations into municipal non-profit enterprises, which should be the basis for the rationalization of providing medical assistance to the population, increase the independence of medical facilities in economic and administrative processes, stimulate the advancement of economic efficiency of the use of existing assets;
(7) opening opportunities for the development of private medical facilities along with municipal ones based on the program of medical guarantees of the NHSU, which should increase the types and improve the quality of medical services;
(8) transformation of the healthcare management system based on additions to the classifier of professions and introduction of such new positions as General Director (Director)/Chief (Head) of HCF, Deputy General Director, Medical Director in Healthcare, and Chief (Head, Leader) of structural subdivision of the HCF. The positions of Chief Physicians of the treatment and prevention institutions have been excluded from the classifier of professions; regional, central city, city, central district, and district hospitals; Deputy Chief Physician of a regional city, central city, city, central district, and district hospitals; Deputy Chief Medical Officer;
(9) introduction of delimitation of managerial functions in the HCF between the General Director (Director) and the Medical Director as a factor in increasing the management efficiency of such specialists and increasing the productivity indicators of the HCF;
(10) change of inefficient approach to financing the activities of medical institutions, based on the multilevel distribution of funds between different budgets and the introduction of the principle of "Money follows the patient." From now on, HCF is receiving funding from the NHSU according to the tariff for primary healthcare for each patient who has signed a declaration with the doctor of this institution;
(11) transformation of the system of accounting and information support of HCF management and transition from accounting and reporting standards for the public sector to standards for the private sector (change of the Chart of Accounts, the system of accounting ledgers, structure and forms of reports);
(12) development and implementation of a two-tier Electronic Healthcare System (eHealth), which functions as the state-central database and solutions of the Medical Information System (MIS). As a specialized type of software, MIS aims to ensure comprehensive informatization of the HCF and automation of the work of medical and administrative staff.

The innovations introduced in Ukraine should create the environment for rationalized medical care provision, promote the effective functioning of public and private HCF on the principles of independence, and open new opportunities to increase the types and improve the quality of medical services.

References

Batsenko D., Braginsky P., & Buchma M. (2018). How to organize a system of primary healthcare at the local level. Operational Manual, Ministry of Health of Ukraine, USAID HIV Services Reform in Action Project, Ukraine Agency LLC, Kyiv.

Biermann, F., Hickmann, T., Sénit, C. A., Beisheim, M., Bernstein, S., Chasek, P., Grob, L., Kim, R. E., Kotzé, L. J., Nilsson, M., Llanos, M. A., Okereke, C., Pradhan, P., Raven, R., Sun, Y., Vijge, M. J., van Vuuren, D., & Wicke, B. (2022). Scientific evidence on the political impact of the sustainable development goals. *Nature Sustainability*, *5*, 795–800. https://doi.org/10.1038/s41893-022-00909-5

Born, P., Kip Viscusi, W., & Baker, T. (2009). The effects of tort reform on medical malpractice insurers' ultimate losses. *Journal of Risk and Insurance*, *76*(1), 197–219. https://doi.org/10.1111/j.1539-6975.2009.01294.x

Born, P. H., Bradley Karl, J., & Viscusi, W. K. (2017). The net effects of medical malpractice tort reform on health insurance losses: the Texas experience. *Health Economics Review*, *7*(1), 42. https://doi.org/10.1186/s13561-017-0174-2

Cerin, P. (2006). Bringing economic opportunity into line with environmental influence: A discussion on the case theorem and the Porter and van der Linde hypothesis. *Ecological Economics*, *56*, 209–225. https://doi.org/10.1016/j.ecolecon.2005.01.016

Danzon, P. M. (1994). Tort reform: The case of medical malpractice. *Oxford review of economic policy* (Vol. 10, pp. 84–98). Oxford University Press. http://www.jstor.org/stable/23606301

D'Arcy, S. P. (1986). Legislative reform of the medical malpractice tort system in Illinois. *The Journal of Risk and Insurance*, *53*(3), 538. https://doi.org/10.2307/252404

ElDahshan, K. A., AlHabshy, A. A., & Abutaleb, G. A. (2020). Data in the time of COVID-19: A general methodology to select and secure a NoSQL DBMS for medical data. *PeerJ Computer Science*, *6*, e297. https://doi.org/10.7717/peerj-cs.297

Fernando, K. D. U. D., Tharanga, T. M. N., Dewasiri, N. J., Sood, K., Grima, S., & Thalassinos, E. (2023). Insurance penetration and institutional spillover on economic growth: A dynamic spatial econometric approach on the Asian and Europe region. *Journal of Risk and Financial Management*, *16*(8), 365.

Fionik, D. (2017). Ukrainians die early. Why is this happening and who is holding back the reform of medicine (in press). Retrieved May 30, 2017, from https://texty.org.ua/articles/76893/Ukrajinci_pomyrajut_rano_Chomu_tak_vidbuvajetsa_i-76893/

Gils, T., Laxmeshwar, C., Duka, M., Malakyan, K., Siomak, O., Didik, V., Lytvynenko, N., Terleeva, Y., Donchuk, D., & Isaakidis, P. (2020). Preparedness of outpatient health facilities for ambulatory treatment with all-oral short DR-TB treatment regimens in Zhytomyr, Ukraine: A cross-sectional study. *BMC Health Services Research*, *20*(1), 890. https://doi.org/10.1186/s12913-020-05735-z

Gutsalenko, L., Wasilewski, M., Mulyk, T., Marchuk, U., & Mulyk, Y. (2018). Accounting control of capital investment management: Realities of Ukraine and Poland. *Economic Annals-XXI*, *170*(3-4), 79–84. https://doi.org/10.21003/ea.v170-14

Harrison, S. (2002). New labour, modernisation and the medical labour process. *Journal of Social Policy*, *31*(3), 465–485. https://doi.org/10.1017/s0047279402006694

Health Care. (1977). *On amendments to the handbook of qualification characteristics of workers' professions. Order of the ministry of health of Ukraine. Handbook of qualification characteristics of workers' professions*, 1977(78). Retrieved October 31, 2018, from https://moz.gov.ua/article/ministry-mandates/nakaz-moz-ukraini-vid-31102018-1977-pro-vnesennja-zmin-do-dovidnika-kvalifikacijnih-harakteristik-profesij-pracivnikiv-vipusk-78-ohorona-zdorovja

Huang, J., Gong, X., Gu, Q., Liu, R., Shi, J., Yu, W., Zu, P., Ma, X., Lin, J., Sun, J., Yang, Y., & Wang, Z. (2020). The effect of family doctor policy practice on primary healthcare workers' health in Hongkou District of Shanghai, China: varied by occupational divisions? *BMC Family Practice*, *21*(1), 205.

Kaur, S., Kumar, R., Singh, K., & Huang, Y. L. (2024). Leveraging artificial intelligence for enhanced sustainable energy management. *Journal of Sustainability for Energy*, *3*(1), 1–20. https://doi.org/10.56578/jse030101

Kvitka, S., Starushenko, G., Koval, V., Deforzh, H., & Prokopenko, O. (2019). Marketing of Ukrainian higher educational institutions representation based on modeling of webometrics ranking. *Marketing and Management of Innovations*, *3*, 60–72. https://doi.org/10.21272/mmi.2019.3-05

Lyashenko, A. (2018). *Accounting KNP: Organizational aspects*. https://uteka.ua/ua/publication/budget-13-byudzhet-buxgalterskij-uchet-otchetnost-i-kaznachejskoe-obsluzhivanie-52-buxuchet-knp-organizacionnye-momenty

Marchuk, U. (2016). Relationship of operational control and operational accounting. *Economic Annals-XXI*, *161*(9-10), 91–94. https://doi.org/10.21003/ea.v161-20

Mensah, J. (2019). Sustainable development: Meaning, history, principles, pillars, and implications for human action: Literature review. *Cogent Social Sciences*, *5*, 202286357. https://doi.org/10.1080/23311886.2019.1653531

Ministry of Health of Ukraine. (2018). *The method of recommendation on the transformation of healthcare facilities from budgetary institutions into municipal non-profit enterprises from February 14, 2018*. https://moz.gov.ua/uploads/0/3555-moz_metod_recomendations_autonomization_2018_ua_final_web.pdf

Ministry of Health of Ukraine (2020). How should a medical institution approach the choice of a medical information system (MIS)? https://moz.gov.ua/uploads/3/18559-ak_obrati_mis.pdf

Nagorny, O. (2018). *Accounting in KNP: Where to start?* https://uteka.ua/ua/publication/commerce-12-xozyajstvennye-operacii-9-buxgalterskij-uchet-v-knp-s-chego-nachat

National Health Service of Ukraine. (2020). Electronic map of places of primary care. https://nszu.gov.ua/en/e-data/dashboard/pmd-map

National Health Service of Ukraine. (2020). Health care packages: content and approach to healthcare contracting (Vol. 59). Retrieved https://nszu.gov.ua/storage/editor/files/paketi-medichnikh-poslug-07022020_1581100466.pdf

National Health Service of Ukraine. (2020). *Vendor payments medical assistance program medical safeguards*. https://nszu.gov.ua/en/e-data/dashboard/pmg-pay (in Ukr.).

Ndekwa, A. G., Kalugendo, E., Sood, K., & Grima, S. (2023). An analysis of agribusiness digitalisation transformation of the sub-Saharan African countries small-scale farmers' production distribution. *Research on World Agricultural Economy*, *4*(3), 63–78.

Özen, E., & Grima, S. (2018). Analysis of the influencing factors on the farmers' take-up of greenhouse agricultural insurance cover: A case study. *International Journal of Economics and Business Administration*, *VI*(4), 14–33.

Pajic, V., Andrejic, M., & Sternad, M. (2023). FMEA-QFD approach for effective risk assessment in distribution processes. *Journal of Intelligent Management Decision*, *2*(2), 46–56.

Petrushka, O. V. (2017). Features of the functioning of health insurance models in economically developed countries. *Economy and Society 13*, 1189–1192. http://www.economyandsociety.in.ua/journal/13_ukr/199.pdf

Ramlogan, R. (2008). Institutional reform in American medical research. *Science and Public Policy*, *35*(5), 373–375. https://doi.org/10.3152/030234208x317142

Rijal, S., Nursaputra, M. A. C., & Dari, H. U. (2024). Flood susceptibility analysis using Frequency Ratio method in Walanae watershed. *International Journal of Sustainable Development and Planning*, *19*(3), 823–832. https://doi.org/10.18280/ijsdp.190302

Shygun, M. M., Bezverkhiy, K. V., & Kovach, S. I. (2019). Development of integrated enterprise reporting structure. *Financial and Credit Activity: Problems of Theory and Practice*, *2*(29), 258–268. https://doi.org/10.18371/fcaptp.v2i29.172308

Skliar, I., Pedchenko, N., Strilec, V., Novikova, V., & Kozmenko, Y. (2020). Assessment of the reforms and program results of Ukraine's economy sustainable development through neural networks. *Problems and Perspectives in Management*, *18*(3), 81–92.

Sood, K., & Özen, E. (2024). A systematic review of ESG in the insurance industry: Navigating the path to sustainability. *International Journal of Sustainable Development and Planning*, *19*(3), 807–821. https://doi.org/10.18280/ijsdp.190301

Statista. (2020). *The population of selected European countries in 2020*. https://www.statista.com

Suprun, U. (2019). *64% of hospitals in Ukraine are already autonomous*. Espresso. https://espreso.tv/news/2019/11/08/v_ukrayini_vzhe_avtonomizovano_64_likaren_suprun

Sustainable Development Goals. (2022). *Goal 3: Ensure healthy lives and promote well-being for all at all ages*. https://www.un.org/sustainabledevelopment/health/

The National Health Service of Ukraine (NHSU). (2022). *The population of Ukraine and the average population for periods of the year*. https://www.ukrstat.gov.ua/operativ/operativ2021/ds/kn/arh_kn2021_u.html

World Health Organization. (2020). *World health statistics 2019: Monitoring health for the SDGs, sustainable development goals* (in press). https://apps.who.int/iris/bitstream/handle/10665/332070/9789240005105-eng.pdf

Wu, T. T., Liu, W. W., Zou, M., Lei, X., Yang, Q., Sharma, Q., Zhao, Y., & Shi, Z. M. (2020). Changes in preventive care utilization and its influencing factors among Chinese adults before and after the healthcare reform: cross-sectional evidence from the China Health and Nutrition Survey in 2004–2015. *BMJ Open*, *10*(10), PMC7534708. https://doi.org/10.1136/bmjopen-2020-038763

Yackee, S. W. (2009). Private conflict and policy passage: Interest-group conflict and state medical malpractice reform. *Policy Studies Journal*, *37*(2), 213–231. https://doi.org/10.1111/j.1541-0072.2009.00311.x

Yang, L., Peng, H., Yang, Y., Ouyang, L., & Li, Y. (2020). Situation and countermeasures of the management team of the elderly care institutions from the perspective of the combination of medical and healthcare: A cross-sectional study. *Journal of Healthcare Engineering*, *2020*, 1–8. https://doi.org/10.1155/2020/8826007

Yerpude, S., Sood, K., & Grima, S. (2022). Blockchain-augmented digital supply chain management: A way to sustainable business. *Journal of Risk and Financial Management*, *16*(1), 7.

Zakon. (1999). *On accounting and financial reporting in Ukraine law of Ukraine on July 16, 1999 № 996-XIV*. https://zakon.rada.gov.ua/laws/show/996-14#Text

Zakon. (1999). *On approval of the Chart of Accounts and Instructions on its application*, Ministry of Finance of Ukraine, Order, Plan on November 30, 1999, № 291. https://zakon.rada.gov.ua/laws/show/z0892-99#Text.

Zakon. (2016). *On the approval of the concept of reform of financing healthcare system. Order of the cabinet of Ministers of Ukraine*. Retrieved November 30, 2016 from https://zakon.rada.gov.ua/laws/show/1013-2016-%25D1%2580

Zakon. (2017). *About the state financial guarantees of medical services for the population, law of Ukraine*. Retrieved October 19, 2017, from https://zakon.rada.gov.ua/laws/show/2168-19

Chapter 13

Tourism Sector Sustainable Development: Evidence from Kuakata, Bangladesh

Mohammad Badruddoza Talukder[a], *Sanjeev Kumar*[b] *and Iva Rani Das*[c]

[a]*International University of Business Agriculture and Technology, Dhaka, Bangladesh*
[b]*Lovely Professional University, Phagwara, India*
[c]*Daffodil Institute of IT, Dhaka, Bangladesh*

Abstract

Purpose: This chapter aims to give thought to tourism marketing and local community development of Kuakata, and we strive to determine how community-centric marketing initiatives contribute to the sustainable development of the tourism sector and the local community in Kuakata, Bangladesh.

Design/methodology/approach: We employ this chapter with secondary data from the previous literature of the relevant study of research papers. The design allows for an understanding marketing strategies' impact on community development in beach tourism marketing in Bangladesh.

Findings: The findings reveal that community-centric marketing initiatives in Kuakata impact beach tourism and local community development. Collaborative efforts, such as community-led tours and cultural festivals, contribute to increased tourist engagement, revenue, and improved community well-being in the tourism industry in Bangladesh.

Research limitations: The study is based on marketing concepts and local community development in Kuakata. Future research could explore additional marketing factors influencing the success of community-centric marketing and assess their applicability in diverse settings intended for tourism development in Bangladesh.

Practical implications: Practically, this study provides valuable insights for tourism stakeholders, policymakers, and local communities seeking

Green Management: A New Paradigm in the World of Business, 231–247

Published under exclusive licence by Emerald Publishing Limited
doi:10.1108/978-1-83797-442-920241013

to enhance the symbiotic relationship between tourism marketing and community development.

Originality/value: The study's originality lies in exploring community-centric marketing strategies as catalysts for positive change, providing valuable lessons for sustainable tourism development globally. The study emphasizes collaborative approaches' potential in fostering mutually beneficial outcomes for tourists and local communities.

Keywords: Beach tourism; tourism marketing; local community development; sustainable tourism; community engagement; tourism revenue; Kuakata

JEL Classifications: M30; M31; M39

1. Introduction

Marketing concepts and the socioeconomic development of local communities are a notable issue of scholarly investigation and practical significance in the vivid tapestry of global tourism (Fu et al., 2022). This chapter takes us on an extensive journey, focusing on the complicated interplay between tourism marketing and community development, with Kuakata, a gorgeous coastal jewel, as our main point. We aim to elucidate the multifaceted influence of tourist marketing on local communities while assessing the efficacy of community-centric initiatives in creating sustainable tourism practices.

The tourism industry's contribution to economic growth is significant as it grows (Thommandru et al., 2023). However, the dangers of cultural dilution, environmental stress, and socioeconomic inequities must not be underestimated. We integrate qualitative insights from previous literature with tourist thoughts and a thorough tourism study. Kuakata, with its distinct seaside charm and cultural diversity, is an ideal setting for exploring the challenges and opportunities in the delicate balance between tourism development and community preservation (Nabi & Salimullah, 2022).

However, this study seeks to illuminate the specific dynamics at work in Kuakata and to give valuable insights that transcend this region, expanding the worldwide discourse on sustainable tourism practices. By following this, we delve into the varied nature of tourist marketing, researching various techniques to promote destinations and tracking the growing trends in this dynamic industry. Following that, we immerse ourselves in an in-depth portrayal of Kuakata as a unique tourist destination, emphasizing its distinguishing features that attract local and foreign visitors (Talukder & Hossain, 2021). A closer look at the region's geographical location and a detailed map illuminate the spatial context of Kuakata, improving our knowledge of its tourism development potential (Dahirul Islam, 2021). Furthermore, we investigate the conceptual framework of marketing specifically adapted for tourism development, primarily emphasizing community-based techniques that prioritize local inhabitants' engagement and well-being.

Kuakata's coastal setting, with its panoramic panoramas and proximity to the Bay of Bengal, establishes it as a marine sanctuary for travelers looking for a unique blend of seaside beauty and maritime activities (Rakib et al., 2021). Our debate goes beyond traditional tourist destinations, delving into maritime experiences that contribute to the region's allure, carving out a particular niche within the larger spectrum of tourism options.

We reveal the critical function of involving local communities of Kuakata Beach in maintaining authenticity and mutual benefit for tourists and inhabitants as we traverse the landscape of community engagement in tourism marketing. This will go into a detailed case study of Kuakata, delving into specific community-centric marketing strategies and evaluating their outcomes regarding increased tourism revenue, improved infrastructure, and higher community well-being.

Finally, we recommend and give future study directions on the obstacles and opportunities discovered, providing practical advice for long-term tourism marketing. By doing so, it hopes to contribute to the empowerment of local populations in Kuakata and the broader goal of building resilient tourism practices that may be utilized and adapted in various global places.

2. Tourism Marketing Landscape

2.1. Overview of Tourism Marketing

Tourism marketing is a dynamic and expanding field inextricably linked to the expansion and transformation of the global tourism industry (Streimikiene et al., 2021). This section aims to provide a complete overview of the historical evolution and current trends impacting the tourism marketing landscape.

2.1.1. Historical Evolution

This part digs into the rich tapestry of the tourism marketing narrative, tracking its historical evolution. The story develops from the early twentieth-century introduction of mass tourism, which necessitated destination promotion, to the mid-twentieth-century strategic branding efforts (Gil-de-Arriba & Larrinaga, 2023). The industry's trajectory is shaped by key events such as the post-World War II rise in international travel and the late-20th-century transition towards customer-centric approaches. The rise of the internet in the 1990s redefined outreach, while the 21st century saw the rise of experiential marketing (Foffa, 2022). This short examination uncovers important milestones, paradigm shifts, and emerging methods that have shaped the dynamic landscape of tourism marketing.

2.1.2. Contemporary Trends

Building on the historical story, contemporary trends delve into the current landscape of tourism marketing. It identifies and examines the prevalent themes that characterize how destinations and tourism businesses present themselves in the modern era (Bastidas-Manzano et al., 2021). From the pervasiveness of digital platforms and the significance of user-generated content to the rise of sustainable tourism as a fundamental paradigm, this investigation offers insight into the dynamic methods that shape the industry's current landscape (Wider et al., 2023).

2.2. Marketing Strategies and Tools

2.2.1. Digital Marketing

Digital marketing has emerged as the linchpin of contemporary tourism strategies. Online platforms, social media, and digital technologies are essential for reaching and engaging with target audiences in the digital age (Kelly et al., 2015). Websites, search engine optimization (SEO), and online travel agencies (OTAs) facilitate information dissemination (Talukder, 2021). At the same time, social media platforms provide interactive spaces for dialogue and Promotion. Email marketing, content creation, and influencer collaborations enhance the digital footprint, allowing destinations like Kuakata to craft compelling stories and engage with a global audience (Karim, 2022).

2.2.2. Experiential Campaigns

Beyond traditional advertising, experiential campaigns create immersive and memorable experiences for potential tourists (Smith & Hanover, 2016). Initiatives include curated travel encounters, interactive events, and participatory activities that transcend the conventional promotional model (Wong et al., 2023). By emphasizing personal engagement and emotional connections, experiential campaigns, whether virtual or physical, enhance a destination's allure, fostering a more profound and lasting connection with the audience.

2.2.3. Collaborative Partnerships

Collaborative partnerships constitute a strategic component, emphasizing the importance of alliances between various stakeholders (Gajda, 2004). Tourism boards, local businesses, and communities can form synergies to enhance overall marketing efforts. These partnerships provide a more holistic representation of the destination, leveraging collective resources, expertise, and local insights. Hostels can amplify their marketing impact by fostering collaboration, ensuring a more comprehensive and authentic portrayal.

2.2.4. Destination Branding

Destination branding involves crafting a distinctive identity for a locale to shape perceptions and attract specific market segments (Qu et al., 2011). This strategy often incorporates visual elements, storytelling, and unique selling propositions. By establishing a solid brand, destinations can differentiate themselves, making a lasting impression on potential travelers and influencing their decision-making processes (Sirgy & Su, 2000).

2.2.5. Personalization and Data Analytics

Personalization, driven by data analytics and artificial intelligence, tailors marketing messages to individual preferences. Destinations can customize their marketing strategies by leveraging data on traveler behavior, preferences, and demographics, offering personalized recommendations and experiences (Del Vecchio et al., 2018). This approach enhances engagement and increases the likelihood of conversion by aligning promotional efforts with the specific interests of the target audience.

2.2.6. Sustainable Tourism Practices

Sustainable tourism practices have evolved from a trend to a fundamental paradigm shift. Destinations increasingly adopt environmentally and socially responsible strategies in their marketing (Madanaguli et al., 2022). From promoting eco-friendly accommodations to showcasing conservation efforts, sustainability has become a compelling narrative that resonates with the conscientious traveler, contributing to the long-term viability of tourism destinations.

Fig. 13.1 illustrates the foundational pillars of the Evolution of Marketing Concept, confirming the progression of marketing development from the past to the present. The figure also highlights that the scope of marketing encompasses digital dominance, sustainability, and crisis management, potentially influencing developments in the tourism industry. Furthermore, the evolution of the marketing concept impacts the scope of future tourism development.

3. Kuakata as a Tourist Destination

This exploration delves into the myriad facets that make Kuakata a compelling destination, from its natural beauty to its cultural richness.

3.1. Geographical Splendor

Kuakata's allure begins with its geographical positioning. Situated at the confluence of the Bay of Bengal, Kuakata boasts an unbroken 30-km stretch of wide sandy beach. This natural expanse offers visitors an immersive experience where the horizon seems to meet the sea in an endless embrace Talukder, 2020b; (Vinnakota et al., 2023). The pristine beauty of the beach, coupled with the rhythmic sound of the waves, creates a serene and rejuvenating environment that beckons those seeking tranquillity.

3.2. Sunrise and Sunset Panorama

One of Kuakata's most distinguishing features is its reputation as the only place in Bangladesh where sunrise and sunset are visible over the sea (Nabi & Salimullah, 2022). The beach faces the southeast, allowing early risers to witness the breathtaking spectacle of the sun ascending from the Bay of Bengal. Conversely, as the day concludes, the sun majestically descends into the same

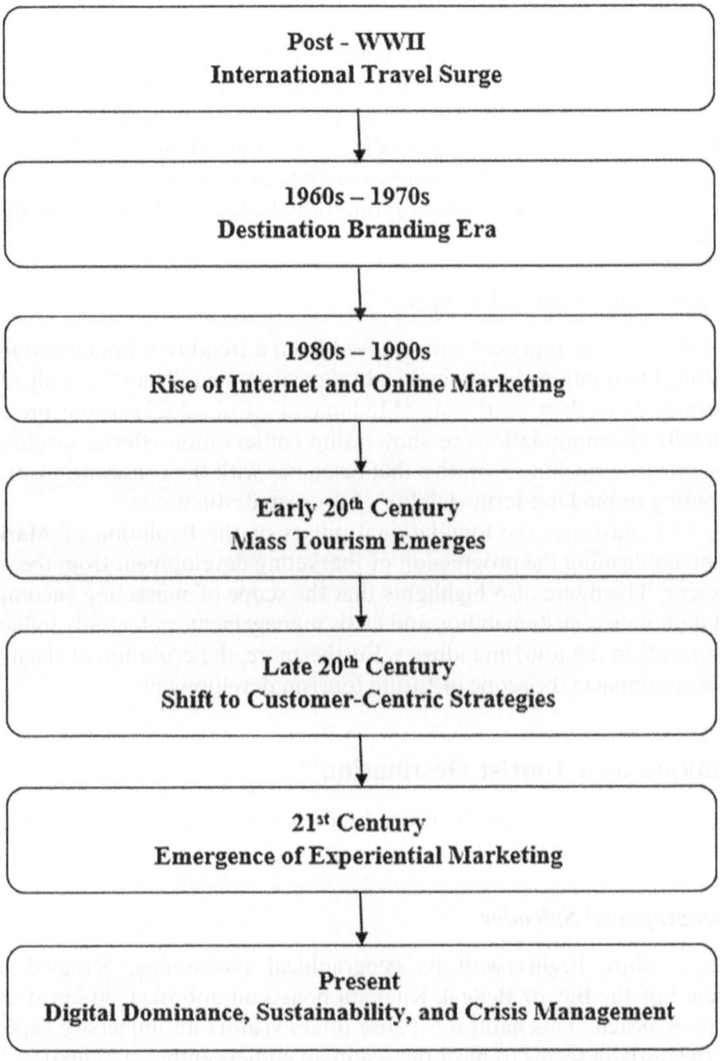

Fig. 13.1. Evolution of Marketing Concept. *Source*: Authors' compilation.

waters, painting the sky with hues of orange and red. This dual celestial phenomenon has bestowed Kuakata with the title "Daughter of the Sea." It is a magnetic draw for nature enthusiasts and photographers alike.

3.3. Cultural Richness

Beyond its natural splendor, Kuakata is steeped in cultural richness. The indigenous Rakhine community's distinctive traditions and practices contribute to the region's cultural tapestry. Visitors can engage with local customs, sample traditional cuisine, and partake in festivities that reflect the vibrant heritage of the area (Putra et al., 2023). The presence of ancient Buddhist temples, such as the Fatrar Char and Kua-Para Buddha Bihar, adds a spiritual dimension to the cultural mosaic of Kuakata.

3.4. Maritime Tourism

Kuakata's proximity to the Bay of Bengal positions it as a hub for maritime tourism. Fishing villages dot the coastline, providing visitors with an authentic glimpse into the lives of the local fishing communities (Graham, 2021). Boat rides on the sea, offering a chance to witness fishermen's daily activities and experience the Bay's vastness, are popular among tourists seeking a maritime adventure.

3.5. Adventure and Eco-tourism

For the adventurous traveler, Kuakata offers opportunities for eco-tourism and exploration. The nearby Lebur Char, an estuarine island, is a haven for migratory birds, making it a birdwatcher's paradise. The lush greenery and biodiversity of the area provide a stark contrast to the coastal landscape, allowing tourists to appreciate the diverse ecosystems that coexist in this enchanting region.

3.6. Tourist Infrastructure and Accommodation

Kuakata has witnessed a growth in tourism infrastructure, with accommodations, restaurants, and recreational facilities catering to visitors' needs (Alauddin et al., 2021). From budget-friendly options to more luxurious resorts, tourists can choose accommodations that suit their preferences, ensuring a comfortable stay while immersing themselves in the beauty of Kuakata.

4. Impacts of Tourism on Local Communities

Economic growth and cultural exchange tourism profoundly impact local communities (Iqbal & Ahmed, 2022). The positive and negative consequences can influence social, economic, cultural, and environmental dimensions. This exploration delves into the multifaceted impacts of tourism, recognizing the need to understand its effects on the communities that serve as hosts.

4.1. Economic Impacts

Positive: Tourism can inject vital economic resources into local communities. Increased employment opportunities arise in the hospitality, transportation, and retail sectors. Small businesses, including local markets and crafts, often thrive due to heightened demand. The economic influx can lead to infrastructure development, benefiting the tourism sector and the community (Storonyanska et al., 2021).

Negative: Tourism for economic sustenance can create vulnerabilities like seasonal fluctuations, and external factors, such as economic downturns or global crises, may lead to instability. Moreover, the influx of tourists can drive up prices, making residents' goods and services less affordable (Mikulić et al., 2021).

4.2. Social and Cultural Impacts

Positive: Cultural exchange has a significant positive impact on tourism. Exposure to diverse perspectives fosters mutual understanding and tolerance. Local traditions, arts, and customs may gain recognition and appreciation from a global audience (Aririguzoh, 2022). Social interaction between tourists and locals can create enriching experiences for both parties.

Negative: The influx of tourists can sometimes lead to cultural dilution or commodification. The demand for "authentic" experiences may result in exploiting local traditions for commercial gain, potentially eroding their authenticity. Social disruption may occur as traditional ways of life are altered to cater to tourist expectations (Wright, 2022).

4.3. Environmental Impacts

Positive: Tourism can contribute to environmental conservation efforts when managed sustainably. Revenues generated from eco-tourism initiatives may be reinvested in preserving natural habitats, wildlife, and landscapes (Makwela, 2022). Also, heightened environmental awareness among tourists may increase support for conservation initiatives.

Negative: Unsustainable tourism practices pose significant threats to the environment. Overdevelopment, pollution, and habitat destruction can result from poorly managed tourist activities. Fragile ecosystems may suffer irreparable damage, impacting local flora and fauna and exacerbating climate change (McElwee, 2021).

4.4. Infrastructure Development

Positive: Tourism often triggers infrastructure development, such as the construction roads, airports, and accommodation facilities. Improved infrastructure benefits tourists and locals, enhancing accessibility and connectivity (Szymańska et al., 2021). Local communities may experience enhanced public services and upgraded facilities.

Negative: The rapid development driven by tourism can sometimes outpace local capacity and planning. This can lead to issues such as inadequate waste management, strain on water resources, and disruptions to the local way of life. The balance between accommodating tourists and maintaining the integrity of the community becomes crucial (Sara et al., 2021).

4.5. Community Well-being

Fig. 13.2 illustrates the dual impacts of tourism on local communities, encompassing positive effects such as economic prosperity, cultural enrichment, environmental

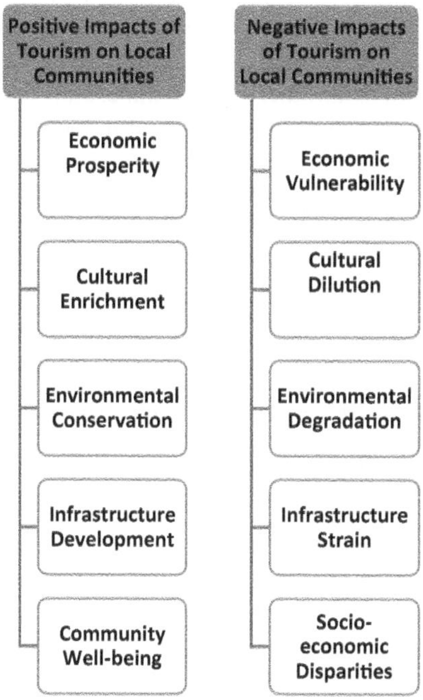

Fig. 13.2. Dual Impacts of Tourism on Local Communities. *Source*: Authors' compilation.

conservation, infrastructure development, and community well-being. Conversely, negative impacts include economic vulnerability, cultural dilution, environmental degradation, infrastructure strain, and socioeconomic disparities.

5. The Role of Community Engagement in Tourism Marketing

Community engagement in tourism marketing is a transformative process that redefines the traditional relationship between a destination and its residents (Pascoli, 2021). It positions communities as integral contributors and stakeholders in promoting the goal, recognizing that the success of tourism initiatives is linked to the well-being and active involvement of the local population. Community engagement supports authentic destination representation by involving residents in storytelling, capturing the essence of the community's culture, traditions, and unique identity (Hay et al., 2022). This approach resonates with modern travelers' desire for genuine and immersive experiences.

Community engagement facilitates the co-creation of experiences, allowing locals to actively participate in the design of tours, events, and cultural activities (Talukder, 2020a). This approach extends to sustainability integration, where local communities play a vital role in decision-making processes that align tourism initiatives with their long-term interests.

Cultural preservation and enrichment emerge as significant outcomes of community engagement, as engaged communities serve as cultural ambassadors, actively preserving and promoting local traditions (Arkhurst et al., 2023). Economic empowerment is another crucial dimension, as community engagement opens up entrepreneurial opportunities for locals, contributing to individuals' financial well-being and the community's overall development. However, community engagement in tourism marketing is transformative, evolving from a transactional relationship to a collaborative and mutually beneficial partnership (Baba et al., 2021). This approach is a guiding principle for responsible and impactful destination marketing in an era where travelers increasingly seek authentic, meaningful, and sustainable experiences.

6. Kuakata's Community-centric Marketing Initiatives

6.1. Overview of Marketing Initiatives

Kuakata's marketing strategy is a community-centric approach, involving local community involvement in storytelling sessions, integrating cultural events, and promoting the destination's vibrancy. This approach empowers local businesses with enhanced marketing skills and encourages community participation in shaping the destination's online narrative. The Tourism Ambassadors Program adds a personalized touch to visitor interactions, celebrating cultural richness and sustainable development (Sormin & Sihombing, 2023).

6.2. Community-led Tours and Events

Kuakata's marketing strategy focuses on community-led tours and events involving residents as guides and hosts. These tours offer authentic experiences of the destination, allowing visitors to immerse themselves in the community's daily life. The marketing initiatives also feature local festivals, performances, and celebrations, empowering residents to promote their cultural identity (Chang et al., 2022). This approach fosters genuine connections between visitors and the local community, aligning with Kuakata's sustainable tourism and community engagement.

6.3. Collaborative Promotional Campaigns

Kuakata's marketing initiatives involve local stakeholders in collaborative promotional campaigns, showcasing the destination's cultural heritage, scenic beauty, and vibrant community life. These campaigns often feature local artisans, entrepreneurs, and performers, enhancing authenticity and fostering community pride. By integrating tourism promotion and community empowerment, Kuakata creates a more vibrant and sustainable destination, highlighting the synergy between tourism promotion and community empowerment (Horaira & Devi, 2021).

7. Assessing the Outcomes

7.1. Increased Tourism Revenue

Kuakata's community-centric marketing initiatives have significantly increased tourism revenue. Key metrics show a tangible economic impact on the local community. Residents' strategic involvement in crafting the destination's narrative and promoting unique cultural events have attracted more visitors, leading to increased demand for local businesses (Carvalho et al., 2021).

7.2. Improved Infrastructure

Tourist-driving investments in roads, sanitation facilities, and healthcare services improved the infrastructure in Kuakata. Collaborative efforts between community and tourism stakeholders have directed resources toward critical infrastructure development, aligning with sustainable tourism goals and fostering holistic destination development. Kuakata's experience demonstrates the potential of aligning tourism promotion with community well-being, creating a win-win scenario for residents and visitors.

7.3. Enhanced Community Well-being

An excellent marketing initiative has significantly improved community well-being in terms of sustainable tourism development. Local businesses thrive by involving residents in the tourism narrative, leading to increased employment opportunities and entrepreneurial ventures (Noorashid & Chin, 2021). Community well-being ensures equitable distribution of benefits, ultimately enhancing the overall well-being of the local community.

7.4. Key Success Factors

The local community shapes the destination's narrative, integrates local cultural events, and promotes community-led tours, which are attributed to active involvement (Talukder et al., 2023). Collaborative promotional campaigns showcase local entrepreneurs' talents, leading to increased tourism revenue, improved infrastructure, and enhanced community well-being.

8. Challenges and Opportunities

8.1. Challenges in Implementing Community-centric Strategies

Community-centric tourism strategies have succeeded and face challenges such as balancing cultural authenticity with tourism development, managing environmental impact, and addressing socioeconomic disparities (Chen & Kong, 2021). However, adaptive strategies like sustainable practices, community education, and responsible tourism guidelines can mitigate environmental concerns and address socioeconomic disparities. Embracing challenges as opportunities for growth and innovation is crucial for the continued success and sustainability of Kuakata's community-centric strategy for tourism development.

8.2. Opportunities for Sustainable Tourism

Kuakata faces challenges implementing sustainable tourism due to its unique natural beauty and cultural richness (Rakib et al., 2021). However, sustainable practices could be resolved by investing in eco-friendly infrastructure, promoting responsible tourism behavior, and developing eco-friendly accommodations. By embracing these opportunities, Kuakata can become a beacon for sustainable tourism, contributing to its community's well-being and preserving its natural and cultural heritage.

8.3. Lessons Learned from Kuakata

Addressing environmental strain and socioeconomic disparities requires proactive measures and inclusive community engagement that prioritizes community well-being alongside tourism development. Leveraging cultural and natural assets highlights the potential for destinations to differentiate themselves through authentic experiences for Kuakata Beach (Amin, 2021). Collaborative efforts between communities, businesses, and government entities demonstrate shared responsibility for sustainable tourism goals. Kuakata's adaptability and resilience in transforming challenges into opportunities offer insights into building a sustainable future for tourism.

Fig. 13.3 illustrates the marketing concept of tourism and local community development in Kuakata, encompassing tourism marketing strategies and resources. The marketing concept of tourism also involves local community development, economic impact, community-centric marketing initiatives, enhanced community well-being, infrastructure, sustainable tourism practices, and community empowerment.

9. Recommendations for Sustainable Tourism Marketing

The above reveals that community-centric marketing initiatives in Kuakata impact beach tourism and local community development. Collaborative efforts could improve community well-being in the tourism industry in Bangladesh. Furthermore, the following recommendations to put the marketing concept for tourism and local community development into action:

- The term "community engagement" refers to encouraging the participation of community people in decision-making processes linked to tourism planning, infrastructure development, and cultural preservation activities.
- To reduce the adverse effects of tourism activities on the environment in Kuakata, it is essential to implement eco-friendly measures such as waste

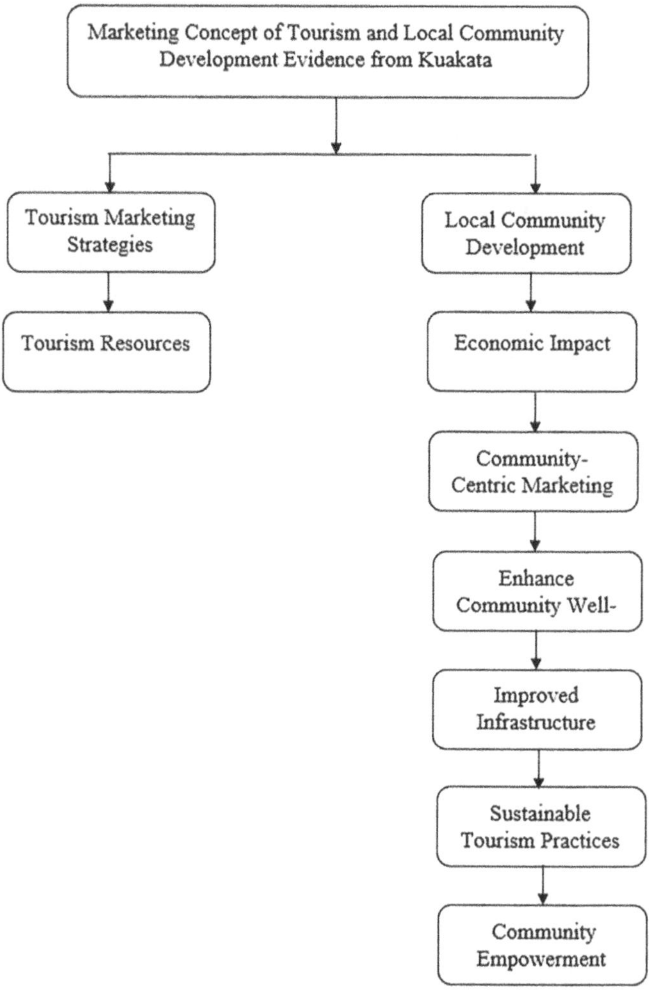

Fig. 13.3. The Marketing Concept of Tourism and Local Community Development in Kuakata. *Source*: Authors' compilation.

management programs, renewable energy projects, and sustainable transportation options. This can be accomplished through the implementation of sustainable tourism practices.

- Increasing the visibility of Kolkata's cultural attractions and community-based activities can be accomplished through digital platforms, social media channels, and tourism websites. By utilizing user-generated content and storytelling, potential visitors can be engaged in marketing and promotion efforts.
- Within the Kuakata Monitoring and Evaluation scope, a monitoring and evaluation framework should be established to track the development of tourist activities and their influence on economic indicators and the community's well-being.

- In addition to government agencies, non-profit organizations, companies from the corporate sector, and academic institutions combine knowledge, Assist in the Promotion of Kuakata as a responsible tourism destination on a worldwide scale by participating in regional and international collaborations to exchange best practices, leverage financial opportunities, and promoting in general.

10. Conclusion and Future Research

Finally, the marketing concept for tourism and local community development of Kuakata Beach has yielded valuable insights into modern destination management in Bangladesh. The success of community-centred initiatives in Kuakata demonstrates the effectiveness of strategies prioritizing local participation and well-being, which could be beneficial in promoting a beautiful Bangladesh. However, obstacles remain, underlining the need for continuing efforts to achieve a sustainable equilibrium and contributing the above recommendations to practices to enlarge tourism revenue. Moving ahead, future studies should focus on other tourism destinations in Bangladesh. More studies are required to document the long-term effect of community-centric projects, which are essential for better understanding the long-term advantages and possible issues that may develop. Technological integration into marketing plans and community engagement procedures should be investigated to harness the potential of digital platforms so that Kuakata will be a more popular destination for tourists. The inclusion of more research in tourism on visitor perceptions will lead to more comprehensive and socially responsible destination management. Finally, an in-depth assessment of policy frameworks and governance structures is critical for finding regulatory measures that may promote sustainable growth while protecting the distinctive characteristics of destinations such as Kuakata. These future research directions aim to refine and expand our knowledge base, contributing to the ongoing debate on responsible tourism practices and providing actionable insights for destination managers, policymakers, and stakeholders involved in the delicate task of balancing tourism growth and community preservation in Kuakata and other similar destinations around the world.

References

Alauddin, M., Dipu, S. M. M. A., & Uddin, M. R. (2021). Tourism products and services in Bangladesh: Challenges and suggestions. In *Tourism products and services in Bangladesh: Concept analysis and development suggestions* (pp. 445–459). Springer.

Amin, S. B. (2021). *Economy of tourism in Bangladesh*. Springer.

Aririguzoh, S. (2022). Communication competencies, culture and SDGs: Effective processes to cross-cultural communication. *Humanities and Social Sciences Communications*, *9*(1), 1–11.

Arkhurst, K., Oduro, I., Dodoo, N., Adu, M., & Edusei, C. (2023). Choir management in Ghana: Overcoming challenges to sustain musical culture and community engagement. *European Journal of Philosophy, Culture and Religion*, *7*(1), 64–78.

Baba, S., Mohammad, S., & Young, C. (2021). Managing project sustainability in the extractive industries: Towards a reciprocity framework for community engagement. *International Journal of Project Management*, *39*(8), 887–901.

Bastidas-Manzano, A.-B., Sánchez-Fernández, J., & Casado-Aranda, L.-A. (2021). The past, present, and future of smart tourism destinations: A bibliometric analysis. *Journal of Hospitality & Tourism Research*, *45*(3), 529–552.

Carvalho, M., Kastenholz, E., & Carneiro, M. J. (2021). Interaction as a central element of co-creative wine tourism experiences—Evidence from Bairrada, a Portuguese wine-producing region. *Sustainability*, *13*(16), 9374.

Chang, J.-J., Chen, R.-F., & Lin, C.-L. (2022). Exploring the driving factors of urban music festival tourism and service development strategies using the modified SIA-NRM approach. *Sustainability*, *14*(12), 7498.

Chen, P., & Kong, X. (2021). Tourism-led commodification of place and rural transformation development: A case study of Xixinan Village, Huangshan, China. *Land*, *10*(7), 694.

Dahirul Islam, K. (2021). *Investigation of wind energy potential in Asia-Pacific Region: Thailand, South Korea and Bangladesh perspectives*. Prince of Songkla University.

Del Vecchio, P., Mele, G., Ndou, V., & Secundo, G. (2018). Creating value from social big data: Implications for smart tourism destinations. *Information Processing & Management*, *54*(5), 847–860.

Foffa, A. (2022). The digital turn in architectural trade literature the case of "The Architects' Journal", 1990–2010. *La Rivista Di Engramma*, *2022*(188).

Fu, X., Kirillova, K., & Lehto, X. Y. (2022). Travel and life: A developmental perspective on tourism consumption over the life course. *Tourism Management*, *89*, 104447.

Gajda, R. (2004). Utilizing collaboration theory to evaluate strategic alliances. *The American Journal of Evaluation*, *25*(1), 65–77.

Gil-de-Arriba, C., & Larrinaga, C. (2023). Configuring the northern coast of Spain as a privileged tourist enclave: The cities of San Sebastián and Santander, 1902–1931. *Journal of Tourism History*, *15*(2), 201–223.

Graham, S. C. (2021). Authentic culinary tourism experiences: The perspectives of locals. *Journal of Gastronomy and Tourism*, *5*(2), 65–82.

Hay, N. A., Chien, P. M., & Ruhanen, L. (2022). Tell me your story: Branding destinations through residents' (place) stories. *Journal of Vacation Marketing*, *28*(3), 319–334.

Horaira, M. A., & Devi, A. (2021). Cultural tourism in Bangladesh, a potential and profound tourism destination: Developing a model for cultural tourism development in Bangladesh. *International Tourism and Hospitality Journal*, *4*(10), 1–22.

Iqbal, Z., & Ahmed, S. (2022). Antecedents and consequences of community-based tourism in border district of Jammu and Kashmir. *International Journal of Tourism Cities*, *8*(3), 569–587.

Karim, M. (2022). *USAID_Feed the Future Bangladesh_Quarterly Progress Report_Jan 2022-Mar 2022*.

Kelly, B., Vandevijvere, S., Freeman, B., & Jenkin, G. (2015). New media but same old tricks: Food marketing to children in the digital age. *Current Obesity Reports*, *4*, 37–45.

Madanaguli, A., Srivastava, S., Ferraris, A., & Dhir, A. (2022). Corporate social responsibility and sustainability in the tourism sector: A systematic literature review and future outlook. *Sustainable Development*, *30*(3), 447–461.

Makwela, S. E. (2022). The effects of eco-tourism on rural land transformation in Mapungubwe National Park, Limpopo Province, South Africa. *International Journal of Contemporary Business Research*, *2*, 164.

McElwee, P. (2021). Climate change and biodiversity loss: Two sides of the same coin. *Current History*, *120*(829), 295–300.

Mikulić, J., Vizek, M., Stojčić, N., Payne, J. E., Časni, A. Č., & Barbić, T. (2021). The effect of tourism activity on housing affordability. *Annals of Tourism Research*, *90*, 103264.

Nabi, R., & Salimullah, A. H. M. (2022). Promoting catamaran tourism in Bangladesh: The challenges of blue economy. In *Technology application in tourism fairs, festivals and events in Asia* (pp. 181–208). Springer.

Noorashid, N., & Chin, W. L. (2021). Coping with COVID-19: The resilience and transformation of community-based tourism in Brunei Darussalam. *Sustainability, 13*(15), 8618.

Pascoli, M. (2021). Community involvement in tourism: Exploring the place image guided by the locals. *Cuadernos Europeos de Deusto, 64*, 111–136.

Putra, F. K. K., Putra, M. K., & Novianti, S. (2023). Taste of ASEAN: Traditional food images from Southeast Asian countries. *Journal of Ethnic Foods, 10*(1), 20.

Qu, H., Kim, L. H., & Im, H. H. (2011). A model of destination branding: Integrating the concepts of the branding and destination image. *Tourism Management, 32*(3), 465–476.

Rakib, M. R. H. K., Islam, M. N., & Hassan, A. (2021). Product and service offers diversification for beach tourism in Bangladesh. In *Tourism products and services in Bangladesh: Concept analysis and development suggestions* (pp. 115–133). Springer.

Sara, I. M., Saputra, K. A. K., & Larasdiputra, G. D. (2021). Community service activities for development of potential tourism villages in Bali (A study based on community service in Siangan Village, Gianyar). *PalArch's Journal of Archaeology of Egypt/ Egyptology, 18*(4), 6358–6369.

Singh, S., Nicely, A., Day, J., & Cai, L. A. (2022). Marketing messages for post-pandemic destination recovery – A Delphi study. *Journal of Destination Marketing & Management, 23*, 100676.

Sirgy, M. J., & Su, C. (2000). Destination image, self-congruity, and travel behavior: Toward an integrative model. *Journal of Travel Research, 38*(4), 340–352.

Smith, K., & Hanover, D. (2016). *Experiential marketing: Secrets, strategies, and success stories from the world's greatest brands*. John Wiley & Sons.

Sormin, A., & Sihombing, H. (2023). Empowering youth for sustainable cultural tourism: A case study Tipang village, Baktiraja district, Humbang Hasundutan regency, Indonesia. *Jurnal Ilmu Pendidikan Dan Humaniora, 12*(1), 56–68.

Storonyanska, I., Dub, A., Grafska, O., Hrynchyshyn, I., Bilanyuk, O., & Pierscieniak, A. (2021). The tourist infrastructure of local communities in Ukraine: Current state and impact on local economic development. *Agricultural and Resource Economics: International Scientific E-Journal, 7*, 102–118.

Streimikiene, D., Svagzdiene, B., Jasinskas, E., & Simanavicius, A. (2021). Sustainable tourism development and competitiveness: The systematic literature review. *Sustainable Development, 29*(1), 259–271.

Szymańska, E., Panfiluk, E., & Kiryluk, H. (2021). Innovative solutions for the development of sustainable transport and improvement of the tourist accessibility of peripheral areas: The case of the Białowieża forest region. *Sustainability, 13*(4), 2381.

Talukder, M. B. (2020a). An appraisal of the economic outlook for the tourism industry, specially Cox's Bazar in Bangladesh. *I-Manager's Journal on Economics & Commerce, 2*(1), 23–35.

Talukder, M. B. (2020b). The future of culinary tourism: An emerging dimension for the tourism industry of Bangladesh. *I-Manager's Journal on Management, 15*(1), 27. https://doi.org/10.26634/jmgt.15.1.17181

Talukder, M. B. (2021). An assessment of the roles of the social network in the development of the tourism industry in Bangladesh. *International Journal of Business, Law, and Education, 2*(3), 85–93. https://doi.org/10.56442/ijble.v2i3.21

Talukder, M. B., & Hossain, M. M. (2021). Prospects of future tourism in Bangladesh: An evaluative study. *I-Manager's Journal on Management, 15*(4), 1–8. https://doi.org/10.26634/jmgt.15.4.17495

Talukder, M. B., Kumar, S., Sood, K., & Grima, S. (2023). Information technology, food service quality and restaurant revisit intention. *International Journal of Sustainable Development and Planning*, *18*(1), 295–303. https://doi.org/10.18280/ijsdp.180131

Thommandru, A., Espinoza-Maguiña, M., Ramirez-Asis, E., Ray, S., Naved, M., & Guzman-Avalos, M. (2023). Role of tourism and hospitality business in economic development. *Materials Today: Proceedings*, *80*, 2901–2904.

Vinnakota, S., Mohan, M. D., Boda, M. J., Askarzai, W., Devkota, M. P., Shetty, M. S., Wangmo, M. T., & Choden, M. T. (2023). Venturing into virtuality: Exploring the evolution, technological underpinnings, and forward pathways of virtual tourism. *Educational Research (IJMCER)*, *5*(6), 8–49.

Wider, W., Gao, Y., Chan, C. K., Lin, J., Li, J., Tanucan, J. C. M., & Fauzi, M. A. (2023). Unveiling trends in digital tourism research: A bibliometric analysis of co-citation and co-word analysis. *Environmental and Sustainability Indicators*, *20*, 100308.

Wong, I. A., Lu, M. V., Lin, S., & Lin, Z. (2023). The transformative virtual experience paradigm: the case of Airbnb's online experience. *International Journal of Contemporary Hospitality Management*, *35*(4), 1398–1422.

Wright, K. Q. (2022). "It changed the atmosphere surrounding the baby I did have": Making sense of reproduction during the COVID-19 pandemic. *Journal of Marriage and Family*, *84*(4), 1105–1128.

Chapter 14

The Role of Green Energy on Economic Aspects of Sustainable Development

Anita Tanwar[a], *Reet Kaur*[a] *and Arvinder Kaur*[b]

[a]*Chitkara Business School, Chitkara University, India*
[b]*University School of Business, Chandigarh University, India*

Abstract

Introduction: Energy is an indispensable element of all economies and is extensively utilized to meet the growing demands of many life forms on the earth.

Purpose: This paper aims to investigate the relationship between green energy resources, popularly known as renewable energy resources, and gross domestic product.

Methodology: For the analysis top seven emerging countries of the world: Brazil, India, Mexico, Turkey, China, Indonesia, and Russia during the period 1990–2020 were chosen as per their economic performance in 2023. For testing the hypothesis, the authors used data from the World Bank database with gross domestic product (GDP) as a dependent variable and green energy resources (GERs) as an independent variable. For analysing the hypothesis, Johansen cointegration test along with ordinary least squares regression (OLS) regression is applied.

Findings: In India, a strong and very positive linear connection is observed, indicating that the independent variables have a significant impact on the dependent variable. While in China, the connection between independent and dependent variable is relatively less prominent. Furthermore, Brazil exhibits a strong positive linear correlation, suggesting that the independent factors have a substantial influence on dependent variable. The aforementioned variables also exert a substantial impact on Mexico's economic dynamics, as demonstrated by the robust positive correlation is observed

Green Management: A New Paradigm in the World of Business, 249–266

doi:10.1108/978-1-83797-442-920241014

between them. A moderate positive correlation between the variables of Russia indicates the noticeable association among the variables.

Implications: Policymakers, economists, and academicians can utilize these insights to develop informed forecasts and make decisions, taking into account the distinctive economic conditions of each country.

Keywords: Green energy; green growth; sustainable development; green; gross domestic product; emerging economies; energy efficiency; panel data analysis

JEL Classifications: A11; A12; C01; C23; C31; F21; G21; G23; G24; O16; Q50; Q4; Q43

Introduction

The globe is rapidly transforming into a global community as the demand for energy from the entire global population continues to grow, while the physical state of the earth remains unchanged. The demand for energy and its associated services to meet the needs that contribute to social and economic progress has grown substantially. Every society needs energy to fulfill fundamental human requirements, including healthcare, illumination, food preparation, transportation, and communication, as well as to support productive activities (Bhargave & Tandon, 2022; Owusu & Asumadu-Sarkodie, 2016).

The conflict between economic progress and environmental preservation is evident in numerous environmental reports, climate change studies, and discussions on sustainable development (Wang et al., 2020). Furthermore, climate change is progressively intensifying, adversely affecting the overall economic progress, generating ecological disparities, and leading to unsustainable development (Kumar et al., 2010). Undoubtedly, it is imperative for all governments, organizations, and enterprises to urgently seek solutions to climate change that facilitate the attainment of growth objectives while mitigating environmental effects (Gao et al., 2022). Companies must prioritize adopting green investments to foster green growth economies, including Vietnam's green growth policy. To eliminate the negative impacts of post-crisis and climate change, it is imperative to not only rely on the financial banking system to reorganize the financial system but also to undertake the reorganization of the economy, which is crucial for enterprises (Eyraud et al., 2013; Ndekwa et al., 2023; Sood & Ozen, 2024; Yerpude et al., 2023).

Several policies, documents, and publications, like the one from the Intergovernmental Panel on Climate Change (IPCC), operate under the assumption that economic growth will remain a fundamental aspect of prosperous future societies (Hickel & Kallis, 2020). Nevertheless, if the expansion of the economy coincides with escalating resource utilization and emissions, it could jeopardize the prospects of achieving future sustainability transformation objectives and attaining objectives such as the Sustainable Development Goals (SDGs) (TWI2050, 2018). It demands eliminating greenhouse gas (GHG) emissions by about 2050.

It necessitates significant cutbacks in the consumption of riches, such as energy or materials, in many places across the globe. Net negative emissions can be obtained in many situations by promoting tree plantation and other land-based "nature-based solutions" (Griscom et al., 2017) or technology that removes carbon dioxide from the atmosphere post-2050 is necessary to take action to restore the climate to the desired target level when it has exceeded the goals set for climate change mitigation. The necessity for "negative emissions" arises in all situations if there is a failure to achieve adequate reductions in carbon emissions for the early part of the century (IPCC, 2014; IPCC, 2018).

In light of the significance of maintaining a sustainable environment and promoting environmentally friendly economic growth, authorities are currently directing their attention on transitioning the energy sector from utilizing non-renewable energy sources such as coal, gas, and oil to adopting renewable alternatives such as wind, solar, biofuel, and nuclear power. The shift in energy structure primarily relies on implementing green financing and accurately valuing the external costs associated with energy production. More than merely implementing a pricing mechanism for emissions is required to address the challenge of environmental sustainability (Li & Ullah, 2022). The IMF also emphasized that only pricing the external costs may not address the challenge posed by global warming and climate change (Lagarde & Gaspar, 2019). Improved public investments in the form of green financing shall have a notable impact on carbon emissions control and the development of a more efficient energy system. Financial policies facilitate the mobilization of private investment to accelerate the process of transitioning to a low-carbon economy (Ullah et al., 2021). The continuous patterns of economic development give rise to new challenges and responsibilities for the government in determining the path for future progress. Hence, it is imperative to address the concerns above to establish an economic, social, and ecological framework that can effectively accomplish the objectives and milestones of sustainable development (Vasylieva, 2019). As per the European Union's Agenda, sustainable development is the primary focus for creating and implementing policies across all areas. This approach aims to enhance the country's competitiveness and create better opportunities for companies and society (Dabyltayeva et al., 2019; Dalevska et al., 2019). Hence, the European Union regards the attainment of sustainability through the utilization of renewable resources as a means to eradicate both the conflicting effects of change climate and to foster tangible economic advantages by diminishing reliance on imported fuel (Brożyna et al., 2017; Kaur et al., 2024; Rijal et al., 2024).

Energy is an indispensable element of all economies and is extensively utilized to meet the growing demands of life forms on the earth. Fuss et al. (2014), although energy plays a crucial role in advancing society, nations face a challenging endeavor in establishing sustainable economic growth in the long term. The current energy system's dependence on fossil fuels is a significant catalyst for pollution and climate change (Yuan et al., 2022). Hence, the degradation of the environment and the alteration of climatic patterns have become the primary issues of this century. The energy sector has witnessed groundbreaking research and development, prompting international organizations and major economies to prioritize measures that prioritize efficient statistics and power use, the utilization of renewable energy sources, and the mitigation of harmful emissions (Guo et al., 2022). The prominent developing countries must exhibit solidarity in their worldwide endeavors to combat global warming by addressing the issues of environmental deterioration, particularly by diminishing the release of hazardous substances into the environment (Chen et al., 2022).

Literature Review

Recently, numerous academics have identified a correlation between Gross Domestic Product (GDP) and greenhouse gas emissions (Lapinskiene et al., 2017). According to Vasylieva et al. (2019), Ukraine has found a significant correlation between gross domestic product and greenhouse gases. Specifically, a per capita increase in GDP can facilitate the adoption of clean energy sources over the long run. The Environmental Kuznets curve hypothesis states that increasing economic development is the means via which environmental safety and quality of life metrics can be raised. Therefore, emerging nations should adopt an economic growth strategy since it will ultimately enable them to attain eco-friendly and economic objectives. Simultaneously, government policy, exclusively prioritizing environmental safety, hinders economic expansion. The theory can be visually represented by an inverted U-shaped curve (Webber & Allen, 2010).

To ascertain the enduring effects of carbon dioxide emissions and consumption of energy on the GDP in Turkey between 1960 and 2010 analyzed by Bozkurt and Yusuf (2014), it was discovered that in the country of Turkey, energy consumption has a beneficial influence on economic growth, whereas carbon dioxide gas emissions have an adverse impact. In a separate study (Ozturk & Acaravci, 2010), the authors aimed to demonstrate the correlation between the use of energy, carbon dioxide emissions, and the rise in Turkey's GDP. They discovered direct long-term correlation estimates of emissions in connection to energy consumption. Additionally, it was discovered that (Furkan et al., 2023) there is a positive relation between the rise in gross domestic product per capita and the rise in carbon emissions per capita. In Canada, there is a one-way causal relationship where the consumption of energy and economic growth lead to greenhouse gas emissions. This indicates a connection between economic expansion and greenhouse gases (Hamit-Haggar, 2012; Kaur et al., 2023). A study conducted in Bangladesh demonstrated the correlation between the growth of the economy and carbon dioxide (CO_2) emissions. The author has determined a direct correlation between the increase in CO_2 emissions and the expansion of the GDP contribution from the industry and services sectors (Alam, 2014). A study conducted on 16 Asian countries revealed that there is a bidirectional Granger causality association between the consumption of energy, the gross domestic product, and greenhouse gas emissions.

Similarly, there is also a bidirectional Granger causation relationship among GDP, emissions of greenhouse gases, and energy consumption (Lu, 2017). Research on carbon capture and storage (CCS) demonstrated that implementing CCS technology can result in a 54% reduction in CO_2 emissions inside the European Union and a 33% reduction globally by 2025. However, more than this decrease is needed to achieve climate stability. Consequently, it is necessary to enhance energy efficiency. The objective of this project is to develop a model that combines econometric and emission statistics for greenhouse gases with supplementary information on understanding the law, size of population, and openness of trade. The aim is to determine the most effective way to utilize economic growth to reduce emissions of greenhouse gases (Stangeland, 2007). The trends in energy efficiency measured by final energy vary across countries and industries within countries. The primary factors driving gains in fuel efficiency are the powerfulness and availability effect (Bhargave & Tandon, 2022; Cunha et al., 2018).

The escalating trajectory of CO_2 emissions poses a grave risk to human existence on Earth (Ali et al., 2014). Green finance encompasses the realms of sustainable, environmental, carbon, and climate financing. Sustainable finance encompasses the areas of corporate governance and social responsibility, whereas environmental finance focuses on the protection of the environment. Carbon finance is specifically aimed at reducing carbon dioxide emissions, while green financing addresses the eradication of and adaptation to environmental-friendly change to attain an energy-efficient economy (Noh, 2010). Hongo (2019) explores the significance of green investment and analyses the key elements that influence CO_2 emissions. As per the findings of the OECD, neither an Environmental Kuznets Curve's association nor a natural relation between gross domestic product and energy was discovered (Arango-Miranda et al., 2018). Increasing consumption typically leads to higher emissions, but decreases in emissions intensities somewhat offset this pattern (resulting in relative decoupling). Identifies increasing amounts of greenhouse gas (GHG) emissions contained within products from developing countries (Kaur & Tanwar, 2024; Liu et al., 2019).

Akram et al. (2020) analyzed the environmental impacts resulting from enhanced energy efficiency in 66 developing countries from 1990 to 2014. The findings indicate that improving the utilization of energy resources could assist in the reduction of CO_2 emissions in these countries (Saidi & Hammami, 2015). The authors contend that enhancing energy efficiency has a disproportionately significant effect on decreasing CO_2 emissions in severely polluted developing nations, while also promoting the use of renewable energy sources. Lei et al. (2022), theemphasized the importance of enhancing energy efficiency to support the EKC hypothesis, particularly from the viewpoint of developing countries.

Fig. 14.1 depicts the gross domestic product patterns of Brazil, China, Indonesia, India, Mexico, Russia, and Turkey from 1990 to 2020. The x-axis denotes the chronological progression of years, while the y-axis signifies the monetary amount of GDP measured in current USD. China's remarkable and unwavering economic growth has propelled it to become a dominant force in the global economy. India witnessed noticeable economic growth during the 2010s, derived from a large youth population and expanding service industries. On the other side, Brazil experienced fluctuations, characterised by o period of economic development in the 2000s chased by subsequent periods of uncertainty. Indonesia sustains consistent economic expansion, surmounting obstacles such as the 1997 financial crisis. The stacked graph of Mexico illustrates alternating phases of expansion and contraction, whereas Russia's economic trajectory is influenced

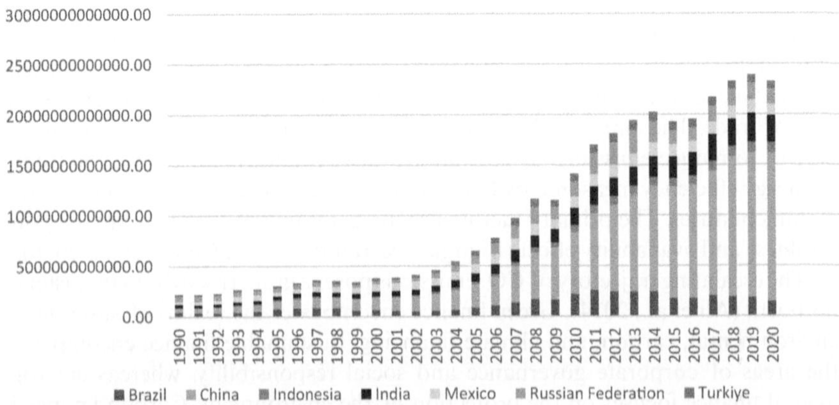

Fig. 14.1. Gross Domestic Product Trend. *Source*: World Bank Data.

by variables such as oil prices and geopolitics. Turkey's Gross Domestic Product (GDP) demonstrates an upward trend, interrupted by instances of financial crises and political instability (World bank, 2023).

Fig. 14.2 depicts the renewable energy usage patterns of Brazil, China, Indonesia, India, Mexico, Russia, and Turkey from 1990 to 2020. The x-axis denotes the chronological progression of years, while the y-axis signifies the renewable energy consumption in percentage of total energy consumption. The stacked graph depicts the fluctuating trends in the adoption of renewable energy in the selected countries. Brazil Continues to have a prominent position in the field of renewable energy, depending on hydroenergy and sugarcane ethanol. China shows a great increase, especially in wind and solar energy capabilities as a result of government initiatives (World Bank, 2023).

Indonesia is expanding its energy portfolio by focusing on hydro, bioenergy, and geothermal sources. India is experiencing a noticeable expansion in solar and

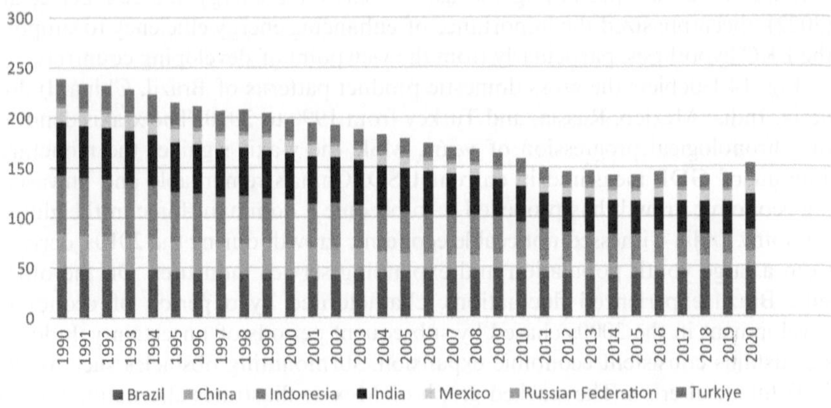

Fig. 14.2. Green Energy Resources Trend. *Source*: World Bank Data.

wind power, which is being facilitated by government regulations and policies. Furthermore, Mexico is also experiencing an increasing emphasis on wind and solar energy, propelled by favorable legislation. In addition to it, Russia, which was traditionally dependent on fossil fuels, has recently experienced an increase in its wind and solar energy capabilities. Finally, Turkey is making advancements in wind, solar, and hydropower, in line with the government's goals of increasing the integration of renewable energy.

Data and Methodology

Emerging economies are economies that have an outstanding economic performance in terms of economic growth (Forbes India, 2023). For the analysis, the following seven economies, namely, Brazil, India, Mexico, Turkey, China, Indonesia, and Russia, during 1990–2020 were chosen based on their economic performance in terms of economic growth as reported by the World Economic Outlook published by the International Monetary Fund in 2023.

The measurement of GDP is often conducted by the expenditure approach, which entails aggregating expenditures on newly produced consumer items, investment spending, government spending, and the value of net exports. In the majority of countries worldwide, the gross domestic product (GDP) varies by the different stages of economic cycles, while also experiencing overall economic growth over an extended period. Nevertheless, the leading economies, as determined by GDP, have a remarkable resistance to change in their respective rankings. Table 14.1 shows the GDP performance of emerging markets.

Hypothesis

$H_{0.}$ There is no correlation between Green Energy Resources and Gross Domestic Product.

$H_{1.}$ There is a correlation between Green Energy Resources and Gross Domestic Product.

Table 14.1. Nominal GDP of Emerging Seven Economies.

COUNTRY	NOMINAL GDP in Current US Dollars
BRAZIL	1.92 trillion
INDIA	3.39 trillion
MEXICO	1.41 trillion
TURKEY	905.99 billion
CHINA	17.96 trillion
INDONESIA	1.32 trillion
RUSSIA	2.24 trillion

Source: World Bank Database (Updated data:2023).

For testing the hypothesis, the authors used data from the World Bank database with **GDP** (GDP is an acronym that stands for Gross Domestic Product. It serves as an indicator of a nation's economic activity and overall well-being. GDP represents the aggregate monetary worth of all products and services generated and exchanged inside a nation within a specific timeframe. The duration of this time often spans one year) as **the dependent variable**, and **GER** (Green Energy Resources is a type of energy that is derived from renewable sources and does not cause harm to the environment. It is generated through the use of renewable energy technologies including wind power, biomass, solar energy, geothermal energy, and others) as **the independent variable**.

For further analysis of the economic component of sustainable development, the authors used the following model:

GDP = mGER + b

where GDP = Gross Domestic Product;
M = Represents the impact of GER on GDP;
GER = Green Energy Resources;
B = Y-intercept.

For the research, panel data of selected top seven countries have been analyzed to study the impact of climate-friendly energy resources through green investment, which has a direct relation with greenhouse gases and an indirect relation with GDP on sustainable development. To test the hypotheses, the following tests were applied using EViews software: Johansen cointegration test (Johansen, 1991) to find out the association between independent variable (GHG) and dependent variable (GDP) and ordinary least squares regression (OLS) (Davidson, 2000), which is widely used method for estimating the coefficients of linear regression equations that model the long-run connection between one or more independent quantitative variables and a dependent variable.

Empirical Results

For India

$H_{oa.}$ There is no correlation between Green Energy Resources and Gross Domestic Product.

$H_{1a.}$ There is a correlation between Green Energy Resources and Gross Domestic Product.

Table 14.2 represents the eigen-value test under the Johansen cointegration test. Based on the Johansen cointegration test, conducted at a 5% significance level, there is conclusive evidence of the presence of at least one cointegrating vector in the dataset. The trace statistic (20.84) surpasses the critical value (25.87) for the null hypothesis of no cointegration, showing a substantial long-term connection among the variables. However, when analyzing a single cointegrating vector, the test does not provide enough evidence to reject the null hypothesis

Table 14.2. Johansen Cointegration Test of India for GER and GDP.

Hypothesized	Eigen Value	Trace Statistic	0.05 Critical Value	P Value
At 0	0.35	20.84	25.87	0.18
At most 1	0.24	8.17	12.51	0.23

Source: Compiled by authors using Excel.

(P value = 0.23). The findings indicate a likely cointegrating link with a 5% significance level, emphasizing a durable and enduring connection between the variables.

For China

$H_{ob.}$ There is no correlation between Green Energy Resources and Gross Domestic Product.

$H_{1b.}$ There is a correlation between Green Energy Resources and Gross Domestic Product.

The results suggest that there is at most one cointegrating vector, with an eigenvalue of 0.04 and a trace statistic of 1.28 present in Table 14.3. However, both numbers are below the critical threshold of 3.84. Consequently, the existing evidence is insufficient to justify the rejection of the null hypothesis at a significance level of 5%. Therefore, it is important to acknowledge the complex interactions between the variables in this dataset, as the exact number of cointegrating vectors remains uncertain. In summary, the findings gained from doing the Johansen cointegration test provide valuable insights into understanding the complex interactions between the variables over a long time frame.

For Brazil

$H_{oc.}$ There is no correlation between Green Energy Resources and Gross Domestic Product.

$H_{1c.}$ There is a correlation between Green Energy Resources and Gross Domestic Product.

Table 14.3. Johansen Cointegration Test of China for GER and GDP.

Hypothesized	Eigen Value	Trace Statistic	0.05 Critical Value	P Value
At 0	0.39	15.73	15.49	0.04
At most 1	0.04	1.28	3.84	0.25

Source: Compiled by authors using Excel.

However, when assuming the existence of only one cointegrating vector, the eigenvalue and trace statistic reduce to 0.922 and 0.03, respectively, shown in Table 14.4. These values are considerably lower than the critical value of 3.84. However, with a significance threshold of 5%, the P value of 0.33 indicates that it is not viable to reject the null hypothesis. This dataset highlights the intricate nature and potential lack of a unified, lasting link within the dataset, suggesting doubt over the coexistence of the variables. In summary, the results of the Johansen test emphasize the complex relationship between the variables, thereby prompting further exploration and consideration of different analytical approaches.

The findings of the Johansen cointegration test offer crucial insights into the interaction of variables, with a significance threshold of 5%. Both the eigenvalue of 0.16 and the trace statistic of 6.18 for the hypothesis of zero cointegrating vectors are below the critical threshold of 15.49. Therefore, we do not reject the null hypothesis. This dataset suggests that there is insufficient information to establish a consistent and enduring association between the variables.

For Mexico

H_{od}: There is no correlation between Green Energy Resources and Gross Domestic Product.

H_{1d}: There is a correlation between Green Energy Resources and Gross Domestic Product.

When examined with a significance level of 5%, the Johansen cointegration test produces statistically significant outcomes. The trace statistic of 14.92 and eigenvalue of 0.37, which support the hypothesis of zero cointegrating vectors, do not surpass the critical threshold of 15.49 presented in Table 14.5. Therefore, the null

Table 14.4. Johansen Cointegration Test of Brazil for GER and GDP.

Hypothesized	Eigen Value	Trace Statistic	0.05 Critical Value	P Value
At 0	0.16	6.18	15.49	0.67
At most 1	0.03	0.922	3.84	0.33

Source: Compiled by authors using Excel.

Table 14.5. Johansen Cointegration Test of Mexico for GER and GDP.

Hypothesized	Eigen Value	Trace Statistic	0.05 Critical Value	P Value
At 0	0.37	14.92	15.49	0.06
At most 1	0.03	1.13	3.84	0.28

Source: Compiled by authors using Excel.

hypothesis is not disproven. There is just a small amount of evidence that suggests a consistent and enduring association between the variables when they are at the zero vector, as illustrated by this.

The trace statistic lowers to 1.13, and the eigenvalue decreases to 0.03, both falling below the crucial value of 3.84. This supports the hypothesis that there is only one cointegrating vector. However, based on a significance level of 5%, the P value of 0.28 does not provide enough evidence to reject the null hypothesis. The presence of uncertainty in the cointegration of the variables highlights the intricate nature of the dynamics and the potential absence of a consistent long-term relationship. It has been reflected from the test that there is an intricate relationship between dependent and independent variables.

For Russia

H_{oe}. There is no correlation between Green Energy Resources and Gross Domestic Product.

H_{1e}. There is a correlation between Green Energy Resources and Gross Domestic Product.

The results shown in Table 14.6 of the Johansen cointegration test, performed at a 5% significance level, are as follows. According to the hypothesis of zero cointegrating vectors, both the trace statistic of 11.11 and the eigenvalue of 0.27 are below the critical threshold of 15.49. As a result, we cannot reject the null hypothesis. This table indicates a lack of empirical evidence to establish a consistent and enduring relationship between the variables in the case of zero vectors.

Under the assumption that there exists a single cointegrating vector, the trace statistic rises to 1.79, while the eigenvalue decreases to 0.05. However, both values remain lower than the crucial threshold of 3.84. With a significance threshold of 5%, the P value of 0.18 suggests that there is insufficient evidence to reject the null hypothesis. This outcome indicates the necessity for establishing assurance regarding the cointegration among the variables, highlighting the intricate interaction and potential lack of a coherent, lasting relationship. This result shows an intricate relationship between the variables.

Table 14.6. Johansen Cointegration Test of Russia for GER and GDP.

Hypothesized	Eigen Value	Trace Statistic	0.05 Critical Value	P Value
At 0	0.27	11.11	15.49	0.20
At most 1	0.05	1.79	3.84	0.18

Source: Compiled by authors using Excel.

Table 14.7. Johansen Cointegration Test of Turkiye for GER and GDP.

Hypothesized	Eigen Value	Trace Statistic	0.05 Critical Value	P Value
At 0	0.35	20.84	25.87	0.18
At most 1	0.24	8.17	12.51	0.23

Source: Compiled by authors using Excel.

For Turkiye

H_{of}. There is no correlation between Green Energy Resources and Gross Domestic Product.

H_{1f}. There is a correlation between Green Energy Resources and Gross Domestic Product.

The results presented in Table 14.7 of the Johansen test show that while testing the hypothesis of no cointegrating vectors in the system (At 0), the estimated Trace Statistic of 20.84 is lower than the critical value of 25.87 at the 5% significant level. In addition, the P value associated with this is 0.18, which is greater than 0.05. Based on these findings, we can conclude that there is not enough evidence to reject the null hypothesis, suggesting that the system does not have any cointegrating vectors.

The Trace, Statistic is 8.17, which is below the critical value of 12.51 at the 5% significance level, with a maximum of 1. The P value associated with the data is 0.23, which is greater than the predetermined requirement of 0.05. Consequently, we lack sufficient evidence to dismiss the null hypothesis that the system includes a maximum of one cointegrating vector. When considering only one possible cointegrating vector, this indicates a lack of evidence supporting the presence of cointegration among time series variables.

For Indonesia

H_{og}. There is no correlation between Green Energy Resources and Gross Domestic Product.

H_{1g}. There is a correlation between Green Energy Resources and Gross Domestic Product.

The Johansen cointegration test, shown in Table 14.8, provides insights into the associations among the variables at a 5% significance level. The null hypothesis is rejected when considering the hypothesis of zero cointegrating vectors because the eigenvalue of 0.35 and the trace statistic of 20.84 exceed the critical value of 25.87. This outcome indicates compelling evidence of the existence of at least one cointegrating vector, indicating a stable, long-term connection between the

Table 14.8. Johansen Cointegration Test of Indonesia for GER and GDP.

Hypothesized	Eigen Value	Trace Statistic	0.05 Critical Value	P Value
At 0	0.35	20.84	25.87	0.18
At most 1	0.24	8.17	12.51	0.23

Source: Compiled by authors using Excel.

variables. Conversely, when considering the hypothesis of having only one cointegrating vector, the trace statistic decreases to 8.17 and the eigenvalue decreases to 0.24. Both values are lower than the critical value of 12.51. The P value of 0.23 indicates that we cannot reject the null hypothesis at the 5% significance level. This raises doubts about the exact number of cointegrating vectors. To summarize, while the evidence indicates a consistent long-term connection, the exact number of cointegrating vectors remains to be determined.

Table 14.9 shows a significant positive linear correlation (R-value of 0.90) between the dependent and independent variables, which is the result of a regression study carried out in India. The model is well-fitting, explaining a significant portion of the variability seen in the dependent variable, according to the adjusted R^2 value of 0.90. The T statistic of 0.00 denotes the statistical significance of the computed coefficients when combined with a P value of 0.00.

The R-value of 0.64 indicates that the linear association with China is positive but comparatively less significant. According to the adjusted R^2 value of 0.63, the model fits the data well. The accompanying P value of 0.00 and the T symbol 10.18 signify that the computed coefficients are statistically significant.

The regression analysis carried out for Brazil indicates that there is a strong positive linear correlation (R = 1.00) between the dependent and independent variables. An adjusted R^2 value of 1.00 for a model indicates a good degree of fit because it explains a sizable amount of variability in the dependent variable. A P value of 0.00 and a T-Ratio of 3.71 highlight the statistical significance of the derived coefficients.

Table 14.9. Ordinary Least Square Result of E7 Countries.

Variable	India	China	Brazil	Mexico	Russia	Turkey	Indonesia
R-Value	0.90	0.64	1.00	0.77	0.40	0.82	0.87
Adjusted R^2 Value	0.90	0.63	1.00	0.76	0.38	0.82	0.87
T Statistic	0.00	10.18	3.71	98.59	20.00	141.00	212.0
P Value	0.00	0.00	0.00	0.00	0.00	0.00	0.00

Source: Compiled by authors using Excel.

The R-value of 0.77 indicates that there is a positive linear association in Mexico. According to the corrected R^2 value of 0.76, the model fits the data well. The T Statistic of 98.59 and the associated P value of 0.00 demonstrate that the computed coefficients are statistically significant.

Russia demonstrates a relatively positive linear connection (R = 0.40) between the dependent and independent variables. The model's adjusted R^2 score of 0.38 suggests that it fits reasonably well. A P value of 0.00 and a T statistic of 20.00 suggest that the computed coefficients have a high level of statistical significance.

Turkey demonstrates a strong positive linear association, as indicated by an R-value of 0.82. The model's adjusted R^2 score of 0.82 suggests a strong match. The statistical analysis reveals that the computed coefficients are highly significant, as indicated by a P value of 0.00 and a T statistic of 141.00. The regression analysis findings for Indonesia indicate a robust positive linear correlation between the dependent and independent variables (R = 0.87). The model's modified R2 value of 0.87 suggests that it fits well and explains a significant portion of the observed variability in the dependent variable. The statistical analysis reveals that the computed coefficients are highly significant, as indicated by a P value of 0.00 and a T statistic of 212.0.

Conclusion

Sustainable Development Goal 13 (SDG 13) specifically targets climate action intricately connected to green investment. Green investments typically focus on initiatives that aim to diminish the release of greenhouse gases, particularly through projects associated with infinite energy sources (such as solar, wind, and hydropower), energy efficiency enhancements, and low-carbon technologies. Investments in environmentally friendly initiatives can bolster infrastructure projects, agricultural methods, and water management systems that improve the ability to withstand climate-related difficulties. Green investments encompass endorsing carbon markets and financial instruments that incentivize reducing emissions. This research helps us to attain climate objectives as described in Sustainable Development Goal 13. Collaboration among governments, corporations, and financial institutions can be undertaken to make green investments to accomplish the targets outlined in Sustainable Development Goal 13. Public-private partnerships can gather resources and specialized knowledge to expand sustainable enterprises.

Sustainable Development Goal 13 urges nations to swiftly and decisively address the threat of global heating. The concept of green growth prompted by green financing, which entails engaging in carbon-free economic activities, has emerged as the most viable solution to address the issue of global heating and to meet the need for sustainable development. Green investment has a significant role to play in this matter. Hence, the analysis seeks to investigate the impact of greenhouse gas emissions on the growth rate denoted by gross domestic product of the top five world economies in terms of GDP for

Table 14.10. The Hypothesis and Relationship Between Dependent and Independent Variable.

Hypothesis	Accepted or Rejected	Relationship
H_{oa}	Rejected	Long Term
H_{ob}	Rejected	Long Term
H_{oc}	Accepted	Intricate relationship
H_{od}	Accepted	Intricate relationship
H_{oe}	Accepted	Intricate relationship
H_{of}	Accepted	Intricate relationship
H_{og}	Accepted	Intricate relationship

Source: Compiled by authors using Excel.

the promotion of environmentally sustainable economic growth with a precise focus on green investment.

Table 14.10 represents the hypothesis and relationship between the independent and dependent variables. The regression study conducted across several nations sheds light on the links between the dependent and independent variables in India, China, Brazil, Mexico, Russia, Turkey, and Indonesia in a significant manner. In India, a strong and very positive linear connection is observed, indicating that the independent variables have a significant impact on the dependent variable. While China is generally seen positively, the connection is relatively less prominent. Brazil exhibits a strong positive linear correlation, suggesting that the independent factors have a substantial influence. The aforementioned variables exert a substantial impact on Mexico's economic dynamics, as demonstrated by the robust positive correlation observed between them. A correlation of moderate positivity indicates that Russia has a discernible albeit moderate impact. The strong and direct positive relationship shown in Turkey emphasizes the significant influence of the independent variables on the country's economic conditions. Indonesia exhibits a robust positive correlation, where the independent variables have a substantial impact on the dependent variable.

The presence of adjusted R^2 values in all nations provides empirical support for the adequacy of the models. The results suggest that the chosen variables can account for a substantial amount of the observed variation in the dependent variable. The credibility of the regression results is further supported by the T and P values, which validate the statistical significance of the calculated coefficients. These findings improve our understanding of the intricate connections between the selected factors and the economy of the analyzed countries. Policymakers, economists, and academics can utilize these insights to develop informed forecasts and make decisions, taking into account the distinctive economic conditions of each country.

References

Akram, R., Majeed, M. T., Fareed, Z., Khalid, F., & Ye, C. (2020). Asymmetric effects of energy efficiency and renewable energy on carbon emissions of BRICS economies: Evidence from nonlinear panel autoregressive distributed lag model. *Environmental Science and Pollution Research International*, *27*(15), 18254–18268.

Alam, J. (2014). On the relationship between economic growth and CO_2 emissions: The Bangladesh experience. *IOSR Journal of Economics and Finance (IOSR-JEF)*, *5*(6), 36–41.

Arango-Miranda, R., Hausler, R., Romero-Lopez, R., Glaus, M., & Ibarra-Zavaleta, S. P. (2018). Carbon dioxide emissions, energy consumption and economic growth: A comparative empirical study of selected developed and developing countries. "The role of exergy". Energies, *11*(10), 2668–2684.

Bhargave, H., & Tandon, D. (2022). A survey study impact of mergers on Indian banking industry. *ECS Transactions*, *107*(1), 8769–8776.

Bozkurt, C., & Yusuf, A. K. A. N. (2014). Economic growth, CO_2 emissions and energy consumption: The Turkish case. *International Journal of Energy Economics and Policy*, *4*(3), 484–494.

Brożyna, J., Mentel, G., & Szetela, B. (2017). Renewable energy and economic development in the European Union. *Acta Polytechnica Hungarica*, *14*(7), 11–34.

Cunha, F. A. F. D. S., Meira, E., & Orsato, R. J. (2021). Sustainable finance and investment: Review and research agenda. *Business Strategy and the Environment*, *30*(8), 3821–3838.

Dabyltayeva, N., & Rakhymzhan, G. (2019). The Green Economy Development path: Overview of economic policy priorities. *Journal of Security & Sustainability Issues*, *8*(4).

Chen, Z., Mirza, N., Huang, L., & Umar, M. (2022). Green banking—Can financial institutions support green recovery? *Economic Analysis and Policy*, *75*, 389–395.

Dalevska, N., Khobta, V., Kwilinski, A., & Kravchenko, S. (2019). A model for estimating social and economic indicators of sustainable development. *Entrepreneurship and Sustainability Issues*, *6*(4), 1839.

Davidson, J. (2000). *Econometric theory*. Wiley-Blackwell. United Kingdom. ISBN 0-631-21584-0.

Eyraud, L., Clements, B., & Wane, A. (2013). Green investment: Trends and determinants. *Energy Policy*, *60*, 852–865.

Forbes India. (2023). The top 10 largest economies in the world in 2024. Retrieved December 10, 2023, from https://www.forbesindia.com/article/explainers/top-10-largest-economies-in-the-world/86159/1

Furkan, H. B., Rakibul Hasan, K. M., & Uddin, M. J. (2023). Greenhouse gas emission, GDP, tertiary education, and rule of law: A comparative study between high-income and lower-middle income countries. *Heliyon*, *9*(6), e16265.

Fuss, S., Canadell, J. G., Peters, G. P., Tavoni, M., Andrew, R. M., Ciais, P., & Yamagata, Y. (2014). Betting on negative emissions. *Nature Climate Change*, *4*(10), 850–853.

Griscom, B. W., Adams, J., Ellis, P. W., Houghton, R. A., Lomax, G., Miteva, D. A., … & Fargione, J. (2017). Natural climate solutions. *Proceedings of the National Academy of Sciences*, *114*(44), 1645–11650.

Gao, B., Ozturk, I., & Ullah, S. (2022). A new framework to the green economy: Asymmetric role of public-private partnership investment on environment in selected Asian economies. *Economic Research-Ekonomska Istraživanja*, *36*(1), 1960–1971.

Guo, X., Liang, C., Umar, M., & Mirza, N. (2022). The impact of fossil fuel divestments and energy transitions on mutual funds' performance. *Technological Forecasting and Social Change*, *176*, 121429.

Hamit-Haggar, M. (2012). Greenhouse gas emissions, energy consumption and economic growth: A panel cointegration analysis from Canadian industrial sector perspective. *Energy Economics*, *34*(1), 358–364.

Hongo, H. (2019). Renewable and green energy resources technologies: Lessons learnt in sub-Saharan Africa (SSA). *Renewable Energy Sources and Their Applications*, 17.

Hickel, J., & Kallis, G. (2020). Is green growth possible? *New Political Economy*, *25*(4), 469–486.

IPCC. (2014). *Climate change 2014, synthesis report*. IPCC, Geneva, Switzerland. Retrieved June 17, 2019, from http://www.ipcc.ch/pdf/assessmentreport/ar5/syr/SYR_AR5_FINAL_full_wcover.pdf.

IPCC. (2018). *Global warming of 1.5°C*. Retrieved December 10, 2023, from https://www.ipcc.ch/sr15/

Johansen, S. (1991). Estimation and hypothesis testing of cointegration vectors in Gaussian vector autoregressive models. *Econometrica*, *59*(6), 1551–1580.

Kaur, A., & Tanwar, A. (2024). Adoption potential and challenges of artificial intelligence in banking. In *Sustainable investments in green finance* (pp. 271–293). IGI.

Kaur, A., Tanwar, A., Kaur, H., & Singh, J. (2023). *A study on linkage between global warming indicators and climate change expenditure* [Conference session]. IOP Conference Series: Earth and Environmental Science, Vol. 1110(1), pp. 12059–12077.

Kaur, S., Kumar, R., Singh, K., & Huang, Y. L. (2024). Leveraging artificial intelligence for enhanced sustainable energy management. *Journal of Sustainable Energy*, *3*(1), 1–20. https://doi.org/10.56578/jse030101

Kumar, A., Kumar, K., Kaushik, N., Sharma, S., & Mishra, S. (2010). Renewable energy in India: Current status and future potentials. *Renewable and Sustainable Energy Reviews*, *14*(8), 2434–2442.

Lagarde, C., & Gaspar, V. (2019). *Getting real on meeting Paris climate change commitments*. IMF Blog. Retrieved on November 25, 2023 from https://www.imf.org/en/Blogs/Articles/2019/05/03/blog-getting-real-on-meeting-paris-climate-change-commitments

Lapinskiene, G., Peleckis, K., & Slavinskaite, N. (2017). Energy consumption, economic growth and greenhouse gas emissions in the European Union countries. *Journal of Business Economics and Management*, *18*(6), 1082–1097.

Lei, W., Ozturk, I., Muhammad, H., & Ullah, S. (2022). On the asymmetric effects of financial deepening on renewable and non-renewable energy consumption: Insights from China. *Economic Research-Ekonomska Istraživanja*, *35*(1), 3961–3978.

Li, X., & Ullah, S. (2022). Caring for the environment: How CO_2 emissions respond to human capital in BRICS economies? *Environmental Science and Pollution Research*, *29*(12), 18036–18046.

Liu, D., Guo, X., & Xiao, B. (2019). What causes growth of global greenhouse gas emissions? Evidence from 40 countries. *Science of the Total Environment*, *661*(3), 750–766.

Lu, W. C. (2017). Greenhouse gas emissions, energy consumption and economic growth: A panel cointegration analysis for 16 Asian countries. *International Journal of Environmental Research and Public Health*, *14*(11), 1436.

Noh, H. J. (2010). Financial strategy to accelerate innovation for green growth (pp. 2–3). Korea capital market institute.

Ndekwa, A. G., Kalugendo, E., Sood, K., & Grima, S. (2023). An analysis of agribusiness digitalisation transformation of the sub-Saharan African countries small-scale farmers' production distribution. *Research on World Agricultural Economy*, *4*(3), 63–78.

Owusu, P. A., & Asumadu-Sarkodie, S. (2016). A review of renewable energy sources, sustainability issues and climate change mitigation. *Cogent Engineering*, *3*(1), 1167990.

Ozturk, I., & Acaravci, A. (2010). CO_2 emissions, energy consumption and economic growth in Turkey. *Renewable and Sustainable Energy Reviews*, *14*(9), 3220–3225.

Rijal, S., Nursaputra, M. A. C., & Dari, H. U. (2024). Flood susceptibility analysis using frequency ratio method in Walanae watershed. *International Journal of Sustainable Development and Planning*, *19*(3), 823–832. https://doi.org/10.18280/ijsdp.190302

Saidi, K., & Hammami, S. (2015). The impact of CO_2 emissions and economic growth on energy consumption in 58 countries. *Energy Reports*, *1*(C), 62–70. https://doi.org/10.1016/j.egyr.2015.01.003

Sood, K., & Özen, E. (2024). A systematic review of ESG in the insurance industry: Navigating the path to sustainability. *International Journal of Sustainable Development and Planning*, *19*(3), 807–821. https://doi.org/10.18280/ijsdp.190301

Stangeland, A. (2007). A model for the CO_2 capture potential. *International Journal of Greenhouse Gas Control*, *1*(4), 418–429.

TWI2050. (2018). The World in 2050. Transformations to Achieve the Sustainable Development Goals. Report prepared by World in 2050 initiative. International Institute for Applied Systems Analysis (IIASA), Laxenburg, Austria. Retrieved from www.twi2050.org

Ullah, S., Ozturk, I., & Sohail, S. (2021). The asymmetric effects of fiscal and monetary policy instruments on Pakistan's environmental pollution. *Environmental Science and Pollution Research International*, *28*(6), 7450–7461.

Vasylieva, T., Lyulyov, O., Bilan, Y., & Streimikiene, D. (2019). Sustainable economic development and greenhouse gas emissions: The dynamic impact of renewable energy consumption, GDP, and corruption. *Energies*, *12*(17), 3289.

Wang, L., Su, C. W., Ali, S., & Chang, H. L. (2020). How China is fostering sustainable growth: the interplay of green investment and production-based emission. *Environmental Science and Pollution Research*, *27*(31), 39607–39618.

Webber, D. J., & Allen, D. O. (2010). Environmental Kuznets curves: mess or meaning? *International Journal of Sustainable Development & World Ecology*, *17*(3), 198–207.

World Bank. (2023). Data Retrieved November 27, 2023 from https://data.worldbank.org/indicator//NY.GDP.MKTP.CD?locations=IN

Yeoh, W. K., Ali, A., & Forney, C. F. (2014). Effects of ozone on major antioxidants and microbial populations of fresh-cut papaya. *Postharvest Biology and Technology*, *89*, 56–58.

Yerpude, S., Sood, K., & Grima. S. (2023). Blockchain-augmented digital supply chain management: A way to sustainable business. *Journal of Risk and Financial Management*, *16*(1), 7.

Yuan, X., Su, C.-W., Umar, M., Shao, X., & Lobon, T. O.-R. (2022). The race to zero emissions: Can renewable energy be the path to carbon neutrality? *Journal of Environmental Management*, *308*, 114648.

Chapter 15

The Role of Shareholder Engagement in Sustainability: A Bibliometric Review

Rajesh Tiwari[a], *Sanjay Taneja*[a] *and Bimal Anjum*[b]

[a]*Graphic Era (Deemed to be University), Dehradun, India*
[b]*DAV College, Chandigarh, India*

Abstract

Purpose: The regulatory framework for corporate governance has focused on enhancing transparency, disclosure, and the role of independent directors. The supply side issues have dominated the attempts to enforce better governance. Rising cases of shareholder activism indicate the lacunas in supply-driven governance enforcement. Developing an ecosystem of shareholder engagement will spur demand-driven corporate governance. Shareholder's active participation provides scope for enforcing good governance. The role of shareholder engagement in enhancing sustainability and value addition has been ignored.

Research methodology: The bibliometric study attempts to explore work done by countries, institutions, and researchers on shareholder engagement to explore the developments in shareholder engagement and the scope for further study. The Scopus online database was used for the study. Bibliometric analysis was done using VOSviewer (version 1.6.18).

Finding: It was found that shareholder engagement attracts researchers' attention. Developed economies dominate the studies on shareholder engagement. Developing economies have relatively underexplored the concept of shareholder engagement.

Originality/value: Firms diversifying from customer engagement to shareholder engagement have the scope to enhance value addition and sustainability.

Keywords: Shareholder engagement; Scopus; bibliometric; sustainability; governance; developed economies; developing economies

JEL Classifications: G10; M10; G34

Green Management: A New Paradigm in the World of Business, 267–284

doi:10.1108/978-1-83797-442-920241015

1. Introduction

The need for shareholder engagement was fled when capital was sourced from diverse investors in the United States after the Second World War (Knight, 2010). The 1970s and 1980s witnessed activists using borrowed funds to acquire high stakes in public companies (Fronda, 2016). The instances of shareholder activism are less hostile now (Klein & Zur, 2009). Shareholder engagement has evolved from a routine superficial activity to a strategic imperative. Despite company management's potential benefits and willingness, constructive shareholder engagement is not attainable for most public companies (Johnson & MacGregor, 2017). The engagement of shareholders has gained significance. The social media has provided an alternative medium of engagement (Carr, 2013; Wessel, 2011). The customers' active participation in company social media updates creates value for the company, and customers become part of the company's value chain (Vargo & Lusch, 2004). Companies have proactively engaged customers (Verhoef et al., 2010). Rising cases of shareholder activism have shifted the focus on shareholder engagement (Johnson & MacGregor, 2017). Shareholder activism is rising in India (Korada & Rajasekharan, 2022).

The emergence of social media has attracted firms' attention to customer engagement using social media. It is observed that customers can destroy and create value (Libai et al., 2010; Verhoef et al., 2010). Customer engagement through social media has yielded mixed results. Customer engagement reduces market value, as shareholders are concerned about backfiring these initiatives (Sanders et al., 2018). Customer engagement initiatives of McDonald's and General Motors have a negative impact as customers highlighted the negative aspects of the products (Verhoef et al., 2010). Customer engagement initiatives that spread word of mouth and use social media are found to be less negative than those that seek customer feedback (Sanders et al., 2018). Van Doorn et al. (2010) considered customer engagement to be beyond purchase behavioral manifestations of customers due to motivational drivers. Transaction and non-transaction activities have been combined by various studies into engagement value, which provides customer lifetime value (Kumar et al., 2010; Pansari & Kumar, 2017). Sanders et al. (2018) considered nontransactional value for customer engagement. Customer engagement initiatives can create value for companies that do not focus on advertisements, while companies with an established corporate image and goodwill may not benefit from such initiatives (Sanders et al., 2018). Customer engagement initiatives are meaningful if they create value for the company and positively impact the bottom line and share price. Customer engagement was found to have a positive impact on the performance of the company by Kumar and Pansari (2016). Online chat and word of mouth positively influence the performance of the firm and shareholder value (Gopinath et al., 2014; Liu, 2006). Porter et al. (2011), on the contrary, found that half of the customer engagement initiatives through firm-sponsored online communities have a negative impact on the market value of the firm.

Shareholder engagement has been discussed in the backdrop of corporate governance. Regulatory authorities have taken many initiatives to enhance shareholder engagement. The Council of the European Union, while reviewing the Shareholder Rights Directive (SRD), observed that shareholder engagement is needed to ensure the sustainability of companies. The corporate governance deficits have led to the financial crisis. The focus of shareholder engagement is on transparency. The OECD Principles of Corporate Governance also emphasize the significant role of institutional investors. The Companies Act (2013) in India has added provisions to enhance the power of shareholders. Indian regulatory framework is focused on clearing out the Benami ownerships in companies, identifying the real owners, and decoding the complex structures made using group companies with cross holdings. Article 3g of SRD provides for public disclosure of the engagement policy of institutional investors (Kaur, 2021).

Regulatory authorities in India are struggling with basic corporate governance issues. Companies are restricted from disclosure norms and are pushing institutional investors to disclose their voting records (SEBI, 2010). Shareholder engagement refers to methods through which management and board shares its perspectives with shareholders and shareholders share their ideas, concerns and views to the board and management (Chapman & Cutler, 2016). The separation of ownership and control in a corporation has been associated with stress between shareholders and managers (Koppell, 2011).

Chapman et al. (2022) found that regular engagement with investors creates trust and cordial relations between the shareholders and management. A two-way dialogue between investors and management is needed. It further reduces the chances of shareholder activist action and avoids the negative consequences of shareholder activism and associated campaigns. The earnings conference call was considered a dedicated investor engagement function. A robust investor engagement framework of the company enhances the success rate of addressing shareholder activism (Deloitte, 2015). Satisfaction enhances continued usage and adoption (Chand et al., 2022). The investor engagement activities are focused on the central theme of trust (Brown et al., 2019).

Shareholder activism came to the limelight in India with the case of Escorts VS LIC of India. The Supreme Court observed that LIC, as an institutional investor, can exercise all rights as a shareholder along with the requisition of an Extra-Ordinary General Meeting (Jaiswal, 2020). With just 1 percent shareholding, the Children's Investment Fund sued Coal India Limited for fuel supply agreements (Jacob, 2013). The Insurance Regulatory and Development Authority of India (IRDAI) issued a stewardship code for insurance companies to frame and disclose policies for their conduct at meetings of their investee companies (IRDAI, 2017). SEBI came up with a similar Stewardship Code effective in 2020 for mutual funds and alternative investment funds. Shareholder engagement is relevant for institutional investors with regard to fiduciary obligation towards their investors (Jaiswal, 2020). Pressure is mounting on Institutional investors to actively engage with the management as they have a large investor base, resulting in a large pile of money (Downes et al., 1999). Bhasin (2012) argued that institutional investors have failed to engage and detect malpractices actively, as is evidenced by many corporate failures, including the case of Satyam Computers. Applying and explaining policy has the potential in India to shift the focus to the disclosure of the outcome of their actions instead of the plans of investors (Aiyappa, 2021). In a study on BSE 500 firms in India, Kansil (2021) found that non-promoter institutional shareholders can play an important role in the engagement of shareholders and corporate governance.

In India, a large number of companies are controlled by promoters. The short-term approach of companies has led to a rise in shareholder activism by institutional shareholders (Fried & Wang, 2017). The share buyback decisions of information technology companies in India benefitted the promoters and group companies. Such decisions raise the issue of viability and sustainability (Mandavia, 2017). Frequent engagement enhances interpersonal familiarity and builds up trust (Brochet et al., 2014; Gulati, 1995). Shareholder engagement initiatives are constrained by the time constraints of shareholders (Johnson & MacGregor, 2017). The shareholder engagement activities have been focused on enhancing the visibility of the firm among the participants of the capital market (Bushee et al., 2017; Chapman et al., 2019). The impact of shareholder engagement on the market value of a firm is ignored in research. Shareholder engagement is a non-starter in small and mid-cap companies (Johnson & MacGregor, 2017). Preetha (2021) explored the regulatory reforms and events in the Indian corporate world to enhance shareholder engagement.

Shareholder engagement is constrained by a limited number of people in governance departments interacting with companies. The sheer size of the number of companies that they are dealing with restricts adequate research on important matters. (Johnson & MacGregor, 2017). Shareholder activism needs to be promoted for better governance. However, hostile attempts by institutional investors to control the company by misusing the regulatory framework are a cause of concern for companies. The Zee-Invesco dispute highlights the friction between institutional shareholder actions being considered as interference by the company management. The involvement of institutional investors in day-to-day matters of the company is increasing in India (Korada & Rajasekaran, 2022). Institutional investors have the ability to destabilize the company by exercising their rights, as evident from the cases of Escorts and DCM (Jaiswal, 2020). The shareholding pattern restricts shareholder activism in India.

Based on the inputs from investor relations professionals, Hockerts and Moir (2004) argued that there is rising awareness about CSR, and investor relations are now evolving from a broadcasting model to an engagement model. Clark and Hebb (2005) evaluated the role of institutional investors in CSR and Governance. Institutional investors have a significant on financial markets. Good CSR performance and transparency minimize the reputation risk. Higher standards of social responsibility and transparency provide better long-term returns to investors. Institutional investors have the potential to compel firms to enhance social responsibility and governance. Stakeholder engagement is influenced by the integrated efforts of global and local players (Wang & Lee, 2007). Estélyi and Nisar (2016) examined the role of diversity of the board with the inclusion of foreign directors in governance. It was found that diverse boards positively influence governance as well as performance. Financial performance and governance for sustainability provide contrasting choices for investors. Shareholders find it difficult to understand the relationship between performance and sustainability (Lo, 2010).

Stakeholder engagement is crucial for novelty-driven technology firms with less visibility (Tylecote & Ramirez, 2006). Gifford (2010) also highlighted that institutional investors have become more involved in the governance issues of the firms. Values of managers and business propositions influence stakeholder salience. Ben-Nasr and Ghouma (2018) examined agency theory and stakeholder theory to predict a downfall in stock prices. Both theories provide contradictory views on the impact of employee welfare on stock prices. Stakeholder theory supports employee welfare as it leads to better involvement of employees and financial performance, reflected in higher stock prices. On the contrary, agency theory considers employee welfare to be a limitation for sustainable performance. The employees are less likely to blow the whistle in case of any wrongdoings to support their own welfare. It was found that agency theory was more effective in predicting a downfall in stock prices. Labor-intensive firms are more likely to be impacted by agency theory.

Responsible investments are significantly influenced by religious organizations. Religious values strongly determine investment behavior toward sustainable investing (Louche et al., 2012). Crifo and Forget (2013) examined the dynamics of investors in private equity for governance. The ESG focus on mainstream institutional investors has also affected private equity investments. Private equity investments also incorporate governance parameters. The private equity governance push is driven by the strategic intent of new avenues of value creation and risk management besides incorporating diversification.

Goodman et al. (2014) argued that institutional investors are increasingly becoming more vocal on governance issues. Religious organizations focus on raising their voices even after their exit from the firm. Political priorities dominate economic returns for investment by religious organizations. Mackenzie et al. (2013) found that the risk of expulsion from an index compels organizations to make governance issues a priority. Liberal market economies demonstrate higher compliance. The development of an index based on governance and responsible investment philosophy will be more effective in ensuring compliance from organizations for good governance.

Wang (2014) found that the duration of investment, investment strategy, and block ownership influence governance push by institutional investors. Active investment managers are more proactive and vocal about governance issues. Short-term institutional investors are less concerned with governance issues. Ferraro and Beunza (2018) explored linkages between different approaches that lead to stakeholder engagement for governance. It was found that strategic and communicative approaches work together to create a common framework for activists and firms. Goodman and Arenas (2015) investigated the role of "social stakeholder engagement" in consideration of minority shareholder concerns. It was observed that social stakeholder engagement plays a constructive role in voicing concerns of minority shareholders regarding firms' decisions that affect these institutional investors. The separation of economic and political intent in investing was also questioned. The reflexive form of corporate governance imposed by statutory governance codes is shallow. Accountability is confined to the mere disclosure of information. Instead of a single loop, a double loop reflexivity is recommended (Veldman & Willmott, 2016).

Internally managed pension funds are more active for governance. Pension funds with distant fund managers are less active in the governance of investee firms. Shareholder engagement provides a solution for corporate governance issues (Tilba & McNulty, 2013). Ying and Wang (2013) argued that state-owned investment firms are more concerned about governance. The need for refinancing drives the intent of state-owned investment firms. Shareholder engagement by state-owned investment firms also leads to improved operational performance. Kolbel et al. (2020) investigated the impact of sustainable investing on the achievement of social goals. Sustainable investing does have a positive impact on governance, but in the absence of a strong policy framework, deeper transformation in governance is questionable.

Cantista and Tylecote (2008) explored the dynamics of stakeholder engagement and supplier relations and innovation. It was found that stakeholder engagement is positively associated with customer-supplier relations and innovation. The innovation-driven firms have long-term associations with suppliers and long-term investors. Yamahaki and Frynas (2016) examined the dynamics of the regulatory framework on shareholder engagement on ESG issues of investee firms. It was found that regulation is not very effective in shareholder engagement, though it influences attitudes toward responsible investing. It was also found that emerging market regulatory frameworks should be customized to take care of their economic and market needs.

Dhir (2012) examined regulations for controlling the dominance of extractive firms. Government interventions are needed to counterbalance the adverse impacts of investment and control by the extractive investment firms. Activism by shareholders has the potential to improve the condition of human rights in third-world economies. Allen et al. (2012) argued that shareholder engagement influences the governance of companies in the extractive sector. Jahnke (2019) argued that institutional investors engage due to the low cost of engagement as compared to exit. Disclosure of engagement efforts by large institutional investors would be helpful for governance (Kaur et al., 2024; Ndekwa et al., 2023; Rijal et al., 2024).

2. Research Questions

We formulate the research questions to identify the pattern of articles and explore the scope for future research. These questions will help to understand the trend of publications and gaps. The interlinkages among authors, institutions, and counties will be revealed. The following research questions are framed for the study:

Q1. Which countries and institutions are involved in research on shareholder engagement?

Q2. What is the year-wise growth trend of publications on shareholder engagement in relation to citations?

Q3. Which articles and authors are influential in shareholder engagement research?

3. Methods

The Scopus database was used for the study. Scopus is an extensive database that provides quality research papers from all across the world. Scopus search results can be directly exported to VOSviewer (version 1.6.18) for detailed analysis. The search results with citation information, bibliographical information, abstract, keywords, funding details, tradenames, conference information, and references were saved into CSV format. The date of search and retrieval was July 25, 2022. Keywords used were "Shareholder engagement," "investor engagement," and "stockholder engagement." One hundred forty-eight documents were obtained in the online Scopus database. The search yielded 145 studies. The search yielded 97 articles, 24 book chapters, 12 reviews, 7 conference papers, 6 books, 1 conference review, and 1 note. After excluding book chapters, reviews, conference papers, books, conference reviews, and 1 note, 97 papers were obtained. The next exclusion criteria applied were based on source type. Book series and trade journals were excluded. After excluding book series and trade journals, 94 papers were obtained and 2 papers were not in English, so they were excluded. After excluding non-English papers, 92 articles were finally included in the study. TITLE-ABS-KEY ("shareholder engagement" OR "investor engagement" OR "stockholder engagement") AND (LIMIT-TO (DOCTYPE, "ar")) AND (LIMIT-TO (SRCTYPE, "j")) AND (LIMIT-TO (LANGUAGE, "English")).

4. Results

The cumulative publications have grown from just 1 in 2003 to 92 in 2022 till July 25 2022. From 2018 onwards, shareholder engagement has attracted the attention of researchers. Twelve papers were published in 2018, 9 in 20119, 11 in 2021, and 8 papers were published in 2022 till July 25, as shown in Fig. 15.1. The recent increase in publications shows the growing significance of shareholder engagement.

The leading countries in shareholder engagement research are shown in Table 15.1. The United Kingdom published the highest number of 31 papers, followed by Germany with 10 papers with 547 citations. The United States published nine papers. Canada, France, Netherlands, and Spain published six papers each. The citations of France (182), Canada (123), Spain (127), and the Netherlands (64) are more than those of the United States. Denmark and Sweden published five papers each, followed by Australia with four papers. The leading country in shareholder engagement is the United Kingdom, as shown in the density visualization in Fig. 15.2. The research is predominantly confined to the European region. There is a lot of scope for further research in other parts of the world.

Fig. 15.3 depicts the prominent cited journals. *Journal of Business Ethics* is the leading journal with 289 citations. Environment and Planning A is ranked 2nd with 171 citations, followed by *Journal of Corporate Finance* with 122 citations. *Corporate Governance: An International Review* has 99 citations, followed by *Corporate Social Responsibility and Environment Management* with 68 citations.

Fig. 15.4 depicts the journals with the highest number of document publications. *The Journal of Sustainable Finance and Investment* is the leading journal

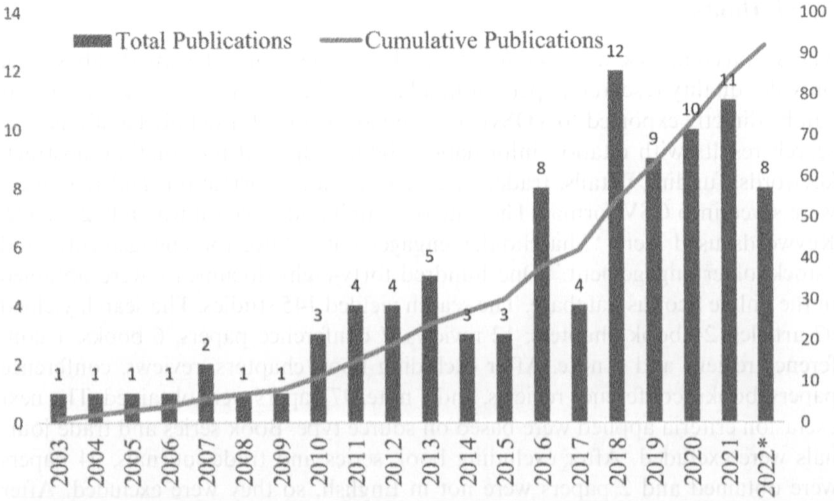

Fig. 15.1. Number of Publications and Cumulative Publications on a Year-on-Year Basis. *Source*: Authors' compilation.*2022 publications till 25th July 2022.

Table 15.1. Top 10 Countries in Publications.

S. No.	Country	Total Publications	Total Citations	Total Link Strength
1	United Kingdom	31	547	13
2	Germany	10	55	4
3	United States	9	51	1
4	Canada	6	123	18
5	France	6	182	17
6	Netherlands	6	64	19
7	Spain	6	127	24
8	Denmark	5	39	7
9	Sweden	5	23	5
10	Australia	4	69	6

Source: Authors' compilation.

with eight papers, followed by *Journal of Business Ethics* with six papers. *Corporate Governance: An International Review and European Business Law Review* each has five papers.

Aarhus University is the leading organization with four papers. The University of Glasgow, University of Oxford, Ramon Llull University, and Ghent University had three papers each. The difference in a number of papers is narrow between the universities, as shown in Fig. 15.5.

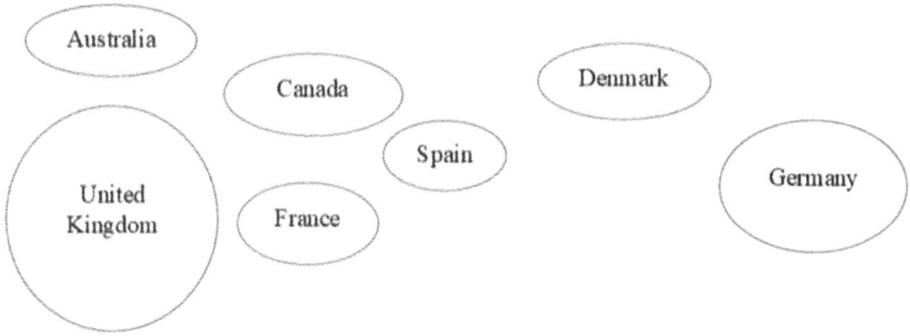

Fig. 15.2. Density Visualization of Countries of Publication. *Source*: Authors' compilation.

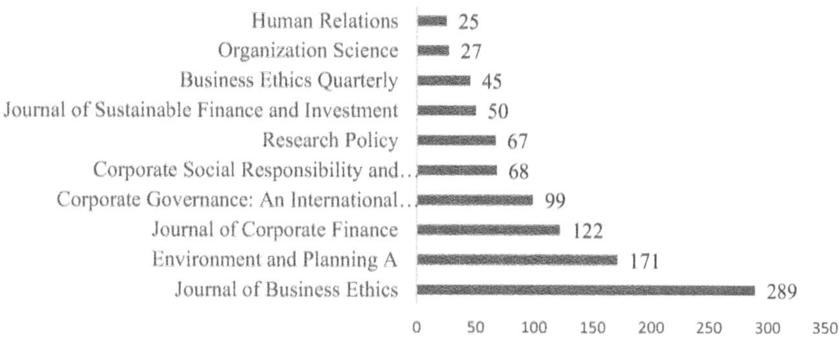

Fig. 15.3. Top 10 Journals with Maximum Citations. *Source*: Authors' compilation.

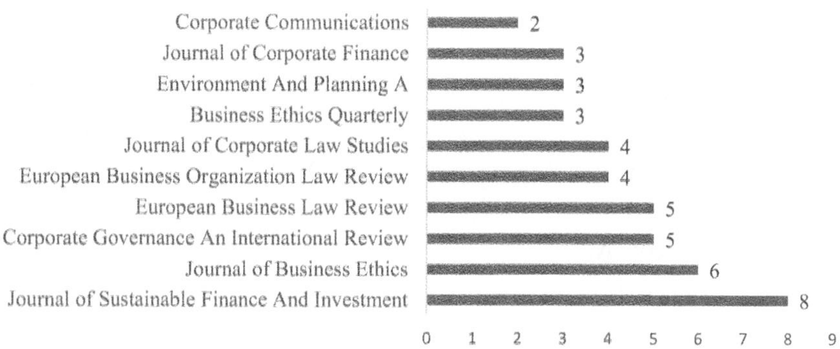

Fig. 15.4. Top 10 Journals with Maximum Publications. *Source*: Authors' compilation.

Arenas D is the leading author with three papers and 100 citations as shown in Table 15.2. Ferraro F also has three papers with 27 citations. Hebb T has 2 papers with 107 citations. Tylecote A (86 citations), Louche C (73), Van Cranenburgh K C (73), Nisar (72), Goodman (57), Beunza D (27), and Yamahaki C (21) have two papers each. The network visualization of authors is shown in Fig. 15.6.

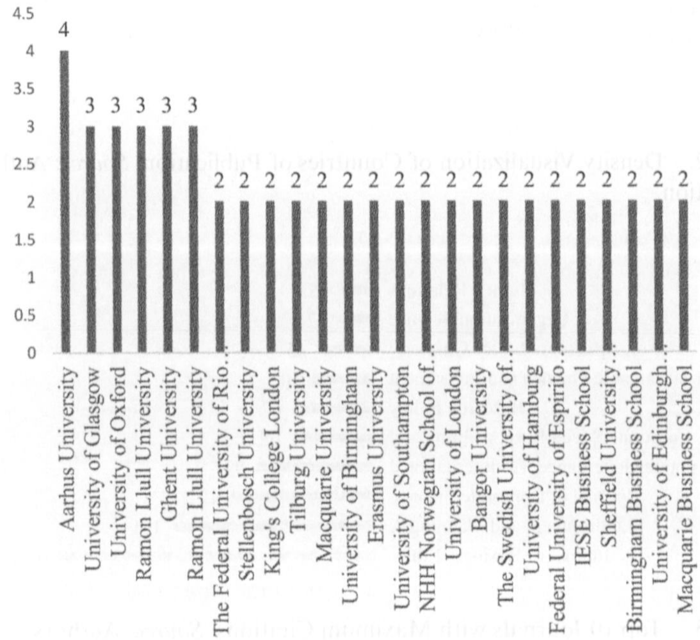

Fig. 15.5. Leading Organisations with Maximum Publications. *Source*: Authors' compilation.

Table 15.2. Top 10 Authors with Maximum Citations.

S. No.	Author	Total Documents	Total Citations
1	Arenas D.	3	100
2	Ferraro F.	3	27
3	Hebb T.	2	107
4	Tylecote A.	2	86
5	Louche C.	2	73
6	Van Cranenburgh K.C.	2	73
7	Nisar T.M.	2	72
8	Goodman J.	2	57
9	Beunza D.	2	27
10	Yamahaki C.	2	21

Source: Authors' compilation.

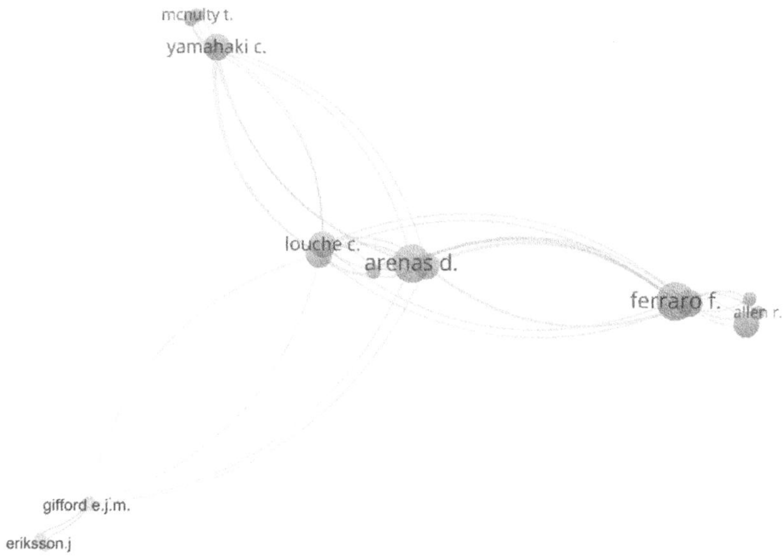

Fig. 15.6. Map of Top Cited Authors. *Source*: Authors' compilation.

The United Kingdom is the leading country in co-authorship, with 31 documents, 547 citations, and a total link strength of 9. Germany ranks 2nd with 10 documents, 55 citations, and a link strength of 7. The United States ranks 3rd with nine documents, 51 citations, and a link strength of 5. Canada, France, and Netherlands each have six documents, Denmark and Sweden each have five documents, and Austria and Belgium each have four documents. Fig. 15.7 represents the map of countries co-authoring. After considering total link strength and citations, Arenas, Louche, Van Cranenburgh, and Goodman emerged as the top 4 in co-authorship, as depicted in Fig. 15.8.

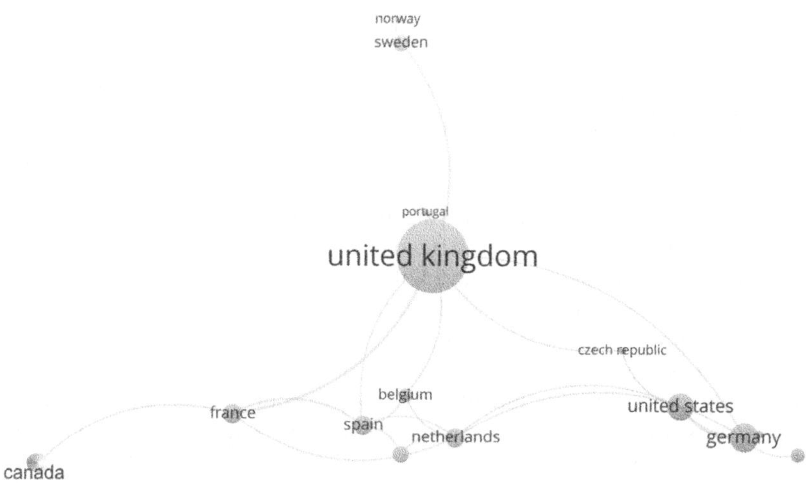

Fig. 15.7. Co-authorship Map of Countries. *Source*: Authors' compilation.

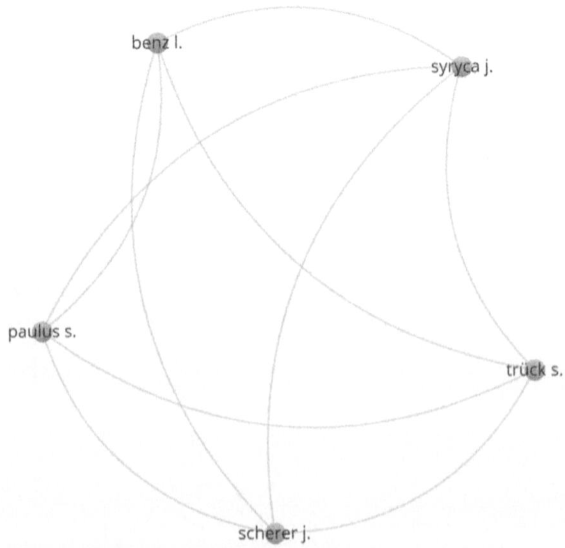

Fig. 15.8. Co-authorship Map. *Source*: Authors' compilation.

Table 15.3. Top Keywords.

Rank	Keyword	Occurrences	Total Link Strength
1	Shareholder engagement	31	31
2	Corporate Governance	26	27
3	Institutional investors	10	11
4	Responsible investment	8	12
5	Corporate social responsibility	6	9
6	Shareholder activism	6	10
7	Engagement	5	4
8	Socially responsible investment	5	8

Source: Authors' compilation.

Author keywords were analyzed using five keywords as the threshold limit. Out of 291 keywords, 8 met the threshold listed in Table 15.3. Shareholder Engagement had maximum occurrences (31) with a link strength of 31. Corporate Governance was the 2nd most prevalent keyword, with 26 occurrences and 27 link strength. Institutional investors had ten occurrences, followed by responsible investment (8), corporate social responsibility (6), and shareholder activism (6). Engagement and socially responsible investment each had five occurrences. Authors have used the keywords with the most link strength. The visualization map of keywords is depicted in Fig. 15.9.

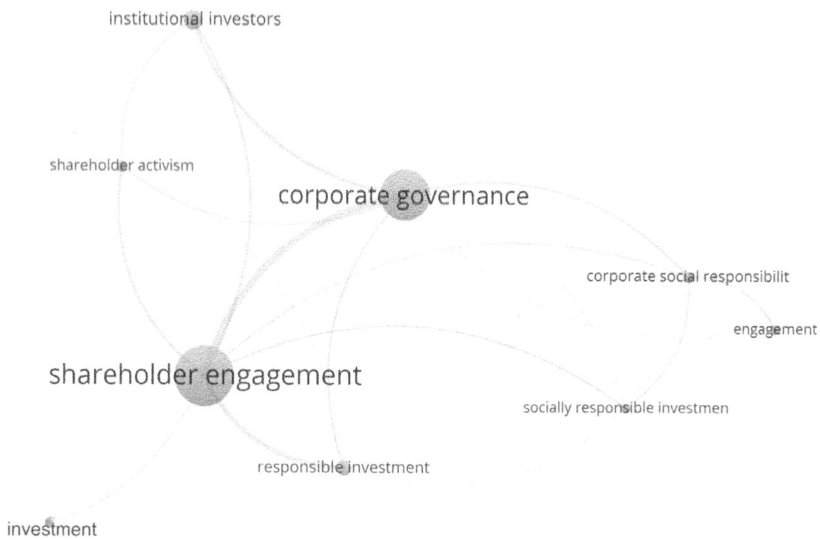

Fig. 15.9. Visualisation of Co-occurrence of Author Keywords. *Source*: Authors' compilation.

5. Discussion

This study examined 92 publications on shareholder engagement in the Scopus database. The cumulative number of papers has increased from 1 in 2003 to 92 in 2022 till July 25. The United Kingdom is the topmost contributor to the research on shareholder engagement. The leading journals in publications were *The Journal of Sustainable Finance and Investment, Journal of Business Ethics, and Corporate Governance: An International Review*. The most cited journals were the *Journal of Business Ethics, Environment and Planning A, Journal of Corporate Finance, Corporate Governance: An International Review, and Corporate Social Responsibility and Environment Management*. The leading organizations with maximum publications included Aarhus University, University of Glasgow, University of Oxford, Ramon Llull University, and Ghent University. Shareholder engagement was found to have the strongest link, followed by corporate Governance, Institutional investors, responsible investment, corporate social responsibility, and shareholder activism. Arenas D of Ramon Llull University, ESADE, Barcelona, Spain, was the top author with 100 citations and three papers. Arenas D collaborated with Louche, Van Cranenburgh, and Goodman. The research on shareholder engagement is gaining attention in European Countries. The studies are based on the themes of corporate governance, responsible investing, and the role of institutional investors.

6. Limitations and Future Scope

The present study was focused on the Scopus online database. The study suffers from the limitation of excluding other databases. The inclusion of other databases can provide additional inputs for further studies to explore shareholder engagement. Since the studies on shareholder engagement focus on developed economies, Further studies can be done to compare the findings of studies on shareholder engagement in developed and developing economies. Non-English articles were excluded from this study due to translation constraints. The inclusion of all language articles can be useful in further research.

7. Conclusion

The supply-driven shareholder engagement has not yielded the desired results. Engagement of only customers restricts the value addition chain. There is an opportunity to diversify from only the customer engagement model to a diversified model focused on both customer engagement and shareholder engagement. Shareholder engagement has been restricted to brief discussions on financial performance. The institutional investors are not very keen on shareholder engagement due to capacity constraints. Retail investors are not willing or have the resources to engage actively with company management. The preconceived notion that retail investors are passive should be avoided. Alternative platforms for engaging retail investors should be explored. Engagement should be planned with clarity on goals to provide regular and frequent interactions to make it a part of corporate culture. Shareholder engagement is an opportunity to share the stories of the company and go beyond mandatory disclosures to convert shareholders into a value creator. Shareholder engagement will provide a mutually beneficial association for management and shareholders. Management will understand the concerns of shareholders and their interests. Management will enhance trust among shareholders and become an attractive investment decision. Shareholders will understand the priorities of management and allocate capital efficiently.

References

Aiyappa, M. (2021). *SEBI's stewardship code, 2019 & Institutional investors in corporate governance*. SSRN. Retrieved from https://papers.ssrn.com/sol3/papers.cfm?abstract_id=3853007

Allen, R., Letourneau, H., & Hebb, T. (2012). Shareholder engagement in the extractive sector. *Journal of Sustainable Finance & Investment*, *2*(1), 3–25.

Ben-Nasr, H., & Ghouma, H. (2018). Employee welfare and stock price crash risk. *Journal of Corporate Finance*, *48*, 700–725.

Bhasin, M. (2012). India's Satyam accounting scandal: How the story unfolded? *Interdisciplinary Review of Economics and Management*, *2*(1), 22–33.

Brochet, F., Miller, G. S., & Srinivasan, S. (2014). Do analysts follow managers who switch companies? An analysis of relationships in the capital markets. *The Accounting Review*, *89*(2), 451–482.

Brown, L. D., Call, A. C., Clement, M. B., & Sharp, N. Y. (2019). Managing the narrative: Investor relations officers and corporate disclosure. *Journal of Accounting and Economics*, *67*(1), 58–79.

Bushee, B. J., Jung, M. J., & Miller, G. S. (2017). Do investors benefit from selective access to management? *Journal of Financial Reporting*, *2*(1), 31–61.

Cantista, I., & Tylecote, A. (2008). Industrial innovation, corporate governance, and supplier-customer relationships. *Journal of Manufacturing Technology Management*, *19*(5), 576–590.

Carr, D. (2013, October 7). Using Twitter to move the markets. *The New York Times*. Retrieved April 12, 2023, from https://www.nytimes.com/2013/10/07/business/media/using-twitter-to-move-the-markets.html

Chand, K., Tiwari, R., & Sapna. (2022). Effect of perception and satisfaction on preference for mobile wallet. *FIIB Business Review*, 23197145221077365

Chapman and Cutler LLP. (2016). Considering a shareholder engagement policy: The what, why and how. Chapman Insights. Retrieved October 18, 2023. From https://www.chapman.com/media/publication/689_Chapman_Considering_Shareholder_Engagement_Policy092916.pdf

Chapman, K., Miller, G., & White, H. (2019). Investor relations and information assimilation. *The Accounting Review*, *94*(2), 105–131.

Chapman, K. L., Miller, G. S., Neilson, J. J., & White, H. D. (2022). Investor relations, engagement, and shareholder activism. *The Accounting Review*, *97*(2), 77–106.

Clark, G. L., & Hebb, T. (2005). Why should they care? The role of institutional investors in the market for corporate global responsibility. *Environment and Planning A*, *37*(11), 2015–2031.

Crifo, P., & Forget, V. D. (2013). Think global, invest responsibly: Why the private equity industry goes green. *Journal of Business Ethics*, *116*(1), 21–48.

Deloitte. (2015). Investor engagement and activist shareholder strategies. Harvard Law School Forum on Corporate Governance. Retrieved December 9, 2023, from https://corpgov.law.harvard.edu/2019/02/19/investor-engagement-and-activist-shareholder-strategies/

Dhir, A. A. (2012). Shareholder engagement in the embedded business corporation: Investment activism, human rights, and TWAIL discourse. *Business Ethics Quarterly*, *22*(1), 99–118.

Downes, G. R., Houminer, E., & Hubbard, R. G. (1999). *Institutional investors and corporate behavior*. AEI Press, Washington, DC.

Estélyi, K. S., & Nisar, T. M. (2016). Diverse boards: Why do firms get foreign nationals on their boards? *Journal of Corporate Finance*, *39*, 174–192.

Ferraro, F., & Beunza, D. (2018). Creating common ground: A communicative action model of dialogue in shareholder engagement. *Organization Science*, *29*(6), 1187–1207.

Fried, J. M., & Wang, C. C. (2017). *Short-termism and shareholder payouts: Getting corporate capital flows right*. Working Paper. Harvard Law School.

Fronda, A. (2016). *The rebranding of corporate raiders*. Retrieved January 18, 2024, from https://www.worldfinance.com/strategy/the-rebranding-of-corporate-raiders

Gifford, E. J. M. (2010). Effective shareholder engagement: The factors that contribute to shareholder salience. *Journal of Business Ethics*, *92*, 79–97.

Goodman, J., & Arenas, D. (2015). Engaging ethically: A discourse ethics perspective on social shareholder engagement. *Business Ethics Quarterly*, *25*(2), 163–189.

Goodman, J., Louche, C., Van Cranenburgh, K. C., & Arenas, D. (2014). Social shareholder engagement: The dynamics of voice and exit. *Journal of Business Ethics*, *125*(1), 193–210.

Gopinath, S., Thomas, J. S., & Krishnamurthi, L. (2014). Investigating the relationship between the content of online word of mouth, advertising, and brand performance. *Marketing Science*, *33*(2), 241–258.

Gulati, R. (1995). Does familiarity breed trust? The implications of repeated ties for contractual choice in alliances. *Academy of Management Journal*, *38*(1), 85–112.

Hockerts, K., & Moir, L. (2004). Communicating corporate responsibility to investors: The changing role of the investor relations function. *Journal of Business Ethics, 52*, 85–98.

IRDAI. (2017). *Guidelines on stewardship code for insurers in India*. Retrieved February 7, 2024, from https://irdai.gov.in/document-detail?documentId=393635

Jacob, S. (January 23, 2013). *TCI bought into Coal India while raising pricing objections*. Business Standard. Retrieved October 5, 2023, from https://www.business-standard.com/article/companies/tci-bought-into-coal-india-while-raising-pricing-objections-112120600155_1.html

Jahnke, P. (2019). Ownership concentration and institutional investors' governance through voice and exit. *Business and Politics, 21*(3), 327–350.

Jaiswal, P. (2020). *SEBI's stewardship code for institutional investors*. Retrieved December 14, 2023, from https://vinodkothari.com/wp-content/uploads/2020/02/SEBIs-Stewardship-Code-for-Institutional-Investors-1.pdf

Johnson, T., & MacGregor, A. (2017, March). Shareholder engagement: An evolving landscape. In *Harvard Law School Forum on Corporate Governance* (Vol. 9). Harvard Law School Forum.

Kansil, R. (2021). Ownership structure segmentation of Indian listed firms: A governance perspective. *International Journal of Monetary Economics and Finance, 14*(3), 197–211.

Kaur, K. (2021). *Customer relationship management practices an empirical study of selected banks in Udaipur city*. Retrieved July 11, 2023, from Businessjournal.ac.in website: http://www.businessjournal.ac.in/2021/January/4.pdf

Kaur, S., Seth, S., & Singh, J. (2024). Value and quality investing strategy in Indian stock market. *Managerial Finance*.

Klein, A., & Zur, E., (2009). Entrepreneurial shareholder activism: Hedge funds and other private investors. *The Journal of Finance, 64*(1), 187–229.

Knight, R. (2010). *Some background on investor relations: its growth and spread*. Retrieved from http://www.irs.org.uk/files/A_brief_history_of_investor_relations1.doc

Kolbel, J. F., Heeb, F., Paetzold, F., & Busch, T. (2020). Can sustainable investing save the world? Reviewing the mechanisms of investor impact. *Organization & Environment, 33*(4), 554–574.

Koppell, J. G. (Ed.). (2011). Shareholder advocacy and the development of the corporation: The timeless dilemmas of an age-old solution. In *Origins of Shareholder advocacy* (pp. 1–26). Palgrave Macmillan US.

Korada, H., & Rajasekaran, V. (January 23, 2022). *Rising shareholder activism in India*, The Hindu Business Line. Retrieved December 17, 2023, from https://www.thehindubusinessline.com/business-laws/rising-shareholder-activism-in-india/article64910251.ece

Kumar, V., Aksoy, L., Donkers, B., Venkatesan, R., Wiesel, T., & Tillmanns, S. (2010). Undervalued or overvalued customers: Capturing total customer engagement value. *Journal of Service Research, 13*(3), 297–310.

Kumar, V., & Pansari, A. (2016). Competitive advantage through engagement. *Journal of Marketing Research, 53*(4), 497–514.

Libai, B., Bolton, R. N., Bugel, M. S., de Ruyter, K., Gotz, O., Risselada, H., & Stephen, A. T. (2010). Customer-to-customer interactions: Broadening the scope of word-of-mouth research. *Journal of Service Research, 13*(3), 267–282.

Liu, Y. (2006). Word of mouth for movies: Its dynamics and impact on box office revenue. *Journal of Marketing, 70*(3), 74–89.

Lo, S. F. (2010). Performance evaluation for sustainable business: a profitability and marketability framework. *Corporate Social Responsibility and Environmental Management, 17*(6), 311–319.

Louche, C., Arenas, D., & Van Cranenburgh, K. C. (2012). From preaching to investing: Attitudes of religious organizations towards responsible investment. *Journal of Business Ethics*, *110*, 301–320.

Mackenzie, C., Rees, W., & Rodionova, T. (2013). Do responsible investment indices improve corporate social responsibility? FTSE4Good's impact on environmental management. *Corporate Governance: An International Review*, *21*(5), 495–512.

Mandavia, M. (June 8, 2017). *TCS: Tata Sons pockets over Rs. 10,000 crores from TCS buyback*. The Economic Times. Retrieved November 21, 2023, from https://economictimes.indiatimes.com/markets/stocks/news/tatasons-pockets-over-rs-10000-crore-from-tcs-buyback/articleshow/59039417.cms

Ndekwa, A. G., Kalugendo, E., Sood, K., & Grima, S. (2023). An analysis of agribusiness digitalisation transformation of the Sub-Saharan African Countries small-scale farmers' production distribution. *Research on World Agricultural Economy*, *4*(3), 63–78.

Pansari, A., & Kumar, V. (2017). Customer engagement: The construct, antecedents, and consequences. *Journal of the Academy of Marketing Science*, *25*(3), 294–311.

Preetha, S. (2021). Emerging prospects of shareholder engagement in India. *Indian Journal of Corporate Governance*, *14*(2), 226–247.

Porter, C. E., Donthu, N., MacElroy, W. H., & Wydra, D. (2011). How to foster and sustain engagement in virtual communities. *California Management Review*, *53*(4), 80–110.

Rijal, S., Nursaputra, M. A. C., & Dari, H. U. (2024). Flood susceptibility analysis using frequency ratio method in Walanae watershed. *International Journal of Sustainable Development and Planning*, *19*(3), 823–832. https://doi.org/10.18280/ijsdp.190302

Saunders, B., Sim, J., Kingstone, T., Baker, S., Waterfield, J., Bartlam, B., Burroughs, H., & Jinks, C. (2018). Saturation in qualitative research: Exploring its conceptualization and operationalization. *Quality and Quantity*, *52*(4), 1893–1907. https://doi.org/10.1007/s11135- 017-0574-8

SEBI. (2010). Mandatory disclosures by the media of its stake in corporate sector, Retrieved July 11, 2023, from Gov.in website: https://www.sebi.gov.in/media/press-releases/aug-2010/mandatory-disclosures-by-the-media-of-its-stake-in-corporate-sector_1455.html

Sood, K., Özen, E. (2024). A systematic review of ESG in the insurance industry: Navigating the path to sustainability. *International Journal of Sustainable Development and Planning*, *19*(3), 807–821. https://doi.org/10.18280/ijsdp.190301

Tilba, A., & McNulty, T. (2013). Engaged versus disengaged ownership: The case of pension funds in the UK. *Corporate Governance: An International Review*, *21*(2), 165–182.

Tylecote, A., & Ramirez, P. (2006). Corporate governance and innovation: The UK compared with the US and 'insider' economies. *Research Policy*, *35*(1), 160–180.

Van Doorn, J., Lemon, K. N., Mittal, V., Nab, S., Pick, D., Pirner, P., & Verhoef, P. C. (2010). Customer engagement behavior: Theoretical foundations and research directions. *Journal of Service Research*, *13*(3), 253–266.

Vargo, S. L., & Lusch, R. F. (2004). Evolving to a new dominant logic for marketing. *Journal of Marketing*, *68*(1), 1–17.

Veldman, J., & Willmott, H. (2016). The cultural grammar of Governance: The UK Code of Corporate Governance, reflexivity, and the limits of 'soft' regulation. *Human Relations*, *69*(3), 581–603.

Verhoef, P. C., Reinartz, W. J., & Krafft, M. (2010). Customer engagement as a new perspective in customer management. *Journal of Service Research*, *13*(3), 247–252.

Wang, J. H., & Lee, C. K. (2007). Global production networks and local institution building: the development of the information-technology industry in Suzhou, China. *Environment and Planning A*, *39*(8), 1873–1888.

Wang, M. (2014). Which types of institutional investors constrain abnormal accruals? *Corporate Governance: An International Review*, *22*(1), 43–67.
Wessel, R., (March 24, 2011). *Activist investor turns to social media to enlist support.* New York Times. Retrieved December 19, 2023, from https://dealbook.nytimes.com/2011/03/24/activist-investors-turn-to-social-mediato-enlist-support/
Yamahaki, C., & Frynas, J. G. (2016). Institutional determinants of private shareholder engagement in Brazil and South Africa: The role of regulation. *Corporate Governance: An International Review*, *24*(5), 509–527
Ying, Q., & Wang, L. (2013). Propping by controlling shareholders, wealth transfer and firm performance: Evidence from Chinese listed companies. *China Journal of Accounting Research*, *6*(2), 133–147.

Chapter 16

Redefining Sustainability: The Role of a Happy Planet Index in Enhancing SDG

Eduard Mihai Manta[a], *Cristina Maria Geambasu*[a] *and Adriana AnaMaria Davidescu*[a,b]

[a]*Bucharest University of Economic Studies, Bucharest, Romania*
[b]*National Scientific Research Institute for Labour and Social Protection, Bucharest, Romania*

Abstract

Purpose: The study aims to enrich sustainable development assessments by integrating the Happy Planet Index (HPI) with Sustainable Development Goals (SDGs) using locally weighted scatterplot smoothing (LOESS) regression, revealing complex trade-offs among well-being, environmental efficiency, and broader sustainability objectives to guide more nuanced and effective policy actions.

Need for study: This study is needed to address the limitations of traditional economic metrics in sustainable development by offering a holistic framework that incorporates well-being and environmental sustainability, thus providing a more comprehensive understanding of and approach to achieving global sustainability goals.

Methodology: The methodology involves using LOESS (locally weighted scatterplot smoothing) regression to analyse the nuanced interactions between the HPI scores and SDGs, facilitating a deeper understanding of the complex relationship among environmental efficiency, well-being, and sustainability.

Findings: The optimal LOESS model adjustment of SDG scores with the HPI highlights stark national disparities: countries like North Macedonia, Cyprus, and Turkey underperform due to urbanization, inequality, instability, and environmental issues, whereas Finland, Sweden, and Denmark

Green Management: A New Paradigm in the World of Business, 285–302

Published under exclusive licence by Emerald Publishing Limited
doi:10.1108/978-1-83797-442-920241016

excel in SDG achievements, likely due to robust welfare, environmental policies, political stability, and infrastructure.

Practical implications: This study's practical implications suggest that integrating HPI with SDGs can guide policymakers towards more effective, balanced strategies for sustainable development, acknowledging the trade-offs between well-being and environmental efficiency to achieve global sustainability goals.

Keywords: LOESS regression; sustainable development goals; happy planet index; SDG; SDG adjustments; HPI; well-being

JEL Classifications: C01; I31; Q01

1. Introduction[1]

The United Nations developed the Sustainable Development Goals (SDGs) in 2015 as an ambitious global agenda to address complex concerns such as poverty, inequality, climate change, and environmental degradation. While the SDGs provide a comprehensive framework for guiding international development efforts, critics have pointed out that they rely solely on traditional economic metrics and fail to adequately capture the intricacies of human well-being and ecological sustainability.

In response to these constraints, there is a rising demand to supplement the SDGs with other measurements that provide a more comprehensive assessment of progress toward sustainable development. The Happy Planet Index (HPI), created by the New Economics Foundation (NEF) and later sponsored by groups such as the Wellbeing Economy Alliance (WEAll), is one example. The HPI assesses countries' performance using three important indicators: life expectancy, experienced well-being (measured through surveys), and ecological footprint.

Adjusting the SDGs with the HPI index has enormous potential to deepen our understanding of development outcomes and guide policy actions down more sustainable and equitable paths. The parts that follow go into detail on why the SDG score was adjusted with HPI, as well as the numerous benefits of this method and its implications for advancing global sustainability (Ndekwa et al., 2023; Sood & Özen, 2024; Yerpude et al., 2022).

This paper argues that by considering subjective well-being and environmental sustainability in addition to traditional development metrics, the combined framework provides a more nuanced and inclusive perspective on progress, one that prioritizes the well-being of both current and future generations while protecting our planet's health.

In this context, LOESS (locally weighted scatterplot smoothing) regression emerges as a critical methodological strategy for altering the SDG score while including the HPI. LOESS regression facilitates the identification of nonlinear interactions

[1]Figure colour descriptions are present, and the digital version contains colour figures.

between variables, allowing for a more nuanced understanding of how well-being and sustainability indices interact in various socioeconomic circumstances.

By including LOESS regression alongside the HPI and SDGs, this research aims to provide a holistic assessment methodology that goes beyond traditional measures. This integrated approach not only broadens our understanding of development outcomes but also directs policymakers toward more targeted and effective policies. This study seeks to shed light on the transformative potential of using LOESS regression to adjust the SDG score taking into account the HPI, hence supporting more inclusive, sustainable, and equitable development trajectories around the world.

2. Literature Review

The Sustainable Development Goals (SDGs), which is a global action, aim to eradicate poverty, protect the environment, and guarantee that everyone lives in peace and prosperity by the year 2030. A more multifaced approach is to measure these objectives by the combination of sophisticated statistical techniques like LOESS regression with alternative measurements like the Happy Planet Index (HPI). By combining ecological efficiency and human well-being, the HPI assesses sustainable well-being and offers a composite metric that may be used to supplement the framework of the SDGs (Kaur et al., 2024; Rijal et al., 2024).

Iriarte and Musikanski emphasize the significance of using subjective well-being and happiness measurements in addition to conventional economic and social indices. This change recognizes that employment rates and GDP alone are insufficient indicators of actual success. Rather, knowing people's actual experiences, levels of pleasure, and perceived quality of life enhances our knowledge of development and gives the SDGs greater personal significance (Iriarte & Musikanski, 2019).

To give a more complete picture of sustainable development, recent research highlights the integration of happiness and subjective well-being alongside conventional economic and social metrics. The Community Happiness Index (CH-index), developed by Musa, Yacob, Abdullah, and Ishak (Musa et al., 2018), emphasizes the critical role that urban design is playing in boosting subjective well-being and advancing sustainable development. In a similar vein, Diener (2000) emphasizes the significance of happiness in sustainable initiatives and pushes for its inclusion as a crucial aim and measure in policymaking.

Cloutier and Pfeiffer are bringing into discussion a framework focused on happiness as a pathway to sustainable community development, making a point for the interdependence between individual well-being and community sustainability (Cloutier & Pfeiffer, 2015). This further explores the complex relationship between happiness and sustainable development. In their 2013 study, Awasthi and Saxena (2013) are investigating how happiness influences sustainable behaviors and laws, putting forth an ecosystem-wide strategy for advancing cultural and environmental sustainability in addition to individual well-being. All these studies point to a paradigm shift in favor of subjective well-being as a crucial component of sustainable development, highlighting the fact that pursuing happiness and well-being can result in more sustainable actions and laws that benefit both people and communities as a whole.

The study by Patrick et al. (2019) emphasizes the close connection that exists between environmental health and human well-being, and it suggests using the HPI as a local index to motivate efforts to achieve the SDGs. The study highlights the need for composite indicators that integrate environmental and human health to promote sustainable development (Patrick et al., 2019).

An analytical framework for evaluating health-related SDG indicators is provided by a study by Lim et al. (2016) on the global burden of disease and its relationship to the SDGs, highlighting the significance of statistical techniques in measuring progress towards the SDGs. This demonstrates how complicated, non-linear correlations included in SDG data may be analyzed using LOESS regression (Lim et al., 2016).

Recent uses of sophisticated statistical approaches in geotechnical and environmental research demonstrate the great promise of methods like LOESS regression in handling intricate data patterns present in a variety of domains. Sunspot counts were modeled and predicted using LOESS regression by Fadel and Al-Hashimi, demonstrating the method's applicability to intricate, non-linear data patterns, especially in the environmental and earth sciences (Fadel & Al-Hashimi, 2022). The advancement of knowledge in areas that directly affect the SDGs, particularly those pertaining to climate action, depends heavily on this kind of analysis. Additionally, Gong (2021) investigated the stability of loess slopes with a combination of particle swarm optimization (PSO)-optimized BP neural networks and partial least-squares regression (PLSR). This work highlights the critical relevance of advanced statistical techniques in analyzing complex geotechnical data, even though it does not only use LOESS regression. This clearly links to the SDGs that are focused on sustainable cities and life on land.

Hu, Du, Lai, and Xie and Yaming carried out research that assessed the susceptibility of landslides on the Loess Plateau of China and the resilience of infrastructure to environmental problems, respectively, further extending the utility of advanced statistical analysis. The wide applicability of techniques such as LOESS regression is highlighted by studies conducted by Hu et al. (2019) on the effects of cover depth on tunnel deformation and by Yaming et al. (2020) on a comparative examination of several statistical models for environmental risk. These approaches not only improve our comprehension of environmental and infrastructure resilience, but they also make a direct contribution to the accomplishment of SDGs pertaining to infrastructure, industry, innovation, and lowering the risk of natural disasters. All of these research show how important it is to use cutting-edge statistical techniques to address the complex issues of sustainable development by showcasing the adaptability of regression techniques like LOESS in the environmental sciences.

A progressive method of tackling global issues is the incorporation of the HPI and the application of LOESS regression in the analysis of the Sustainable Development Goals. Incorporating comprehensive measures for well-being and environmental sustainability coupled with sophisticated statistical techniques can provide researchers and policymakers with a more profound understanding of how the SDGs are being achieved. Creating policies that genuinely strike a balance between planetary health and human development requires this multifaceted viewpoint.

3. Data and Methodology

This research employs the 2021 SDG score (overall) and HPI data of 34 countries. The countries included in this study are Austria, Belgium, Bulgaria, Croatia, Cyprus, Czechia, Denmark, Estonia, Finland, France, Germany, Greece, Hungary, Iceland, Ireland, Italy, Latvia, Lithuania, Luxembourg, Malta, Netherlands, North Macedonia, Norway, Poland, Portugal, Romania, Serbia, Slovak Republic, Slovenia, Spain, Sweden, Switzerland, Türkiye, and United Kingdom.

SDGs stand for Sustainable Development Goals, practically, those are a collection of 17 connected global goals calculated with the intention to become a blueprint to achieve a better and more sustainable future. Since the SGDs are integrated, any change made in one area could affect the outcomes from another, consequently, the development must be balanced between social, environmental, and economical sustainability. The 17 SDGs are:

1. **No Poverty**: The SDG aims to end poverty in all forms.
2. **Zero Hunger**: The goal is to end hunger and achieve food security and improved nutrition promoting sustainable agriculture.
3. **Good Health and Well-being**: The aim is to ensure healthy lives and promote well-being for all at all ages.
4. **Quality Education**: Ensure inclusive and equitable quality education and promote lifelong learning opportunities for all.
5. **Gender Equality**: Achieve gender equality and empower all women and girls.
6. **Clean Water and Sanitation**: Ensure availability and sustainable management of water and sanitation for all.
7. **Affordable and Clean Energy**: Ensure access to affordable, reliable, sustainable, and modern energy for all.
8. **Decent Work and Economic Growth**: Promote sustained, inclusive, and sustainable economic growth, full and productive employment, and decent work for all.
9. **Industry, Innovation, and Infrastructure**: Build resilient infrastructure, promote inclusive and sustainable industrialization, and foster innovation.
10. **Reduced Inequality**: Reduce inequality within and among countries.
11. **Sustainable Cities and Communities**: Make cities and human settlements inclusive, safe, resilient, and sustainable.
12. **Responsible Consumption and Production**: Ensure sustainable consumption and production patterns.
13. **Climate Action**: Take urgent action to combat climate change and its impacts.
14. **Life Below Water**: Conserve and sustainably use the oceans, seas, and marine resources for sustainable development.

15. **Life on Land**: Protect, restore, and promote sustainable use of terrestrial ecosystems, sustainably manage forests, combat desertification, and halt and reverse land degradation and halt biodiversity loss.
16. **Peace, Justice, and Strong Institutions**: Promote peaceful and inclusive societies for sustainable development, provide access to justice for all, and build effective, accountable, and inclusive institutions at all levels.
17. **Partnerships for the Goals**: Strengthen the means of implementation and revitalize the global partnership for sustainable development.

In this research, the SDG score developed by the United Nations is used. The overall score indicates the entire progress made toward accomplishing all 17 SDGs. One way to interpret the score is as a percentage of SDG accomplishment. When all SDGs are scored at 100, they are considered accomplished.

Looking into the summary statistics (Table 16.1), it can be noticed that 70.6 is the lowest SDG score that was recorded. This implies that certain nations—such as Turkey—perform comparatively less when it comes to reaching the Sustainable Development Goals. Finland achieved the highest SDG score of 86.40. This shows the maximum amount that can be accomplished to meet the Sustainable Development Goals. 75% of the recorded SDG scores, according to the third quartile, are lower than the score of 81.54. It offers further context for the score distribution and indicates that a sizable percentage of the data fall below this threshold.

The Happy Planet Index (HPI), extracted from the Happy Planet Index report (WEA11, 2021) evaluates long-term well-being. It analyzes the efficiency with which citizens in various countries use natural resources to live long and healthy lives. Equation 1 approximates how HPI scores are calculated.

$$\text{Happy Planet Index} \approx \frac{\text{Life Expectancy*Experienced Wellbeing}}{\text{Ecological Footprint}} \tag{1}$$

Equation 2 completely describes the statistical modifications; thus, this equation is only an approximation. To prevent a single component from dominating overall HPI scores, technical adjustments must be made to the particular formula used to calculate them

$$\text{Happy Planet Index} \approx \frac{\propto \text{*Life Expectancy*}(\text{Ladder} + \beta) - \gamma}{\text{Ecological Footprint} + \varepsilon}, \tag{2}$$

where $\alpha = 0.75$, $\beta = 2.92$, $\gamma = 54.92$, and $\epsilon = 6.39$.

The HPI is calculated by combining three important components:

- Life expectancy: It is a measure of how long an average newborn in a country is expected to live under current mortality levels, reflecting the population's general health.
- Experienced wellbeing: It is measured using a survey question that asks people to rate their current life satisfaction on a scale of 0 to 10, often known as

Table 16.1. SDG Score Summary Statistics.

Min	70.6
1st Quartile	77.86
Mean	79.51
Median	79.66
3rd Quartile	81.54
Max	86.40

Source: Author's computations.

the "Ladder of Life," which provides an indication of people's overall assessment of their quality of life.

- Ecological Footprint: The average amount of land necessary per person to support a country's consumption habits, taking into account resources consumed, infrastructure, and absorbed carbon emissions. It is displayed in worldwide hectares, indicating that consumption has a greater environmental impact than production.

Looking into the summary statistics table of the HPI (Table 16.2), it can be noticed that there are regions that have lower levels of well-being and environmental sustainability, the lowest HPI score recorded is 31.7 and it was registered for Luxembourg. On the other side, the highest value is registered for Switzerland, having a HPI of 62.3. 75% of the recorded HPIs, according to the third quartile, are lower than 53.03.

To better understand the countries overall progress towards sustainability and wellbeing, the SDG overall score was adjusted by the Happy Planet Index. The HPI measures subjective well-being and life satisfaction, two critical components of sustainable development. Adjusting the SDG score with the HPI allows you to include measurements of happiness and life satisfaction in the evaluation, providing insights into a country's overall quality of life. The adjustment of the SDG was done through LOESS regression.

Cleveland and Devlin (1988) present LOESS regression, a technique for estimating a regression surface via a multivariate smoothing process, highlighting

Table 16.2. HPI Summary Statistics.

Min	31.7
1st Quartile	45.33
Mean	49.7
Median	49.08
3rd Quartile	53.03
Max	62.3

Source: Author's computations

its usefulness for nonparametric regression surface generation, data exploration, and diagnostic testing of parametric models. The previously mentioned fundamental work showcases the adaptability of LOESS, giving it a valuable instrument for studying SDG data, which frequently displays intricate and non-linear patterns (Cleveland & Devlin, 1988).

The use of LOESS as a powerful yet straightforward method for fitting smooth curves to empirical data in the social sciences is covered by Jacoby (2000). This work emphasizes LOESS's flexibility in responding to different data patterns, which is particularly useful for SDG data analysis, as it eliminates the need for presumptive characterization of the link between variables (Jacoby, 2000).

LOESS (locally weighted scatterplot smoothing) regression is a nonparametric technique for fitting a smooth curve or surface to a scatterplot of data points. The general methodology of LOESS regression consists of the following steps (Fig. 16.1):

1. *Data Preparation*: Start with a dataset of paired observations (x,y). Ensure that the data are clean and clear of outliers, as LOESS is sensitive to extremes.
2. *Local Regression Fitting*: Fit a low-degree polynomial regression model (often linear or quadratic) to each data point using a subset of nearby data points. The bandwidth, often known as the span, is a user-defined smoothing parameter that determines the nearest spots.
3. *Weighting*: Assign weights to nearby points according to their distance from the point of interest. Typically, a tri-cube or Gaussian weight function is utilized, with closer points receiving heavier weights and farther locations receiving lighter weights.
4. *Local Regression Calculation*: Run a weighted least squares regression on the bandwidth-defined local neighborhood. This entails reducing the sum of squared residuals between observed y-values and fitted values from the polynomial regression model.
5. *Smoothing* involves combining the local regression estimates to create a smooth curve or surface that runs through the data points. This is accomplished by

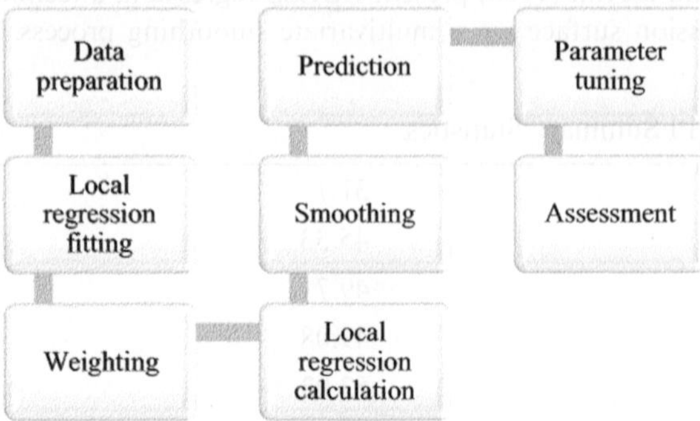

Fig. 16.1. LOESS Regression Methodological Steps. *Source*: Author's computation.

averaging the fitted values from nearby local regressions, using weights dependent on distance from the site of interest.

6. *Prediction*: After fitting the LOESS model, it can be used to forecast new x values by assessing the smoothed curve at those points.
7. *Parameter Tuning*: Change the smoothing parameter (bandwidth) to alter the amount of smoothing. A greater bandwidth creates a smoother curve, whereas a narrower bandwidth absorbs more local variability.

    - The span parameter specifies the size of the local neighborhood surrounding each data point used to fit the local regression model. It is usually reported as a percentage of the total number of data points or as a predetermined number of nearest neighbors.
    - Smoothing and Flexibility: A greater span creates a smoother curve or surface by including more data points into each local regression. In contrast, a smaller span captures more local variability but may result in a more jagged or noisy fit.
    - Bandwidth Selection: Choosing an adequate span is critical for balancing bias and variation in the LOESS model. A large span may oversmooth the data, resulting in the loss of significant features, whereas a narrow span may result in overfitting and increased sensitivity to noise.
    - Cross-validation: To select the best span, techniques such as cross-validation can be used, in which the data is divided into training and validation sets and different spans are evaluated based on their prediction ability.
    - Empirical Rule: In practice, choosing a span generally requires some trial and error or domain knowledge. A general rule of thumb is to begin with a span that covers a respectable part of the data, such as 25% to 50%, and then adjust as needed based on the desired level of smoothing and the dataset's properties.

8. *Assessment*: Use diagnostic plots, such as residual plots or scatterplots of observed against predicted values, to evaluate the LOESS model's goodness of fit.

After the optimal loess model is chosen, the next step is to calculate the SDG Happy Planet performance using the formula:

$$\text{SDG Happy Planet Performance} = 100 * \left(\frac{\text{Actual SDG score}}{\text{Expected SDG score}} - 1 \right).$$

4. Empirical Results

To explore the relationship between the SDG score and the Happy Planet index, a LOESS regression was applied. The plot of the regression can be seen in Fig. 16.1. The OX axis represents HPI score, while the OY axis is representing the overall SDG score. The black dots indicate specific observations or data points that demonstrate the relationship between the "Happy Planet" index and the "SDG" score. The blue line depicts the LOESS smoothed curve. This curve is fitted to the data using local polynomial regression to demonstrate the trend without assuming a certain type of relationship (such as linear or quadratic).

Fig. 16.2 shows a nonlinear link between the "Happy Planet" index and the "SDG" score. Initially, as the "Happy Planet" score expands from the left side of the graph, the "SDG" score falls, hitting a low point around a "Happy Planet" value of 40. This could imply that in the lower HPI score range, increases in long-term well-being and environmental efficiency may come at the expense of progress toward the SDGs. This might indicate that the initial efforts to promote well-being and environmental efficiency are not in line with a wider spectrum of sustainability objectives.

Beyond this point, as the "Happy Planet" score rises, so does the "SDG" score, reaching a high of roughly 50. Following this peak, the "SDG" score looks to level and possibly fall somewhat as the "Happy Planet" score rises over 50. This highlights a complex link between extremely high levels of long-term well-being and progress toward the SDGs. It may imply decreasing benefits or potential trade-offs at higher levels of HPI, when additional increases in well-being and environmental efficiency might not always translate into equivalent gains in SDG scores.

The width of the confidence interval at various positions on the HPI scale indicates varying degrees of conviction about SDG score forecasts. The confidence interval is wider at the HPI scale's extremes, reflecting a lower level of assurance in the association between HPI and SDG scores. In Fig. 16.2, the grey area represents the confidence interval while the blue line is the fitted line.

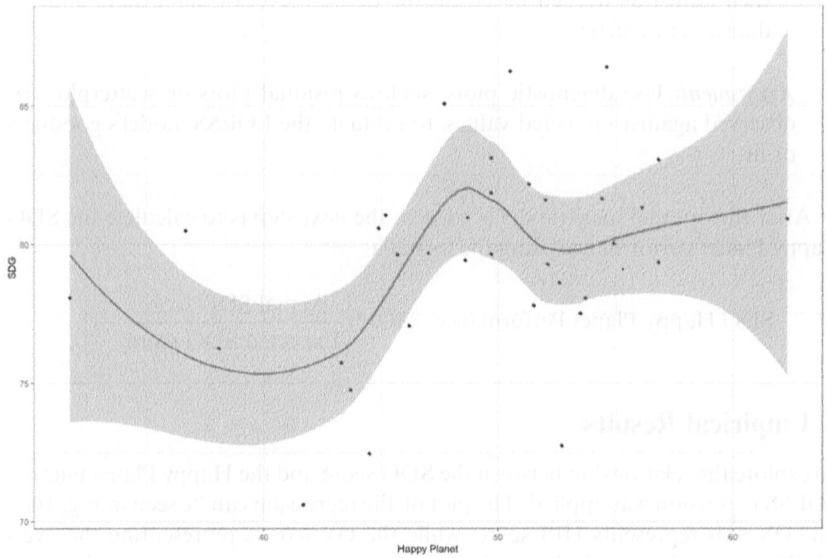

Fig. 16.2. Loess Regression Plot. *Source*: Author's computation.

The LOESS regression shows that the association between the HPI and progress toward the SDGs is not straightforward and may vary depending on the degree of HPI. This complexity may reflect the multidimensional structure of these indices, as well as the multiple trade-offs and synergies between diverse aspects of long-term well-being, environmental efficiency, and the SDGs' broad list of targets.

The next step is running the LOESS regressions at different spans to explore how the choice of bandwidth may affect the fitted curve and the overall model performance. Varying the span allows testing the LOESS model's sensitivity to varied levels of smoothing. By comparing the fitted curves and model performance, it can be seen how the model reacts to variations in the amount of smoothing applied to the data. A greater span produces a smoother curve with reduced variation but potentially higher bias, whereas a shorter span captures more local variability with higher variance but potentially lower bias.

The summary of each model can be seen in Table 16.3. The table contains information for each model about:

- RMSE: Calculates the model's prediction error. A lower RMSE suggests a better match.
- R-square: Represents the percentage of the dependent variable's variation explained by the model's independent variable. A higher R-squared value suggests a stronger explanatory fit.
- MAE: Measures the average magnitude of errors in a group of predictions, regardless of their direction. A lower MAE indicates a better fit with fewer errors.

The model with span = 0.6 has the lowest RMSE and MAE, indicating that it has the highest predictive accuracy of the models provided. However, its R-squared is not the highest, implying that it may not explain as much variability in the SDG score as other spans.

The model with span = 0.4 has the highest R-squared, indicating that it accounts for a considerable portion of the variability in SDG score. Nonetheless, this model's RMSE and MAE values are not as low as some of the others, implying some trade-offs in predicting accuracy.

Table 16.3. Cross-Validation Summary of the LOESS Models.

Loess Regression Span	RMSE	R-squared	MAE
0.5	5.486530	0.5521735	4.052281
0.6	3.810225	0.3796445	3.073404
0.7	4.069888	0.4669789	3.241751
0.8	3.315989	0.4316071	2.809451
0.9	3.249869	0.3546405	2.795450

Source: Author's computation.

The models with greater spans (0.8 and 0.9) exhibit low RMSE and MAE values, indicating high predictive ability, but lower R-squared values, showing less explanatory power.

The table implies that a middle ground, at the 0.8 span, could provide a good mix of prediction accuracy and explanatory power for this dataset.

Fig. 16.3 depicts the robustness analysis graph, which shows multiple LOESS regression models, each represented by a different color line that corresponds to a distinct span parameter. In a LOESS model, the span parameter determines how much smoothing is applied. Red line corresponds to a 0.5 span, blue line to a 0.6 span, green line to a 0.7 span, orange line to a 0.8 span, and yellow line to a 0.9 span.

As the span expands, the LOESS curves smooth out and become less sensitive to variations in the data points. For example, the red curve (span = 0.5) tracks the data points more closely than the yellow curve (span = 0.9).

The varying fits of the models imply various assumptions about the underlying data. Models with a smaller span presume that the data are more complicated and varied in structure. Large-span models, on the other hand, presume that the data may be explained by a simpler, more general trend.

The next step of the analysis is to adjust the SDG overall score using the HPI using the optimal LOESS regression model. The SDG Happy planet performance (or gap) can be seen in Table 16.4. The SDG Happy planet performance variates between a minimum of −100 to a maximum +100.

Fig. 16.4 displays the matrix SDG score vs SDG Happy Planet performance for the overall SDG. The matrix is split into four sectors depending on the SDG score level and SDG Happy Planet performance level:

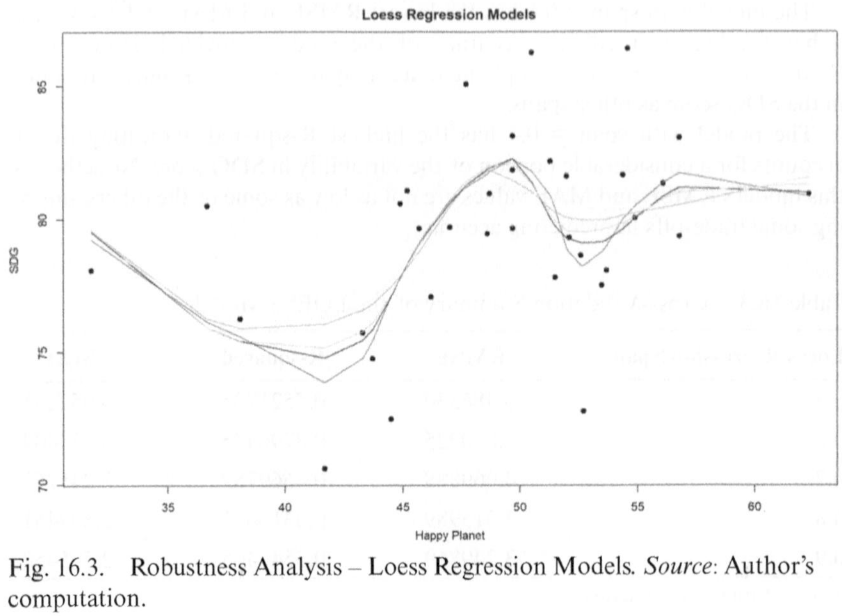

Fig. 16.3. Robustness Analysis – Loess Regression Models. *Source*: Author's computation.

Table 16.4. Overall SDG Happy Planet Performance.

Code	Country	SDG	HPI	Adjusted SDG
CH	Switzerland	80.93417	62.3	−0.79819
DE	Germany	83.04504	56.8	3.127214
NL	Netherlands	79.34623	56.8	−1.46606
UK	United Kingdom	81.32364	56.1	1.126046
ES	Spain	80.03038	54.9	−0.25494
FI	Finland	86.40249	54.6	7.758778
FR	France	81.64901	54.4	1.883858
IS	Iceland	78.06476	53.7	−2.40228
RS	Serbia	77.5088	53.5	−3.05338
CY	Cyprus	72.74472	52.7	−9.02071
IT	Italy	78.61611	52.6	−1.69397
IE	Ireland	79.28003	52.1	−0.95169
HR	Croatia	81.61353	52	1.94926
GR	Greece	77.79652	51.5	−3.04485
NO	Norway	82.16652	51.3	2.232135
SE	Sweden	86.25593	50.5	6.460227
AT	Austria	83.1075	49.7	2.03698
CZ	Czechia	81.84415	49.7	0.485874
SK	Slovakia	79.64198	49.7	−2.21788
SI	Slovenia	80.95571	48.7	−1.06332
BE	Belgium	79.43236	48.6	−2.91057
DK	Denmark	85.07741	47.7	4.696195
PT	Portugal	79.68157	47	−0.99889
RO	Romania	77.07099	46.2	−2.97265
HU	Hungary	79.63266	45.7	1.087878
EE	Estonia	81.05898	45.2	3.676915
PL	Poland	80.57459	44.9	3.48119
MK	North Macedonia	72.45932	44.5	−6.45643
BG	Bulgaria	74.74184	43.7	−2.68456
MT	Malta	75.72376	43.3	−1.12776
TR	Türkiye	70.59903	41.7	−7.16684
LT	Lithuania	76.25647	38.1	0.470305
LV	Latvia	80.48915	36.7	5.551242
LU	Luxembourg	78.07504	31.7	−1.85449

Source: Author's computation.

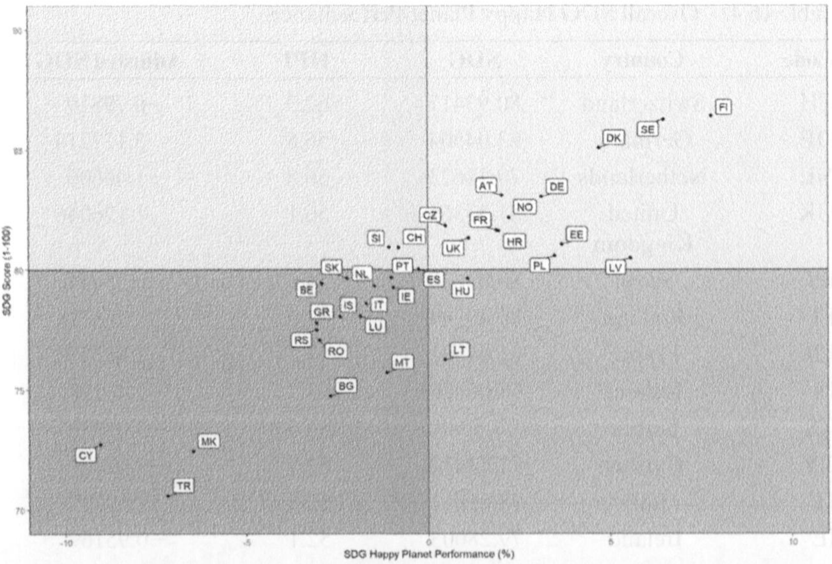

Fig. 16.4. Matrix of SDG Score Versus SDG Happy Planet Performance for the Overall SDG. *Source*: Author's computation.

- ☐ Red zone: covers countries with low score and low performance.
- ☐ Orange zone: cover countries with low SDG score but higher performance.
- ☐ Yellow zone: is populated by countries that present a higher SGD score, but lower performance.
- ☐ Green zone: populated by countries that have both a high performance and a high SDG score.

According to Fig. 16.4, Cyprus, Turkey, and North Macedonia are the countries that present the smallest SDG score, and the smallest SDG Happy Planet performance. Several factors could be responsible for this weak performance:

- ☐ Environmental Degradation: These countries may suffer environmental degradation difficulties such as deforestation, pollution, and habitat loss, all of which can have an influence on their SDG scores and HPI. For example, the study by Miltiadou et al. (2021) shows how locals in Cyprus view forest degradation and climate change. The results of the study are highlighting that a significant portion of the population has observed significant degradation in coniferous forests, despite Cyprus being identified as vulnerable within the EU, particularly to carbon emissions. This implies that in order to lessen the effects of climate change and assist Cyprus in reaching its Green Deal goals, specific education and policymaking are required.
- ☐ Economic inequality, as well as inequities in access to resources and opportunities, can have a negative impact on well-being and sustainability. For instance, Duman explores the subtleties of institutional convergence and

income between Turkey and the EU in his study, concentrating on long-term patterns in social inclusion, poverty, and inequality. This investigation revealed that although Turkey has made significant economic progress in recent decades, there are still obstacles to be overcome to guarantee equal opportunities, a fair regulatory environment, and access to markets and resources for all of its citizens (Duman & Duman, 2021).

- Political instability, conflicts, and governance challenges can impede progress toward sustainable development goals and have a detrimental influence on overall well-being. For example, Gomes highlights the difficulties posed by governance issues on environmental and sustainability efforts when discussing the policies surrounding the Western Balkan countries' accession to the European Union and climate change, including North Macedonia, against a backdrop of political and economic instability (Gomes, 2019).
- Urbanization and Infrastructure Challenges: Rapid urbanization and inadequate infrastructure can strain resources, resulting in environmental deterioration and decreased well-being. Studies conducted on the environmental competitiveness of Macedonia (Jianping et al., 2014) and the urban issues facing Turkey (Kulińska & Gruszka, 2019) highlight the vital necessity of comprehensive policies and initiatives aimed at reducing the negative impacts of urbanization and advancing sustainable development.

On the opposite pole, the countries with the highest SDG score and the highest performance are Finland, Sweden, and Denmark. Finland, Sweden, and Denmark are well known for their strong social welfare systems, which stress equal access to healthcare, education, and social services. These systems promote higher levels of well being and social cohesion, as seen by their high HPI scores. These countries have made considerable investments in environmental protection, renewable energy, and sustainable development programs. Finland, for example, is well-known for its sustainable forestry methods, whilst Sweden has aggressive climate legislation in place. Also, these countries have stable political systems, little corruption, and good governance. These qualities foster an environment conducive to long-term development endeavors while also increasing citizen trust and satisfaction.

5. Conclusions

A complex, non-linear link between the HPI and SDGs scores is revealed by the study using LOESS regression, indicating a subtle interaction between environmental efficiency, well-being, and sustainability goals.

First results show a decrease in SDG scores with an increase in HPI up to a certain point, then a rise, a plateau, or a little reduction, suggesting possible trade-offs at greater levels of environmental efficiency and well-being. This complexity draws attention to the complex relationship between well-being and sustainability measures, highlighting the need for well-rounded strategies that improve both without sacrificing larger sustainability goals.

The reason for this complexity is that these measures take into account a wide range of issues, such as social, environmental, economic, and personal well-being aspects. Sustainable development involves achieving a careful balance among social inclusion, economic progress, and the preservation of the environment. It is often thought of as addressing existing demands without sacrificing the ability of future generations to meet their own needs. On the other hand, well-being includes elements that enhance the total quality of life, such as equity, health, education, and the environment, in addition to financial prosperity and comforts.

The analysis reveals that advances in long-term well-being and environmental efficiency, as evaluated by the HPI, may not always correspond linearly to progress toward the SDGs, which represent a larger set of sustainability goals.

The sensitivity of the model to data smoothing is revealed by further research into the resilience of the LOESS regression models over various spans; the spread of 0.8 stands out as particularly successful in prediction accuracy without fully reflecting the variability in SDG scores. This implies a careful balancing act between preserving a broadly applicable trend across data points and capturing local variances.

Significant differences between the countries are then revealed by applying the optimal LOESS model for adjusting SDG scores based on the HPI. North Macedonia, Cyprus, and Turkey exhibit low performance, which may be related to issues with urbanization, economic inequality, political unpredictability, and environmental degradation. As a model for striking a balance between well-being and sustainable development, nations like Finland, Sweden, and Denmark, on the other hand, have excellent SDG ratings and performance. These nations probably benefit from strong social welfare systems, environmental regulations, political stability, and infrastructure.

Acknowledgment

This research study has been elaborated within the Data Science Research Lab for Business and Economics of the Bucharest University of Economic Studies.

References

Awasthi, P., & Saxena, S. (2013). Happiness and wellbeing for sustainable development. *Purushartha: A Journal of Management Ethics and Spirituality*, *6*, 268–299.

Cleveland, W., & Devlin, S. (1988). Locally weighted regression: An approach to regression analysis by local fitting. *Journal of the American Statistical Association*, *83*, 596–610. https://doi.org/10.1080/01621459.1988.10478639

Cloutier, S., & Pfeiffer, D. (2015). Sustainability through happiness: A framework for sustainable development. *Sustainable Development*, *23*, 317–327. https://doi.org/10.1002/SD.1593

Diener, E. (2000). Subjective well-being. The science of happiness and a proposal for a national index. *The American Psychologist*, *55*(1), 34–43. https://doi.org/10.1037/0003-066X.55.1.34

Duman, A., & Duman, A. (2021). *Economic growth, income distribution, and social exclusion in Turkey* (pp. 268–299). Oxford Academic. https://doi.org/10.1093/OSO/9780197545706.003.0008

Fadel, I., & Al-Hashimi, M. (2022). Locally weighted regression for sunspots estimation and prediction. *Iraqi Journal of Statistical Sciences, 19*, 15–23. https://doi.org/10.33899/iqjoss.2022.176200

Gomes, T. (2019). The European union accession and climate change policies in the Western Balkan countries. In *Climate change and global development*. Springer. https://doi.org/10.1007/978-3-030-02662-2_8

Gong, B. (2021). Study of PLSR-BP model for stability assessment of loess slope based on particle swarm optimization. *Scientific Reports, 11*, 17888. https://doi.org/10.1038/s41598-021-97484-0

Hu, Z., Du, K., Lai, J., & Xie, Y. (2019). Statistical analysis of influence of cover depth on loess tunnel deformation in NW China. *Advances in Civil Engineering, 10*, 464. https://doi.org/10.1155/2019/2706976

Iriarte, L., & Musikanski, L. (2019). Bridging the gap between the sustainable development goals and happiness metrics. *International Journal of Community Well-Being, 1*, 115–135. https://doi.org/10.1007/S42413-018-0012-2

Jacoby, W. (2000). Loess: A nonparametric, graphical tool for depicting relationships between variables. *Electoral Studies, 19*, 577–613. https://doi.org/10.1016/S0261-3794(99)00028-1

Jianping, L., Minrong, L., Jinnan, W., Jianjian, L., Hongwen, S., & Maoxing, H. (2014). *Report on the global environment competitiveness of Macedonia* (pp. 589–592). Springer. https://doi.org/10.1007/978-3-642-54678-5_87

Kaur, S., Kumar, R., Singh, K., & Huang, Y. L. (2024). Leveraging artificial intelligence for enhanced sustainable energy management. *Journal of Sustainable Energy, 3*(1), 1–20. https://doi.org/10.56578/jse030101

Kulińska, E., & Gruszka, M. (2019). Green cities – Problems and solutions in Turkey. *Transportation Research Procedia, 39*, 242.

Lim, S. S., Allen, K., Dandona, L., Forouzanfar, M. H., Fullman, N., Goldberg, E. M., Hay, S. I., Holmberg, M., Kutz, M. J., Larson, H. J., Lopez, A. D., McNellan, C. R., Mokdad, A. H., Mooney, M. D., Naghavi, M., Olsen, H. E., Pigott, D. M., Vos, T., Wang, H., ... Yoon, S. (2016). Measuring the health-related sustainable development goals in 188 countries: A baseline analysis from the global burden of disease study 2015. *Lancet (London, England), 388*, 1813–1850.

Miltiadou, M., Antoniou, E., Theocharidis, C., & Danezis, C. (2021). Do people understand and observe the effects of climate crisis on forests? The case study of Cyprus. *Forests, 12*, 1152. https://doi.org/10.3390/f12091152

Musa, H., Yacob, M., Abdullah, A., & Ishak, M. (2018). Enhancing subjective well-being through strategic urban planning: Development and application of community happiness index. *Sustainable Cities and Society, 38*, 184–194. https://doi.org/10.1016/J.SCS.2017.12.030

Ndekwa, A. G., Kalugendo, E., Sood, K., & Grima, S. (2023). An analysis of agribusiness digitalisation transformation of the sub-Saharan African countries small-scale farmers' production distribution. *Research on World Agricultural Economy, 4*(3), 63–78.

Patrick, R., Shaw, A., Freeman, A., Henderson-Wilson, C., Lawson, J., Davison, M., Capetola, T., & Lee, C. (2019). Human wellbeing and the health of the environment: Local indicators that balance the scales. *Social Indicators Research, 146*, 1–17. https://doi.org/10.1007/S11205-019-02140-W

Rijal, S., Nursaputra, M. A. C., & Dari, H. U. (2024). Flood susceptibility analysis using frequency ratio method in Walanae watershed. *International Journal of Sustainable Development and Planning, 19*(3), 823–832. https://doi.org/10.18280/ijsdp.190302

Sood, K., & Özen, E. (2024). A systematic review of ESG in the insurance industry: Navigating the path to sustainability. *International Journal of Sustainable Development and Planning, 19*(3), 807–821. https://doi.org/10.18280/ijsdp.190301

Wellbeing Economy Alliance (WEAll). (2021). *Happy Planet index report*. http://www.happyplanetindex.org.

Yaming, T., Feng, F., Guo, Z., Wei, F., Zhengguo, L., Wang, J., Sun, Q., Ma, H., & Yan'e, L. (2020). Integrating principal component analysis with statistically-based models for analysis of causal factors and landslide susceptibility mapping: A comparative study from the loess plateau area in Shanxi (China). *Journal of Cleaner Production*, *277*, 124159. https://doi.org/10.1016/J.JCLEPRO.2020.124159

Yerpude, S., Sood, K., & Grima, S. (2022). Blockchain-augmented digital supply chain management: A way to sustainable business. *Journal of Risk and Financial Management*, *16*(1), 7.

Chapter 17

Adaptation of Blockchain Technology into the Letter of Credit (LC) Arrangement: An Overview of the Sustainable Business Practice in Asia

Afroza Sultana and Shahidul Alam

Department of Business Administration, Premier University, Chattogram, Bangladesh

Abstract

Purpose: This study aims to explore the efforts of several Asian countries adopting blockchain-enabled letter of credit (LC) processes and highlight the key challenges hindering blockchain adoption into the entire LC system.

Need for the study: As trade volume among countries grows, nations should agree on the technology's application mechanism to prevent disputes over discrete practices. As blockchain is a borderless approach, the global context of the applications should be considered, incorporating the cases of Asia, the hub of intraregional collaboration in trading.

Methodology: This chapter has surveyed the existing literature to identify the dichotomy between blockchain-enabled LC and traditional LC. Ten Asian countries were selected considering their adaptation motivations, number of use cases, and economic outlook. The case-study method was applied to compare the counties.

Findings: Countries reported blockchain-enabled LC as time-efficient, less costly, and secure. Interoperability, scalability, the absence of legal and administrative infrastructure, stress for new skills, and cyber security concerns are the most cited challenges among users. Instances of regulatory sandbox and collaborative effort were found among some countries, although some countries have yet to publish application guidelines.

Green Management: A New Paradigm in the World of Business, 303–337

Published under exclusive licence by Emerald Publishing Limited
doi:10.1108/978-1-83797-442-920241017

Practical implication: The study provides comparative pictures of blockchain-enabled LC systems adopted by several Asian countries. This will contribute to future collaboration between Asian countries to create a unified and standardised trade financing platform. The study will also contribute to the future formulation of guidelines for administrative methodologies of the permissioned blockchain application in the trade finance section.

Keywords: Sustainability; blockchain; letter of credit (LC); blockchain-enabled LC; Asia

JEL Classifications: G21; G23; F36

1. Introduction

The fourth industrial revolution innovations like Artificial Intelligence (AI), blockchain, and the Internet of Things (IoT) are paving the way for achieving the most desirable 17 Sustainable Development Goals (SDGs) of the United Nations (UN). Though the revolution has yet to reach its full potential, it supports the SDG9 of "build resilient infrastructure, promote inclusive and sustainable industrialisation, foster innovation" (World Economic Forum. PWC, 2020). Business organisations worldwide are not out of the team for achieving the most appreciated endeavour of the UN, and the ongoing revolution has initiated the thinking of combining the existing business process with these emerging technologies.

Regarding the SDG goals, sustainability is considered a vital indicator of economic progress. Sustainability is achievable through business models which ensure circular business processes, decentralisation, collaboration, data sustainability, and less use of natural energy (Schulte, 2013). Sustainable finance is the predicted output of this novel practice. European Commission defines sustainable finance as business practices that involve considering environmental, social, and governance (ESG) factors when making financial investments to support a more sustainable economy (European Commission, 2024). Technological innovations primarily support establishing this ESG, and blockchain garners the top list in this regard (Khamzaeva et al., 2023).

By ensuring less transaction costs and time, increased efficiencies, transparency, decentralisation, and collaboration, blockchain technology contributes to sustainable business practice through less carbon footprint in a circular economy system (Upadhyay et al., 2021). The circular economy rejects the old idea of "make, use, dispose" and emphasises "reduce, reuse, and recycle" natural resources (Murray et al., 2017). Cluster analysis showed that reviewing 85 articles confirmed the ability of blockchain technology to create sustainable applications in several disciplines of sustainable operation management, digital tool management, sustainable solid waste management, and, most importantly, the growth of the circular economy (Ren et al., 2023a). As a phase of creating a circular economy, wireless power transfer by utilising blockchain technology reduces energy loss for green and secure IoT (Jiang et al., 2019).

Blockchain was primarily criticised for its over-consumption of energy and carbon emissions due to its mining activities (Jiang et al., 2021). However, the ever-increasing nature of blockchain applications could hardly be restrained. The later efforts emphasise the sustainable use of blockchain which emphasises the minimisation of carbon footprint and reduction of energy consumption (Rana et al., 2019). Renewable energy sources like wind power or solar have become the new trend in deploying sustainable blockchain (Gawusu et al., 2022). A longitudinal study of energy consumption between 2015 and 2023 in Texas showed a significant reduction in electricity consumption with the deployment of blockchain in the energy sector. This reduction happened because of the peer-to-peer trading feature of blockchain that ensures efficiency, transparency, and sustainability (Ren et al., 2023b). The basic model of blockchain facilitates less use of manual paperwork and less energy-demanding hardware, which results in economic sustainability and the cheapest electricity prices (Giungato et al., 2017). A study shows that private and consortium blockchains being used in LC are partially decentralised, saving much energy (Vranken, 2017).

Blockchain has emerged as one of the remarkable innovations of the current industrial revolution, initiating disruption in existing business systems. Blockchain is a tamperproof global record-keeping database that stores data decentralised without a central authority. Though the first application was on the functioning of the cryptocurrency Bitcoin, it has explored various applications beyond its narrow primary realm of digital and cryptocurrencies. It has become the highest agenda for business firms, disrupting how businesses run by tracking each transaction in real-time. It facilitates a consensus among participants, as everyone has the authority to verify each transaction, which creates an audit trail and ensures the correctness and integrity of each transaction (Muheidat et al., 2021). A study showed that the funding for the blockchain-based start-up was 4.1 billion in 2018. This study also estimated that the adaptation of blockchain into business firms will be worth USD 17.5 billion by 2025, which will be more than USD 3 trillion by 2030. Among the current adaptation rate, 15% was devoted to financial services (MeitY, 2021; MOSTI, 2021).

It was found that managers who intend to steer the strategic decision do not bother about the cost and new changed demand-supply dynamics when designing the new blockchain-adopted system (Sahu et al., 2023). 54% of the stakeholders expressed that the firm will lose competitiveness if blockchain is not adopted into business processes (MOSTI, 2021). There are pieces of evidence that blockchains have supported business processes where the confidentiality of data and the privacy of the participants were the concern. However, one study also showed that security and privacy are still concerns when adopting the technology (Sahu et al., 2023). On the other hand, the combined application of blockchain with radio frequency identification (RFID) and the Industrial Internet of Things (IIoT) has proven to enhance transparency in systems where several partners and customers are involved (Zelbst, 2020). This secured temper-prevented facility for several partners in blockchain platforms drew the attention of letters of credit (LC) practitioners, as LCs involve security and assurance to several parties in a single arrangement.

LC has been widely recognised as the primary instrument in international trade. This document is generally acknowledged as an international contract, which plays a critical role in safeguarding the interests of all parties in global trade transactions. Its paramount importance lies in its ability to ensure payment security for international trade dealings. Among the other trade financing options, the dependency on LCs in facilitating such trade arrangements is increasing for its risk reduction characteristics (Abdallah Alrabei, 2017; Al-Amaren et al., 2020). By 2017, the trade guarantees by paper-based LC were worth over $2 trillion (Barreto, 2017). An estimation showed that LCs usually finance 10% to 15% of global trade (IMF, 2019). One of the surprising facts is that between the years 2020 and 2021, when economies were recovering from the adverse effect of the COVID-19 pandemic on the economy, the default rate on import and export LCs was much lower than in the pre-pandemic periods (ICC, 2022).

Despite LC's secured trade financing shreds of evidence, open accounts are primarily issued in international trade as LC involves a lengthy process of verification of compliance and confirmations from several parties (ICC, 2022). A survey by contour, the largest network for global trade, reported that 86% of the users of LC found it intolerable for banks and corporates because of its overreliance on paper documentation (Insight, 2020a). Process complexity, excess costs, and human resource-intensive workflows create barriers to adopting LC arrangements in several potential fields like small and medium enterprises (SMEs), which are indulged in the export-import process only 5% to 40% (OECD, 2021). A time-efficient platform is expected to be needed for the entire LC functioning to explore the untapped opportunities of this secured trade finance tool. Adapting blockchain technologies to the system might serve the cause well.

In line with this expectation, blockchain is being adopted in trade finance scenarios. Trade finance becomes a lucrative use case for blockchain as trade financing does not need legacy investment for automation (Bank, 2017). Introducing blockchain to the LC system has reduced the transactional turn-around time of LC processing to almost a quarter or even less than what it used to take through the conventional method. Information latency due to several intermediaries was a significant problem of traditional LC processing, and a solution was found by adopting blockchain (Chang et al., 2020). Moreover, blockchain keeps providing real-time data distribution with all the counterparties, reducing the chances of discrepancy. It speeds up the settlement process between banks and other counterparties (Vedapradha & Ravi, 2023). A study showed up to 97% increased efficiency in the business process after applying blockchain to the LC process (Khalil et al., 2021).

As blockchain is a borderless approach, the global context of the application needs to be considered (OECD, 2019). Moreover, to achieve the full potential of the technology, it must be applied to the entire financial system, not merely to individual firms. As cross-border financial activities are rising, countries' collaboration is also needed to develop the infrastructure for technological advancement smoothly. In this regard, Asia has become a magnificent example of maintaining intraregional collaboration, where 60% of goods are traded among all Asian economies (Tonby et al., 2019). As of 24 April 2023, ranking number one regional economy in terms of the total population of 4,752,173,554, Asia constitutes 59.76% of the world population (Worldometer, 2023). From 2007 to 2017, Asia's share of global goods trade increased from 27% to 33% (Tonby et al., 2019). Regarding technology adaptation, several countries have become the front-runners here. By 2021, the number of blockchain-based start-ups was 900, and the Venture Capital (VC) for such start-ups was 20% in Asia Pacific (MOSTI, 2021). The region is dreaming of having an Asian Blockchain Hub, and Singapore, being the first country, has announced that it would grant research funds that contribute to creating the hubs (Oh & Shong, 2017). So, exploring Asian countries to identify the aspiration of technology adaptation will be interesting.

Considering all the above issues, the study has explored the adaptation of blockchain technology into LC processing in Asia by identifying the opportunities and challenges accompanying blockchains' adoption. Blockchain applications in trade finance are mostly on permissioned blockchain networks, so we have discussed the challenges of private or consortium blockchain, leaving the drawbacks of public blockchain domains. In some cases, countries' initiatives for the smooth functioning of permission-less crypto assets are reviewed, expecting them to pave the way further for developing a permissioned blockchain platform.

Our study guides researchers and practitioners alike in explorations that focus on the dichotomy of the traditional LC and blockchain-enabled LC and offers research directions for blockchains in international trade, focusing on the opportunities and challenges faced by several Asian countries. The remainder of this paper has been organised as follows. First, we presented vital concepts of blockchain and traditional LC processing and introduced the fundamental concepts associated with blockchain-enabled LC processing. We then continued discussing the practice of blockchain-adopted LC processing in several Asian countries. Finally, a comparative picture has been presented, highlighting each country's initiatives, practices, and efforts.

2. Blockchain

Blockchain, also known as distributed ledger technology (DLT), keeps records of transactions between parties on a peer-to-peer platform. Here, each transaction generates a block of data containing immutable relevant information. This block is then validated across all nodes in the system, and subsequent transactions create additional blocks that are gradually added to the legacy blocks (Deloitte, 2018). Each block in a blockchain consists of two essential elements: the header and the contents. The header contains a solitary reference number, block generation timing, and legacy block connections. In contrast, the contents compose information about the sender, receiver, and executed amount or exchanged information for future records (Mulligan, 2017).

Blockchain technology is based on two digital ideas: asymmetrical cryptography and a distributed computer network. Asymmetrical cryptography has two separate keys in its system: the public and private keys. These two encrypt and decrypt information, data, and documents. The distributed computer network is an IT network where the participants are interconnected with computers.

Each party has permission to access, transfer, and monitor data independently without any intervention from third parties (PWC, 2018). Transactions on the blockchain are verified using complex cryptographic algorithms. Once confirmed, the transaction cannot be altered or deleted, ensuring the data's integrity (Narayanan et al., 2016). As these transactions are updated with the approval of all the participants on the platform, it becomes impossible to temper, which confirms permanent, unchangeable, and transparent transactions (Saberi et al., 2019; Zheng et al., 2017).

The process also creates smart contracts, self-executing unique contracts where the agreement conditions between parties involved are written into lines of code and can automate various processes. Smart contracts can be executed automatically in compliance with specific agreement terms, reducing the chance of fraud or any other contractual disputes between the parties (Karim, 2022). Smart contracts create a legal binding between trade finance parties, confirming that they will ensure a guarantee if the prerequisites and requisites are met (Javaid et al., 2022).

Blockchain has three types. A Public Blockchain is a fully decentralised system where anyone can participate, access, and transact. In this arrangement, pseudo-anonymity is maintained, so several unverified participants may join here, making it unattractive to use in the financial sector. This blockchain functions for crypto assets (Bitcoin, Ethereum, etc.). The second one is the Consortium Blockchain, where a pre-selected number of nodes is required for a block to be valid. For example, if there is a consortium of 10 financial institutions, when each is considered as a node, 8 of the nodes must sign digitally for each block to be valid. This blockchain is a partially decentralised one. The last one is the Private Blockchain, a centralised database with one or multiple authorities controlling the entire network and approving a limited number of participants. It is helpful for cost reduction without losing control of the entire system and is highly appreciated by companies and financial institutions. In Consortium and Private Blockchains, rules can be altered with permission of the central authority, and participants are identifiable (Gonzalez, 2018; Oh & Shong, 2017). The consortium and private blockchains are called Permissioned Blockchain, offering enhanced privacy, improved auditability, and increased operational efficiency (Chitranshi & Chawla, 2020). Eighty companies, including IBM and Intel, joined this platform to develop business-level blockchains, especially for use cases of finance. Some prominent permissioned blockchain platforms are Ripple, Quorum, and R3 Corda (Ahmed, 2021). Among them, Corda is a popular one, which performs under the governance of R3, the worldwide consortium for financial and other supporting organisations.

Blockchain technology can increase efficiency by eliminating intermediaries. It can reduce the need for manual processes to streamline transactions and reduce time and costs (Khalil et al., 2021). Six significant contributions were found in applying blockchain to several systems: security, time-cost efficiency, fraud reduction, record-keeping, transparency, and decentralisation (MOSTI, 2021). These contributions can be particularly beneficial in industries such as finance, where using intermediaries and manual processes can lead to delays and errors.

Extensive literature found 34 probable application segments of blockchain to finance, including, among others, the trade finance scenarios, and emphasised the cost-reduction aspect as fewer bank resources are needed after the adaptation (Javaid et al., 2022). The application, specifically in the banking industry, increases banking business processes' transparency, trustworthiness, and traceability (Saheb & Mamaghani, 2021).

3. Letter of Credit (LC)

A letter of credit (LC) is a commercial-purpose agreement that enables the promise of payment to a beneficiary (Mooney & Blodgett, 1995). As the issuer, the bank promises to the third party, the beneficiary, payment upon fulfilment of prerequisite conditions on behalf of the 'account party' or the purchaser. The issuing bank necessarily transfers non-payment risk from the account party to itself. More specifically, an LC is a standard method used in trade to sell and exchange goods, where the seller will receive payment for the goods they have shipped if he meets the terms and conditions specified in the LC. On the other hand, LC also protects the buyer by ensuring that payment is only made once the goods have been shipped and the seller has provided the necessary documentation (Quoc et al., 2022). This mechanism ensures all parties' interest throughout the transactions. Buyers get the desired product, sellers get assurance for payment, and the intermediary banks receive a commission for their services.

In Fig. 17.1, the LC process involves several stages, as outlined in the study on international trade procedures and Uniform Customs and Practice for Documentary Credits (UCP 600), a standard of documentary credit formulated by the International Chamber of Commerce (ICC). Fig. 17.1 highlights the entire process. First, it needs to understand the LC, which involves the buyer and seller agreeing on the terms and conditions of the document and includes the type of LC to be used. Then, to make comparisons, the buyer compares the terms of the LC with those of other payment methods to determine the most suitable option (Quoc et al., 2022). Once the LC has been agreed upon, the buyer applies for the LC to his bank, known as the issuing bank. After that, the issuing bank sends the LC to the seller's advising bank. The advising bank immediately notifies the seller that the LC has been received and lets the seller know about the terms and conditions of the LC (Alavi, 2016). Upon the preparation of the shipment, the seller ships the goods to the buyer and presents the necessary documents, such as bills of lading and invoices, to the advising bank. The advising bank verifies the terms and conditions of the LC and forwards these to the LC issuing bank (Quoc et al., 2022). If the documents fully comply with the terms, the issuing bank pays the seller via the advising bank. On the other hand, when the documents are not in order, the issuing bank may request the seller via the issuing bank to provide the corrected documents. Upon successful payment of dues, the buyer receives the documents and can disburse the goods from customs with the bill of lading (Alavi, 2016). The entire process is shown in Fig. 17.1.

The traditional LC process is fraught with numerous challenges that impede its effectiveness. One of the significant issues is the reliance on manual work and

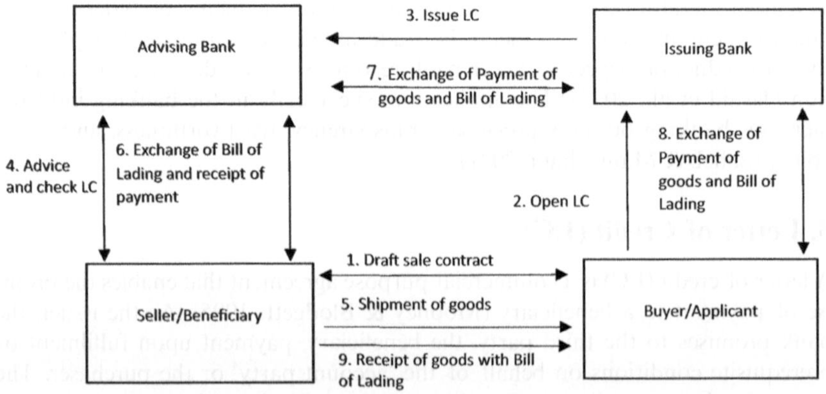

Fig. 17.1. Traditional Letter of Credit Process. *Source*: WTO (2018).

paper-based documentation, which results in increased complexity and delays in processing (Khalil et al., 2021). The lack of effective automation of human resources and weak visibility of the process further exacerbates the problem (Sepanloo, 2019). The LC process requires excessive human intervention and workforce, including presenting bills of lading and sending them to buyers, which increases the uncertainty of the tracking down of the documents (Khalil et al., 2021). This results in delayed timelines, which can be problematic, especially in the case of short-distance voyages (Al-Abri et al., 2020; Al-Amaren et al., 2020).

Another challenge is the time it takes for the LC to be issued and approved by the banks involved in the transaction (Chmielewska, 2005). This time duration can cause delays in the shipment of goods. LC may need up to twenty parties to complete a single transaction, leading to communication and coordination problems and negatively impacting user experience (Chang et al., 2019; Khalil et al., 2021).

The arrangement lacks integration as different parties record the transaction individually into their database. This may create the problem of duplication of the information and require amendment by all the parties in case any errors happen (Caudevilla, 2021). Furthermore, the long and complicated nature of the LC process has an undesirable effect on cost, which can be a significant burden for businesses (Al-Amaren et al., 2020; Chang et al., 2019). The arrangement's complicated nature sometimes produces documentation errors, which can cause delays and additional costs. The risk of fraud, like several LCs in a single LC or duplicative bill of lading, and the authenticity of documents also pose significant challenges. The manual nature of the Anti-Money Laundering review procedure also increases the risk of fraud (Khalil et al., 2021).

4. Blockchain-Enabled LC

The blockchain-enabled LC functions in a manner that starts with the buyer's request in the blockchain network to open a new LC, as shown in Fig. 17.2. The blockchain system notifies the issuing bank of the application. The system is a permissioned platform so the issuing bank can approve or reject the application

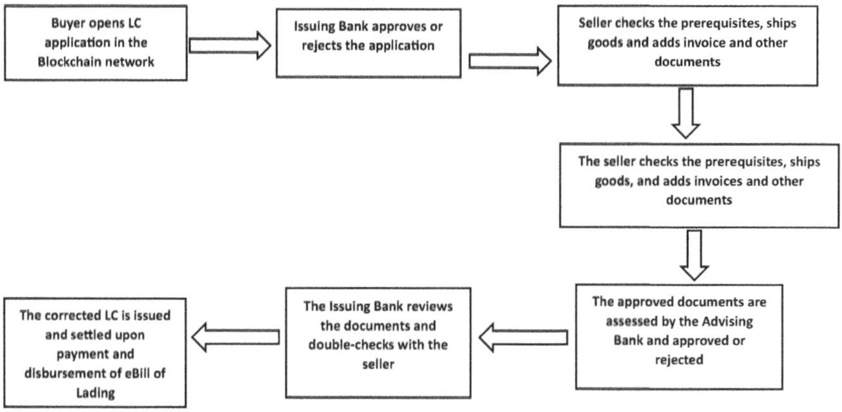

Fig. 17.2. Basic Flowchart of Blockchain-Enabled Letter of Credit Process. *Sources*: Al-Abri et al. (2020), Al-Amaren et al. (2020), Khalil et al. (2021), and InfoSystems (2017).

from its node. The advising bank also verifies the LC requirements and approves or rejects the application of the LC using its authorisation. The seller must comply with the terms and conditions of the LC, and eventually, shipment is made. The advising bank automatically notifies the system about the seller's documentation; it reviews the documents and requests the buyer to check for any discrepancies. If all parties approve and validate the documents and conditions, the final approval is permanently issued, settled, and added to the distributed ledger. Upon payment, the eBill of Lading and other documents are exchanged, and disbursement of goods is ensured (Al-Abri et al., 2020; Al-Amaren et al., 2020; Khalil et al., 2021). The entire treatment is a permissioned blockchain system that requires the approved participation of parties by a central entity that facilitates identity verification and data privacy.

Blockchain technology has several features that can effectively address the challenges of the traditional LC process. For one, it is distributed, immutable, and can be permissioned, making it more secure and transparent than traditional LC processes. Additionally, it is multicenter and less intermediated, reducing counterparty risk and enabling decentralised contract execution. Furthermore, blockchain technology provides real-time reviews, automated payments, and regulatory transparency (Chang et al., 2019).

Integrating blockchain reduces the risk of counterfeiting and malicious alteration, as the technology is more secure, transparent, auditable, and automated. Moreover, it removes the necessity of presenting physical documents and manual paperwork, lowering costs and increasing transaction speed. (Al-Abri et al., 2020; Chang et al., 2019). Applying to agreement-based smart contracts, blockchain also enquires whether parties are following the terms and conditions of the agreement or not (Muheidat et al., 2021). In a simulation study comparing paper-based LC and blockchain-enabled LC, the latter concluded the transaction within 10–23 h, while the former took 15 to 30 days (Khalil et al., 2021). Moreover, blockchain technology can facilitate the anti-money laundering initiatives by banks and the Know Your Customer (KYC) procedure, making it a versatile tool in the finance industry (India, 2017).

5. Overview of Current Application in Asian Countries

We have selected ten countries of Asia considering the country categorisation of the International Monetary Fund (IMF). Four countries (Japan, South Korea, Singapore, and Hong Kong) were selected from the Advanced Economies category. Five countries (China, India, Thailand, Vietnam, and Malaysia) were taken from the Emerging Economies category. Bangladesh has been taken as the mere case of a Developing Economy (IMF, 2023). Countries' blockchain adaptation motivations, the instances of at least one blockchain-enabled LC, and regulatory application guidelines were searched at the time of country selection. The economic outlook of the international organisations on selected countries has been reviewed to identify the individual economic significance of the countries. Though LCs are being used in domestic and international trade, we have reviewed the export-import scenarios of individual countries to search for any magnitude for international trade. Current initiatives and practices of blockchain adaptation in general and LCs specific have been highlighted for each country's case studies emphasising government-backed policy guidelines.

Fig. 17.3 shows Gross Domestic Product (GDP) growth rates, which indicates that countries experienced a negative economic trend during the COVID-19 pandemic but recovered from the adverse effects right after the year. An exception was Hong Kong, which endured a negative Real GDP in 2022. However, in Fig. 17.4, the IMF projection shows the country's intriguing bounce-back possibility in 2023. Another fact is that during the 2020 pandemic, China, Vietnam, and Bangladesh managed to maintain positive GDP growth.

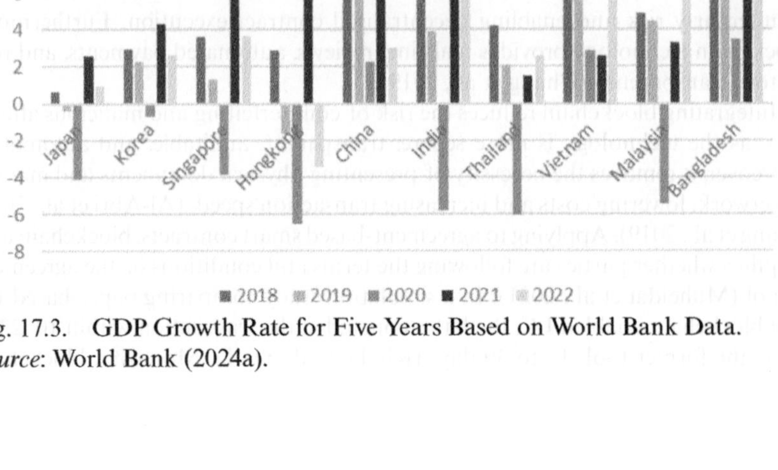

Fig. 17.3. GDP Growth Rate for Five Years Based on World Bank Data. *Source*: World Bank (2024a).

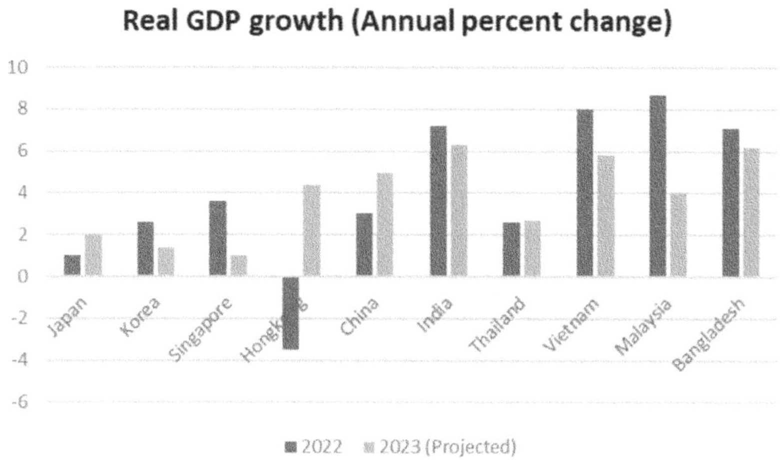

Fig. 17.4. Real GDP Growth Rate for Two Years Based on IMF Data. *Source*: IMF (2024).

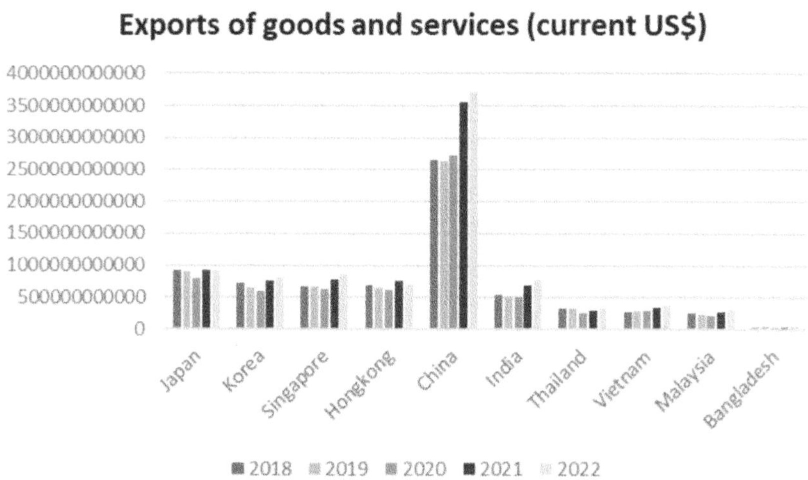

Fig. 17.5. Export of Goods and Services (US$) for Five Years Based on World Bank Data. *Source*: World Bank (2024c).

Figs. 17.5 and 17.6 show the export-import of goods and services over five years, proving that China has emerged as the leading country worldwide in overall trading activities.

Table 17.1 indicates that the annual growth rate of countries' import-export volume is stable, although 2019 and 2020 were two years of negative growth due to the worldwide pandemic crisis.

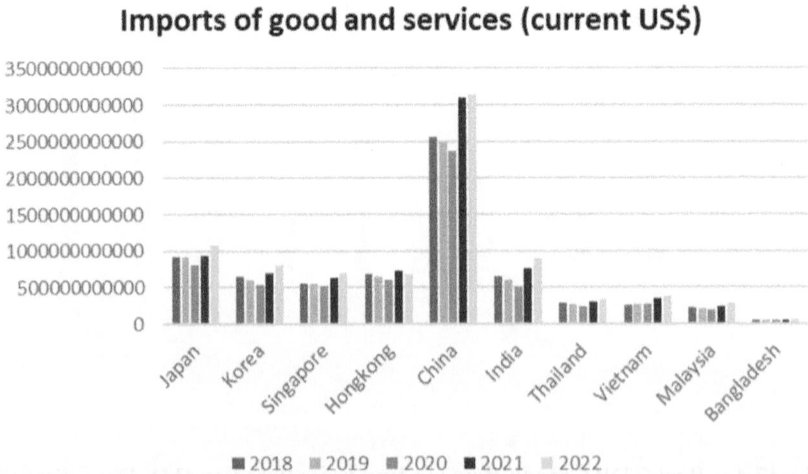

Fig. 17.6. Import of Goods and Services (US$) for Five Years Based on World Bank Data. *Source*: World Bank (2024b).

Table 17.1. The Growth Rate (Annual %) of Import–Export Volume for 5 Years.

	2018 (%)		2019 (%)		2020 (%)		2021 (%)		2022 (%)	
	Import	Export	Import	Export	Import	Export	Import	Export	Import	Export
Japan	11	6	−1	−3	−12	−12	18	16	15	0
Korea	9	8	−6	−10	−11	−8	30	27	16	6
Singapore	12	14	−1	−1	−5	−4	20	23	11	11
Hong Kong	6	6	−6	−5	−6	−6	22	24	−7	−7
China	16	10	−3	−1	−5	4	30	30	1	5
India	10	8	−6	−2	−15	−6	49	36	19	15
Thailand	15	8	−4	−1	−15	−20	28	15	14	10
Vietnam	12	14	7	9	3	3	25	17	10	13
Malaysia	10	10	−5	−3	−12	−13	27	27	20	19
Bangladesh	−19	8	13	13	−15	−15	14	14	34	34

Source: Calculated by the authors, based on The World Bank Open Data Bank (World Bank, 2024b, 2024c).

5.1 Japan

By 2020, 1.7% of Japanese firms had adopted blockchain in their system, and another 13% were in the process of adopting it (Broeckaert, 2022). The primary motivation for adopting these technologies was developing a vibrant cryptocurrency market. In line with its goal, by 30 April 2022, 30 crypto-asset service providers were given licenses here to exchange this virtual currency (Kawai & Nagase, 2022). Despite these developments, the legal standing of crypto assets under Japanese civil law is yet to be formed. As crypto assets are intangible, the transfer of crypto assets is not considered a transfer of legal ownership of such assets under the Civil Act. No individual blockchain application guidelines were found in Japan. Still, the Payment Service Act 2010 is in effect for handling the decentralised finance platform here with the co-application of the Banking Act 1981, Financial Instruments and Exchange Act 2006, and Money Lending Business Act 1983, which depends on the functions of the platform (Kawai & Nagase, 2022).

The first move Japan took to adopt blockchain-enabled LC was in 2017 when Mizuho Bank, in consultation with Mizuho Financial Group, initiated a project under which there will be a fully digitalised blockchain-based LC processing between Australia and Japan in the future (Mizuho, 2017). Japan executed its first blockchain LC transaction in January 2020 through the largest bank, Mitsubishi UFJ Financial Group (MUFG). The MUFG bank formed the Geneva-based digitalised financing platform KomGo-SA, facilitating the first LC to a commodity trader, Mercuria, in London. The users have reported faster and more secure trade finance due to blockchain's immutability and non-manual nature (Insight, 2020b). On 17 April 2023, in another move to digitalise the trade transaction for accelerated import and export with its third largest trading partner, ASEAN, Japan introduced a blockchain-enabled system. It is expected that the new system will facilitate the digitalised processing of LCs of the bank and will exempt the need for paper documents for the entire functioning (Post, 2023).

A significant step taken in Japan was its amendment to the "Payment Service Act" on March 4, 2022, which went into effect on March 4, 2023. Hopefully, the amendment could help the entire LC processing here adopt the blockchain. In this amendment, a prudent move adopted by the Japanese is that the latter will be applied in case of any conflict between the decentralised finance platform and existing finance regulation. This rule also applies to the decentralised lending platform. Moreover, according to the amendment, blockchain-based gaming transactions will not be considered crypto-asset payment transactions (Kawai & Nagase, 2022).

5.2 South Korea

South Korea has been working to establish an infrastructure for digital trade to facilitate cross-border trade and reduce the time and cost of LC processing. One of the initiatives in South Korea's implementation of blockchain technology in LC processing is the Korea Financial Investment Association (KFIA) blockchain-based platform. The association initiated a consortium of 26 technology and financial institutions to promote blockchain-based innovation in the financial sectors (Griffin, 2016). Later, it established a platform designed to provide an automated and secure LC process, enabling faster transactions and reducing the risk of fraud. The platform uses a permitted blockchain that ensures only authorised parties can access the platform. The KFIA platform has demonstrated the potential to reduce the time required for LC processing from several days to just a few hours by enabling the secure exchange of documents and automating the verification process. The platform has also reduced the cost of LC processing by eliminating the need for intermediaries and reducing the risk of fraud (KOFIA, 2023).

Implementing blockchain technology in LC processing requires interoperability with other blockchain networks. The KFIA platform has addressed this challenge using the Hyperledger Fabric framework, designed to enable interoperability with other blockchain networks using different consensus algorithms (Lafourcade & Lamberd-Platet, 2020).

In November 2016, 16 Commercial Banks and 2 Coordination Institutes of Korea, under the authorisation of the central bank, created a consortium to conduct research on document verifications, customer identifications, etc., which is a significant step for digitalising trade finance (Oh & Shong, 2017). In 2019, INEOS Styrolution, a Korean company, exported plastic products to a Vietnamese Company. The platform was the leading trade finance network worldwide, Voltron (Currently known as Contour), facilitating a document exchange of less than 24 h (HSBC, 2019a).

Two notable research papers, Global Standard Mapping Initiative 1.0 (2020) and 2.0 (2021), were published and funded by the Ministry of Science and ICT, giving an overview of the holistic efforts of the country to adopt the technology. Korea has a vast interest in cryptocurrencies, and in 2017, it contributed 12% of the total trade volume of cryptocurrencies. However, in 2018, it became silent after the notable price fall of the currency. The two mentioned papers indicated some blockchain use cases other than cryptocurrency transactions. Nevertheless, trade finance was missing from the list of probable use cases here.

5.3 Singapore

Singapore is playing a leading role in digital adaptation. In 2022, The IMD World Competitiveness Center conducted a digital competitiveness ranking of 63 countries based on 53 criteria measuring their adoption of digital practices. Singapore ranked fourth for initiating substantial digital identity programs (IMD, 2022). It has been proactive in promoting blockchain technology in trade finance and has undertaken several initiatives to explore the use of blockchain in LC processing.

In 2016, 15 banks in Singapore created a collaboration to adopt blockchain-based smart contracts on the R3 Corda platform to implement accounts receivable buy-sell and LC transactions. The same year, Bank of America Merrill Lynch (BofAML), the Infocomm Development Authority of Singapore (IDA), and HSBC Singapore adopted blockchain into their LC transactions to support their customers (Persio, 2016). Another unique step here is the bilateral collaboration of the Hong Kong Monetary Authority (HKMA) and the Monetary Authority of Singapore (MAS) to tackle paper-based inefficiencies like fraud and errors in case of trade transactions between the two countries by introducing blockchain-based systems (Barreto, 2017). In 2019, a shipment of oil from Thailand to Singapore was made through a blockchain-enabled LC platform with the support of Standard Chartered Bank (Standard Chartered, 2019). In 2020, Singapore executed another cross-bank LC transaction with Vietnam, which is mentioned in the section of the country discussion of Vietnam.

One of the key initiatives in Singapore's adoption of blockchain technology in LC processing is the TradeTrust platform in 2020 (VentureBeat, 2020). TradeTrust is a blockchain-based platform that aims to simplify the exchange of trade documents and enhance the security and efficiency of trade finance transactions. The platform is built on the Ethereum blockchain. The TradeTrust platform enables the secure exchange of documents between buyers, sellers, banks, and other intermediaries in the LC process (Yuh, 2022). One of the significant challenges in implementing blockchain technology in LC processing is the need for interoperability between different blockchain networks. The TradeTrust platform has addressed this challenge by using a common data format and a set of standard application programming interfaces (APIs) that enable the platform to connect with different blockchain networks. This initiative has enabled the platform to be interoperable with other blockchain networks, such as the Corda network, which several banks use in Singapore for LC processing (Times, 2019).

Another challenge in implementing blockchain technology in LC processing is standardising data and processes. The TradeTrust platform has addressed this challenge by working with industry stakeholders to develop a set of standard data elements and processes for trade documents. This effort has enabled the platform to streamline the document verification process and reduce the need for manual intervention.

5.4 Hong Kong

The Hong Kong Monetary Authority (HKMA) has been driving several blockchain initiatives to improve the efficiency and security of the financial system, one of which is the use of blockchain technology in trade finance, specifically in the LC process. This application effort of blockchain technology in LC processing has faced several challenges and opportunities. One of the main challenges is ensuring that the technology is interoperable with existing systems and standards, such as the SWIFT messaging system used by banks to exchange transaction information (News, 2021). Another challenge is ensuring compliance with local regulations and international trade laws, such as the United Nations Convention on Contracts for the International Sale of Goods (CISG) (Chang et al., 2019).

To address these challenges, the HKMA has worked with industry partners to develop a blockchain-based trade finance platform called eTradeConnect. The platform is built in collaboration with 12 banks in Hong Kong (Caudevilla, 2021). This platform facilitates secure and efficient trade finance transactions, including LC, while complying with local regulations and international trade laws. One of the key benefits of the eTradeConnect platform is that it allows banks and other trade finance participants to share transaction data and documentation in real time, reducing the risk of fraud and errors. The platform also offers greater transparency and visibility into the trade finance process, enabling faster resolution of disputes and more accurate risk assessments (Hong Kong Monetary Authority, 2016).

In addition to eTradeConnect, other blockchain-based trade finance platforms have been developed in Hong Kong, such as the Trade Finance Platform (TFP) developed by HSBC and the Voltron platform developed by a consortium of banks including HSBC, BNP Paribas, and Standard Chartered (Chang et al., 2019).

Two notable papers were published by HKMA, Whitepaper 1.0 in 2016 and Whitepaper 2.0 in 2017, which indicated the key features, benefits, and risks of blockchain applications. Both the Whitepapers highlighted the entire blockchain ecosystem, where trade finance, especially LC processing, was of extra importance. In 2019, MTC Electronic, a Hong Kong-based company, exported electronic products to its parent company, Shenzhen MTC China. The arrangement was the first blockchain-enabled LC transaction in Hong Kong facilitated by HCBC. It reduced the turnaround time to 24 h from the previous ten days (John, 2019).

5.5 China

China's view is "no Bitcoin but accept blockchain." China banned Cryptocurrency Initial Coin Offerings (ICO) and prohibited investment in the metaverse, citing the disruption these offerings are causing to the financial order (Osborne, 2017). Though the ICO market is small compared to the total economy, it is a speedy one that is hard for overpopulated countries like China to control (Acheson, 2021). On the other hand, the adoption of blockchain in China is gradually increasing.

China Academy of Information and Communication Technology (CAICT), in partnership with Trusted Blockchain Initiatives, developed two White Papers in 2018 and 2022 exploring the entire blockchain ecosystem in the country. According to White paper 2.0 in 2022, China is taking the global lead regarding the number of blockchain firms. With 1400 blockchain firms alone in China, the USA, and China constitute 50% of the total blockchain companies globally. Moreover, at least 48 educational institutes in China offer blockchain-based curriculum courses. Whitepaper 2.0 has also identified four development areas where blockchain applications will benefit China the most. One of the four was the area of cross-border payments, where document verification between parties is the highest priority (COINGEEK, 2022).

As China is the number one exporting country in the world and deals with several volatile economies, LC has become the first payment option for cross-border trade here. However, unlike the world business practice, China follows a different LC recording system. It records LCs as a liability in Advising Bank's book when required documents are presented, regardless of whether the conditions are met (IMF, 2017). This practice creates an additional risk for the banks of China and demands more cautious verification of the credibility of the clients. Considering the facts, China has been one of the countries that have adopted blockchain technology in the LC process, intending to improve business processes' efficiency, security, and transparency.

China started its blockchain-enabled LC journey in 2018 to import iron ore from Australia, which takes only 2 h to execute. After that, several blockchain-enabled LC transactions occurred on the Contour platform. In 2019, another three blockchain arrangements happened with Australia and UAE (CONTOUR, 2020a).

However, implementing blockchain technology in the LC process in China has faced challenges and opportunities. One key challenge has been ensuring interoperability and compatibility between different blockchain platforms used by various banks and financial institutions (Grandin & Eriksson, 2021). Additionally, challenges related to the regulatory environment and the need to comply with local laws and regulations can vary significantly from one jurisdiction to another.

Despite these challenges, implementing blockchain technology in the LC process in China has also brought several opportunities. The key opportunities are the potential to reduce the time and costs involved in the process and enhance efficiency, transparency and security (Lian, 2022). Various solutions have been developed in China to overcome the challenges faced in the implementation process. For example, some banks have developed proprietary blockchain platforms, while others have adopted third-party platforms to ensure interoperability and compatibility (Grandin & Eriksson, 2021). A significant step in China is forming a Blockchain-based Service Network (BSN) in 2020. The cloud-based interoperable network comprises more than 100 nodes, each representing one city capable of operating all blockchain-distributed applications (DApps). This initiative has reduced the cited problem of interoperability here in China. The country also initiated a National Blockchain Technology Innovation Center with the Chinese Ministry of Science and Technology authorisation to promote blockchain-based innovations to boost the local economy(Dzhondzhorov, 2023).

5.6 India

A study found that blockchain adoption in India was 5% in 2018, projected to be 6% from 2021 to 2023 (PWC, 2018). It stood fourth in the 2022 Global Crypto Adoption Index assessed by Chainalysis (2022). In 2021, the Ministry of Electronics & Information Technology, Government of India (MeitY) published a national guideline stating blockchains' nature, initiative, and probable use cases. It identified 44 key areas where blockchain could be employed; among them, the validation of bill of lading for cross-border trade was one of the major ones (MeitY, 2021). Several other government-affiliated bodies are also working to create a vibrant technological infrastructure here.

In India, the LC system faces various challenges and believes that blockchain has the potential to address the challenges faced by the LC system and increase efficiency in the process. Empirical studies believe implementing blockchain in India's letter of credit system can enable faster, more secure, and transparent transactions (Taneja et al., 2023). In line with these beliefs, the State Bank of India has implemented blockchain technology in its LC system to streamline the process and reduce transaction turnaround time. The bank partnered with Intellect Design Arena, a fintech software provider, to create a blockchain-based platform that provides real-time visibility and transparency to all parties involved. The platform has also automated the process, eliminating the need for manual intervention and reducing the risk of errors and fraud (Times, 2020).

In 2018, HSBC India and ING Bank Brussels executed blockchain-enabled, real-time trade finance transactions with exporter Reliance Industries and importer Tricon Energy on an R3 Corda-powered platform to facilitate the shipment. The arrangement reduced the document exchange time from 7 to 10 days to less than one day (Pathak, 2018; Shivendu, 2019). On January 30, 2023, Tata Power Company of India affiliated with Contour. By joining the network, Tata Power is implementing a blockchain-enabled digital LC settlement process that will present LC documents in less than 24 hours instead of the usual 5 to 10 days of an existing manual process (Power, 2013). The process would also help prevent fraud involving several LCs on a single invoice (Vahia, 2021).

In 2021, the Reserve Bank of India initiated a collaboration with 11 private and four public sector banks. The collaboration, named Indian Banks' Blockchain Infrastructure Company Private Limited (IBBIC) that is worked for blockchain-based applications in the new regulatory sandbox environment. The initiative is also looking for a solution to the issues in processing LCs, e-way bills, and GST invoices (BFSI, 2021). India expects to support their medium and small-scale enterprises (MSMEs) through collaboration (Vahia, 2021).

However, implementing blockchain in the LC system faced some challenges. One of the challenges was the need for more standardisation in the banking industry. Different banks use different processes and systems, making it challenging to create a uniform blockchain-enabled platform. Another challenge was the need for more awareness and understanding of the technology among stakeholders, which led to resistance and scepticism toward implementing the blockchain. India, an overpopulated country, stressed the need to form a central Know Your Clients (KYC) platform to reduce duplication of customer onboarding efforts (India, 2017).

To overcome these challenges, the State Bank of India conducted extensive training and awareness programs for all stakeholders, including staff, customers, and regulators, to help them better understand the technology and its benefits. Additionally, the bank worked with other banks in the country to standardise processes and systems, creating a uniform blockchain-based platform that all banks can use (Times, 2020).

5.7 Thailand

Thailand took a gradual blockchain adaptation initiative known as Blockchain 1.0 in 2008 by embracing digital currencies. It stood eighth in the 2022 Global Crypto Adoption Index assessed by Chainalysis, which surveyed over twenty countries (Chainalysis, 2022). Two endeavours, Blockchain 2.0 and Blockchain 3.0, were taken in 2013 and 2015 to apply smart contracts and decentralise the applications. The recent one is Blockchain 4.0, which is focused on applications in broader industries and was initiated in 2018 (Pongnumkul et al., 2021). In 2020, the Bank of Thailand launched the first government blockchain saving bond of $1.6 billion worth, which is expected to ensure a fast and secure system for selling government savings bonds in the future. Regulators also see blockchain as a means of exploring financing options for SMEs in Thailand, as the industry is suffering liquidity problems due to the unreliability of documents (GOV.UK, 2019).

61.7% of Thailand's GDP relies upon its exports, so operational efficiency in trade finance has become a significant issue (Krungthai, 2023). Until 2021, most blockchain adaptations were in the finance domain in Thailand, contributing 42.6% of the total blockchain projects here, mostly for letters of payment guarantees, letters of confirmation, and domestic or international transfers (Pongnumkul et al., 2021). 2019 GC Marketing of Thailand exported Polyethylene products to the Indonesian firm PT.Bukitmega Masabadi on the Contour network. The arrangement reduced the turnaround time from 10 days to 24 hours (CONTOUR, 2020a). In 2019, a consortium of 22 commercial banks and 15 corporations in Thailand began to issue blockchain-enabled LC to facilitate business and trade. The collaboration is expected to increase the competitive capacity and reduce costs by performing in a shared platform and blockchain technologies.

Though the Electronic Transactions Act 2001 of Thailand was amended once in 2019, the new digital business operations could not reach the desired standard of stability in Thailand due to the outdated nature of the law that does not accommodate the blockchain application adequately (Boonyanan, 2019). The government of Thailand has initiated a "sandbox" where all the commercial banks of Thailand could develop and test their blockchain-based systems, which would not subject the country's existing financial system or pose undue risk to the clients (IBM, 2020). An application into the land project found that the blockchain application may violate the land law as the law still needs to be updated. Lack of expertise was also cited as a challenge for blockchain applications in Thailand (Pongnumkul et al., 2021).

5.8 Vietnam

Vietnam claimed to be one of the five leading countries in the field of blockchain, which is expected to create 40 million new blockchain-based jobs by the end of 2030. Currently, 7 out of 200 top blockchain-based companies are formed in Vietnam, and 10 startups here are valued at US$100 million (Dharmaraj, 2022). On 17 May 2022, the Ministry of Home Affairs, Vietnam, formed two entities, the Vietnam Blockchain Union and Vietnam Blockchain Association, intending to promote Vietnam's digital economy. These organisations facilitate research, potential application, training, and investment in blockchain innovation.

The current application is for digital asset and cryptocurrency management. It stood first in the 2022 Global Crypto Adoption Index assessed by Chainalysis, the popular blockchain data platform operated in 70 countries worldwide (Chainalysis, 2022). Prime Minister of Vietnam has assigned the Ministry of Finance, Ministry of Justice, State Bank of Vietnam, and other relevant ministries to develop a legal framework for managing and applying these digital assets and virtual currencies. Without specific laws, the government's concern is that, like many other innovations (computers, the internet, etc.), technology may not cause any legal issues. Still, applying such technologies to different areas may create further legal disputes (Quang et al., 2022). There is also a classification problem, as Vietnamese laws do not currently classify cryptocurrencies as a legal payment platform or mention them as an asset or a currency (Prodent, 2022).

On September 11, 2020, Vietnam took its first step in applying blockchain to trade finance with Contour Network. The transaction involved importing US$50,000 worth of plastic products from Thailand through a cross-border LC with the partnership of the Asian Development Bank (ADB), Bank for Investment and Development of Vietnam, and Standard Chartered Bank (Thai). The adaptation reduced the LC processing time from five days to seven hours (Standard Chartered, 2020). Following the event, another successful LC processing in the blockchain platform was conducted by VPBank for purchasing coffee, which completed the entire process within only two hours, which used to be a week or even months (News, 2021). Another commercial bank in Vietnam, MB Bank, partnered with the Contour Network to offer blockchain-enabled LC to its clients (Review, 2021).

5.9 Malaysia

The Ministry of Science, Technology, and Innovation (MOSTI) in Malaysia has published a National Blockchain Roadmap from 2021 to 2025. The paper surveyed 278 stakeholders and found that blockchain could improve 77% business efficiency, 76% risk reduction, and 64% for better transaction integrity and visibility (MOSTI, 2021).

In 2018, Cargil, Argentina, exported soybeans to Cargil, Malaysia, with blockchain-enabled LC on the Contour network, where HSBC was the issuing bank (CONTOUR, 2020b). In October 2019, HSBC implemented another blockchain-enabled LC deal to import resin from a Singapore firm (HSBC, 2019b). HSBC Malaysia was the issuing bank, and HSBC Singapore was the advising bank. The deal was a live pilot transaction to support the accelerated import to Malaysia from Singapore, valued at US$85 billion in 2018 (Star, 2019). The importer of the deal, Simple Packing, is a medium-sized firm in Malaysia, unlike the other LC users, which are mostly large corporations (Insight, 2019). This initiative may be significant for 1,226,494 micro-, small-, and medium-sized enterprises (MSMEs) in 2021, which constitute 97.4% of total business establishments in Malaysia (SMECorp, 2021).

Though the shipping of goods used to take only 48 hours to be completed, the lengthy process of document transferring and checking took 5 to 10 days. The blockchain platform has facilitated a compatible tenure for the whole process of LC checking to a 24-hour duration (HSBC, 2019a). In 2018, nine banks in Malaysia teamed up to collaborate on trade financing activities enabled by the blockchain platform (Zhao, 2018). However, there is still a concern about regulatory clarity for blockchain adaptation and interoperability of the systems between different agencies in Malaysia (MOSTI, 2021).

5.10 Bangladesh

In recent years, Bangladesh has seen a growing interest in blockchain technology, particularly in international trade and finance. Due to its decentralised nature, acquiring cryptocurrency is prohibited in Bangladesh. The country's governance and financing activities mostly dominate its blockchain adaptation aspiration. Implementing blockchain technology in LC processes in Bangladesh can address some of the critical challenges traditional paper-based systems face. It can also address the limitations of specialised digital payment platforms.

In 2010, the Bangladesh Bank launched a platform called the "Bangladesh Electronic Fund Transfer Network" (BEFTN) to facilitate interbank transactions, including LC transactions. The BEFTN platform aims to reduce the time and cost associated with interbank transactions, including issuing and processing LC documents (Bank, 2010). Implementing the BEFTN platform needed more awareness and understanding among stakeholders in the banking and finance industry, which was a significant challenge (Rahman et al., 2017). To overcome this challenge, the Bangladesh Bank conducted extensive training and awareness-raising programs for stakeholders, including bankers, regulators, and policymakers. The bank also organised workshops and seminars to discuss the potential benefits and risks of using this technology in the letter of the credit process. Another challenge faced by the BEFTN platform was integrating with existing banking systems and the need to standardise data formats and protocols (Rahman et al., 2017). The Bangladesh Bank addressed this challenge by working closely with other banks and financial institutions to develop a standard data format and protocol for interbank transactions. The bank also established a centralised data repository for stakeholder sharing and collaboration.

Despite these challenges, implementing the BEFTN platform has significantly benefited Bangladesh's LC process. The platform has enabled faster and more secure processing of interbank transactions, reducing the time and cost associated with issuing and processing LC documents (Bank, 2010). The platform has also improved transparency and accountability in the LC process, reducing the risk of fraud and errors. Blockchain technology can support the effective running of this existing system.

In 2020, Bangladesh's Information and Communication Technology Division published the National Blockchain Strategy. The paper highlighted common misconceptions about blockchain and suggested probable use cases for blockchain. Among 13 other application domains, trade finance was one of the majors. Trade activities are significant in Bangladesh as trade (total import-export volume) to GDP increased by 1.45% in 2021 from the previous year to 27.72% (Macrotrends, 2023).

In August 2020, Standard Chartered Bank implemented a blockchain-enabled LC for Viyellatex Ltd, an RMG company based in Bangladesh. The Standard Chartered Bank acted as the issuing bank in this arrangement, where Contour was the facilitating platform (Hasan, 2020). In the same year, HSBC Bank performed a cross-border blockchain transaction. The bank opened a cross-border LC to import 20,000 tonnes of fuel from Singapore using blockchain technology in favour of United Mymensingh Power Limited. Following the successful completion of the LC, United Mymensingh Power Limited noted that while it previously took five to ten days to execute the LC, blockchain technology facilitated the process in less than 24 hours (Desk, 2020).

Prime Bank, a Bangladeshi financial institution, has claimed to have executed the first interbank blockchain-enabled LC transaction in Bangladesh in December 2020 with HSBC Bank. The pilot transaction was carried out via Contour, whereby Prime Bank opened an inland LC on behalf of Ananta Group, Bangladesh, to import raw materials from another company in Bangladesh, Tamishna Group, an HSBC Bangladesh customer (Bank, 2020). In 2021, City Bank partnered with the International Islamic Trade Finance Corporation (ITFC) and executed the first Shariah-based LC arrangement for the Debonair Group, which intended to export apparel to Apparel Link of Hong Kong. The arrangement conducts the entire process in only 38 minutes, which used to be 24–72 hours (Bank, 2021).

These successful blockchain transactions demonstrate the potential of blockchain technology in streamlining cross-border trade processes by increasing efficiency, reducing the time required to execute transactions, and enhancing transparency. As such, more financial institutions in Bangladesh and beyond will likely seek to explore adopting blockchain technology in the future.

Table 17.2 presents a comparative picture of countries' efforts in the blockchain adaptation processes.

A regulatory sandbox creates a platform for testing technological innovations that do not violate a country's legal or regulatory environment. Blockchain-based innovations also need a sandbox for safe testing before bringing it to actual practices. Table 17.2 shows that maximum countries have initiated the Sandbox platform, a significant step for future blockchain adaptation. Governments of the selected countries have published guideline papers for better coordination among application efforts of financial institutions, though some countries have yet to publish their guideline. All the guidelines published were about the overall blockchain applications, where the administrative model for permissioned blockchain applications in the trade finance system was mainly avoided. Country-specific LC-processed trade financing volume was not found.

Collaborative efforts were made by financial institutions, which are expected to create a uniform global trade finance system. Hong Kong and Singapore created a cross-border collaboration in this regard. The contour network was found to be the leading platform for blockchain-enabled LC processing when HSCB Banks became the initiator for most of the adaptation instances.

All the countries reported blockchain adaptation in LC processing as a time-efficient, less costly, and secure practice. Interoperability between different platforms was the most cited concern on which some countries are working well, while it is still a concern for some countries. India, Thailand, and Malaysia highlighted the future benefit of blockchain-enabled LC applications to the SME sector of the countries as the sector faces financing problems due to the unreliability of the documents.

Table 17.2. Comparative Picture of Selected Countries.

Countries	**Regulatory Sandbox**	**Government-Affiliated Publications**	**Number of Instances of Blockchain-Enabled LC Found**	**Financial Institutions' Collaboration**	**Notable Initiatives**
Japan	Yes	Not Found	3	No	Amendment in Payment Service Act 2019
Korea	Yes	Global Standard Mapping Initiative 1.0 and 2.0	1	Yes	Korea Financial Investment Association (KFIA)
Singapore	Yes	Not Found	2	Yes	TradeTrust
Hong Kong	Yes	Whitepaper 1.0 and 2.0	1	Yes	eTradeConnect
China	No	Whitepaper 1.0 and 2.0	4	No	Blockchain-based Service Network (BSN)
India	Yes	National Strategy on Blockchain	2	Yes	Indian Banks' Blockchain Infrastructure Company Private Limited (IBBIC)
Thailand	Yes	Not Found	1	Yes	Blockchain 1.0 to 4.0
Vietnam	Yes	Not Found	2	No	Vietnam Blockchain Union and Vietnam Blockchain Association
Malaysia	Yes	National Blockchain Roadmap 2021−2025	2	Yes	Roadmap 2021–2025 by MOSTI
Bangladesh	No	The National Blockchain Strategy	4	No	Bangladesh Electronic Fund Transfer Network (BEFTN)

Source: Authors' compilation.

6 The Challenges Ahead

Though blockchain adaptation is growing, there are several concerns over its applicability. An initiative by The Organization for Economic Cooperation and Development (OECD), welcoming expressions of 1600 stakeholders, opined that blockchain is not a panacea and needs critical evaluation before applying it to each use case (OECD, 2019). A perception study on blockchain adaptation indicated blockchain as a critical strategic priority (MOSTI, 2021). World Bank has highlighted the problems of cyber security, dispute and recourse framework, scalability, and interoperability when applied to the financial sectors (Bank, 2017). Country-specific cases, international organisations' reports, and several research papers have indicated challenges that future permissioned blockchain adaptation into the finance section, especially the LC processing, would face.

6.1 Interoperability

Interoperability is the most cited challenge in almost all countries. Incompatibility was considered one of the major problems in adopting blockchain (Bischoff & Seuring, 2021). However, one study also said it was less significant when the management strategy-building scenario was surveyed (Sahu et al., 2023). Interoperability is the ability of two or more systems, networks or processes to understand and exchange data (Hodapp & Hanelt, 2022). Blockchain needs to be interoperated with other ledger systems in three cases: when a node needs to move to a new blockchain platform when a node participates in different blockchain platforms, and when a new blockchain platform needs to be formed for exhausted storage capacity of the existing one (MeitY, 2021). It was found that the interoperability of the banking system would be the main concern for future payment and value exchange (Harris & Wonglimpiyarat, 2019). The process requires a substantial cost and collaboration between stakeholders, which imposes extra efforts and costs for the businesses (Bank, 2017).

6.2 Scalability

Scalability is the capability of a network, system, or process to handle an increasing number of activities at a specific unit of time (Bondi, 2000). Scalability is a significant challenge for public blockchain in terms of verification speed and transaction speed due to the narrow size of the block. At present, the scalability of the platforms ranges from 7tps (transactions per second) to 3500tps (MeitY, 2021). The attempt to increase scalability takes a substantial time to spread throughout the network, which can exacerbate the forking problem. Our concern is the permissioned blockchain network, where scalability is higher as it can process higher volumes of data. However, the challenge here is that the higher scalability comes at the expense of a less transparent, more centralised network system that removes most of the advantages of the public blockchain (Bank, 2017). Another issue is that though the transaction scale in the real economy is enormous, the capability of payment systems through the network is still low (Oh & Shong, 2017).

6.3 False data

The nature of blockchain is such that it cannot prohibit corrupted data from being entered into the system (Division, 2020). The blockchain ledger is not immune to the input of false information. In contrast, LC fraud typically involves issuing false documents, and blockchain technology cannot fully address legal hurdles associated with the bill of lading (CheHashim & Mahdzan, 2014). However, studies show that the co-application of blockchain and artificial intelligence (AI) will improve financial institutions' fraud reduction and risk management (Bank, 2021).

6.4 Cyber-Security

As the entire trade finance system is private or permissioned, anonymous entities are prohibited from entry, which could be a target area for cyber-attacks (Bank, 2017). When the private key system is hacked, there is no remedy to the problem (Oh & Shong, 2017).

6.5 Skilled Human Resources

Blockchain requires a clear system understanding, and some countries stress skilled human resources (MeitY, 2021). The workforce must learn cross- and multidisciplinary technological skills like several operating systems, cryptography, network communication, programming languages, etc. Some countries should arrange more training and educational programs incorporating these skills (CAICT, 2018).

6.6 Building Infrastructure

As blockchains are not being used in trade financing but in other sectors of an economy, several applications may create coordination problems in the future. Appropriate sandbox, incorporation of best practices, and resolution of cited disputes need a single infrastructure for smooth functioning. India has highlighted the concern for the common infrastructure (MeitY, 2021).

6.7 Privacy Concern

Though the permissioned blockchain allows only selected parties to access the data, some organisations are reluctant to disclose confidential information to approved members. Zero-knowledge proof is a recent technique studied by practitioners claiming to filter sensitive data in the network. Bangladesh has indicated the issue in its policy guidelines (Division, 2020).

6.8 Users' awareness

Blockchain demands technological expertise from facilitators and users. Lack of users' technological awareness and complexity in setting up the system may compromise reliability (Sahu et al., 2023).

6.9 Administrative Authority

An administrative model for a permissioned blockchain network must exist. In case of network interruptions, cyber-attacks, or other disputes, the administrative team should be authorised to reverse the hassle and get the network back into regular operation. Nevertheless, the administrative methodologies have yet to be formulated (Hong Kong Monetary Authority, 2016).

6.10 Legal Implication

In permissioned blockchain, participating parties share personal data. Proper provision should be formulated referring to the purpose of data collection and specific future use. There should be specified legal implications for using the data in the future for a new initiative. Moreover, the legal system should address the bearing of any financial costs arising from bug attacks or defective codes (Hong Kong Monetary Authority, 2016). There is a need to establish internationally agreed-upon arrangements in this area that are harmonised with national laws.

6.11 New Legal Infrastructure

In the blockchain ecosystem, the computer codes are the law, but the code itself is not considered law in the existing legal system (CAICT, 2018). Though some of the LC examination process, which relies on human judgment, cannot be automated through a smart contract, there are substantial clauses of LC that would be captured in smart contracts in the future (Al-Amaren et al., 2020). So, in the future, the legal society and law firms should incorporate smart contracts into their practices. Tremendous efforts and training are needed to execute such contracts written in codes (Hong Kong Monetary Authority, 2016).

7 Conclusion

As trade volume among countries is growing at the pace of globalisation, there should be a consensus among countries on the application mechanism of several technologies. Disputes may arise in the case of discrete technological applications in an individual country. As Blockchain technology is still in its experimental stage in most application domains, the overview of the country-wise scenarios of the concepts, technological characteristics, governance, and supervision of the technology is needed to constitute consensus among them. The chapter has attempted to overview the application efforts of several Asian countries, which might motivate countries to create a unified and standardised trade financing platform in future. Countries' initiatives for facing challenges can be a learning point for other countries who need to catch up. A separate study is needed for a clarified guideline of administrative methodologies of the permissioned blockchain application in the trade finance section. More research is needed to ensure the success of blockchain-enabled LC applicability in several business sections, especially SME businesses. Training, educational courses, seminars, and workshops must be conducted to support the new infrastructural transitions. Financial institutions' coordinated team-based efforts would create a dynamic finance system worldwide.

References

Abdallah Alrabei, A. M. (2017). Perception of Jordanian bank employees on the relationship between accounting information quality (AIQ) and documentary credits. *International Journal of Applied Business and Economic Research, 15*(26), 409–419.

Acheson, N. (2021). China's ICO ban: Understandable, reasonable and (probably) temporary. *CoinDesk*. Retrieved March 21, 2024, from https://www.coindesk.com/markets/2017/09/12/chinas-ico-ban-understandable-reasonable-and-probably-temporary/

Ahmed, A. (2021). How permissioned blockchains can revolutionise Bangladesh's financial institutions. *The Business Standard*. Retrieved March 21, 2024, from https://www.tbsnews.net/features/panorama/how-permissioned-blockchains-can-revolutionise-bangladeshs-financial-institutions

Alavi, H. (2016). Documentary letters of credit, legal nature and sources of law. *Journal of legal studies, 17*(31), 106–121.

Al-Abri, K. M., Al-Shukaili, A. R., Al-Maqrshi, S. R., & Al-Badi, H. M. (2020). Modernizing letter of credit with blockchain technology in Oman. *Journal of Student Research*, 1–5. https://doi.org/10.47611/jsr.vi.980

Al-Amaren, E. M., Ismail, C. T. B. M., & Nor, M. Z. B. M. (2020). The blockchain revolution: A game-changing in the letter of credit (l/c)? *International Journal of Advanced Science and Technology, 29*(3), 6052–6058. 10.20961/sersc.org/journals/index.php/IJAST/article/view/6747

Bank, B. (2010, August). *Bangladesh electronic funds transfer network*. Payment Systems Division, Department of Currency Management and Payment Systems. Bangladesh Bank. Retrieved March 21, 2024, from https://www.bb.org.bd/aboutus/regulationguideline/beftn_operatingrules.pdf

Bank, C. (2021). *City bank executes first ever cross-border Shariah-based blockchain LC transaction Partnering with ITFC*. City Bank. Retrieved March 21, 2024, from https://www.thecitybank.com/newsevent/city-bank-executes-first-ever-cross-border-shariah-based-blockchain-lc-transaction-partnering-with-itfc#:~:text=Login-,City Bank Executes First Ever Cross-border Shariah Based, LC Transaction Partnering with ITFC&text=

Bank, P. (2020). *Prime Bank becomes the first Bangladeshi Bank to execute interbank blockchain LC transaction*. Prime Bank. Retrieved March 21, 2024, from https://www.tbsnews.net/economy/banking/prime-bank-becomes-first-bangladeshi-bank-execute-interbank-blockchain-lc-166393

Bank, W. (2017). Distributed ledger technology (DLT) and blockchain. *FinTech Note, 1*, 1–60. Retrieved March 21, 2024, from https://documents.worldbank.org/en/publication/documents-reports/documentdetail/177911513714062215/distributed-ledger-technology-dlt-and-blockchain

Barreto, E. (2017). Hong Kong, Singapore to link up trade finance blockchain platforms. *Reuters*. Retrieved March 21, 2024, from https://www.reuters.com/article/us-hongkong-singapore-fintech-idUSKBN1CU0JY

BFSI. (2021). *How Indian banks are leveraging blockchain technology*. Retrieved March 21, 2024, from https://bfsi.economictimes.indiatimes.com/news/banking/how-indian-banks-are-leveraging-blockchain-technology/88027231

Bischoff, O., & Seuring, S. (2021). Opportunities and limitations of public blockchain-based supply chain traceability. *Modern Supply Chain Research and Applications*, *3*(3), 226–243. https://doi.org/10.1108/mscra-07-2021-0014

Bondi, A. B. (2000). *Characteristics of scalability and their impact on performance* [Conference session]. Proceedings Second International Workshop on Software and Performance WOSP 2000, April, pp. 195–203. https://doi.org/10.1145/350391.350432

Boonyanan, P. (2019). Electronic transaction law on Blockchain as a legal measure for the emerging digital economy. *The Association of Thai Professionals in the European Region*. Retrieved March 21, 2024, from https://atper.eu/wp-content/uploads/2019/07/Electronic-Transaction-Law-_PBoonyanan.pdf

Broeckaert, L. (2022). Digital transformation in Japan: Assessing business opportunities for EU SMEs. *EU-Japan Center for Industrial Cooperation, February*. Retrieved March 21, 2024, from https://www.eu-japan.eu/sites/default/files/publications/docs/Digital-Transformation-Japan-Assessing-opportunities-forEU-SMEs.pdf

CAICT. (2018). Blockchain White Paper. *China Academy of Information and Communication Technology*. https://doi.org/10.2139/ssrn.4176506

Caudevilla, O. (2021). Blockchain-based trade finance offers opportunities. *China Daily*. Retrieved March 21, 2024, from https://www.chinadaily.com.cn/a/202108/06/WS610cdb05a310efa1bd66737d.html

Chainalysis. (2022). *The 2022 Global Crypto Adoption Index*. Retrieved March 21, 2024, from https://www.chainalysis.com/blog/2022-global-crypto-adoption-index/

Chang, S. E., Chen, Y. C., & Wu, T. C. (2019). Exploring blockchain technology in international trade: Business process re-engineering for letter of credit. *Industrial Management and Data Systems*, *119*(8), 1712–1733. https://doi.org/10.1108/IMDS-12-2018-0568

Chang, S. E., Luo, H. L., & Chen, Y. (2020). Blockchain-enabled trade finance innovation: A potential paradigm shift on using the letter of credit. *Sustainability (Switzerland)*, *12*(1), 188. https://doi.org/10.3390/su12010188

CheHashim, R., & Mahdzan, N. S. (2014). Fraud in letter of credit transactions: The experience of Malaysian bankers. *International Journal of Law, Crime and Justice*, *42*(3), 224–236. https://doi.org/10.1016/j.ijlcj.2014.01.008

Chitranshi, U., & Chawla, S. K. (2020). Application view towards Blockchain: Demystifying the myths. *Cryptocurrencies and Blockchain Technology Applications*, pp. 281–295. https://doi.org/10.1002/9781119621201.ch15

Chmielewska, M. K. (2005). Documentary letter of credit: A pivotal case for the inefficiency of the law of contract. *Revue Générale de Droit Documentary*, 35(4), 487–532. https://doi.org/10.7202/1027179ar

COINGEEK. (2022). *China in the global lead with over 1,400 blockchain firms: Report*. Retrieved March 21, 2024, from https://coingeek.com/china-in-global-lead-with-over-1400-blockchain-firms-report/#:~:text=In a document titled "2022, the world's biggest blockchain hubs

CONTOUR. (2020a). The network of networks: Digitalizing trade finance. *Contour Network*, 1–10. https://doi.org/10.4337/9781783478668.00013

CONTOUR. (2020b). Contour facilitates the first blockchain Letter of Credit in Bangladesh. *Contour Network*. Retrieved March 21, 2024, from https://www.contour.network/press-release/contour-facilitates-first-blockchain-letter-of-credit-in-bangladesh/

Deloitte. (2018). What is a blockchain? *Modus*, pp. 1, 20–23. Retrieved March 21, 2024, from https://www2.deloitte.com/content/dam/Deloitte/uk/Documents/Innovation/deloitte-uk-what-is-blockchain-2016.pdf

Desk, S. B. (2020). HSBC executes the country's first cross-border blockchain LC transaction. *The Daily Star*. Retrieved March 21, 2024, from https://www.thedailystar.net/business/news/hsbc-executes-countrys-first-cross-border-blockchain-lc-transaction-1987393

Dharmaraj, S. (2022). Blockchain Technology on the Rise in Vietnam. *OPENGOV Vietnam*. Retrieved March 21, 2024, from https://opengovasia.com/blockchain-technology-on-the-rise-in-vietnam/

Division, C. T. (2020). National Blockchain strategy: Bangladesh information and communication technology division. *ResearchGate, January*. Retrieved March 21, 2024, from https://www.researchgate.net/publication/343574573_National_Blockchain_Strategy_Banglades

Dzhondzhorov, D. (2023). *China establishes national blockchain organization*. Retrieved March 21, 2024, from https://cryptopotato.com/china-establishes-national-blockchain-organization-report/#

European Commission. (2024). Sustainable finance. *European Commission*. https://doi.org/https://joint-research-centre.ec.europa.eu/scientific-activities-z/sustainable-finance_en?prefLang=mt

Gawusu, S., Zhang, X., Ahmed, A., Jamatutu, S. A., Miensah, E. D., Amadu, A. A., & Osei, F. A. J. (2022). Renewable energy sources from the perspective of blockchain integration: From theory to application. *Sustainable Energy Technologies and Assessments*, *52*. https://doi.org/10.1016/j.seta.2022.102108

Giungato, P., Rana, R., Tarabella, A., & Tricase, C. (2017). Current trends in sustainability of bitcoins and related blockchain technology. *Sustainability (Switzerland)*, *9*(12). https://doi.org/10.3390/su9122214

Gonzalez, M. (2018). Blockchain in Japan. *EU-Japan Center for Industrial Cooperation*. Retrieved March 21, 2024, from https://www.eu-japan.eu/sites/default/files/publications/docs/blockchaininjapan-martagonzalez.pdf

GOV.UK. (2019). *Thailand: Ministry of commerce and British embassy join forces to bring blockchain for trade facilitation*. Retrieved March 21, 2024, from https://www.gov.uk/government/news/thailand-ministry-of-commerce-and-british-embassy-join-forces-to-bring-blockchain-for-trade-facilitation

Grandin, A., & Eriksson, M. (2021). *International payments, trade finance & blockchain: A qualitative study about the impact of blockchain implementation*. Retrieved March 21, 2024, from https://umu.diva-portal.org/smash/get/diva2:1571481/FULLTEXT02.pdf

Griffin, O. (2016). Korea Financial Investment Association launches blockchain consortium with 26 technology and financial firms. *StarupBeat*. Retrieved March 21, 2024, from https://startupbeat.com/blockchain-consortium-korea/24301/

Hasan, M. (2020). StanChart executes Bangladesh's first-ever blockchain LC transaction. *The Daily Star*. https://www.thedailystar.net/business/news/stanchart-executes-bangladeshs-first-ever-blockchain-lc-transaction-1945733

Harris, W. L., & Wonglimpiyarat, J. (2019). Blockchain platform and future bank competition. *Foresight*, *21*(6), 625–639. https://doi.org/10.1108/FS-12-2018-0113

Hodapp, D., & Hanelt, A. (2022). Interoperability in the era of digital innovation: An information systems research agenda. *Journal of Information Technology*, *37*(4), 407–427. https://doi.org/10.1177/02683962211064304

Hong Kong Monetary Authority. (2016). Whitepaper on distributed ledger technology. *Astri*, p. 98. Retrieved March 21, 2024, from http://www.hkma.gov.hk/media/eng/

doc/key-functions/finanical-infrastructure/Whitepaper_On_Distributed_Ledger_Technology.pdf

HSBC. (2019a). *HSBC executes the first live blockchain letter-of-credit transaction in Korea and Vietnam. July*. Retrieved March 21, 2024, from https://www.tokenpost.com/HSBC-executes-first-blockchain-LC-transaction-between-Korea-and-Vietnam-2780

HSBC. (2019b). *HSBC leads Malaysia's first pilot blockchain letter-of-credit transaction **The first-ever live pilot blockchain Letter-of-Credit transaction in Malaysia** **Shows that blockchain solutions can be used by large corporates as well as smaller firms** **Enco. October* 1–3. Retrieved March 21, 2024, from https://www.about.hsbc.com.my/-/media/malaysia/en/news-and-media/191014-release-hsbc-leads-malaysias-first-pilot-blockchain-lc-transaction.pdf

IBM. (2020). Bank of Thailand launches world's first government savings bond on IBM blockchain technology. *IBM Newsroom*. Retrieved March 21, 2024, from https://newsroom.ibm.com/2020-10-05-Bank-of-Thailand-Launches-Worlds-First-Government-Savings-Bond-on-IBM-Blockchain-Technology

ICC. (2022). ICC trade register report: Global risks in trade finance. *International Chamber of Commerce, 33*(1), 1–12. Retrieved March 21, 2024, from https://iccwbo.org/news-publications/policies-reports/icc-trade-register-report/

IMD. (2022). *World digital competitiveness ranking 2022*. Retrieved March 21, 2024, from https://www.imd.org/centers/wcc/world-competitiveness-center/rankings/world-digital-competitiveness-ranking/

IMF. (2017). *IMF Committee on Balance of Payments Statistics*, 11. https://doi.org/10.5089/9781475583342.044

IMF. (2019). *Thirty-second meeting of the IMF committee on balance of payments statistics recording of letters of credit in external sector statistics*. Retrieved March 21, 2024, from https://www.imf.org/external/pubs/ft/bop/2019/pdf/19-16c.pdf

IMF. (2023). *World economic outlook: A Rocky REcovery* (Issue April). Retrieved March 21, 2024, from https://www.imf.org/-/media/Files/Publications/WEO/2023/April/English/text.ashx

IMF. (2024). *Real GDP growth (Annual percent change)*. Retrieved March 21, 2024, from https://www.imf.org/external/datamapper/NGDP_RPCH@WEO/OEMDC/ADVEC/WEOWORLD

India, R. B. (2017). *Applications of Blockchain technology: To banking and financial sector in India* (pp. 272–295). Institute for Development and Research in Banking Technology. https://doi.org/10.4135/9781526435651.n11

InfoSystems. (2017). The seven steps to a blockchain-based Letter of Credit (LC) transaction. Retrieved March 21, 2024, from https://infosystems.mu/the-seven-steps-to-a-blockchain-based-letter-of-credit-lc-transaction

Insight, L. (2019). *HSBC executes blockchain letters of credit in Malaysia*. Retrieved March 21, 2024, from https://www.ledgerinsights.com/hsbc-blockchain-letter-of-credit-malaysia/

Insight, L. (2020a). HSBC, ING-backed letter of credit blockchain contour launches in Singapore. *Ledger Insight*. Retrieved March 21, 2024, from https://www.ledgerinsights.com/letter-of-credit-blockchain-contour-hsbc-ing/

Insight, L. (2020b). *MUFG executes blockchain letters of credit using Komgo*. Retrieved March 21, 2024, from https://www.ledgerinsights.com/mufg-blockchain-letter-credit-komgo/

Javaid, M., Haleem, A., Singh, R. P., Suman, R., & Khan, S. (2022). A review of Blockchain Technology applications for financial services. *Bench Council Transactions on Benchmarks, Standards and Evaluations*, *2*(3), 100073. https://doi.org/10.1016/j.tbench.2022.100073

Jiang, L., Xie, S., Maharjan, S., & Zhang, Y. (2019). Blockchain empowered wireless power transfer for green and secure internet of things. *IEEE Network*, *33*(6), 164–171. https://doi.org/10.1109/MNET.001.1900008

Jiang, S., Li, Y., Lu, Q., Hong, Y., Guan, D., Xiong, Y., & Wang, S. (2021). Policy assessments for the carbon emission flows and sustainability of Bitcoin blockchain operation in China. *Nature Communications*, *12*. https://doi.org/10.1038/s41467-021-22256-3

John, A. (2019). HSBC processes the first blockchain letter of credit using Chinese yuan. *Reuters*. Retrieved March 21, 2024, from https://www.reuters.com/article/us-hsbc-hldg-blockchain-idUSKCN1VN1QL

Karim, S., Rabbani, M. R., & Bawazir, H. (2022). Applications of blockchain technology in the finance and banking industry beyond digital currencies. In S. Khan, M. Syed, R. Hammad, & A. Bushager (Eds.), *Blockchain technology and computational excellence for society 5.0* (pp. 216–238). IGI Global. https://doi.org/10.4018/978-1-7998-8382-1.ch011

Kawai, K., & Nagase, T. (2022). Blockchain 2022. *Anderson Mori & Tomotsune*. Retrieved April 17, 2023, from https://practiceguides.chambers.com/practice-guides/blockchain-2022/japan

Khalil, M. A., Kerbache, L., & El Omri, A. (2021). Digitizing trade finance using blockchain technology illustration of letter of credit process [Conference session]. *Proceedings of the International Conference on Industrial Engineering and Operations Management*, pp. 1580–1591. Retrieved March 21, 2024, from https://ieomsociety.org/proceedings/2021rome/563.pdf

Khamzaeva, A. M., Menshchikova, V. I., Karbekova, M. Z., & Tazhiyeva, Z. N. (2023). Applied solutions for ESG management of entrepreneurship in digital economy markets with the help of blockchain. *Smart Green Innovations in Industry 4.0*, 195–202. https://doi.org/10.1007/978-3-031-45830-9

KOFIA. (2023). *Korea financial investment association (KOFIA)*. Retrieved March 21, 2024, from http://icsa.global/korea-financial-investment-association-kofia

Krungthai. (2023). *Krungthai and Contour launch digital L/C, advancing trade finance and empowering Thai businesses in the global market*. Krungthai Compass Research Center. Retrieved March 21, 2024, from https://www.ryt9.com/en/prg/265159

Lafourcade, P., & Lamberd-Platet, M. (2020). About blockchain interoperability. *Information Processing Letters*, *161*. https://doi.org/10.1016/j.ipl.2020.105976

Lian, G. (2022). Research on credit algorithm of international trade enterprises based on blockchain. *Mathematical Problems in Engineering*, *2022*. https://doi.org/10.1155/2022/4768868

Macrotrends. (2023). *Bangladesh trade to GDP ratio 1960-2023*. Retrieved March 21, 2024, from https://www.macrotrends.net/countries/BGD/bangladesh/trade-gdp-ratio#:~:text=Trade is the sum of a 5.31%25

MeitY. (2021). National strategy on Blockchain. *Ministry of Electronics & Information Technology, Government of India*, *1*(1), 1–52. https://doi.org/10.5937/zz0702059r

Mizuho. (2017). Conclusion of trade transaction using blockchain and distributed ledger technology. In (Vol. 87, Issue 1,2). Retrieved March 21, 2024. Mizuho Financial Group, Inc. from https://www.sompo-japan.co.jp/-/media/SJNK/files/english/news/sjnk/2017/e_20170707_1.pdf?la=ja-JP

Mooney, J. L., & Blodgett, M. (1995). Letters of credit in the global economy: Implications for international trade. *Journal of International Accounting, Auditing and Taxation*, *4*(2), 175–183. https://doi.org/10.1016/1061-9518(95)90016-0

MOSTI. (2021). *National blockchain roadmap*. Retrieved March 21, 2024, from https://www.mosti.gov.my/wp-content/uploads/2022/08/National-Blockchain-Roadmap-2021-2025.pdf

Muheidat, F., Patel, D., Tammisetty, S., Tawalbeh, L. A., & Tawalbeh, M. (2021). Emerging concepts using blockchain and big data. *Procedia Computer Science*, *198*, 15–22. https://doi.org/10.1016/j.procs.2021.12.206

Mulligan, C. (2017). Blockchain – a brief overview. *Imperial College London*. Retrieved March 21, 2024, from https://na.eventscloud.com/file_uploads/b4d722450d854c8b-9fdaf14823c49a0c_MULLIGAN_Blockchain-brief-overview.pdf

Murray, A., Skene, K., & Hayne, K. (2017). The circular economy: An interdisciplinary exploration of the concept and application in a global context. *Journal of Business Ethics*, *140*(3), 369–380. https://doi.org/10.1007/s10551-015-2693-2

Narayanan, A., Bonneau, J., Felten, E., Miller, A., & Goldfeder, S. (2016). Bitcoin and cryptocurrency technologies. *Journal of Information Technology*, *21*(4). https://doi.org/10.1016/S1353-4858(16)30074-5

News, V. (2021). *VPBank successfully tests blockchain LC*. Retrieved March 21, 2024, from https://vietnamnews.vn/economy/1031211/vpbank-successfully-tests-blockchain-lc.html#:~:text=A

OECD. (2019). The policy environment for blockchain innovation and adoption: 2019 OECD global blockchain policy forum summary report. *OECD Blockchain Policy Series*. Retrieved March 21, 2024, from www.oecd.org/finance/2019-OECD-Global-Blockchain-Policy-Forum-Summary-Report.pdf

OECD. (2021). Trade finance for SMEs in the digital era. *OECD SME and Entrepreneurship Papers*, *24*(24). Retrieved March 21, 2024, from https://dx.doi.org/10.1787/e505fe39-en

Oh, J., & Shong, I. (2017). A case study on business model innovations using Blockchain: focusing on financial institutions. *Asia Pacific Journal of Innovation and Entrepreneurship*, *11*(3), 335–344. https://doi.org/10.1108/apjie-12-2017-038

Osborne, C. (2017). *China bans cryptocurrency ICOs*. Retrieved March 21, 2024, from https://www.zdnet.com/article/china-bans-cryptocurrency-icos/

Pathak, K. (2018). *Reliance receives India's first LC payment via blockchain*. Retrieved March 21, 2024, from https://www.livemint.com/Companies/XFxvBWrOho03bxwZOKCaRJ/Reliance-receives-Indias-first-LC-payment-via-blockchain.html

Persio, S. L. (2016). Banks bring blockchain innovation to letters of credit. *Global Trade Review*. Retrieved March 21, 2024, from https://www.gtreview.com/news/asia/banks-blockchain-innovation-letters-of-credit/

Pongnumkul, S., Bunditlurdruk, T., Chaovalit, P., & Tharatipyakul, A. (2021). A cross-sectional review of blockchain in Thailand: Research literature, education courses, and industry projects. *Applied Sciences (Switzerland)*, *11*(11). https://doi.org/10.3390/app11114928

Post, T. A. (2023). *Digitalising Japan & ASEAN Trade With Blockchain*. Retrieved March 21, 2024, from https://theaseanpost.com/article/digitalising-japan-asean-trade-blockchain

Power, T. (2013). Tata power partners with contour for a blockchain-based digital trade finance network. *Tata Power*. Retrieved March 21, 2024, from https://www.tatapower.com/media/PressReleaseDetails/2002/tata-power-partners-with-contour-for-blockchain-based-digital-trade-finance-network

Prodent, L. (2022). *Vietnam tasks government agencies to prepare legal framework for cryptocurrencies, virtual assets*. Vietnam Briefing. Retrieved March 21, 2024, from https://www.vietnam-briefing.com/news/vietnam-tasks-government-agencies-prepare-legal-framework-cryptocurrencies-virtual-assets.html/

PWC. (2018). Building block (chain) for a better planet. *Pwc, September*, 1–51. Retrieved March 21, 2024, from https://www.pwc.com/gx/en/sustainability/assets/blockchain-for-a-better-planet.pdf

Quang, T. N., Hang, N. T., & Duong, N. D. (2022). *How to classify and regulate crypto in Vietnam?* YKVN. Retrieved March 21, 2024, from https://www.lexology.com/library/detail.aspx?g=88a6df76-f9a8-4794-9417-3e7747ea3b0c

Quoc, K. L., Trong, P. N., Van, H. L., Vo, H. K., Huong, L. H., Dang, K. T., Gia, K. H., Phu, L. V. C., Quoc, D. N. T., Tran, N. H., Nghia, H. T., Khanh, B. L., & Tuan, K. L. (2022). Letter-of-credit chain: Cross-border exchange based on blockchain and smart contracts. *International Journal of Advanced Computer Science and Applications, 13*(8), 890–899. https://doi.org/10.14569/ijacsa.2022.01308103

Rahman, M., Saha, N. K., Sarker, N. I., Sultana, A., & Prodhan, A. Z. M. (2017). Problems and prospects of electronic banking in Bangladesh: A case study on Dutch-Bangla bank limited. *American Journal of Operations Management and Information Systems, 2*, 42–53. https://doi.org/10.11648/j.ajomis.20170201.17

Rana, R. L., Giungato, P., Tarabella, A., & Tricase, C. (2019). Blockchain applications and sustainability issues. *Amfiteatru Economic, 21*(Special Issue 13), 669. https://doi.org/10.24818/EA/2019/S13/861

Ren, Y.-S., Ma, C.-Q., Chen, X.-Q., Lei, Y.-T., & Wang, Y.-R. (2023a). A peer-to-peer trading model to enhance resilience: A blockchain-based smart grids with machine learning analysis towards sustainable development goals. *Research in International Business and Finance, 64*. https://doi.org/10.1016/j.ribaf.2022.101871

Ren, Y. S., Ma, C. Q., Chen, X. Q., Lei, Y. T., & Wang, Y. R. (2023b). Sustainable finance and blockchain: A systematic review and research agenda. *Research in International Business and Finance, 64*(November 2022), 101871. https://doi.org/10.1016/j.ribaf.2022.101871

Review, V. I. (2021). *MB becomes the first Vietnamese commercial bank offering blockchain-enabled L/C services.* Retrieved March 21, 2024, from https://vir.com.vn/mb-becomes-the-first-vietnamese-commercial-bank-offering-blockchain-enabled-lc-services-89965.html

Saberi, S., Kouhizadeh, M., Sarkis, J., & Shen, L. (2019). Blockchain technology and its relationships to sustainable supply chain management. *International Journal of Production Research, 57*(7), 2117–2135. https://doi.org/10.1080/00207543.2018.1533261

Saheb, T., & Mamaghani, F. H. (2021). Exploring the barriers and organisational values of blockchain adoption in the banking industry. *Journal of High Technology Management Research, 32*(2), 100417. https://doi.org/10.1016/j.hitech.2021.100417

Sahu, A. K., Katyayan, A., Khandey, U., Jangde, P., Sahu, A. K., & Sahu, N. K. (2023). Adaptation of blockchain technology in SCM for steering managerial strategies: investigative study under Indian context. *Journal of International Logistics and Trade*, 21(1), 18–40. https://doi.org/10.1108/jilt-06-2022-0020

Schulte, U. G. (2013). New business models for a radical change in resource efficiency. *Environmental Innovation and Societal Transitions, 9*, 43–47. https://doi.org/10.1016/j.eist.2013.09.006

Sepanloo, H. (2019). A blockchain-based approach towards overcoming fraud in issuing letter of credit [Conference session]. *8th Annual Conference of Electronic Banking and Payment System*, pp. 1–12. Retrieved March 21, 2024, from https://conf.mbri.ac.ir/ebps8/assets/Articles/Paper-1548.pdf

Shivendu, S. (2019). National strategy for blockchain India. *National Institute for Smart Government, December* 1–41. Retrieved March 21, 2024, from https://4c44db83-35be-491f-a87f-fc7c6a312fd0.filesusr.com/ugd/cc85ab_6dd677ce70124618b88c70be071f3eac.pdf

SMECorp. (2021). *Profile of MSMEs in 2016-2021.* Retrieved March 21, 2024, from https://www.smecorp.gov.my/index.php/en/policies/2020-02-11-08-01-24/profile-and-importance-to-the-economy

Standard Chartered. (2019). We have completed our first cross-border Letter of Credit blockchain transaction in the oil industry with PTT Group. *Standard Chartered.* Retrieved March 21, 2024, from https://www.sc.com/en/press-release/weve-completed-our-first-cross-border-letter-of-credit-blockchain-transaction-in-the-oil-industry-with-ptt-group/

Standard Chartered. (2020). *We have completed our first cross-bank Letter of Credit blockchain transaction between Vietnam and Thailand*. Retrieved March 21, 2024, from https://www.sc.com/en/press-release/weve-completed-our-first-cross-bank-letter-of-credit-blockchain-transaction-between-vietnam-and-thailand/

Star, T. (2019). *HSBC leads Malaysia's first blockchain letter-of-credit deal*. Retrieved April 17, 2023, from https://www.thestar.com.my/business/business-news/2019/10/14/hsbc-leads-malaysia039s-first-blockchain-letter-of-credit-deal

Taneja, S., Gupta, M., Bhushan, P., Bhatnagar, M., & Singh, A. (2023). Cultural marketing in the digital era. In *Cultural marketing and metaverse for consumer engagement* (pp. 109–122). IGI Global. https://doi.org/10.4018/978-1-6684-8312-1.ch008

Times, S. (2019). *Seven banks completed successful blockchain trials for LCs*. Retrieved April 17, 2023, from https://www.straitstimes.com/business/banking/seven-banks-complete-successful-blockchain-trial-for-lcs

Times, T. E. (2020). *State Bank of India deploys blockchain for trade finance*. Retrieved April 17, 2023, from https://economictimes.indiatimes.com/industry/banking/finance/banking/state-bank-of-india-deploys-blockchain-for-trade-finance/articleshow/73528868.cms

Tonby, O., Woetzel, J., Choi, W., Eloot, K., Dhawan, R., Seong, J., & Wang, P. (2019). The future of Asia. *McKinsey Global Institute*. Retrieved March 21, 2024, from https://www.mckinsey.com/~/media/mckinsey/featured insights/asia pacific/the future of asia asian flows and networks are defining the next phase of globalization/mgi-future-of-asia-flows-and-trade-discussion-paper-sep-2019.pdf

Upadhyay, A., Mukhuty, S., Kumar, V., & Kazancoglu, Y. (2021). Blockchain technology and the circular economy: Implications for sustainability and social responsibility. *Journal of Cleaner Production*, *293*, 126130. https://doi.org/10.1016/j.jclepro.2021.126130

Vahia, S. (2021). SBI, HDFC, ICICI and 12 other banks are joining forces to use blockchain to power Letters of Credit—a move that could be a boon for MSMEs. *Business Insider India*. Retrieved March 21, 2024, from https://www.businessinsider.in/cryptocurrency/news/sbi-hdfc-icici-and-12-others-banks-are-joining-forces-to-use-blockchain-to-power-letters-of-credit-a-move-that-could-be-a-boon-for-msmes/articleshow/83570874.cms

Vedapradha, R., & Ravi, H. (2023). Blockchain: an EOM approach to reconciliation in banking. *Innovation and Management Review*, *20*(1), 17–27. https://doi.org/10.1108/INMR-05-2020-0060

VentureBeat. (2020). *TradeTrust: Singapore, ICC, and 17 companies back trade digitalisation*. Retrieved March 21, 2024, from https://venturebeat.com/business/tradetrust-singapore-and-16-companies-back-perlin-blockchain-for-global-trade-platform/

Vranken, H. (2017). Sustainability of bitcoin and blockchains. *Current Opinion in Environmental Sustainability*, *28*, 1–9. https://doi.org/10.1016/j.cosust.2017.04.011

World Bank. (2024a). GDP growth (Annual %). *World Bank Open Data*. Retrieved March 21, 2024, from https://data.worldbank.org/indicator/NY.GDP.MKTP.KD.ZG

World Bank. (2024b). Imports of goods and services (current US$). *World Bank Open Data*. Retrieved March 21, 2024, from https://data.worldbank.org/indicator/NE.IMP.GNFS.CD?locations=US

World Bank. (2024c). Exports of goods and services (current US$). *World Bank Open Data*. Retrieved March 21, 2024, from https://data.worldbank.org/indicator/NE.EXP.GNFS.CD

World Economic Forum. PWC. (2020). Unlocking technology for the global goals: As part of frontier 2030: Fourth industrial revolution for global goals platform. *World Economic Forum, January*, 48. Retrieved March 21, 2024, from http://www3.weforum.org/docs/Unlocking_Technology_for_the_Global_Goals.pdf

Worldometer. (2023). *Asia Population (Live)*. Retrieved March 21, 2024, from https://www.worldometers.info/world-population/asia-population/#:~:text=Asia population is equivalent to,%22)%2C ordered by population

WTO. (2018). *Can Blockchain revolutionize international trade? World trade organization*. Retrieved March 21, 2024, from https://www.wto.org/english/res_e/booksp_e/blockchainrev18_e.pdf

Yuh, K. R. (2022). TradeTrust: Digitalising documents used in international trade. *Infocomm Media Development Authority of Singapore*. Retrieved March 21, 2024, from chrome-extension://efaidnbmnnnibpcajpcglclefindmkaj/https://www.unescap.org/sites/default/d8files/event-documents/APTFF%20CB%202022%20Session%204-2%20Mr.%20KAY%20Ren%20Yuh.pdf

Zelbst, P. J., Green, K. W., Sower, V. E., & Bond, P. L. (2020). The impact of RFID, IIoT, and Blockchain technologies on supply chain transparency. *Journal of Manufacturing Technology Management*, *31*(3), 441–457. https://doi.org/10.1108/JMTM-03-2019-0118

Zhao, W. (2018). 9 Malaysian banks team up for trade finance blockchain apps. *CoinDesk*. Retrieved March 21, 2024, from https://www.coindesk.com/markets/2018/03/23/9-malaysian-banks-team-up-for-trade-finance-blockchain-apps/

Zheng, Z., Xie, S., Dai, H., Chen, X., & Wang, H. (2017). An overview of blockchain technology: Architecture, consensus, and future trends [Conference session]. Proceedings - 2017 IEEE 6th International Congress on Big Data, BigData Congress 2017, October, pp. 557–564. https://doi.org/10.1109/BigDataCongress.2017.85

Chapter 18

Cradle of Research Gaps: Reflections on Green Orientation

Anuradha Iddagoda[a], Rohitha Abeysinghe[b], Hiranya Dissanayake[c], Narayanage Jayantha Dewasiri[d] and W. P. Richard Wickramaratne[e]

[a]*University of Sri Jayewardenepura, Sri Lanka*
[b]*National Defence College, Sri Lanka*
[c]*Wayamba University of Sri Lanka, Sri Lanka*
[d]*Sabaragamuwa University of Sri Lanka, Sri Lanka; University Center for Research and Development (UCRD), Chandigarh University, Punjab, India*
[e]*University of Peradeniya, Sri Lanka*

Abstract

Purpose: This chapter examines the concept of "green orientation" within corporate environments by systematically reviewing literature indexed in Scopus from 2000 to 2023. The focus is on addressing knowledge gaps related to understanding green orientation, emphasising sustainability and stability as indispensable components for organisational success.

Methodology: Utilising a bibliometric analysis, a statistical panorama of the literature landscape is presented. The study identifies and delineates five discernible research gaps, constructing a conceptual framework or nomological network.

Findings: Noteworthy discoveries emanate from this study, notably identifying research lacunae and developing a conceptual framework delineating the interrelatedness among the discerned constructs. The framework accentuates the significance of High-Performance Work Practices, authentic leadership, green orientation, employee engagement, and job performance in cultivating corporate sustainability.

Implications: In practical terms, this research provides valuable insights for organisations aspiring to augment their sustainability endeavours. The comprehension of interrelationships among the identified constructs

Green Management: A New Paradigm in the World of Business, 339–357

Published under exclusive licence by Emerald Publishing Limited
doi:10.1108/978-1-83797-442-920241018

serves as a strategic guide for decision-making, empowering businesses to align with the principles of green orientation and advocate for environmentally friendly practices.

Originality: The significance of this research lies in its systematic response to the imperative for comprehensive investigations into green orientation. The formulated conceptual framework introduces a distinctive perspective, establishing a groundwork for subsequent research endeavours. Moreover, it constitutes an original synthesis of quantitative and qualitative knowledge in the field, thereby advancing scholarly understanding.

Keywords: Green orientation; high-performance work practices; authentic leadership; employee engagement; employee job performance; research gaps; military context

JEL Classifications: D22; L21; M14; M51

1. Introduction

An increasing number of individuals value adopting an eco-friendly lifestyle due to their commitment to abstaining from detrimental practices towards the environment or nature – Arulrajah (2014) associates "green" with eco-friendliness. Shaharudin et al. (2015) elucidate that orientation, as mentioned by Iddagoda et al. (2022), is the fundamental awareness or underlying ideology shaping businesses' internal and external practices. As defined by Iddagoda et al. (2022), green orientation involves transforming an individual's core awareness and activities towards ecologically friendly approaches to attain environmentally sustainable objectives.

Meskhi et al. (2020) emphasises the ecological and social orientation of the "green" model, highlighting the potential for societal benefits through the harmonisation of relationships and the consideration of environmental and societal interests by businesses and civil society. Fok et al. (2012) expand the concept of greening to encompass various eco-friendly actions, such as waste reduction, the use of environmentally friendly products, and the provision of organic food. Viola and Marinelli (2014) define green orientation as adopting green practices and ecologically friendly behaviour, including supplying natural resources, metabolising pollutants, and protecting landscape and nature. Hong et al. (2009) posit that successful enterprises prioritise green orientation to produce environmentally sound products, while companies more committed to a green strategy may face significant costs associated with environmental disasters.

The primary objective of this study is to offer an overview of the prevailing state of research on green orientation, with specific research objectives aimed at delineating the scope of the study: (1) to discern current publication trends in green orientation literacy across time, journals, disciplines, authors, and affiliated countries; (2) to identify influential studies and thematic research areas within this domain; (3) to pinpoint research gaps present in the literature on green orientation; and (4) to propose a conceptual framework based on the identified research gaps and trends.

2. Methodology

The primary aim of this study is to employ bibliometric analysis and a systematic literature review (SLR) approach to fulfil its primary objective. Following the framework established by Zupic and Čater (2014), the bibliometric analysis undergoes five key stages: research design, data compilation, analysis, visualisation, and interpretation, as depicted in the research method stated in Fig. 18.1.

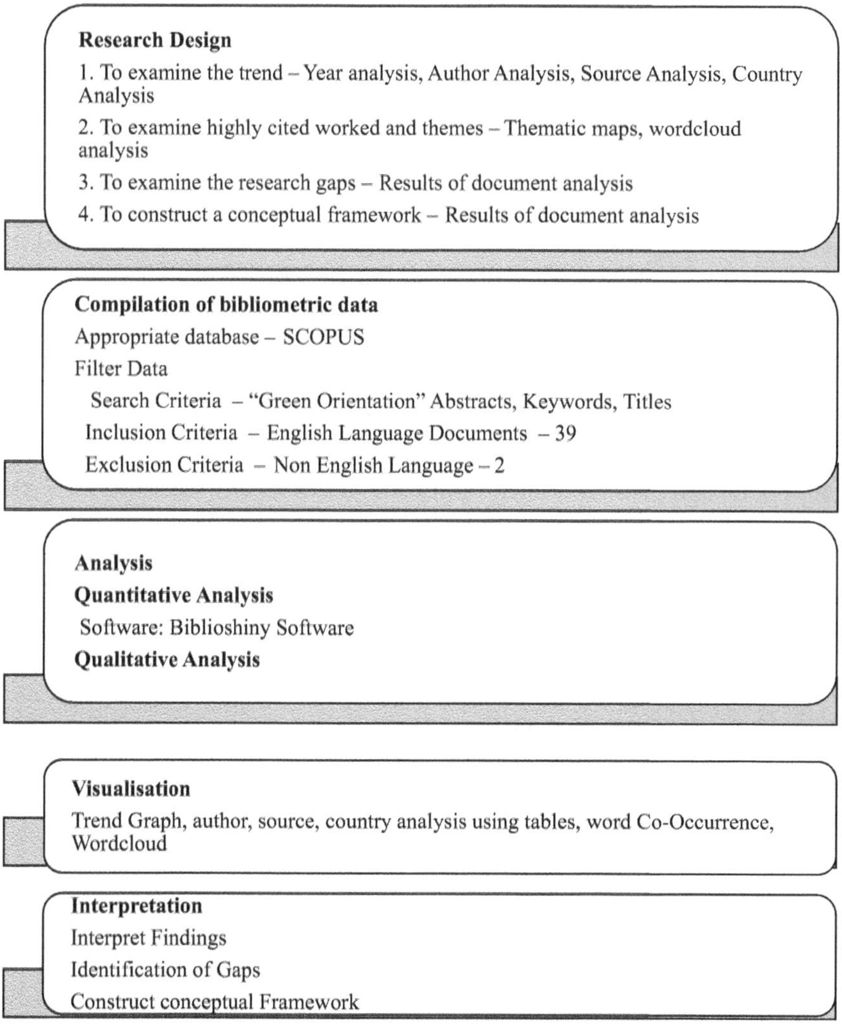

Fig. 18.1. Research Method. *Source*: Adapted from Zupic and Čater (2014).

SLR approach has been utilised to uncover the research gaps as investigated by Dewasiri et al. (2022), Jayawardena and Dewasiri (2023), and Rathnasiri and De-Silva (2023).

Publication trends are scrutinised through bibliometric quantitative analysis, delving into the quantitative aspects of scholarly output. Subsequently, an exploration of influential studies and themes is conducted through bibliometric qualitative analysis, emphasising qualitative attributes of significance. The third objective entails identifying research gaps based on the outcomes of both quantitative and qualitative studies. Finally, the fourth objective involves the construction of a conceptual framework informed by the identified research gaps and trends.

Data for this study were gathered from Scopus, a preeminent database for published papers and citations, in December 2021 to extract pertinent information. The researchers examined data from 2000 to 2021 during this search process conducted in December 2021, utilising the phrase "Green Orientation," which yielded 40 articles. Subsequently, the search was refined to include only English-written articles, resulting in 39 articles after excluding two non-English language documents. The final database comprises 39 articles, and the primary information from this collection is detailed in Table 18.1, subject to bibliometric analysis.

Table 18.1 reveals information about research books and journals serving as sources, indicating that the initial article on green orientation was published in 2000. The average number of years elapsed since publication (calculated by dividing the total years by the number of publications) is 5.64. Additionally, the average number of citations per document is 11.44 (computed by dividing the total citations by the number of records), signifying an average of eleven citations per document.

A qualitative examination was employed to refine the database following the quantitative analysis suggested by Sakshi et al. (2020), Centobelli et al. (2020), and Shroff et al. (2024). Publications underwent scrutiny based on abstracts, and full-length papers were consulted when there was ambiguity regarding their relevance. Articles focusing on social science background or business management were nominated for final analysis to ensure the inclusion of pertinent literature. Consequently, the study researchers selected 18 articles for further qualitative analysis. These 18 articles undergo qualitative scrutiny to identify research gaps and contribute to developing the conceptual framework.

Table 18.1. Main Information About Data.

Timespan	**2000:2023**
Sources (Journals, Books, etc.)	50
Documents	63
Annual Growth Rate %	11.41
Document Average Age	5.65
Average citations per doc	11.44
References	3395

Source: Constructed by the authors with Biblioshiny Software.

Quantitative data analysis is conducted utilising Biblioshiny software and VOSviewer. Trend analysis examines changes in publications from 2000 to 2022, providing insights into the current trajectory of the research area. Author and Source analyses rely on total publications and citations, comprehensively understanding influential contributors and authoritative sources. The country analysis is based on full publications and citations, shedding light on the geographical distribution of research activity.

Additionally, Biblioshiny software is employed to construct word clouds, visually representing the most prominent terms within the selected literature. VOSviewer software generates Co-Occurrence graphs, illustrating the relationships between key terms.

Finally, a qualitative analysis of highly cited documents is undertaken to extract valuable insights. This analysis also serves to identify research gaps, contributing to the overarching objective of constructing a conceptual framework based on a comprehensive understanding of the existing literature.

Indeed, author analysis is instrumental in discerning prominent contributors within the field, facilitating a closer examination of their publications and areas of expertise. This scrutiny aids in identifying key thought leaders and influential voices. Country analysis is crucial for assessing empirical gaps on a global scale, providing insights into the distribution of research efforts and potential regional variations in focus or contribution.

Thematic maps and a review of highly cited documents are pivotal in unravelling research gaps and significant trends within the current landscape. This comprehensive approach ensures a nuanced understanding of the existing literature, enabling the formulation of a conceptual framework that encapsulates the critical dimensions of green orientation research.

3. Results and Discussion

3.1. Trend Analysis

The trend analysis involves assessing the evolution of annual publications, conducting author analysis, scrutinising journals, and analysing the contributions of different countries.

Fig. 18.2 illustrates the publication trend in green orientation research spanning the entire millennium to the conclusion of the twenty-first century. The findings suggest a discernible upward trajectory in exploring topics related to green orientation within the scientific literature. In 2001, specific green orientations such as "ecologism," "mainstream environmentalism," and "market environmentalism" were introduced, each delineating its distinct set of principles. Fig. 18.1 depicts articles addressing green orientation themes that have consistently risen since 2004. From the commencement of 2009, the annual publications in the field of green orientation have maintained a relatively steady level, experiencing a notable increase in 2009 but subsequently declining. Notably, the number of green orientation articles published in 2023 increased after the COVID-19 pandemic. Furthermore, the average number of citations per year has demonstrated a progressive growth throughout this period.

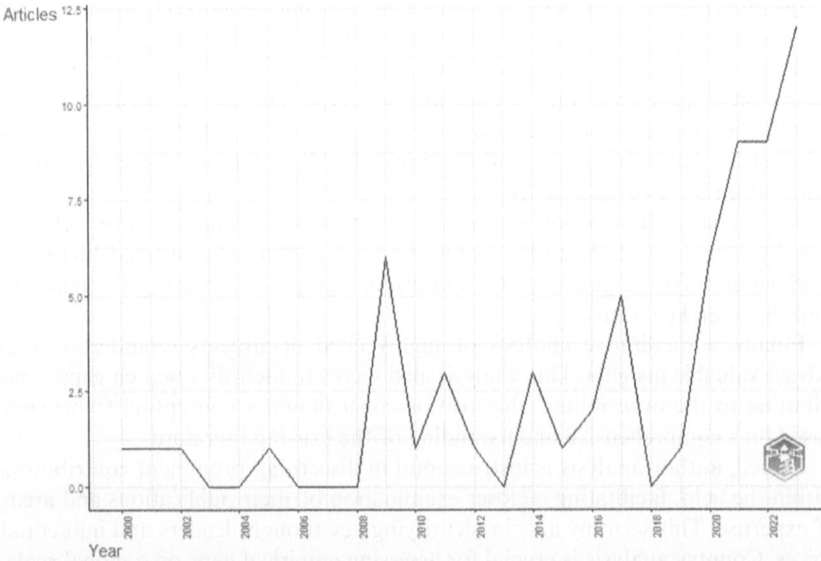

Fig. 18.2. Annual Scientific Production. *Source*: Constructed by the authors with Biblioshiny Software.

Table 18.2. Author Analysis.

Authors	h_index	g_index	m_index	TC	NP	PY_start
Hong P	2	2	0.133	173	2	2009
Kwon H-B	1	1	0.067	139	1	2009
Roh JJ	1	1	0.067	139	1	2009
Choi G	1	1	0.067	79	1	2009
Parsa Hg	1	1	0.067	79	1	2009
Putrevu S	1	1	0.067	79	1	2009
Sigala M	1	1	0.067	79	1	2009
Contò F	1	1	0.143	70	1	2017
Fiore M	1	1	0.143	70	1	2017
Pellegrini G	1	1	0.143	70	1	2017

Source: Constructed by the authors with Biblioshiny Software.

3.2. Author Analysis

Table 18.2 provides a list of the most prolific authors in the field of green orientation. Notably, Hong P. emerges as the author with the highest citation count for their work in this domain, having authored two papers, each garnering an average of 74 citations. Kwon H. B. and Roh J. J. stand out as two particularly influential authors in green orientation, with their publications consistently receiving high acclaim, each attaining an average of over 100 citations per work. This underscores the significant contributions and impact of these authors within the field.

3.3. Source Analysis

The database, comprising 63 items disseminated across 50 journals, emphasises journals with notable citation records. Table 18.3 encapsulates the top ten journals with the highest citation counts for publications about green orientation.

Notably, these selected journals account for 31% of the identified publications. The *European Journal of Innovation Management* stands out with the most citations, boasting 139 citations for a singular document, attesting to its significant impact on green orientation research.

Table 18.3. Source Analysis.

Element	h_index	g_index	m_index	TC	NP	PY_start
European Journal of Innovation Management	1	1	0.067	139	1	2009
Journal of Cleaner Production	3	4	0.429	127	4	2017
Journal of Quality Assurance in Hospitality and Tourism	1	1	0.067	79	1	2009
Sustainability (Switzerland)	2	4	0.250	47	4	2016
Journal of Interactive Marketing	1	1	0.333	38	1	2021
Journal of Physical Chemistry B	1	1	0.042	35	1	2000
International Journal of Health Care Quality Assurance	1	1	0.100	34	1	2014
Business Strategy and Development	2	2	0.500	28	2	2020
Business Strategy and The Environment	1	2	0.250	25	2	2020
IOP Conference Series: Materials Science and Engineering	1	1	0.250	23	1	2020

Source: Constructed by the authors with Biblioshiny Software.

3.4. Country Analysis

This study section examines countries with high productivity and impact in green orientation. The current data analysis reveals contributions from twenty-eight countries and regions in green orientation research over the past few decades. Notably, developed countries emerge as the primary contributors, with China, the USA, Italy, Malaysia, and Canada ranking as the top five nations regarding article publications, as delineated in Table 18.4.

As stated in Table 18.4, the United States, the most prolific country in this sector, has authored 46 articles with a cumulative citation count of 185, underscoring its significant contribution to the body of green orientation literature. In general, industrialised nations dominate the majority of the top 10 countries in terms of paper publications, a trend likely attributable to the favourable inclination of these countries towards green initiatives. Moreover, publications originating from the USA, Italy, Malaysia, China, and Canada garner citations exceeding 40, indicating a higher quality of research in these studies.

3.5. Thematic Analysis

The study employs analyses such as keyword Co-Occurrence, Word Cloud, and Trend topics to discern influential studies and research themes within this domain.

3.6. Keyword Co-Occurrence

The researchers looked at the co-occurrence of keywords and the topic trends of themes to suggest potential future research directions for green orientation research. An academic article's keywords serve as the most sophisticated

Table 18.4. Country Analysis.

Country	TP	TC	Average Article Citations
USA	30	185	46.2
Italy	17	87	17.4
Malaysia	14	75	18.8
China	46	63	6.3
Canada	10	43	14.3
India	8	18	9
Spain	3	15	15
Estonia	3	11	11
Indonesia	4	5	2.5
Portugal	9	2	1
Romania	2	2	2

Source: Constructed by the authors with Biblioshiny Software.

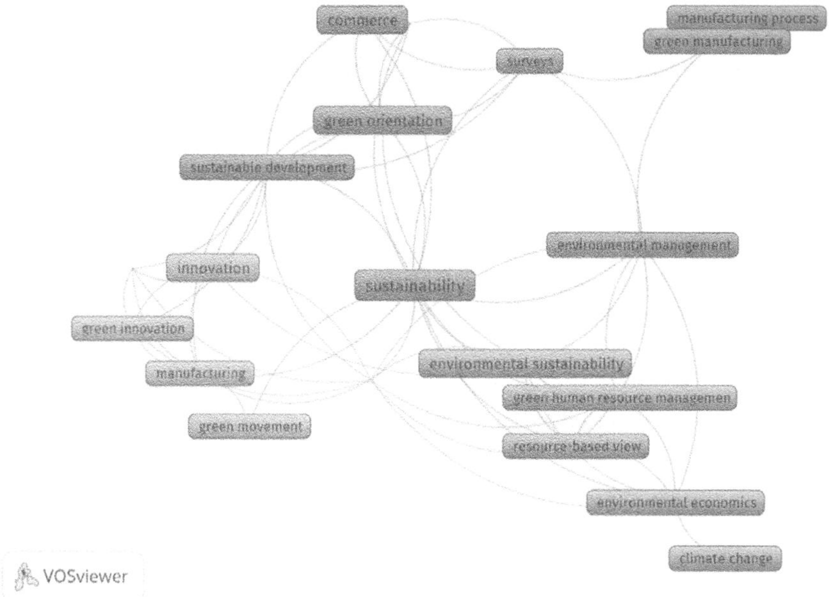

Fig. 18.3. Word Co-Occurrence Graph. *Source*: Constructed by the authors with Biblioshiny Software.

introduction possible. When researchers look at the co-occurrence of terms in a topic, they can immediately identify research hotspots and future research directions in that particular field. VOSviewer generated a term co-occurrence graph, as shown in Fig. 18.3.

The results of this study were analysed using this graph. For the sake of this analysis, the study's researchers required at least two occurrences of a keyword among all 149 keywords, and only 20 keywords met this requirement. Using keyword co-occurrence analysis, a network of subjects and their relationships can be constructed in a scientific field.

In the generated map, the size of each node corresponds to the frequency of the respective keyword's appearance in the documents. The distance between nodes and the thickness of connecting lines indicate the strength of co-occurrence between pairs of keywords. Node colour represents keyword clusters, signifying groups of words frequently occurring together, which can be interpreted as broad research topics. From 2000 to 2021, three overarching clusters encapsulate the critical topics of interest in green orientation:

Cluster 1 (Red)*[1]*: This cluster centers around environmental orientation and sustainable development. It encompasses studies that gather information about the manufacturing industry through surveys and examining manufacturing

[1] Figure colour descriptions are present, and the digital version contains colour figures.

companies. The emphasis is on the pivotal role of green orientation in environmental management and its potential to enhance sustainability.

Cluster 2 (Blue): This cluster focuses on green orientation within green human resource management practices. It underscores the critical role of Green Human Resource Management in achieving environmental sustainability through a resource-based approach. Additionally, this cluster delves into ecological economics and climate change considerations.

Cluster 3 (Green): This cluster explores the concept of green orientation through the lens of green innovation. Articles within this cluster investigate the green movement within the manufacturing sector, emphasizing the role of innovation in fostering environmentally friendly practices.

3.7. Trend Topics

The Trend Topics depicted in Fig. 18.4 reveal a concentration in green orientation research from 2004 to 2020, particularly within the last decade.

The most extensively researched topics encompass green orientation, environmental sustainability, and sustainability. Some emerging keywords, such as resource-based view, Green Human Resource Management, and innovation, are noteworthy but exhibit a low frequency of occurrence. This suggests that while these topics have garnered some attention, they have yet to undergo comprehensive investigation within the field of green orientation research.

3.8. WordCloud

"Environmental sustainability" emerges as the most frequently used keyword among researchers, followed by the pivotal term "green orientation." The keyword "sustainability" holds the third position in terms of frequency of utilisation by authors. This information is visually represented in Fig. 18.5, highlighting the prominence of these keywords in the landscape of green orientation research.

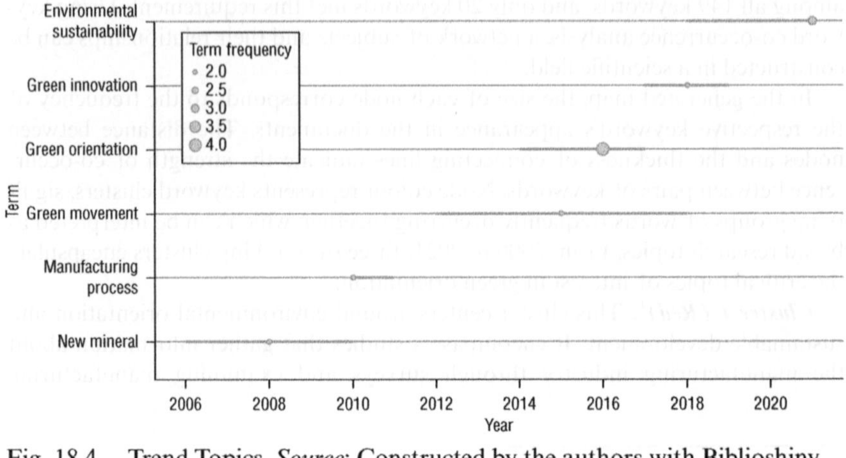

Fig. 18.4. Trend Topics. *Source*: Constructed by the authors with Biblioshiny Software.

Fig. 18.5. WordCloud. *Source*: Constructed by the authors with Biblioshiny Software.

3.9. Towards the Identification of Research Gaps

Based on the documents identified through bibliometric analysis, this section elucidates the research gaps identified through a critical review of 18 journal articles. Perron and Durand (2001) categorise green orientations into three distinct types: Ecologism, mainstream environmentalism, and market environmentalism. The findings affirm the diversity within the green movement, highlighting three discernible ideological orientations among green leaders. These distinctions are rooted in varying perceptions of science and technology and differing views on economic sacrifices. The identified categories include ecologism, mainstream environmentalism, and market environmentalism (Ndekwa et al., 2023; Sood & Özen, 2024; Yerpude et al., 2022).

Choi et al. (2009) observed that the correlations between Greek consumers' attitudes, intentions to take environmentally friendly actions, and willingness to pay differed in magnitude compared to the corresponding relationships among American customers. This underscores that cultural and social variations influence consumers' green attitudes and willingness to pay. The study further indicates that consumers in Greece exhibit more pronounced environmental concerns and a greater willingness to pay than their counterparts in the United States. These findings highlight the significant impact of cultural and societal variables on a consumer's green orientation and their willingness to contribute financially to environmentally friendly practices.

Hwang et al. (2014) suggest an increasing shift towards green orientation and sustainability efforts over lean approaches for effective outcomes such as waste reduction, employee satisfaction, and enhanced customer value, addressing significant competitive challenges within and between organizations (Kaur et al., 2024; Rijal et al., 2024).

In the context of the current scenario in Russia, Meskhi et al. (2020) find that customers perceive environmental concerns differently and are less demanding of the hotel industry's "green" focus. Meskhi et al. propose a strategic shift, positioning ecological hotel services as premium offerings and gradually presenting energy-efficient services as cost-saving measures to reshape the consumer mindset.

Ge et al.'s (2016) empirical findings, derived from data on 235 new Chinese green enterprises, suggest that green start-ups gain a performance advantage by commencing with a proactive green orientation. The study underscores the impact of institutional legitimacy on advancements in green performance, with startups possessing higher legitimacy and achieving better outcomes.

Viola and Marinelli's (2014) research in the food industry emphasises the importance of environmentally friendly processes, products, and marketing innovations within a green approach. Sathasivam et al. (2021) identify green employee involvement, participation, rewards, recycling training, and orientation as essential practices for fostering environmental sustainability in companies. They introduce the concept of Green Human Resource Management (GHRM), aligning HRM techniques with organisational goals of ecological sustainability.

Dahiya's (2020) study, involving 183 employees, explores the moderating role of organisational and coworker green orientations in connecting perceived corporate sustainability policies to employee green behaviour. The findings highlight the significance of psychological processes in linking administrative sustainability policies to green employee behaviour. Nguyen et al. (2020) emphasis the growing customer demand for environmental compliance, reflecting various consumer green orientation activities such as green vendor certification and collaborative green initiatives. Shen et al. (2017), as cited in Bohari et al. (2020), stress the importance of green measures in the procurement delivery process, including energy conservation, recycling, waste management efficiency, and the use of green materials and methods. Bohari et al. (2020) identify three critical factors influencing procurement's green orientation: policies and guidelines, environmental review, and product and process considerations.

Sáez-Martínez et al. (2016) contribute to the literature on open and eco-innovation by examining the link between a firm's green orientation and its interactions with stakeholders. They establish a model evaluating how interactions with clients, suppliers, rivals, and research institutions affect a company's environmental orientation. Fok et al.'s (2012) model, tested in Jamaica and the United States, incorporates constructs such as Individual Green Orientation, Organizational Green Orientation, Organizational Culture, Organizational Performance, and the Impact of the Green Movement. The study reveals that employees in both cultures perceiving organisational alignment with the green movement are likelier to perceive higher corporate culture, supporting quality, and employee satisfaction.

Mets et al. (2021) propose a conceptual model integrating entrepreneurial education into a multidisciplinary green transformation competency framework. Entrepreneurship education is positioned as a strategy for cultivating an active, educated, responsible, sustainable, ecosystem-oriented, and green orientation among individuals in the school system. Hong et al.'s (2009) study on a company's strategic green orientation highlights the importance of past green activities,

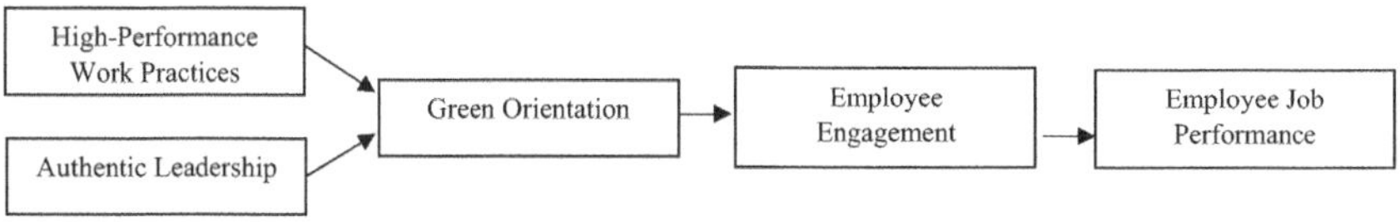

Fig. 18.6. Conceptual Framework/Nomological Network. *Source*: Authors' own work.

adoption of novel environmental improvement programs, and future commitment to ecological practices. The model, encompassing strategic green orientation (SGO), its influence on green performance outcomes (GPO), and business unit performance (through integrated product development and supply chain coordination), reveals research gaps.

Research Gap 1: The existing literature lacks investigations into the extent or degree of green orientation within the Sri Lankan Navy, potentially extending to the international military setting.

Research Gap 2: The absence of both theoretical and empirical support hinders the understanding of the mediating role played by green orientation in the connections between high-performance work practices (HPWPs), authentic leadership, and employee engagement within the Sri Lanka Navy, and possibly within the broader international military context.

Research Gap 3: The absence of theoretical and empirical evidence leaves an unexplored area concerning the influence of high-performance work practices (HPWPs) or authentic leadership on green orientation within a nomological network or conceptual framework in the Sri Lanka Navy and potentially within the international military context.

Research Gap 4: The literature needs theoretical and empirical evidence regarding the mediating impact of employee engagement on the correlation between green orientation and employee job performance.

Research Gap 5: There is an evident gap in the theoretical and empirical exploration of green orientation within a nomological network or conceptual framework specific to the Sri Lanka Navy and conceivably in the broader international military context.

The depiction of the nomological network or conceptual framework in this study is presented in Fig. 18.6, formulated through a comprehensive analysis combining quantitative and qualitative bibliometrics.

4. Variables or the Constructs of the Nomological Network

4.1. High-Performance Work Practices (HPWPs)

Surprisingly, despite its prevalence in management and organisational behaviour, there remains a need for more theoretical and empirical studies on the impact of high-performance work practices (HPWPs) on green orientation. This concept is often referred to by various titles, such as high-participation work practices, high-commitment work practices, and high-performance work practices, all sharing common characteristics (Iddagoda & Opatha, 2018; Rana, 2015). Notably, Iddagoda and Opatha (2018) suggest that high-performance work practices are the most suitable title for this concept.

For instance, practices like "pay for performance" may initially be considered a "scheme," but with frequent implementation, they transform into recognised practices (Iddagoda & Opatha, 2018). The scope of HPWPs encompasses elements such as realistic job previews, pay for performance, employee attitude surveys, self-directed teams, extensive training, frequent assessments, and symbolic egalitarianism, as outlined by Pfeffer (cited in Opatha, 2013).

Despite the prevalence of HPWPs, achieving a widely accepted definition has proven elusive, as Armstrong (2012) acknowledged. Consequently, Iddagoda and Opatha (2018) took the initiative to define HPWPs in 2018 as a collection of human resource practices that disproportionately influence organisational effectiveness.

4.2. Authentic Leadership

A leader is described as a "person or object who leads and is the most successful or advanced in a given sector." Leadership, as defined by Iddagoda (2021), encompasses the ability to motivate, guide, and influence others as needed. The concept of authentic leadership, receiving substantial attention from both academics and practitioners, has undergone significant theoretical and empirical development due to growing interest (Miao et al., 2018).

Authenticity, within this context, is elucidated as "owning one's personal experiences, whether they are ideas, feelings, desires, preferences, or beliefs, processes encapsulated by the mandate to know oneself," and subsequently acting in alignment with one's genuine self (Harter, 2002, as cited in Walumbwa et al., 2008). As Valsania et al. (2016) articulated, authentic leadership represents a behavioural pattern that inspires and cultivates positive psychological capacities and an ethical atmosphere, resulting in performance that surpasses expectations.

Toor and Ofori (2009) assert that authentic leaders adhere to high standards of ethics and morals, exhibiting the utmost integrity, a profound sense of purpose, the courage to forge ahead, passion, and a comprehensive set of leadership competencies.

4.3. Green Orientation

Zameer et al. (2020) posit that green orientation is the fundamental guiding principle for directing a company's environmental initiatives, acknowledged by ecological management as a crucial business tenet. This concept has traditionally held a central role in environmental management studies, as observed by Zameer et al. in 2020. The definition of green orientation, provided by Iddagoda and Opatha in 2022, characterises it as the transformation of an individual's primary consciousness and activities in an ecologically friendly manner to achieve environmentally friendly goals.

4.4. Employee Engagement

Employee engagement has garnered significant attention among practitioners and academics across various social science fields, including management, organisational behaviour, organisational psychology, and human resource development (Rana, 2015). Iddagoda et al. (2016) define employee engagement as cognitive, emotional, and behavioural involvement in their jobs and organisations. Commonly, engagement is associated with participation, passion, excitement, and energy, according to Eldor and Vigoda-Gadot (2017). As Graça et al. (2019) noted, engaged workers tend to exhibit higher satisfaction with their work environment, experience fewer sick days, and express lower turnover intentions. Andrew and Sofian (2013) highlight that engaged employees demonstrate proficiency in teamwork.

Engaged employees, as emphasised by Richman (2006) and Salanova et al. (2005), demonstrate loyalty to the organisation. Therefore, engaged employees are inclined to actively contribute to green-oriented initiatives with their heads, hearts, and hands.

4.5. Employee Job Performance

Prentice and Thaichon (2019) describe employee work performance as how an individual utilises resources to fulfil job criteria. Weis and Sub (2005) view employee work performance as a concept related to human behaviour. Viswesvaran and Ones (2000) define job performance as scalable activities, behaviours, and results that individuals engage in or produce, contributing to organisational goals. Iddagoda et al. (2021b) characterise employee job performance as an individual's contribution to task completion, aiming to create a positive work environment while minimising harmful or destructive activities. Despite the absence of a universally accepted definition for employee job performance, studies like Anitha (2014), Iddagoda and Opatha (2020) suggest that employee engagement influences work performance. Finally, future research endeavours should focus on testing five identified research gaps within the context of the Military organisations as their culture differs, as stated by Iddagoda et al. (2021a).

5. Conclusions and Implications to the Practice

A comprehensive literature analysis has unveiled five distinct research gaps. Research Gap 1 indicates a lack of investigation into the extent or degree of green orientation within the Sri Lankan Navy, possibly within international military operations. Gap 2 highlights the absence of theoretical or empirical evidence regarding the mediating impact of green orientation on the relationships between High-Performance Work Practices (HPWPs), authentic leadership, and employee engagement in the Sri Lanka Navy, potentially in the global military arena. Research Gap 3 points to the absence of more theoretical or empirical evidence concerning how high-performance work practices (HPWPs) or authentic leadership significantly influence green orientation within a nomological network/

conceptual framework in the Sri Lanka Navy. Gap 4 underscores the lack of theoretical or empirical evidence regarding employee engagement as a mediating factor in the connection between green orientation and employee job performance. The fifth research gap emphasises the need for theoretical and empirical evidence on green orientation within a nomological network/conceptual framework. These research gaps encompass practical and theoretical aspects, with Gaps 2, 3, 4, and 5 representing both gaps.

References

Andrew, O. C., & Sofian, S. (2012). Individual factors and work outcomes of employee engagement. *Procedia-Social and Behavioral Sciences*, *40*, 498–508.

Anitha, J. (2014). Determinants of employee engagement and their impact on employee performance. *International Journal of Productivity and Performance Management*, *63*(3), 308–323.

Arulrajah, A. A., Opatha, H. H. D. N. P., & Nawaratne, N. N. J. (2015). Green human resource management practices: A review. *Sri Lankan Journal of Human Resource Management*, *5*(1), 1–16.

Armstrong, M. (2012). *Armstrong's handbook of human resource management practice*. Kogan Page, London.

Bohari, A. A. M., Skitmore, M., Xia, B., Teo, M., & Khalil, N. (2020). Fundamental stakeholder values in encouraging green orientation of construction procurement. *Journal of Cleaner Production*, *270*, 1–47.

Centobelli, P., Cerchione, R., Esposito, E., & Shashi. (2020). Evaluating environmental sustainability strategies in freight transport and logistics industry. *Business Strategy and the Environment*, *29*(3), 1563–1574.

Choi, G., Parsa, H. G., Sigala, M., & Putrevu, S. (2009). Consumers' environmental concerns and behaviours in the lodging industry: A comparison between Greece and the United States. *Journal of Quality Assurance in Hospitality & Tourism*, *10*(2), 93–112.

Dahiya, R. (2020). Do organisational sustainability policies affect the environmental attitude of employees? The missing link of green work climate perceptions. *Business Strategy & Development*, *3*(3), 395–403.

Dewasiri, N. J., Baker, H. K., Banda, Y. K. W., & Rathnasiri, M. S. H. (2022). The dividend decision model: A possible solution for the dividend puzzle. In S. Rana, Sakshi, and J. Singh (Eds.), *Exploring the latest trends in management Literature* (Review of Management Literature, Vol. 1, pp. 249–267). Emerald Publishing Limited, Leeds. https://doi.org/10.1108/S2754-586520220000001013

Eldor, L., & Vigoda-Gadot, E. (2017). The nature of employee engagement: Rethinking the employee–organisation relationship. *The International Journal of Human Resource Management*, *28*(3), 526–552.

Fok, L. Y., Zee, S. M., & Hartman, S. J. (2012). Relationships among individual green orientation, employee perceptions of organisational commitment to the green movement, and corporate culture: A comparative study of Jamaica and the United States. *Journal of Organizational Culture, Communications and Conflict*, *16*(2), 115.

Ge, B., Jiang, D., Gao, Y., & Tsai, S. B. (2016). The influence of legitimacy on a proactive green orientation and green performance: A study based on transitional economy scenarios in China. *Sustainability*, *8*(12), 1–20.

Graça, M., Pais, L., Mónico, L., Santos, N. R. D., Ferraro, T., & Berger, R. (2019). Decent work and work engagement: A profile study with academic personnel. *Applied Research in Quality of Life*, *16*(3), 917–939.

Hong, P., Kwon, H. B., & Roh, J. J. (2009). Implementing strategic green orientation in the supply chain: an empirical study of manufacturing firms. *European Journal of Innovation Management*, *12*(4), 512–532.

Hwang, P., Hwang, D., & Hong, P. (2014). Lean practices for quality results: A case illustration. *International Journal of Health Care Quality Assurance*, *27*(8), 729–741.

Iddagoda, A. (2021). Towards an instrument of measuring the construct of leadership by the 10 Cs for employee engagement. *Annals of Social Sciences*, *13*(1), 1–23.

Iddagoda, A., Abeysinghe, R., & Wickramaratne, W. P. (2022). Green orientation: Conceptualisation and operationalisation. *Academy of Management*, *6*(2), 290–306.

Iddagoda, A., Dewasiri, N. J., & Keppetipola, M. (2021a). Conceptualization and operationalization of military organizational culture. *International Journal of Sustainable Economies Management*, *10*(2), 19–30.

Iddagoda, A., Hysa, E., Bulińska-Stangrecka, H., & Manta, O. (2021b). Green work-life balance and greenwashing the construct of work-life balance: Myth and reality. *Energies*, *14*(15), 1–19.

Iddagoda, Y. A., & Opatha, H. H. D. N. P. (2018). The intensity of implementing high-performance work practices in selected Sri Lankan companies. *Społeczeństwo i Rodzina nr*, *56*(3), 69–95.

Iddagoda, Y. A., & Opatha, H. H. (2020). Relationships and mediating effects of employee engagement: An empirical study of managerial employees of Sri Lankan listed companies. *SAGE Open*, *10*(2), 1–22.

Iddagoda, Y. A., Opatha, H. H. D. N. P., & Gunawardana, K. D. (2016). Towards a conceptualisation and an operationalisation of the construct of employee engagement. *International Business Research*, *9*(2), 85–98.

Jayawardena, N. S., & Dewasiri, N. J. (2023). Food acquisition and consumption issues of south Asian countries: A systematic literature review and future research agenda. *FIIB Business Review*, *26*, 1029–1040. https://doi.org/10.1177/23197145231194113

Kaur, S., Kumar, R., Singh, K., & Huang, Y. L. (2024). Leveraging artificial intelligence for enhanced sustainable energy management. *Journal of Sustainable Energy*, *3*(1), 1–20. https://doi.org/10.56578/jse030101

Meskhi, B., Bondarenko, V., Efremenko, I., Larionov, V., Rudoy, D., & Olshevskaya, A. (2020, December). Technical, technological, and managerial solutions in ensuring environmental safety. In *IOP Conference Series: Materials Science and Engineering* (Vol. 1001, No. 1, p. 012100). IOP Publishing.

Mets, T., Holbrook, J., & Läänelaid, S. (2021). Entrepreneurship education challenges for green transformation. *Administrative Sciences*, *11*(1), 1–15.

Miao, C., Humphrey, R. H., & Qian, S. (2018). Emotional intelligence and authentic leadership: A meta-analysis. *Leadership & Organization Development Journal*, *39*(5), 679–690.

Ndekwa, A. G., Kalugendo, E., Sood, K., & Grima, S. (2023). An analysis of agribusiness digitalisation transformation of the sub-Saharan African countries small-scale farmers' production distribution. *Research on World Agricultural Economy*, *4*(3), 63–78.

Nguyen, H. M., Onofrei, G., Truong, D., & Lockrey, S. (2020). Customer green orientation and process innovation alignment: A configuration approach in the global manufacturing industry. *Business Strategy and the Environment*, *29*(6), 2498–2513.

Opatha, H.H.D.N.P. (2013). Green human resource management: A simplified introduction. *Proceedings of the HR Dialogue*, *1*(1), 12–21.

Perron, J.-G. V., & Durand, B. C. (2001). A global problem for a worldwide movement? An exploratory study of climate change perception by green groups' leaders from Quebec (Canada) and Costa Rica. *Society & Natural Resources*, *14*(10), 837–855.

Prentice, C., & Thaichon, P. (2019). Revisiting the job performance–burnout relationship. *Journal of Hospitality Marketing & Management*, *28*(7), 807–832.

Rana, S. (2015). High-involvement work practices and employee engagement. *Human Resource Development International, 18*(3), 308–316.

Rathnasiri, M. S. H., & De Silva, W. V. (2023). The role of shopping values, cognitive and affective evaluations on the relationship between store environment and store patronage intention: A future research agenda. *Sri Lanka Journal of Management Studies, 5*(1), 100–120.

Richman, A. (2006). Everyone wants an engaged workforce. How can you create it? *Workspan, 49*(1), 36–39.

Rijal, S., Nursaputra, M., A., C., & Dari, H. U. (2024). Flood susceptibility analysis using Frequency Ratio method in Walanae watershed. *International Journal of Sustainable Development and Planning, 19*(3), 823–832. https://doi.org/10.18280/ijsdp.190302

Sáez-Martínez, F. J., Avellaneda-Rivera, L., & González-Moreno, Á. (2016). Open and green innovation in the hospitality industry. *Environmental Engineering & Management Journal, 15*(7), 1481–1488.

Sakshi, S., Cerchione, R., & Bansal, H. (2020). Measuring the impact of sustainability policy and practices in tourism and hospitality industry. *Business Strategy and the Environment, 29*(3), 1109–1126.

Salanova, M., Agut, S., & Peiró, J. M. (2005). Linking organisational resources and work engagement to employee performance and customer loyalty: The mediation of service climate. *Journal of Applied Psychology, 90*(6), 1217–1227.

Sathasivam, K., Abu Bakar, R., & Che Hashim, R. (2021). Embracing organisational environmental sustainability: Experiences in green human resource management. *Business Strategy & Development, 4*(2), 123–135.

Shaharudin, M. R., Zailani, S., & Ismail, M. (2015). Third-party logistics' strategic orientation towards reverse logistics service offerings. *International Journal of Management Practice, 8*(4), 356–374.

Shroff, S. J., Paliwal, U. L., & Dewasiri, N. J. (2024). Unravelling the impact of financial literacy on investment decisions in an emerging market. *Business Strategy & Development, 7*(1), 1–14. https://doi.org/10.1002/bsd2.337

Sood, K., & Özen, E. (2024). A systematic review of ESG in the insurance industry: Navigating the path to sustainability. *International Journal of Sustainable Development and Planning, 19*(3), 807–821. https://doi.org/10.18280/ijsdp.190301

Toor, S. U. R., & Ofori, G. (2009). Ethical leadership: Examining the relationships with full range leadership model, employee outcomes, and organisational culture. *Journal of Business Ethics, 90*(4), 533–547.

Valsania, S. E., Moriano, J. A., & Molero, F. (2016). Authentic leadership and intrapreneurial behaviour: Cross-level analysis of the mediator effect of organisational identification and empowerment. *International Entrepreneurship and Management Journal, 12*(1), 131–152.

Viola, I., & Marinelli, N. (2014). Green orientation in the food industry and labour market. *Calitatea, 15*(S1), 154–158.

Viswesvaran, C., & Ones, D. S. (2000). Perspectives on models of job performance. *International Journal of Selection and Assessment, 8*(4), 216–226.

Walumbwa, F. O., Avolio, B. J., Gardner, W. L., Wernsing, T. S., & Peterson, S. J. (2008). Authentic leadership: Development and validation of a theory-based measure. *Journal of Management, 34*(1), 89–126.

Weis, S., & Sub, H. M. (2005). *Social intelligence–A review and critical discussion of measurement concepts. Emotional intelligence: An international handbook* (pp. 203–230). Hogrefe & Huber Publishers.

Yerpude, S., Sood, K., & Grima, S. (2022). Blockchain-augmented digital supply chain management: A way to sustainable business. *Journal of Risk and Financial Management, 16*(1), 7.

Zameer, H., Wang, Y., Yasmeen, H., & Mubarak, S. (2020). Green innovation as a mediator in the impact of business analytics and environmental orientation on green competitive advantage. *Management Decision*, *60*(2), 488–507.

Zupic, I., & Čater, T. (2014). Bibliometric methods in management and organization. *Organizational Research Methods*, *18*(3), 429–472. https://doi.org/10.1177/1094428114562629

Index

Printed and bound by CPI Group (UK) Ltd, Croydon, CR0 4YY

13/09/2026

14961027-0004